I WOULDN'T START FROM HERE

Among various misadventures in more than 70 countries, **Andrew Mueller** has reported on the Taliban's takeover of Afghanistan, the lifting of the siege of Bihac, the handover of Hong Kong, the invasion of Iraq, the wartime rock'n'roll scene of Sarajevo, an Elvis Presley festival in Tupelo and Ukraine's efforts to launch Chernobyl as a tourist destination. He has ridden the Cresta Run, driven the proverbial Road to Damascus, been given a guided tour of Lebanon by Hizbollah, patrolled Basra with the Welsh Guards, Kabul with the Royal Anglian Regiment, and played the country songwriters' open-mic night at the Bluebird Café in Nashville. Born in Australia, he has been based in London for the last twenty years.

"I am regularly lost. I ask people all the time for directions. They send me to places I never could have imagined . . . a pizza place in Pisa, a club in a cellar in São Paulo . . . the City Lights book shop in San Francisco's tenderloin, Moran's on the weir in the west of Ireland for oysters, brown bread and Guinness . . . Osaka to see and feel Tadao Ando's Church of Light . . . often places of conflict. The east/west crossroads that is Sarajevo . . . Haile Selassie stables in Addis Ababa . . . watching the surfers in El Salvador. I usually want to enter these places when everyone else is queuing up to leave, oftentimes there's just one person in front of me, oftentimes it's Andrew Mueller . . . at the desk in the airport, or in the customs hall at the same counter as me, filling out a similar form. His face has the same expression every time . . . it's a very familiar expression: comic disbelief. He can't believe it's happened to him again . . . he thinks it's the poor directions, the road maps or the unkind stranger who pointed him here. And where is here? Nowhere . . . it's not that he likes to be lost, it's just that he likes the company of the lost. Be very careful reading this book." —**Bono**

"Andrew Mueller is a splendid man and a wonderful writer. But, for his own good, we must make him stop talking common sense. The human brain is not programmed to receive common sense. This may be a Darwinian adaptation. What man would undergo the trials of marriage and family if common sense prevailed? What woman would endure the agonies of childbirth? Mueller's book sales would be greater if he talked drivel. And his life would be longer, because Mueller travels to places where locals are not just deaf to common sense, they revile it. One of these days the natives will twig to what Andrew Mueller is saying. They'll kill him. And we'll lose the best foreign correspondent of this generation." —**P.J. O'Rourke**

"A gung-ho *Candide* with a taste for places it is wiser to avoid . . . the reports collected in *I Wouldn't Start From Here* are graphic, comic, bemused and properly contemptuous of faith and ideology."
—Jonathan Meades, Books of the Year, *Evening Standard*

I WOULDN'T START FROM HERE

THE 21ST CENTURY AND WHERE IT ALL WENT WRONG

ANDREW MUELLER

Soft Skull
Brooklyn

Copyright © Andrew Mueller 2007. The moral right
of the author has been asserted.

First published in Australia in 2007 by Pan Macmillan
Australia Pty Ltd.

Library of Congress Cataloging-in-Publication Data

Mueller, Andrew.
I wouldn't start from here : the 21st century and where it
all went wrong / Andrew Mueller.
p. cm.
ISBN 10: 1-59376-218-6
ISBN 13: 978-1-59376-218-6
"First published in Australia in 2007 by
Pan Macmillan Australia"—T.p. verso.
Includes bibliographical references and index.
1. History, Modern—21st century. 2. World politics—21st century.
3. Social history—21st century. 4. Mueller, Andrew—Travel.
5. Ethnic conflict. 6. Social conflict. 7. War and society. I. Title.
D862.M845 2007
909.83'1—dc22
2008044091

Cover design by Goodloe Byron
Interior design Midland Typesetters, Australia
Printed in the United States of America

Soft Skull Press
An Imprint of Counterpoint LLC
2117 Fourth Street
Suite D
Berkeley, CA 94710

www.softskull.com
www.counterpointpress.com

Distributed by Publishers Group West

10 9 8 7 6 5 4 3 2 1

For Nana and Jungie

'As scary as the world is, and it is . . . it's just a ride.'
Bill Hicks

CONTENTS

FOREWORD TO THE U.S. EDITION OF
I WOULDN'T START FROM HERE

I am pleased to introduce Andrew Mueller's book to probably the most disinterested and confused audience one could pick: America. The United States has always been a bastion of isolationism and xenophobia, and an audience more prone to buying books on losing weight than packing on intellectual muscle. Even though at press time we are currently up to our ample waists in Afghanistan and Iraq, you won't find Americans sporting an Afghan *pakool* at a jaunty angle or humming the latest Iraqi pop hit. To be blunt, we don't like foreign stuff. And we don't trust unshaven scribes who talk or dress funny. We don't like danger here and we prefer to fill our quiet hours with torrid TV tales of knickerless celebutantes and waterskiing squirrels. Oh, and did I mention we don't like to read? We think bookstores are places to buy coffee or pick up smart chicks.

So why do I so enthusiastically endorse a book about places that no one wants to go to, to a nation of which a quarter is proud to admit they don't read books and even fewer have passports? Well because Andrew's *I Wouldn't Start From Here* is that perfect blend of investigation, humor, drama, and above all, insight into the global human condition. Andrew has succeeded in making the world's bent places seem understandable and entertaining. He may have achieved that perfect mix of insight and information that will make America want to read a book to understand why the world has so many seemingly unfathomable backwaters. By tackling a tough and often dull subject with a fresh, engaging approach, Andrew may do what "Sesame Street" did for the alphabet, what "Cops" did for criminals . . . or perhaps even what Borat did for Kazakhstan. Bravo Andrew – now just make sure you keep the countries you slagged off in this book off of your future travel list.

Andrew Mueller is just the man to actually understand these places. He wants us to meet these dodgy celebrities, and he gives equal shrift to odious and melodious characters and places. His view of these places is almost like how Americans view the underside of the US. So I think Americans will love this book if only they would put down their bookstore latte and stop ogling each other over the bookstands long enough to get past my introduction.

Writing books about unpleasant and unpronounceable places is exactly the kind of questionable career move you would expect from someone who gave up the sun and beauty of his native Australia for the grimy, gray world of London. Perhaps that's why he finds places like Cameroon and Gaza ideal for a getaway, and of course ideal subjects for a great collection of funny stories that are woven into a tapestry of misery and woe.

I believe that a writer is defined by his choice of subject matter. Andrew, like his odd-bird subjects and regions, is by any definition an odd bird. Although he comes from the land of Bazza McKenzie, Diggers and square-jawed bronzed Bondi Beach lifeguards, Andrew has the look of a failed poet. I say failed because he doesn't chain smoke, he's not confused and he can barely drink. He has no glaring personality defects and he is cursed with an irritating sense of humor that makes the most unfortunate event funny. Funny as in that increasing cascade of mutual giggles in which you realize that the true joy of living and understanding is being able to take surviving these places in stride. A redeeming character flaw that you will learn to love in this book.

Whenever I have met or traveled with Andrew he is maddeningly disheveled, infuriatingly calm, and perpetually looking like someone that was rudely awakened at 5AM on a Sunday morning. I can see him now: tousle-haired, unshaven, outwardly grumpy, but incessantly curious. His lethal hosts spend an inordinate amount of time sizing him up for criminal purposes but he consistently defeats their evil ideas by constantly asking intelligent and relevant questions.

Usually he is somewhat concerned that complete strangers might dare to shorten his lifespan. As soon as he begins talking to his questionable hosts they quickly learn that Andrew has not only a wicked sense of humor, but a sense of comfort with their country that even his hosts often don't have. His journey to war-torn Baghdad seems to calm excitable Iraqis. But his insistence on bringing along a four-foot tall yellow TeleTubby he christened LaLa Hussein Al-Tikriti soon made his hosts realize that there might have been a very good reasons why Saddam kept out foreigners for so long. His interviews with famous bad men should end with him bouncing down flights of stairs but instead morph into mutual friendships. The bastard is unkillable, unflappable, and always eager to turn down dark alleys rather than head for the closest air-conditioned hotel.

The scariest thing about this book is the reader's concern for Andrew's safety. His constant probing of people who don't like to be probed too deeply. Andrew is the kind of writer that terrorists would drop off at the embassy with a note saying "This fellow doesn't take us seriously, can we have another one please?" You think I jest? Read his tale of West African imprisonment.

I suppose his background as a rock critic has taught Andrew a few things about pathetic posturing, loud angry noises and easily dissected bombast. His choice of topics go beyond political posturing: how you get rid of a dead body in Baghdad, why Palestinians are like Australian Aborigines, and even why even Luxembourg can be, well, scary.

I Wouldn't Start From Here is like a jazz song or a modern painting that at first is chaotic and mesmerizing, but through its choice of colors, tones, and focus, captures something a more pedantic approach could never. This is a book that probably provides more insight into war, strife, and conflict than any number of high dollar pundits or droning PhDs ever could. It is also a inspiration to those who want to dig a little deeper in their lives and travels. After all, if a badly dressed rock reviewer, budding country music singer, and professional curmudgeon like Andrew can make sense of our world, then perhaps there is hope for those who actually have the ability to change things.

Enjoy.

Robert Young Pelton

San Diego, California

INTRODUCTION

LONDON, ENGLAND
MARCH 2007

It's an old joke, usually set in Ireland.

A tourist, hopelessly off course, pulls up alongside a local hick, who is probably wearing a straw hat, toting a pitchfork, chewing on peat, perhaps cradling a piglet beneath one arm. The lost traveller asks the ruddy-cheeked peasant how he might reach the destination he seeks. The rustic hayseed looks up the road, down the road, back up the road, thinks for a bit, and finally replies: 'Well, I wouldn't start from here.'

On New Year's Eve 1999, I did what I usually do on New Year's Eve: nothing. Any calendar contains 364 nights on which I can go out in the reasonable expectation of getting a cab home when I want one, so going out on the one night certain to end in a long trudge home, or chilly, fitful sleep in someone's hedge, makes as much sense as booking a snowboarding holiday in Chad. So I stayed in, by myself, and watched the BBC's coverage of the world's people celebrating the beginning of the twenty-first century as the dawn of 1 January 2000 crept across the globe.

For all that I was alone, I felt unusually connected to the rest of my fellow humans, and in an unusually positive way. When most of the world is mostly thinking about the same thing, it's mostly something ghastly – wars, disasters, British royal weddings. But for hour upon hour, my television surveyed a cornucopia of once-in-a-thousand-years optimism, determination and jovial drunkenness – even those sober out of religious conviction appeared mildly plastered by association. It was, for a day at least, a planet I felt utterly content about living on, and the new era edging towards me loomed like a whole bunch of days worth seizing.

As midnight GMT neared, I scanned my CD shelves for appropriate end credits music for the twentieth century, and an opening theme for the twenty-first. I decided to farewell the century I was born in with 'The Final Countdown'. Not the original, recorded in a best-forgotten year of the 1980s by mullet-cropped Swedish lite-metal prancers Europe, but the uproariously pompous rock-operatic cover version from the 1994 album *NATO*, by Slovenian situationists Laibach, who'd souped up Europe's fatuous hit into Haydn-goes-disco *sturm und drang* sung by what sounded like Fozzie Bear from *The Muppet Show* with a headache.

It seemed right. In the outgoing epoch's closing decade, the country in which Laibach had formed, Yugoslavia, had suffered terminal doses of every foolishness that humanity had visited upon itself in the twentieth century – racism, nationalism, greed, bigotry, vanity, self-pity, ignorance, ideological headbanging, religious fanaticism, arcane historical grudge-bearing, international indifference – and in the 1990s I'd seen a small sample of the results in the countries which were now Croatia and Bosnia-Herzegovina. I suspected that Europe's feather-follicled singer, Joey Tempest, had considered precisely none of these all-too-common human failings when he composed his lyric, but Laibach's grandiloquent interpretation detected, and reflected, a certain idiot savant sagacity in the song. Sung by Tempest, 'The Final Countdown' was a silly tune about flying to Venus. Growled by Laibach's gruff, stentorian Milan Fras, it sounded like a wounded, weirdly dignified plea for an age of reason.

I welcomed the century I would die in – unless online canasta proves to possess as-yet-unheralded life-prolonging properties – with 'Wheels', by the Flying Burrito Brothers. It's on the Burritos' 1969 album *Gilded Palace Of Sin*, and it's my only superstition – playing it is always the last thing I do before leaving the building on any outing that necessitates luggage. 'Wheels' is a standard-issue country trundle, elevated above the ordinary by a discordant guitar riff that buzzes beneath the chorus like a wasp trapped in a lunchbox, an impish flight of pedal steel, and a lyric espousing the cheerfully fatalistic attitude which one should always pack – along with sleeping bag and stomach medicines – as one prepares to sally to parts unknown, resigned to and yet excited by where the road may lead: 'We're not afraid to ride,' croons Gram Parsons. 'We're not afraid to die.'

At that moment, it felt perfect. At that moment, everyone old enough to understand what we were celebrating also understood that they wouldn't be joining in next time the people of Earth counted in a new century. If everybody grasped that, I thought, maybe we could, as a species, set about making the time we have here more pleasant for all of us. It hadn't occurred to me that people who weren't afraid to die were shortly going to become one of the biggest problems we had.

My optimism, like everyone else's, was misplaced.

I Wouldn't Start From Here is a random history of the twenty-first century so far as seen by one peripatetic hack. It's not really a proper reporter's memoir, but then I'm not really a proper reporter, due to chronic lack of discipline, negligible attention span, and a certain juvenile difficulty taking serious things seriously. I am, however, fortunate enough to be able to go to the places that interest me, and meet the people I'm interested in. When I watched the world greet the twenty-first century, there seemed to me no reason why our new era couldn't be a golden age of peace, love and brotherhood. This, as the least observant witness to our times would have noticed, has declined to dawn. This book is an attempt to understand why, a ruminative ramble around the world's past, present and future conflict zones. It works on more than one level, though – it's also a compendium of cheap mockery of querulous foreigners.

At any gathering of honest – well, drunk – journalists, aid workers and others whose jobs remove them from the comfort of the First World, a point will be reached, usually late in the evening. Slightly guilty questions about the subjects of our work – the inhabitants of the Third World – will be furtively whispered. Why don't these bloody people just knock their nonsense off? Why don't they, you know, get with the program? Are they all just thick? When those around these bottle-cluttered tables elaborate, they rarely discuss the headline-grabbing, awesomely terrible stuff: the wars, the pogroms, the pits full of folk who had the wrong surnames or aberrant ideas about God. It's the trivial stuff that any person in any of these places could change with little effort, and doesn't. It's not a sophisticated question, but why – really, why? – is every public convenience east of Vienna so bloody filthy? You can buy bleach and scrubbing brushes in these places; I've seen them myself, in shops. It wouldn't take anyone long.

My overwhelming epiphany in this department occurred in August 2005. I'd been visiting Abkhazia, a wannabe breakaway republic of Georgia. My work done, I'd gotten a lift to the de facto border, negotiated Abkhazia's exit formalities, strolled across the Inguri river bridge into Georgia proper, cleared Georgia's customs post – a chap with a pistol in his waistband, sunbathing on a tree stump – and taken a taxi to the UN compound in Zugdidi, from where I'd arranged for a car to take me back to Georgia's capital, Tbilisi.

I'd suffered Georgian roads before, so I wasn't surprised by what I saw over the next few hours. Georgians are the worst drivers in the world, combining the mindless aggression of Lebanese, the terrifying fatalism of Pakistanis, the adolescent machismo of Italians, and the technical competence of baboons. To drive anywhere in Georgia is to ride with the Reaper sharpening his scythe in the rear-view mirror. On this trip, though, it occurred to me to wonder why it was like this. Why didn't everyone drive sensibly? It isn't difficult – it's easier, indeed, than what they were doing. It decreases the sum of human misery by the expedient of killing, injuring and terrifying fewer people, and damaging less property. It means people get where they're going more quickly, if only because they're obliged to spend less time flagging down passing traffic to find other motorists willing to help them pull their vehicles out of the ditch into which they've veered to avoid being T-boned by some other yahoo trying to overtake two lanes of traffic on a blind corner. And why was everyone in such a hurry, anyway? To get somewhere in *Georgia*?

My driver had been sulking from the off; the first fifteen minutes of our journey were spent in a struggle of wills over my seatbelt, the wearing of which by any of his passengers he regarded as a mortal affront (he was, incidentally, a policeman by profession). Nevertheless, after we'd narrowly, tyre-screechingly dodged yet another terrifying confluence of speeding vehicles, I asked him: why do you people drive like such fucking idiots?

'We drive like this,' he intoned, in that theatrically baleful way ex-Soviets often employ when working up an especially picturesque dose of gnomic ennui, 'because in Georgia, life is short.'

Had he, I asked, considered the possibility that the reason life in Georgia was short was that it was full of people driving like Georgians?

'This is likely,' he conceded.

And what was the deal with the seatbelts? Putting them on was hardly an effort. Wearing them made it more likely that when you had a big accident – which, if you drove like a Georgian, you would – you would survive it. Why didn't anybody use them? Why did Georgians, driving like Georgians, on Georgian roads on which other Georgians were driving like Georgians, let their children sit on the damn dashboards?

'The new government,' the driver said, referring to the reformist, relatively uncorrupt regime brought to power by Georgia's Rose Revolution of November 2003, 'is introducing a seatbelt law. Then everyone will wear seatbelts.'

I wondered if Tbilisi's legislators were also working on a bill enforcing coats and mittens on cold days, but decided there was little to be gained by contesting matters, and tried to sleep. I wasn't tired, but if my eyes were closed, I couldn't see the demented, unnecessary mayhem being wrought in front of us, into which I was being propelled at ludicrous, gratuitous velocity. It's sometimes easier not to know.

* * *

And that's the choice most people make. It is common to bewail the wilful ignorance of citizens of the First World, and it's correct to. There is no excuse for spending our secure, privileged existences, granted us by the ingenuity, luck and sacrifice of our forebears, doing little beyond gratifying ourselves with vacuous amusements. On the occasions when the horrors of the world flicker on our television and computer screens, or catch our eye on a printed page, we don't feel good about them, but we don't care. If we did, it stands to reason, we'd fix them.

Especially now. One of the things that changed most radically about the world in the early twenty-first century was that the internet ceased to be a novelty. We had long taken for granted the manifestation of human genius that allowed us to pick up a phone and communicate with people anywhere in the world who we knew. We now take it for granted that we can switch on a computer and communicate with people anywhere in the world who we don't know yet. At the risk of talking myself and my colleagues out of our immensely enjoyable jobs, nobody has to wait anymore for a magazine article to get a sense of a place they've never been and may never visit. There is now almost no limit upon the circle of people we can choose to care about personally and individually, as opposed to abstractly and en masse. It seems self-evident that this removal of barriers to communication should have made the world a more peaceful place, but it hasn't. I sometimes wonder if it has just made it easier for everyone to loathe each other.

I moved from Sydney to London in 1990, when I was twenty-one, and that's really (really) not so long ago, but back then it was a big deal if a friend from Australia mailed me a letter, and a bigger deal, of the order of a weeping statue, if the Italian postal service delivered any two epistles from my then-girlfriend, Clancy, who was studying in Perugia, in the correct order. When I backpacked around Eastern Europe with Clancy that summer, and by myself in Eastern Europe and the Middle East in 1993, I kept in touch with friends and family via postcards; people who wanted to contact me wrote care of post offices in Helsinki, Vilnius, Warsaw, Budapest,

Bucharest, Istanbul, Damascus and Jerusalem. This now seems as fantastically olde worlde as the stories my mother used to tell me about the horse-drawn cart that delivered ice to her family's home in Albury in the 1950s.

When I started travelling as a journalist, wrangling foreign contacts was a matter of wishfully left messages, desperately pulled connections, turning up and hoping. It is now possible to schedule a week of appointments, in advance, pretty much anywhere, in the couple of hours after an editor has called with an idea for some overseas jaunt. A decade ago, it was difficult to keep in touch with people I'd met on assignment, especially when those people lived in remote and/or dangerous places. It now barely seems remarkable when my first coffee of the day is consumed over ongoing correspon-dence with a translator in Gaza, an activist in Tirana, a secessionist in Bamenda, a heavy metal impresario in Taipei, a country singer in Nashville and a strange Sri Lankan man in Dubai who is unbudgeably convinced that I once wrote a book about South Africa's intelligence services (which, if you're reading this, Mr Srinath, I really didn't). Were it not for the revolution in communications, I would probably never have met any of these people, still less been able to maintain a relationship with them – even, in the case of the persistent Mr Srinath, a reluctant one (seriously, mate, you're confusing me with someone else). But I did, and I do, and so I care about these people, and so I'm interested in what's going on around them. Except Mr Srinath, who is beginning to annoy me.

The indifference of the developed world towards the undeveloped ditto is hardly an original observation. But it does have a neglected corollary. In the world's war zones, famine-pits and heck-holes, there are, also, many people riding with their eyes shut, despite knowing that the steering wheel is in the grip of a lunatic. Humans have been organising societies for thousands of years. It has been the longest, most dangerous experiment ever undertaken. However, by the end of the second millennium to have elapsed since the birth of one man who discovered that propounding commonsense about such matters is a fairly thankless occupation, we had, by and large, figured it out.

Our planet, at the beginning of the twenty-first century, boasted dozens of societies which worked. These societies which worked had things, fairly obvious things, in common: freedom of speech, thought, press and association, along with peace, democracy, transparency, rule of law, property rights, freeish and fairish trade, tolerance (or its more mature cousin, benign indifference) and secularism. Our planet also hosted many societies which didn't work. These places also had things, howlingly obvious things, in common: dictatorship, oppression, corruption, censorship, ethnocentricity, centralised economic meddling, any tendency whatsoever to make the law the servant of faith.

Just as citizens of the First World know, but don't much care, that the Third World suffers in squalor and fear, so the denizens of the Third World know that there are places where nobody's going to pelt you with rocks for giving birth unwed, or deport you to the saltpile for wishing someone else ran the country, or harbour the mildest desire to slaughter your family over some irrelevant quirk of identity. They also know that these places tend to be richer and calmer than the ones they live in, which is why so many of them make such heroic efforts to leave their homes and construct new lives elsewhere – and why nobody has ever smuggled themselves in a potato crate from Stockholm to Kabul. It is not blaming the victim to occasionally ask the people whose societies are pushing their communal handcart to hell if they've considered that there might be better ways of dealing with their problems than ethnic hatred, religious mania, violence and collective sulking.

In December 2004 and January 2005, researching the subjects of ethnic hatred, religious mania, violence and collective sulking, I visited the reliably fertile pasture of the Holy Land. There is more on this journey later, but the single conversation that haunts me most from that trip I will recount here, as an encapsulation of what, if anything, this book is about. I was talking to a Palestinian friend of mine in Ramallah about the funeral of Yasser Arafat, which had taken place a few weeks earlier.

'The most depressing day of my life,' she said.

I expressed surprise that someone of her apparent sense would miss the elderly buffoon so fervently.

'That's not what I mean,' she sighed. 'It was the crowd. It was . . . us. It was knowing that the world was watching, and seeing Palestinians being chaotic, and angry, and stupid, and threatening, and jumping around firing guns in the air. Again.'

I asked what she'd have preferred to see happen.

'Imagine,' she said, 'if that same crowd – but quiet, unarmed, dignified – had walked with Arafat's coffin to the checkpoint at Qalandia, and politely told the Israeli soldiers that we wanted to carry it to Jerusalem.'

They'd have said no, I said.

'That's right,' said my friend. 'So we'd have sat down, all of us, and waited, quietly, with the coffin, until they let us across, or fired tear gas. With every television camera in the world watching, carrying it live, updates every half-hour. Imagine that.'

It was difficult to picture anything that would have discombobulated the government of Israel and its most boneheaded apologists more, or advanced the cause and image of Palestinians further. Many of the stories that follow are stories of bewilderment at people who aren't doing smart things that they should, or are doing daft things they shouldn't. Some of these stories express admiration for people who are accomplishing marvels. It should be reasonably clear which is which. The note that lingers will hopefully be, well, hopeful – because hope is really the only reason any of us have to get out of bed, or go places.

Come on, wheels. Take this boy away.

1

'You are entering Temple Mount, the holiest place in the world.'

I had no idea who the young man was. He was wearing the black and white rig of the Hasidic Jew, though he'd shed the heavy overcoat in deference to the heat, which shimmered off the golden-white stone forming the backdrop to our encounter. His sideburns were curly, thick and splendid, but the lofty standard they set was unmatched by his forlorn, wispy beard, which looked like he'd glued mattress stuffing to his chin in a bid to fool a bottle-shop proprietor into parting with a quart of Jack Daniel's. His unblinking earnestness suggested, however, that furtive drinking was not the sort of activity that often featured in this teenager's evenings. And, also, that it would probably do him a power of good.

'You must dress and behave modestly,' he continued.

We were on a ramp overlooking the Jewish faithful congregating on the Western Wall plaza. I was waiting for my turn at the metal detector through which tourists and sundry infidels had to pass to enter Temple Mount – an area sacred to all the world's monotheistic faiths and, not coincidentally, the most persistently troublesome few acres on Earth, for three thousand years and counting. Temple Mount, known to Muslims as Haram al-Sharif, was the location of the Dome of the Rock, the magnificent shrine to the lumpy porridge-coloured hilltop upon which Abraham, so one story goes, was joshingly instructed by Yahweh to sacrifice his kid Isaac, and from which Mohammed is said to have vaulted into heaven. Temple Mount also hosts the immense Al-Aqsa Mosque, and was the original repository of the Ark of the Covenant, thought by many to be lying around here somewhere still, beneath thirty turbulent centuries' worth of succeeding rubble.

'No eating or smoking is permitted,' he yapped.

His fervour may have been born partly of frustration. Though Temple Mount was sacred to all monotheistic faiths in theory, it was in practise a Muslim sanctuary, into which very few Israeli Jews ventured. He seemed determined that if he couldn't or wouldn't walk further up the ramp himself, he would at least guide the steps of those who did.

In a seat alongside the metal detector, the uniformed Israeli policeman who searched my bag sighed, shook his head and rolled his eyes as the young man sternly issued further strictures. I got the impression that the cop had been wishing for some time that this clearly self-appointed guardian of Temple Mount's sanctity would go and stand outside the Al-Aqsa and read aloud from *The Satanic Verses*.

'And you may not,' the mysterious sentinel concluded, 'indulge in displays of intimacy.'

I wanted to tell him that this shouldn't be a problem, seeing as how I'd come by myself, and it's hard to think of a less likely pick-up spot than Temple Mount. But, I supposed, you didn't want to get too smart with blazing-eyed Jewish zealots with unruly facial hair in Jerusalem, of all places. You didn't know who you might be upsetting.

In the summer of 2000, Jerusalem's Old City, of which the Temple Mount complex constitutes about a fifth, was something of a boom town – due, ironically, to a lull in incidences of that sound echoing in its streets. There had been a few years of relative peace – or, at least, dormant havoc – following the mid-nineties Oslo Accords between Israel and the Palestine Liberation Organisation. There had been the public relations coup of a papal visit. Secular and religious tourists had combined to become the umpteenth invasion force to descend on Jerusalem. The narrow, cobbled alleys of the Old City thronged with lone dreadlocked backpackers and shoals of package pilgrims. The Old City, which had suffered plenty more threatening incursions over the years, was coping fine. It was possible to send emails from the Via Dolorosa – the street up which Christ trudged to Calvary – while drinking sludgy Arabic coffee served from antique brass salvers, and enjoying the competing, yet eerily complementary, soundtracks of Bryan Adams groaning 'Please Forgive Me' on the internet cafe's stereo and the chanting of a crowd of crucifix-carting Christians in the street outside.

My presence represented an exceedingly trivial testament to the prosperity and confidence alive in Jerusalem at the beginning of the twenty-first century. I'd been sent by the *Sunday Times* to write a travel feature – that is, to suggest to a mainstream readership that they might enjoy a holiday in a place which had, in preceding years, been at best slightly dicey, and at worst an outright war zone. I had been installed, by whichever tour operator was underwriting this jolly, in a vast suite at the justly legendary King David Hotel – the same suite, staff told me, that they'd given British prime minister John Major when he'd come out for Yitzhak Rabin's funeral. Most evenings, cheerful functionaries of Israeli ministries with some link to tourism would appear in the lobby and take me out to riotous dinners. They were excited, optimistic, their enthusiasm for the possibilities of the new epoch as extravagant as their expense accounts.

The bonhomie even appeared to be requited by Israel's traditional enemies. In the Old City's Muslim quarter – Jerusalem's largest, busiest and noisiest sector – Palestinian traders stacked their shopfronts with menorahs, crucifixes, Israeli flags and – unbelievably, all things considered – replica Israeli military uniforms, and T-shirts making joking references to the Israel Defense Forces and Israel's feared intelligence service, Mossad (MY JOB IS SO SECRET EVEN I DON'T KNOW WHAT I'M DOING, smirked the Mossad T-shirt). Jerusalem's principal attraction may have been its thousands of years of still-visible history, but it was greeting the new millennium as the most post-modern place imaginable: a city which existed primarily to sell souvenirs of itself. All that was needed to make the vision of cross-community cooperation perfect was for the prim, glass-fronted stores along the quiet, gleaming lanes of the Old City's Jewish quarter to reciprocate, and start selling colour-in Korans, wind-up Yasser Arafat dolls, and garments proclaiming My brother was martyred waging jihad against the Zionist occupier, and all I got was this lousy T-shirt.

For most of its many centuries of existence, Jerusalem had looked like incontrovertible proof that we, as a species, might as well stop trying. On this visit, though, it really did appear a beacon of hope, in spite of everything, and there seemed to be no reason why the twenty-first century – a phrase which had been shorthand for 'the future' all my life – couldn't be a golden age of peace, love, brotherhood and all the rest of the stuff that Jesus of Nazareth had once tried to interest people in, for all the good it had done him.

The Old City was small, startlingly so. I could cross it wall to wall, on foot, in twenty-five minutes, and that was allowing for delays caused by merchants' handcarts, mobs of somnambulant American school-kids being conducted between buildings full of historically important busted crockery in glass cases, veiled women toting pallets of goods on their hidden heads, swaggering Israeli soldiers, and schools of nuns comparing Last Supper refrigerator magnets.

The spot where Christ's personally calamitous agitations on behalf of universal niceness came to their messy end was believed, by much of the faith he founded, to be beneath the Church of the Holy Sepulchre, in the Christian Quarter of the Old City. In the courtyard outside the church a dozen hefty crucifixes were stacked against a wall. Inside, the American tourists who'd dragged them there were being noisily corralled by their tour guides. I was engulfed in a crowd of handicam-encumbered God-pesterers wearing white baseball caps which read, in blue writing, Regina Tours: 1-800-CATHOLIC. A few handed me their cameras and asked me to take their pictures by the smooth stone slab upon which Christ is said to have been laid after his removal from the cross ('Here's Edna, next to where our saviour perished for our sins. Anyone want another Dorito?').

The Church of the Holy Sepulchre was dank, and gloomy. For this heathen visitor, it didn't inspire much beyond bemusement. Beneath the church's dome, true believers were being sorted from dilettantes by a long, nigh immobile, queue for entry to the shrine which allegedly marked the precise location of the Crucifixion. At the head of this wilting, disconsolate line, rival tour guides were attempting to engineer better positions for their own groups. Two of the guides, pushed beyond decorum by heat and frustration, forgot themselves, and began swatting each other about the ears with their brochures. They were dragged outside by their shirtsleeves by a Greek Orthodox cleric whose resigned frown, crumpling his long grey beard, suggested that this was not unusual.

This outbreak of bitch-slapping between pilgrimage organisers was the only conflict I saw in a week. Measured against Jerusalem's lengthy record of scarcely interrupted mayhem, this might almost have reassured Christ that his breath hadn't been wasted. Was it really possible, I could imagine him wondering, as he rubbed another tube of Savlon into his hands and tossed it onto the Everest-sized heap of empties behind his cloud, that the cantankerous breed of bipeds his father had created were getting the idea after all?

When I got around to writing the story, a few weeks after I returned to London, I was still gripped by an uncharacteristic dawn-of-a-new-era optimism engendered by the visit. I rattled up 1700 breezy words enjoining all who read them to visit Jerusalem at the earliest opportunity, and to bask in the hope which dazzled – I may well have written – like the sun reflecting from the golden Dome of the Rock. I emailed the copy to my editor, brewed a cup of coffee, and sat down to watch the news. The top story was a surprise visit to Temple Mount by retired Israeli general and former defence minister Ariel Sharon, a disgraced has-been in the process of launching the most remarkable comeback witnessed in the region since Lazarus decided he didn't feel so bad after all.

Sharon later described his visit to Temple Mount as 'a message of peace', a statement of almost charming preposterousness. Sharon was reviled – and rightly so – throughout the Arab world for his complicity in the 1982 massacres of Palestinian refugees in Lebanon by Israel's Christian Phalangist allies. As if to illustrate a certain lack of confidence about how his 'message of peace' might go over with Temple Mount's Muslim worshippers, Sharon took with him a protective detail of armed Israeli police of sufficient size that it looked rather more like an invasion force – which was exactly how it was perceived. As gestures of reconciliation went, it was akin to the Reverend Ian Paisley leading an Orange Order parade past the Sinn Fein headquarters on Falls Road in Belfast, while belting a lambeg drum and roaring 'God Save the Queen'. The second Palestinian intifada began almost immediately.

My cheerful travel feature on Jerusalem is yet to run, and I'm glad about that for the interring of the hope-dazzling-like-reflected-sun simile, if for no other reason. As well as being somewhat overwrought on its own merits, the device had been, to use the technical term, OBE – overtaken by events. A year or so later, so would be any remaining delusions that the twenty-first century would be much less foolish and barbarous than any of its predecessors.

2

Six weeks after the event, the felling of New York's highest peaks, by criminals armed with the contents of cutlery drawers, still seemed incredible. Crowds gathered at the flower-festooned barricades around Ground Zero, looking up at what was no longer there.

Eighteen months earlier, I'd ridden the Staten Island ferry with an ex-girlfriend who was living in New York, and we'd taken the obligatory pictures of each other in front of the World Trade Center, using the distance to make the Twin Towers look like science-fiction hallucinations: chunky silver aerials sprouting from our heads, or the remaining legs of a robot parrot which had been shot off our shoulders by the laser blaster of an interplanetary pirate. When I boarded the ferry this time, I found the view blocked by people photographing each other against the backdrop of New York City's abrupt, monumental, outrageous absence. Denial and defiance: neither necessarily conscious, but two common reactions to war.

Back on Manhattan, another predictable response to attack was in evidence: aggression, which in New York was manifesting itself as aggressive enterprise. Freelance stallholders hawked T-shirts bearing pictures of military aircraft soaring over slogans like NOW IT'S OUR TURN and THESE COLORS DON'T RUN. New York's barns of tatty tourist bait had cleared their shelves of 'I ♥ NY' ephemera in favour of Osama bin-Laden toilet paper, GO GET 'EM GEORGE fridge magnets, and bumper stickers of Manhattan's skyline, with the vanquished skyscrapers replaced by a fireman and a police officer, above the words

NEW YORK'S OTHER TWIN TOWERS. Tacky dioramas of firemen and cops, frozen in the square-jawed performance of heroics, had flooded shops with almost suspicious haste. One toyshop had constructed a window display of every Matchbox fire engine in the catalogue. I bought one of these, as well as a couple of packets of Operation Enduring Freedom bubblegum cards. I still have a spare of the USS *Carl Vinson*, if anyone wants to swap for an F-16 and Donald Rumsfeld.

On Times Square, the electronic billboards had been adjusted to wave the American flag above or behind the glittering logos. HSBC – the Hong Kong & Shanghai Banking Corporation – was flying the stars and stripes on its advertisement. The American broadcaster NBC had modestly relegated its technicolour peacock symbol to the bottom corner of an Old Glory overwritten with UNITED WE STAND. Apple Computer had put up a red, white and blue apple, above the words YOU DO US PROUD, NEW YORK NEW YORK. On the hoarding of technology company NCR – a vast replica of an automatic teller machine hanging over the corner of Broadway and West 46th – the screen had temporarily abandoned shilling for custom in favour of messages asking New Yorkers to donate blood, and God to bless America. WE LIVE AS MANY, declared blazing orange bulbs beneath a storey-high Diet Coke bottle, WE STAND AS ONE – although that could have been an actual Coca-Cola slogan.

While the positivist panaceas sounded as clumsy and inadequate as they were, the accidental articulacy of Manhattan's improvised memorials was more than making up for it. In Greenwich Village, the forecourt of the fire station of Engine 24, Ladder 5, had become a shrine. Given the proximity to Ground Zero, the men from this station must have been among the first emergency workers to arrive at the scene. When I remembered how dumbstruck I'd been watching the attack on television in London, I found it impossible to imagine how it must have felt to not only witness it live, but be expected to do something about it. The twenty-four firefighters who rode out of this station that morning had tried, and eleven of them never came back. On the front of the building, flags flew over photos of the missing firefighters, drawings by children, and letters, candles and flowers left by grateful citizens. The station's surviving personnel had hung a banner reading THANK YOU AND GOD BLESS YOU.

There is probably no more overused word in the language than 'hero', and probably no more overused observation than the observation that 'hero' is an overused word. I stuffed some notes in the fire station's collection bucket, and wondered if Bill McGovern, Richard Prunty, Vinny Giammona, Mike Warchola, John Santore, Tommy Hannafin, Greg Saucedo, Paul Keating, Louie Arena, Andy Brunn and Faustino Apostol had realised what extraordinary men they were before it was too late.

With every other hack in the world marooned in Peshawar and Dushanbe, trying to plead, sneak or bribe their way to Kabul in order to be war correspondents, I'd flown to New York, one of about twenty passengers on a United Airlines jet, to be a rock journalist. U2 were doing three nights at Madison Square Garden, and seeing U2 here of all places, now of all times, made sense to me. Like a lot of people who'd grown up loving music to an unusual – some may argue unhealthy – degree, probably more of my outlook and philosophy than I cared to admit had been formed by the songs that had echoed in my consciousness over the years. It had taken me a while to get there where U2 were concerned. The first thing I'd ever written about them was for *Melody Maker*, a sneering review of the Sydney show of their 'Rattle & Hum' tour in 1989. This had been a somewhat self-righteous and adolescent piece of writing, for which – when members of U2 had since joshingly raised it – I could offer no excuse beyond having been a somewhat self-righteous adolescent. But 1991's *Achtung Baby*, a resoundingly intelligent record, and the giddying 'Zoo TV' tour that had accompanied it, had won me over, and I'd written about U2 with a convert's zeal ever since, to the extent of arguing passionately in favour of 1997's *Pop* album, which even U2 didn't like all that much.

I wanted to see U2 here of all places, now of all times, because the thing about their music, and their way of engaging with the world, that had finally cracked my critical carapace, was that it was all driven by persistent, indefatigable faith – a faith which, unusually for rock'n'roll, went out of its way to acknowledge the realities it was defying. 'Pride', their encomium to Martin Luther King Jr, was about him being assassinated. Their most ringingly hopeful, lighters-aloft (or, as was increasingly the case by 2001, mobile phones-aloft) anthems, 'Where The Streets Have No Name' and '(I Still Haven't Found) What I'm Looking For', were about getting lost, and being lost. 'Walk On', the best song on U2's then-current album, *All That You Can't Leave Behind*, sounded a hymn of encouragement and solidarity, Edge's guitar managing to resemble an entire choir of angels, but it was essentially an admission that if we try, and if we hope, as we must, then it's because it's really all we can do.

Even for U2, though, this was surely going to be a rough week: how could they project a ray of light through the dust of what New York had just suffered? Did they even dare try? The three shows had already been scheduled, as part of U2's 'Elevation' world tour, and the tickets had gone on sale as planned, after September 11th – there was never, I was told, any thought of cancelling, and I could believe this, on grounds of self-interest if nothing else. For U2, Madison Square Garden was literally a home fixture. Though the four members of the band were all based in their native Dublin, three also owned homes in New York. U2's passion for the city was summarised in an exuberant song named after New York on *All That You Can't Leave Behind*. It was safe to assume, I thought, that the lines about the Irish feeling like they owned the place amounted to one of Bono's more explicitly autobiographical couplets.

Tickets for the shows had sold out in nothing flat. New York seemed to want something from U2, and while U2's sense of occasion was more finely tuned than most, this looked a challenge. If they waved the flag too high, they'd look like gatecrashers at a funeral. If Bono banged on about forgiveness and tolerance, as he'd been known to do, he'd be asking for the broadside of booing that had battered Richard Gere when he'd tentatively floated the concepts at a charity concert at Madison Square Garden just five days previously. For the first time since the first time they played here, U2 would be thinking of New York as a tough crowd. The T-shirts hanging on the Elevation tour's merchandising stalls were emblazoned with a suitcase with a heart on it. It was a very U2 image – have love, will travel – but here of all times, now of all places, it was an incongruous sentiment to be selling.

Four years earlier, I'd flown to Sarajevo to see U2 take their supernaturally gaudy PopMart show to the Bosnian capital's shrapnel-scarred Koševo stadium. It was about a year and a half after the forty-seven-month siege of the city had ended, and though Bono had all but lost his voice that night, the concert had worked. For a start, the very idea of erecting, in a venue which had until recently been an improvised cemetery, a stage backdrop dominated by an immense swizzle stick impaling a neon olive, half the McDonald's logo and a vast lemon-shaped glitterball was always going to appeal to the hyperactively absurdist Bosnian sense of humour. Beyond that, U2 had located a sensibility that felt at once a lament for a ghastly past and celebration of a restored future. The echoing chorus of gloomy Balkan accents accompanying Edge's lovely solo shot at 'Sunday Bloody Sunday' had sounded sad, angry and proud.

The morning after the Sarajevo show, I'd interviewed Bono in his suite in the bullet-pocked Holiday Inn and asked him if pointing out that war was bad was really enough. 'It's not the job,' he'd said, 'of the artist or writer to come up with solutions. We're not politicians, we're a rock band.' Four years later, that last sentence was less true, at least in Bono's case. Even if he wasn't running for office – once, in Miami on the PopMart tour, when I'd half-jokingly suggested a future tilt at Ireland's presidency, he'd replied, 'I wouldn't move to a smaller house' – he was now very much a political figure, conferring with presidents and prime ministers about trade and Third World debt. Bosnia had been a reasonably easy thing for a rock star to take a stand on, even if a bemusing number of political leaders with air forces had failed to apprehend the desirability of preventing genocide. Bono's guiding principle was that all the world's people were, or should be, each other's problem – an idea which had just been depressingly validated by the partial demolition of a modern metropolis by primitivist maniacs acting under the inspiration of a cave-dwelling crank half a planet away. Whatever was going to follow September 11 was surely going to be a tougher arena in which to pick a side. When U2 played Sarajevo in September 1997, Bosnia's war was over. When U2 played New York in October 2001, America's had just begun.

On opening night, there was a palpable sense that U2 were finding their range, figuring out if there were places that New York wasn't quite ready to be taken. Bono's only reference to the previous month's attack on the city was lingeringly embracing an American flag passed from the audience. Instead of lapsing, as I'd feared he might, into one of his sometimes overcooked uplifting homilies, he talked, during an extended instrumental break in a full-band version of 'Sunday Bloody Sunday', about terrorism closer to where he came from. Earlier that day, the Irish Republican Army, doubtless realising that the buckets they passed around New York bars were likely to come back a little lighter from hereon, had offered a typically disingenuous statement on weapons decommissioning. 'In order to save the peace process,' the IRA had loftily concluded, 'we have implemented the scheme agreed with the Independent International Commission on Decommissioning in August.' That is, agreed back before blowing stuff up suddenly became unfashionable in the IRA's key overseas support base.

'The IRA have put their arms to bed,' Bono announced, to a crowd uncertain as to whether they should clap or not. 'We want to thank these men and these women who made this choice.'

As a Londoner, and therefore resident of a city the IRA had attacked dozens of times, I was disinclined to join the cheers at this point, even if the IRA's campaigns had never caused me personal grief beyond making my train late, and once waking me up, along with everyone else trying to sleep in North London, with the Brent Cross bomb in 1992. I didn't have any doubts about Bono's views on Northern Irish paramilitary thuggery – in U2's 1988 movie *Rattle & Hum*, he famously introduced 'Sunday Bloody Sunday' with a scalding anti-IRA tirade inspired by the bombing of a Remembrance Day ceremony in Enniskillen, the key phrase of which was 'Fuck the revolution'; it had earned the singer death threats. I did have doubts about how much applause the IRA were due for announcing that, after thirty-odd years of murdering and maiming, they were going to destroy as much or as little of their illegal arsenal as they deemed expedient. It wasn't until later, when Bono introduced the second encore, 'One', that it became clear where he was going with this. He explained that IRA violence in the seventies, eighties and nineties had sometimes made Britain an uncomfortable place for an Irishman to be.

'People looked at you funny,' Bono told the crowd. 'What we love about New York is that no one looks at nobody else funny. If you're a Muslim, if you're a dignified follower of Islam, you belong in New York City. Catholics, Jews, blacks, weirdos, rock stars, megalomaniacs, peanut sellers . . .'

He was on a roll, and the crowd were going with him. The roars, at this point, were louder than anything U2 had wrung from their speaker stacks in the previous two hours – which, given that they'd played like men with guns at their backs, was saying something. Bono sensed an opportunity to step briefly into his part-time job, as a globe-trotting lobbyist for Third World debt relief.

'Our one prayer,' he said, 'and you can turn a song into a prayer, is that when the dust settles, and this evil is pushed aside, that in the United States and Europe we can do something about what's going on in Africa. We've seen what happens when one country, Afghanistan, implodes . . . imagine what would happen if the entire continent of Africa were left to implode.'

The applause that followed was probably the loudest ever to greet a seminar on geopolitics, but it dwindled quickly as a blue screen rose behind the stage and, as U2 struck up 'One', scrolled through the names of the crews and passengers of the aeroplanes hijacked on September 11, followed by the police officers killed in the rescue effort, followed by the awful, interminable list of dead or missing firefighters. The names of others lost in the World Trade Center were projected onto the venue's ceiling, where they drifted like thousands of bewildered ghosts. By the end, everyone in the venue seemed to be crying or cheering, and a great many were doing both.

A triumph, I thought, though the following morning's *New York*

Post begged to differ. 'So liberal,' thundered the *Post*'s choleric correspondent of Bono, 'so politically correct, he made you want to puke green . . . you wanted to hit him upside the head.'

'Yeah, I saw it,' said Bono, when I asked him about the *Post*'s review a couple of days later. 'I do understand that singing about peace, love and understanding right now will lead to a certain, ah . . . fuck off factor.'

We were in the singer's apartment, overlooking Central Park, at the end of a long interview. We'd run way over our allotted time, and I'd run out of tape, but Bono, typically, had not run out of conversation. He selected a bottle and began ransacking his kitchen for a corkscrew. In Afghanistan, the planet's most advanced power was exacting its vengeance upon a broke and broken country ruled by the most determinedly backward government of modern times: the Taliban, an unpleasant gaggle of obscurantist dingbats who made the Amish look like Vulcans.

'Do you think any of this is ultimately going to do Afghanistan any good?' asked Bono, clattering fruitlessly in his cupboards. I found the corkscrew myself, in the first place I looked, which was the drawer you'd expect the corkscrew to be in, and jangled it at Bono, who was gently tapping the bottle's neck on the side of the granite bench, daring himself to break it off, valiantly risking the ventricles of his insurers, so as not to be a poor host.

From what I remembered of Afghanistan, I answered, it could hardly make it much worse.

3

KABUL, AFGHANISTAN
MARCH 2003

After a few days back in town, I decided that the only way to keep track of the difference between the Kabul of 2003 and the Kabul I remembered was to tally everything that would have been illegal during my previous visit, five years earlier. Back in 1998, Kabul had been a fiefdom of the Taliban, the sensationally batty fundamentalist cult which was part George Orwell's Thought Police and part Monty Python's Spanish Inquisition: terrifying, yet difficult to take entirely seriously. The Taliban had outlawed pretty much everything, on pain of flogging, except facial hair and praying, which they'd made compulsory. They prowled Kabul in Toyota pickups, wearing their signature black turbans and Ray-Ban sunglasses, enforcing with peremptory violence their laws against women inadvertently flashing their ankles or riding in taxis accompanied by men to whom they were unrelated. In a city of undrinkable water and intermittent electricity, their sense of priorities was quaint.

If the Taliban's curious creed of Koran and Kalashnikov had still prevailed in Kabul, then on this trip I could have warranted the lash for committing any or all of the following: taking photographs, talking to women, watching television, listening to music, buying postcards of Bollywood starlets, staying out late, drinking beer, reading magazines, helping children fly kites and, most heinously, employing a barber to give me a shave.

'A miracle from the skies,' Dr Abdullah Sherzai called the new Kabul. 'A complete rebirth.'

While the overwhelming might of their western opposition had been persuading the Taliban fighters holding Kabul that martyrdom might be an overrated option, Dr Sherzai, a neurologist whose family had fled Afghanistan in the 1970s, was watching events unfold on television from his home in America. Now, eighteen months later, he'd given up his comfortable, profitable life in America for a wage of US$40 a month from the Afghan Transitional Authority's Ministry of Health, and a room at Kabul's Mustafa Hotel. The Mustafa was the favoured haunt of visiting press, aid workers, UN staff and members of that mysterious class of carpetbaggers which always descends on post-war environments, invariably equipped with a grant from some Scandinavian government ministry to make a documentary whose subject and purpose will completely confuse the locals, and which will never be watched by anybody.

The Mustafa had a great location, around the corner from the souvenir and rug shops of Chicken Street, and an intoxicating frontier atmosphere. The reception staff in the downstairs lobby kept Kalashnikovs behind the desk. A bullethole in one wall of the hotel's restaurant dated from a dispute between the manager and a patron a couple of weeks before I checked in. I got talking to Dr Sherzai in the restaurant one night, during one of the beer-fuelled salons that erupted around the tables after dinner. Sherzai hadn't visited Afghanistan during the lunatic reign of the Taliban – a well-off exile from the States would not have been the most popular of visitors – but he summed up their Kabul better than I ever did.

'They outlawed all the senses,' he said. 'There was nothing to look at, nothing to listen to, nobody you could touch. Even the food didn't taste of anything.' Sherzai didn't mention smell, but then neither the Taliban's righteous fury nor the reconstruction efforts of Kabul's liberators had found a way to subdue the city's open sewers. 'People are building things now,' said Sherzai. 'People hope.'

This seemed to be the case. People had been fleeing Afghanistan for decades. At the end of 2001, the two countries with the largest refugee populations in the world were Iran and Pakistan, both of which bordered Afghanistan. But my flight from Dubai to Kabul with Ariana Afghan Airlines – known locally, not without reason, as Insh'allah ('If God wills it') Airways – had been crowded. The terminal in Kabul was as near the contradictory idea of a medieval airport as could be imagined. But the mood in the queue at passport control, as we struggled for balance on a marble floor which some genius had polished with engine oil, had been cheerful (that said, these were the same people who, as we'd made our descent, had pointed and laughed at the aircraft wreckage piled at the ends of the runways). Nobody seemed to mind that the conveyor belt for baggage reclaim hadn't moved since about 1982, or that retrieving our luggage necessitated crawling out of the arrivals hall through the hole at the end of the belt, finding our bags on the runway, and then crawling back into the terminal with them, like escaping prisoners emerging from a tunnel with the knapsacks in which we'd secreted our bogus SS uniforms.

Rarely in the field of human conflict can so many have been so grateful for being bombed so much. At the Golden Lotus Hotel, a sign announced READY AGAIN TO SERVE YOU EACH KIND OF INTERNAL AND EXTERNAL DELICIOUS FOODS. Along Chicken Street, shopkeepers were adapting to the new reality with admirable agility. The merchandise I'd seen in 1998 – fur coats, leather bags, lapis lazuli jewellery, assorted hammer-and-sickle-emblazoned Soviet detritus – had been joined by exquisite woodcuts of British regimental cap badges and crockery covered with the flags of the twenty-nine foreign militaries contributing to the International Security Assistance Force (ISAF) in Kabul. ISAF, at this time under joint German–Dutch command, was essentially the good cop to the bad cop of Operation Enduring Freedom, the American-led pursuit of the Taliban and al-Qaeda, based out at the former Soviet airbase at Bagram.

In Habibi Books (HISTORY CALE BOOKS & GREATINGSCARDS, promised the sign out the front, ALL KINDS OF FRINCH & ENGLISH MAGAZINES), I found a locally produced bootleg of *Flashman* – the first in George MacDonald Fraser's series of fictional memoirs of the bully of Thomas Hughes' Victorian novel *Tom Brown's Schooldays*.

Fraser's *Flashman* followed the great anti-hero's progress from his expulsion from Rugby to his bewildered participation in the calamitous British Afghan campaign of 1839–42. The edition in Habibi was subtitled 'Story of British disaster in Afghanistan', and purported to be the 'First Kabul edition, 2002'.

I loved the idea that this racy, cynical novel must have been one of the first books, other than the Koran, published in Afghanistan for years. I'd interviewed Fraser the year before in London. A man whose opinions of military adventurism were formed by his own experience as a teenage sniper-scout in Burma during World War II, he'd been firmly against the 2001 intervention in Afghanistan, for robustly honest reasons which no ostentatiously concerned peacenik would dare utter ('I don't give a damn who runs Afghanistan,' he'd growled. 'Why is it our problem?'). When I got back to London, I posted him the Afghan bootleg of his novel, with a note suggesting that the recent invasion hadn't been a complete waste of blood and treasure. In his reply he proclaimed himself 'delighted and flattered' that his creation had been thus pirated, but I doubted I'd changed his mind.

In Chicken Street's carpet shops, the famous Soviet-era war rugs, with their deftly woven AK-47 rifles, Mi-8 helicopters and T-54 tanks, had been supplanted by new designs: blazing World Trade Centers, cartoonish images of the foreign forces that came to Afghanistan as a result, and picturesquely spelled summaries of the plot: ROUT OF TERORISM (sic), read one, WITH HELP OF AMERICA AND BRITAIN. The 9/11 rugs were spectacular, but I wasn't sure I fancied being reminded of the event every time I walked up my hall. The one I finally settled on was titled WAR AGAINST TERRORIST. Around a map of Afghanistan, it showed a Chinook helicopter, a couple of tanks, a rocket-propelled-grenade launcher, hand grenades, some bullets, and a bomber, helpfully captioned 'B-52'. AFGHANS LIBERATED FROM TERORIST (sic) read woven words. LONG LIVE US SOLDIERS, it said on the bottom.

Other rugs depicted Ahmed Shah Massoud, the legendary anti-Soviet mujahideen leader turned legendary anti-Taliban Northern Alliance commander, who'd been killed by al-Qaeda suicide bombers, posing as journalists, on 9 September 2001. In death, Massoud had become an Afghan Che Guevara – someone whose actual record didn't stand serious scrutiny, but who'd talked a poetic fight and looked cool gazing towards the middle distance in pictures. His rockets had killed thousands of Kabul's citizens during the 1990s, but his portrait was everywhere, including over the WELCOME TO KABUL sign at the airport. It was much harder work finding pictures of Afghanistan's new president, Hamid Karzai. From beyond the grave, Massoud had scooped a mandate with the weirdest electoral strategy in history: 'Vote Ahmed! He only flattened half the capital!'. In one shop, I asked about a dish engraved with Massoud's handsome face, but the seller, who was willing to deal on any other item, wouldn't budge below US$30, as if bargaining over Massoud's image would have been sacrilegious.

I spent days bickering with the shopkeepers on Chicken Street. It was fun, and there are few better ways to get a sense of a place than to ask people how business is. Buying anything on Chicken Street involved interminable glasses of tea, swapping of family photos, and vigorous haggling. The buyer would insinuate that the seller was a pillaging crook, and the seller would dutifully declare that the buyer was a heartless tightwad who would starve a man's family to save ten bucks on a carpet. During these encounters, whenever I asked about the removal of the Taliban and the presence of foreign soldiers in Kabul, I couldn't provoke anything but rejoicing, and I don't think it was just because they were doing such a roaring trade in replica nineteenth-century British army Lee-Enfield rifles.

'I waited a week to make sure the Taliban were gone,' said Allah Mansoor at Yamood Carpet. 'Then I got my beard cut.'

'The Taliban knocked one of my teeth out,' said Said Omer. 'Of course I'm happy they've gone. I hope ISAF stay forever.' Said, all of eleven years old, insisted that he was the proprietor of Said Omer Antiques, and pointed to his name on the business card to prove it. When his father appeared behind the counter, he confirmed this. 'Talk to the boss,' he smiled, nodding at Said. 'Get back to work,' instructed Said, without missing a beat, and then, with a roll of the eyes, whispered, 'He's very lazy.' I bought some lapis lazuli boxes, and

Said gave me a scarf and one of the pakoul-style hats in which Massoud had looked such a hero, and in which I looked a total goose.

The black market money changers outside Kabul's Blue Mosque had cleaned up under the Taliban as Afghanistan's currency, the afghani, peaked and troughed as spectacularly as Afghanistan's scenery, but they wouldn't have had the Taliban back for any amount. In 1998, I'd waddled Kabul's streets with the side pockets of my combats stuffed with thick wads of all but worthless afghanis. Post-Taliban, the afghani had stabilised at around forty to the dollar, officially. The money changers were offering fifty to the dollar. They said business was lousy, but life was much better.

A mechanic called Mohammed told me much the same. 'We are not yet making enough for me to get married,' he said. 'But this was a terrible, boring place under the Taliban. We are free now. I just hope nobody forgets us.'

Kabul's sports scene had also been revived (the Taliban used to grudgingly permit football, with pre-match entertainment of criminals and adulterers getting bits lopped off). I attended a match of Afghanistan's national sport, buzkashi, in which whip-wielding horsemen drag a goat carcass around a paddock. Buzkashi is violent and noisy, and it is impossible to figure out what the participants are doing or how anyone wins. I mention it only in the vague hope that there might be some sort of prize on offer for being the millionth writer to compare buzkashi to Afghan politics.

The people best able to tell me how Kabul had changed were the people who hadn't been able to tell me anything last time I'd been in town: the women. On arrival in Kabul in 1998, I'd been read the riot act at the Taliban's foreign ministry by their press liaison officer, one Dr Aminzai. Of the many rules he'd laid down – no breaking curfew, no photographing people, no going anywhere without my Taliban-appointed translator – he was sternest about one. 'You will not,' he'd said, 'be able to talk to women.' In an effort to lighten the mood, I'd told him not to worry, it was like that at home, but he didn't find my quip amusing. 'It will mean trouble for you,' he'd hissed, 'and worse trouble for them.' I didn't doubt that he was serious, and so didn't push my luck. While the worst that could have happened to me was probably a drive back to the border in a Taliban pickup, followed by an unceremonious heave over the gate back into Pakistan, I didn't want to be the reason some poor woman got flogged. It had been profoundly depressing, though, watching Kabul's women blundering about the unmaintained, potholed, chaotic streets, shrouded in those absurd purple and blue burkas, like extras from an exceedingly low-budget ghost movie.

It would be an exaggeration to report that, Dr Aminzai's employers having been put to flight, Kabul's pavements suddenly clopped with stiletto-shod babes in mini-skirts comparing navel rings as they walked to their astrophysics class. Most women were still wearing the burka, out of fear or habit or peer pressure or – it takes all sorts – preference. A woman's face, even one framed by a scarf, was still unusual enough to be noticeable. I only saw one woman who hid neither her face nor her hair, but one was a start, especially when it was this one.

I met Jamila Mujahid in the AINA compound, which was home to much of Kabul's fledgling media. A thirty-nine-year-old mother of five, Mujahid was the editor of a new English-language publication called *Malalai*, 'A Social and Cultural Magazine for Women'; the March 2003 issue, its tenth, contained beauty tips, recipes and an investigation into whether there are health risks in washing clothes in the Kabul River (executive summary: yes). She was also launching a radio station. It sounded like the frantic activity of someone desperate to make up for lost – or, in her case, stolen – time, and it was. Before the Taliban descended on Kabul, Mujahid was Afghanistan's best-known broadcaster, a fixture on Radio Afghanistan. In 1996, the Taliban renamed the station Radio Shariat, cancelled its programming in favour of an indigestible stew of religious harangues, and sent all the women employees home – where, at colossal risk to herself, Mujahid spent the next five years running secret classes for girls. 'We had to hide the books,' she smiled, 'so those burkas were good for something.'

I wondered what people in Kabul had made of September 11 when it happened, and how quickly they'd understood what it might mean for them.

'I heard about it on the BBC World Service and Voice of America, on an illegal radio,' she said. 'We all knew this would be a fiasco for the Taliban. Everyone was thinking that now we would be rescued, and liberated.'

On 13 November 2001, Mujahid went back to work. Radio Shariat was Radio Afghanistan again.

'I announced the fall of the Taliban on the radio,' she said. 'I took off my burka as soon as the Taliban fled. It was the first time I'd gone out uncovered for five years. I'm not putting it back on.'

Among the foreign soldiers protecting Mujahid's right to see where she was going without being beaten up by some bearded bonehead who thought he was working for God, were 100-odd British soldiers stationed at Camp Souter, formerly a fertiliser factory on the outskirts of town on the road to Jalalabad. The British had history around here, of course. Their first effort to impose a semblance of order on Afghanistan had been that disastrous campaign of the first *Flashman* book. In 1839, Britain wanted to replace an inconveniently independent-minded Afghan Emir called Dost Mohamed with an obliging stooge called Shah Shuja. A mighty force of British and Indian troops marched on Kabul, and established a garrison in support of their favoured puppet. Their failure, over the next few years, to establish a template for benign stewardship of a peaceful Kabul, is best illustrated by the fact that most of what is known about this intervention comes from the recollections of the man who became widely celebrated as its sole survivor: Dr William Brydon, who reached the British lines at Jalalabad, riding a dying horse, on January 6 1842. Subsequent British enterprises, the Second Afghan War (1878–80) and Third Afghan War (1919) were, at best, qualified successes.

The British soldiers serving in what, I was sure, they didn't want anyone calling the Fourth Afghan War (2001–who knows?) had a commendable grasp of history, and a serene attitude to tempting fate. Camp Souter was named after a Captain Souter, who was found wrapped in his regimental standard after the last stand of the 44th Regiment of Foot during the disastrous 1842 retreat. When I arrived at Camp Souter with photographer Damian Bird from *Esquire* magazine, it was also clear that the soldiers were determined to go about their business in as British a fashion as possible. The security protocols at the gate were more relaxed than at any American airport.

'Anything in your rucksack likely to go bang?' asked a corporal. 'No? Jolly good. Come in, I'll get the kettle on.'

Camp Souter's commanding officer, Colonel Mark Theobald, was kind enough to laugh when I asked if he ever woke at night screaming the name of Major General William Elphinstone, who'd led the Kabul garrison to the catastrophe of 1842.

'The circumstances are different,' said Colonel Theobald. 'We're here to help get things back to normal – or rather, I suppose, to normal.'

Such, in this new century of ours, was going to be much of the lot of the modern soldier – training to break and destroy, then going into the field to fix and build. There was plenty of the latter to be done in Kabul – everything in the city needed to be repaved, repainted, reglazed, rewired or dusted – and I'd be returning to Camp Souter later in this visit and spending time with the foreign armies charged with doing it. But Afghanistan was only the latest episode in one of the most popular reality gameshows of the early twenty-first century: *Changing Regimes*, a makeover program in which eager specialists descended on a place, took down the fixtures and fittings which had fallen behind fashion ('Dictatorship? Theocracy? Nobody's doing that anymore'), passed mocking comment as they tossed them into the skip ('Refusal to accede to American hegemony? *Sooo* last century'), and then lectured the people who lived there about how to do it properly.

The title sequence of the Iraq episode was still a few days from rolling, but Afghanistan had been presaged by several one-off specials: Somalia in 1993, Bosnia-Herzegovina in 1995, East Timor in 1999, and, that same year, Kosovo. Which, after all those years and all that money, must surely have become a sunlit upland of democracy, where the national emblems of its constituent peoples, the double-headed white eagle of Serbia and the double-headed black eagle of Albania, had amiably amalgamated to form a doubtless ungainly but nevertheless happy creature, whose four beaks were warbling, in perfect harmony, a soaring, stirring anthem of brotherhood.

4

PODUJEVO, KOSOVO POLJE AND PRISTINA, KOSOVO OCTOBER 2004

Five or so kilometres east of Podujevo, there was a border which wasn't a border, marked by a border post which wasn't a border post. The border post which wasn't a border post looked like a border post – and a pretty serious border post at that, of the sort that once disfigured Europe when there was still a wall across the continent. At the border post which wasn't a border post, there were steel mesh fences crowned with razor wire, sandbagged observation positions, guns probing from camouflage netting, barricades made of gravel poured into enormous plastic sacks, and a carport-like structure beneath which vehicles were being bailed up and searched. A red and white sign warned STOP – CUSTOMS. The border post which wasn't a border post was manned by armed police, and even more formidably tooled-up soldiers, who operated out of a fortified compound at the side of the road. I asked one of the police if the border had been busy, this fine autumn morning. I used the word 'border' deliberately, and he picked up on it instantly.

'This isn't a border,' he grinned, his moustache twitching beneath his silver reflector shades. 'It's an administrative boundary line.'

'Administrative boundary line', it struck me, was a term which could function as a nigh perfect dictionary definition of the word 'border', but at the installation known as Gate 3, the difference between a border and an administrative boundary line was important. Gate 3 was a crossing point between Serbia and Kosovo. Legally, technically and theoretically, Kosovo was a province of the state of what was, then, still Serbia and Montenegro (leave it to the Serbs, a people who'd spent two decades playing what looked like an immense practical joke on themselves, to arrive at a name for their country which abbreviated as the Republic of S&M). On paper, this border – or administrative boundary line – mattered less than the frontier which divided Scotland from England. In reality, it mattered a great deal.

'But, yeah,' said the cop. 'Pretty quiet this morning. Busier in the summer.'

The cop was a retired police officer from Miami. He was here with the dizzyingly multinational police force attached to the United Nations Interim Administration Mission in Kosovo (UNMIK). The efforts of dozens of nations to prevent further violence between the peoples of Serbia and Kosovo was creating surreal bedfellows all over Kosovo, but nowhere more than at Gate 3. The military contingent at Gate 3, part of NATO's Kosovo Force (KFOR), was comprised principally of troops from the Czech Republic and Slovakia. That is, the armies of two Slavic peoples from former Eastern bloc states which had separated from each other during the 1990s – although, in polar contrast to the Yugoslav model, without so much as scratching the furniture. When the American policeman decided I should really speak to his boss, he fetched a Russian colonel decked out in extravagantly braided mess kit.

'Sorry about the fancy dress,' said the colonel, who clicked his boot heels together as we shook hands. 'I'm flying home to Moscow tonight.'

The previous day in Pristina, Kosovo's capital, I'd been hanging out in cafes near the immense UN headquarters in the heart of the city, logging historically incongruous dining partners among the KFOR troops. I saw Irish officers having a beer with British officers. Pakistanis lunching with Indians. Turks sharing coffee with Greeks. The locals weren't taking the hint. Five years after NATO had gone to war to prevent genocide in Kosovo, this was how weird Kosovo had become – Russians commanding Americans seemed, relative to everything else, normal. I asked the colonel how he'd been getting on with his opposite numbers recently. I could see them in the distance: Serbian police, stationed at what, as far they were concerned, wasn't a border post at all – not even a border post which wasn't a border post – but a bogus imposition of a malign international community.

'We're all adults,' said the colonel. 'If there's a problem, we talk. You don't solve anything by confrontation.'

What about March, I asked. In March 2004, seven months before, Kosovo had been convulsed by ethnic violence, which seeped south from its beginnings as a punch-up in Mitrovica to swamp the province. Hundreds of homes, mostly belonging to Kosovo's few remaining Serbs, had been destroyed, and at least nineteen people, mostly Serbs, had been killed.

'Here, March was not so bad,' said the colonel.

'March was hilarious,' interjected another American, this one a plainclothes translator. 'Three waves of 'em – Serbs – came charging down the road, through the checkpoint, all over our position. They took our computers and metal detectors.'

Then what happened?

'A couple of days later the Serbian police brought them all back.'

By the road on the Kosovo side of the border which wasn't a border, there was a cafe, operating out of a rickety caravan. I took a chair at one of the plastic tables arranged in front of it, along with my guide for the day, Captain Thomas Magnusson – a Swedish army reservist who'd driven me up from Pristina. Despite the unglamorous surroundings, the cafe's owner was punctilious about service, bringing excellent Turkish-style coffee in china cups on a silver tray. A car, which had just been permitted to cross the administrative boundary line from Serbia, stopped in front of us.

'Watch this,' Captain Magnusson said.

The driver got out of the red Yugo coupe, fished a screwdriver from his trousers, and removed the front and rear licence plates from the car. This operation completed, he opened his boot, threw the plates in, retrieved two other licence plates and attached them to the bumpers. He looked at us, regarding Captain Magnusson with a somewhat sour expression, and drove off.

'Yugoslav plates off,' explained Captain Magnusson, 'Kosovo plates on. This isn't a good place to be taken for a Serb.'

There would be many who would find it difficult to muster much sympathy for the Serbs on that score. When Kosovo was practically as well as technically a province of Serbia, its ethnic Albanian majority were subject to repressions ranging from petty bigotry to what, in late 1998 and early 1999, was looking like the beginnings of an attempted genocide similar to that which had been perpetrated by Serbia's proxies in neighbouring Bosnia-Herzegovina earlier that decade. When NATO's air forces began a seventy-nine-day bombing campaign against Serbian targets in Kosovo and Serbia, 1.3 million Kosovars – slightly more than half Kosovo's population – became refugees from Serbia's revenge, heading south into Macedonia and west over the mountains into Albania.

In May 1999, I'd met some of the (relatively) fortunate ones, who'd been evacuated to temporary accommodations in Manchester and Leicester.

While I'd been collecting the refugees' stories, I kept thinking that they sounded familiar. It was while I was talking to a young woman from Pristina called Ardiana that I made the connection. She'd had her door kicked in by masked paramilitaries dressed in black. They'd given her family five minutes to pack, then herded them aboard a hideously crowded train, destination unknown. I realised I had heard her story before – on television, told by old Polish women in head-scarves, about the 1940s. Ardiana, a twenty-one-year-old dentistry student in jeans and a T-shirt, was telling me what had happened to her last week. It was difficult not to nod when another refugee who, when asked about Kosovo's future, said, 'There's no going back now. It's ours or it's theirs.'

I went to Kosovo in 2004 in search of an idea of what the West's nation-building attempts in Iraq and Afghanistan might look like five years or so down the track. There were similarities. We'd bombed this place, as we'd bombed Afghanistan and Iraq, for reasons that purported to be at least partly humanitarian. The foreign troops still in Kosovo were an occupying force on Muslim territory, although most Kosovars articulated attitudes to Islam similar to what most Europeans would say of Christianity. It was what they were, they supposed, if anyone asked, but in practice they saved their prayers for bumpy flights and penalty shoot-outs.

At Pristina's modest airport, I struggled through a scrum of Pakistanis who, despite their smart suits, were being noisily deported. Arrivals formalities were minimal. A yawning UNMIK official from Thailand handed me over to a local customs officer. She leafed through my passport, smiled when she spotted the stamps from a visit to Albania the previous year, and planted the UNMIK stamp beneath them. There was no proper Kosovo passport stamp, because there was not a state empowered to issue them – although I'd arrived in time for elections to decide who wasn't governing this country which wasn't there.

I was met outside the airport by my friend Nick, a former British army paratrooper who had been working in the Balkans in various capacities for years, and was running a private security franchise in Pristina. Nick hated the place, but then hating things – loudly, exuberantly, hilariously – was what Nick did. Had he devoted his post-service career to the Foreign and Commonwealth Office, he could have single-handedly plunged Britain into wars larger, bloodier and even further afield than the one they fought here.

'It's a dump,' said Nick, wrestling with the gearstick of his Land Rover like a man throttling a snake. 'End of chat. I mean, look at it.'

I was looking at it, and the view, jolted occasionally as the vehicle ricocheted out of potholes, wasn't encouraging. On first acquaintance, I was thinking that Pristina had better be able to cook, or tell a good joke, or have a cute sister. There's a kind of modern urban architecture whose unremitting ugliness seems too acute to be the result of lack of funds, or necessity for swift building, or even carelessness. There's a lot of it in former communist states, on the outskirts of cities like Moscow, Bucharest and Tbilisi, but you also see a lot of it in London – the view from my lounge room window in Hackney is dominated by a crumbling tenement which resembles a twenty-storey public toilet. It's an ugliness so complete that it can only be a wilful gesture of contempt for every poor sap who will have to live in it or look at it. All of Pristina looked like it had been designed according to this creed, and then daubed in a brown suggestive of the post-match whites of a cricketer who had been patrolling an especially damp outfield, or facing extremely quick bowling.

The balcony of Nick's house provided an ideal vantage point for contemplating Pristina's monumental unattractiveness. Across the stalls of a vast bootleggers' market, the view included a crumbling football stadium, the Grand Hotel – which had acquired a certain lustre as the preferred flophouse for correspondents covering the 1999 war – and an ungainly, angular basketball stadium that looked like either a kit-built Japanese temple that got posted to the wrong country, or a spaceship parked by aliens who'd set out with a particularly poorly researched guide to Earth. Almost everything was brown, and what wasn't brown was grey.

'We didn't bomb it enough,' said Nick.

Taking in the sights, as Nick had confidently predicted, didn't take long. Along Pristina's main road, Mother Teresa Street, there were a couple of cool Soviet-style statues of fallen Kosovo Liberation Army (KLA) veterans, radiating a pride that the drab flats and shops behind them scarcely seemed to merit. There was a statue of Teresa herself – though the dictator-hugging fraud was born in Macedonia, she is claimed as kin by Kosovars and Albanians – and another of Skanderbeg, the fifteenth-century Albanian national hero. The latter, a copy of the statue which presides over Skanderbeg Square in Tirana, was oddly proportioned – Skanderbeg, as the sculptor saw it, was either an extremely big chap, or rode a very small horse.

In front of the Grand Hotel, a thicket of flagpoles flew the banners of the USA, the UN, NATO, Albania and the EU. Further along was Pristina's only genuinely distinguished building – distinguished in that it was ugly even by local standards, and therefore possibly the ugliest building in the world. Looking at Pristina University's library was like being squirted in the eyes with bleach. It was a misshapen concrete wart inexplicably crowned with white domes fashioned from mildewing triangular plastic panels. Every surface was upholstered with trellises of metal bars, possibly fitted as a protective measure aimed at reducing the damage which might be inflicted by an aesthetically outraged truck bomber.

Pristina's more even vertical surfaces were covered in posters touting candidates seeking election to Kosovo's parliament. Most numerous were those bearing the portrait of Dr Ibrahim Rugova, veteran figurehead of the brave and ingenious pre-war campaign of civil disobedience waged by Kosovo's ethnic Albanians, exemplar of the cravat-wearing, pipe-sucking Balkan intellectual, and leader of the LDK – the Democratic League of Kosovo. Almost as plentiful were those bearing the grinning, thumbs-aloft photos of Hashim Thaci and Bajram Rexhepi, the former once a KLA commander, the latter a KLA field doctor. They were leading the ticket of the PDK – the Democratic Party of Kosovo. The parties' platforms were as excitingly divergent as their names. The LDK wanted to see Kosovo independent, whereas the the PDK sought an independent Kosovo.

The trouble for both the PDK and the LDK was that where it was once obvious enough who their oppressors were, and easy enough to marshal hatred and resistance against those oppressors, what stood between Kosovo and statehood now was the same international community which had brought it this far. Kosovo had, in effect, traded being colonised by the Serbs for being colonised by everybody but the Serbs. UN Security Council resolution 1244 formally declared Kosovo a UN protectorate. UNMIK didn't look that big on paper: 656 international civilians, 202 UN volunteers, 2494 local civilians and 2612 civilian police, operating on an annual budget of about US$250 million. But its physical presence in Pristina was massive.

There was the expansive headquarters, bristling with satellite dishes, surrounded by fences. There was the industry that attended it: the cafes, the restaurants, and the vendors of bootleg CDs, DVDs and computer games shifting their product (PlayStation games from two euros, CDs from one euro) to UN employees unbothered that they were subsidising the organised crime they were supposed to be helping to prevent. There were the vehicles: the big white Toyota Land Cruisers, liberally iced by the blackbirds which filled Pristina's sky, parked bumper to bumper all along both sides of Luan Haradinaj Street. Between the UN, KFOR and the countless NGOs running around the place, Pristina resembled the world's largest gathering of SUV enthusiasts. One afternoon, waiting for a lift by an intersection, I passed the time by counting Land Cruisers spangled with the logos of foreign peacekeepers and interloping do-gooders. I recorded thirty-two in twenty minutes, and reflected that next time some hitherto obscure pocket of Europe plunges into chaos, the smart move would be to load up on shares in Toyota.

Kosovo became a battlefield in 1999 partly because it had been a battlefield in 1389. On 28 June that year, the army of Serbia's Prince Lazar had been trounced by Sultan Murad's invading Ottomans, and sections of Serbian society had been sulking about it ever since. Six centuries later, Slobodan Milosevic had stood before a million people on the spot where the battle took place and given a speech which was, effectively, the kick-off whistle for the wars of the former Yugoslavia. Near the climax of his turgid, soppy litany of self-pity and paranoia, Milosevic had noted, 'Now, we are being again engaged in battles and are facing battles. They are not armed battles, although such things cannot be excluded yet.' This rather undermined the praise for multiculturalism he'd recited a few paragraphs previously.

Like Lazar and Murad before me, I arrived at Kosovo Field with an impressive military force – a three-vehicle convoy of Swedish, Czech and Slovak troops, which seemed an overzealous response to the request I'd filed for a lift if anyone was going that way anyway.

'It's a nice day for a drive,' said the Swedish colonel commanding the lead car. 'Anyway, we don't have much else to do.'

The Kosovo Field memorial was a stone tower on a hillside over-looking the battlefield. At the foot of the tower, Lazar's eve-of-battle address was embossed in Cyrillic letters: 'Those who are Serbian and have a Serbian heart and do not come to battle for Kosovo will not have children – neither male nor female – crops or wine. They will be damned until they die.' Lazar had clearly not subscribed to the 'Be all you can be' theory of recruitment. The tower was surrounded by barbed wire, watchtowers, sandbagged gun emplacements and tanks belonging to the Czech and Slovak soldiers who protected it from the vengeance of local Kosovars (the KLA tried to blow it up in 1999, but either the tower was too strong, or the KLA's explosives too weak). The foreign troops were aided in their task by the tower itself, which they used as a lookout, taking turns to bask with a pair of binoculars by a field radio. I asked the Slovak corporal on watch whether his job was as dull as it looked.

'For sure,' he sighed. 'As long as we're here, nobody will try anything, because we'd see them coming from miles away. So we kind of cancel ourselves out. It's much worse up here in the winter, though.'

At the foot of the tower, in the small barracks built from steel demountables, his shirtless comrades played with the menagerie of stray cats and dogs they'd adopted. The Czech and Slovak flags flew side by side at the gate, reminders that the business of nation-dividing could be a peaceful one if everyone involved decided not to be a jerk about it. It takes rare humility, though. While I probably knew enough about Slobodan Milosevic to hold my own in an eponymously themed round of a pub quiz, I couldn't have named the first president of the independent Slovakia with a gun at my head.

'While we are in this area,' said the Swedish colonel, 'you should see Obilic.'

I asked if it was nice.

'No,' chorused several Czech and Slovak accents.

They weren't wrong. Obilic was . . . well, for a start it wasn't really called Obilic anymore. Obilic had originally been named after the Serbian knight Milos Obilic, who had distinguished himself at the battle of Kosovo Field by sneaking into Sultan Murad's tent and clouting him with a sword. On the signs on the outskirts of town, OBILIC had been obliterated by spray paint, and replaced with KASTRIOT – after Georgi Kastrioti, the birth name of Skanderbeg. The reason that Skanderbeg was an Albanian national hero was that he, like Lazar and Obilic, had defended his land and people from marauding Ottomans, but the enemy-of-my-enemy-is-my-friend principle wasn't buying Obilic any friends in Kosovo.

I didn't need to spend long in Obilic/Kastriot to decide that the argument the locals should be having wasn't what to call it, but whether to bulldoze the place or dynamite it. It was a dump. The nearby power station, a vast brown relic resembling a rusty warship which had somehow ploughed inland, belched smoke which rendered the air perceptibly yellow. It stang the eyes, tasted rancid on the tongue, and smelled like a kitchen waste disposal struggling with an unsuccessful paella. The atmosphere also stank in a less tangible, but even more depressing, respect. Since the disturbances of the previous March, Obilic/Kastriot's sectarian tensions had become formalised. The remaining Serbs in the town existed – 'lived' seemed the wrong word – under round-the-clock armed guard provided by KFOR. Seventy-two Serbs, burned or terrorised out of their homes, were staying in a school which had been turned into temporary accommodation, surrounded by sandbags and razor wire. The soldiers on sentry duty were, again, Czechs and Slovaks.

This must just kill you guys, I said.

'What can I say?' asked the Slovak captain. 'Our country didn't work as it was, and it had to separate. But we never hated each other, not like these people. We didn't have these stupid peasant feuds.'

The Serbs they were guarding sat gloomily on benches beneath the trees in the playground. A couple of children teased the pet dogs which had been incarcerated in cages.

'I don't know what's to be done,' said a Czech sergeant. 'The Serbs can't work, because nobody wants them here. But Kosovo is supposed to want its Serbs to stay. There is just no reasoning with anybody in this place.'

One night, Nick took me to Kukri, a pub next to the UN building. Decorated with English and Scottish football shirts, it had once, according to Nick, who'd worked in Pristina shortly after the war, been 'like that spaceport bar in *Star Wars*, full of the most bizarre people you'd ever meet.' Now, in Nick's assessment, Kukri was 'full of wankers, clock-watchers and time-servers, who'd have shat themselves if they'd come here back then.' I didn't have time to make a comprehensive assessment of this claim, but I did get talking to a bunch of internationals, American and European, who reacted to inquiries about Kosovo's viability with well-rehearsed snorts.

'Albanians,' said one, 'are children. Funny and cute, and everything, but helpless.'

'It'll never happen,' slurred another. 'Fucking cabbage-monkeys.'

'Useless,' hiccuped a third. 'Can't do anything for themselves.'

It was funny, I thought, that they should say that. Not long before, I'd been to a place where Albanians, without much help from anyone, were doing remarkably well.

5

From the revolving cocktail lounge atop the city's highest building, I could see the following: a magnificent square, into which were pouring several lanes of expensive cars, mostly Mercedes-Benzes and Audis. In the middle of this superb public space there was a Ferris wheel and other rides for children, whose parents were catered for by the cafe tables on the balcony of the opera house to the right. As the bar rotated, I had a view over a tree-lined district of bars, full of snappily dressed youths. Further around, I looked across a park to gleaming new hotels along the main boulevard. As I completed my circuit, there was a vista of luxury apartment blocks, painted a tropical mix of reds, greens, blues and yellows. I could have been in Miami, or maybe Barcelona. I wasn't, though – and more to the point, I wasn't sure I'd swap. I was in Tirana, Albania, and it wasn't at all what I'd expected.

I'd been sent to the Albanian capital by Andrew Tuck, then editor of the *Independent on Sunday*'s colour supplement. He told me that he'd heard that the adjective 'Albanian' had become playground vernacular in London schools, as a shorthand description for anything shoddy, cheap or dodgy. Children were being teased for wearing 'Albanian' shoes, or sporting 'Albanian' haircuts. This had got Andrew thinking. What did we really know of Albania? He suggested I go and take a look, and I was intrigued enough to say yes. How could I not be? Albania was the crazy, drooling cousin in Europe's cellar, a place intractably associated in the popular imagination with gangsterism, prostitution, drugs, poverty, squalor, violence, illegal immigration, blood feuds and inbreeding. There were viruses hatching in African rivers which had better public images than Albania. It seemed the perfect setting for a thoughtful, chin-stroking feature which might lead to yet another opportunity to attend a soporific awards ceremony, at which I could consume rubbery salmon and grin like a corpse embalmed by the apprentice as someone else lifted the trophy.

Albania's fearsome reputation was the product of a modern history best described as tragicomic – tragic if you had to live there, comic if you didn't. Under the fabulously insane dictator Enver Hoxha, who ruled from 1944 until his death in 1985, Albania had been such an insular, paranoid, communist state that it fell out with every other insular, paranoid, communist state – Hoxha left the Warsaw Pact when the USSR invaded Czechoslovakia, and stopped talking to China when they started speaking to America ('Revisionists!' snorted Hoxha). Hoxha jailed or killed thousands of opponents, and banned religion and foreign travel. Convinced that the world coveted his loopy Ruritanian fiefdom, he ordered the building of hundreds of thousands of semicircular concrete bunkers all over Albania, facing randomly in every direction. The world, whose true feelings towards Albania were bemusement and indifference, left him to it.

Hoxha's death in 1985 came, theoretically, at the right time for his country to catch the wave of freedom that began sweeping across Eastern Europe in 1989. Instead, Albania turned itself from a Balkan North Korea into a Balkan Somalia. During the 1990s, a substantial proportion of Albania's population invested their savings in pyramid schemes. When the schemes collapsed in February 1997, the country went berserk, in a manner for which 'Albanian' did seem a justifiable adjective. Military installations were looted – more than 500,000 guns were suddenly distributed among Albania's 3.5 million people, minus the estimated 20,000 who seized boats and tried to sail them to Italy. Hardly had that fracas subsided when the 1999 war in Kosovo dumped half a million refugees on Albania's northern doorstep.

That was the last time the media had paid attention to Albania, so those were the images that stuck – anarchy, rioting, soggy-socked desperados tramping through mountains. The confidence with which everyone had written Albania off became apparent when I started researching my trip. The *Rough Guide to Eastern Europe* didn't mention Albania. Fodor's *Central & Eastern Europe* also gave it a swerve. Ditto the Eastern Europe edition of *Let's Go* – which did cover such balmy paradises as Bosnia-Herzegovina and Belarus. Lonely Planet did Albania in one of their guides, but the relevant chapter kicked off with the encouraging reminder that 'This pint-sized, sunny slice of Adriatic coast has been ground down for years by poverty, blood vendettas, and too many five-year plans,' and remarked that 'Armed robberies, assaults, mobster assassinations, bombings and carjackings have been reported, and street crime (particularly at night) is a problem.' When I told my friends – educated, enlightened citizens of the world, naturally – that I was going to Albania, their responses were instructive: 'Was Baghdad not dangerous enough?'; 'Can I have your flat?'; 'Bring me back a, erm . . . cabbage?'

I wish I could say I'd been any less ignorant. I'd visited lots of places, some of them pretty awful. I knew Albania's neighbours well enough to know the Serbo-Croat for 'Don't shoot!'. I really thought Tirana was going to resemble the less fashionable districts of Kabul. I packed my Third World travel kit. Money belt. Mosquito net. Water purification tablets. Insect repellent. Stomach medicine. First-aid kit with clean syringes. Spare roll of cash to stuff under sole of boot. The ancient, battered laptop I wouldn't mind handing to, or throwing at, some Kalashnikov-toting carjacker of the type certain to bail us up on the road from the airport. The photographer accompanying me, David Sandison, suffered similar trepidations. He fretted about having his cameras stolen by bandits or confiscated by police. As we waited to change planes at Budapest airport, we contemplated the racks of Hungarian salami in the duty-free stores, and seriously discussed taking our own food.

David cracked first. One morning, after a few amiable days and long nights failing to find the putrid, dangerous hellhole we'd been sent to report on, we were strolling the leafy avenue leading into town from our clean, friendly hotel, slurping delicious gelati.

'Is it just me,' asked David, 'or are we having quite a good time?'

We were. Measured against received wisdom and all our expectations, Tirana was entirely disorienting. It was like accepting an assignment to Brussels, or Copenhagen, or some similar apotheosis of stolid European dullness, and coming under sniper fire and getting kidnapped. True, some footpaths needed maintenance, but I'd tripped over worse in London. There were a few beggars, but not as many as on the Strand. The traffic, by Balkan standards, was only mildly chaotic. Nobody seemed interested in robbing or arresting us. The only way we could get the vaguest thrill of Stalinist oppression was to stand outside Hoxha's dowdy villa and wave cameras around ostentatiously, at which a guard politely asked us to stop. Our embarrassment finally escalated to shame when, after a night in Tirana's excellent bars, I got my 1000 lek notes mixed up with my 100 lek notes and tried to pay a taxi driver ten times what I owed him. He returned my money and carefully plucked the correct fare from my wallet.

Of the Albania of received opinion, of the legendary nest of gangsters and scroungers, plotting to steal our jobs and ravish our women, we found but one sign. Or, rather, he found us, long after we'd given up on our original assignment. Sokul, a gum-chewing wideboy with a rockabilly haircut, accosted us in Rinia Park. He was recently back from America.

'I was there ten years,' he said. 'I worked in building.'

I asked if he'd come back to partake of the Albanian renaissance blossoming around us.

'Not quite,' he said. 'I had some trouble. Drugs, man. Cocaine supply. I did five years in Florida State Penitentiary, then they deported me. You know, when I left here ten years ago, this was total hell, dude. Now look at it. Wow.'

All's well that ends well, I suggested.

'No way, dude,' said Sokul. 'I'm going to get in the back of a truck and go to London. I got to Brussels last year, but they caught me.'

This struck me as ludicrous. Already, my time in Albania had radically altered my view of the swarthy, tracksuited men selling bootleg cigarettes to hostile locals on Holloway Road in London. I never thought they were any threat to civilisation as I knew it. But by now I didn't think they were ambitious immigrants pulling themselves up by their bootstraps, either. I didn't even think they were pitiable economic flotsam with nowhere else to drift. By now, I just thought they were completely crazy. I said as much to Sokul, and observed that the world was full of people who'd row their own front doors across shark-infested oceans to live in places a hundred times worse than Tirana.

'There's no work here, man,' said Sokul.

There were construction projects everywhere, hotels opening on every street. Sokul, a young man with experience and perfect American-accented English, would have had little trouble finding work, as long as prospective employers didn't scrutinise his CV too closely.

'You gotta understand, dude,' said Sokul. 'Minimum wage in the UK is four pounds an hour. I get four dollars a day here. I go to London, I'll share a room with ten other people, I can save some money, then I can come back, or maybe find an English girl and stay there. There's some pretty girls here, though. Wow.'

I wished Sokul well, but I could see why he felt that Tirana held nothing for him now. There was a sense of the rise of a generation who saw what needed to be done as a challenge, rather than a reason to swim to Italy. In the bar of the gleaming new Rognor Hotel, I lunched with Gazmend Haxhia. He managed the Tirana edition of the In Your Pocket guide – witty, irreverent city primers for which I had developed an affection while backpacking in the Baltic states in 1993. Gazmend had left Albania when Hoxha's ban on foreign travel was lifted in 1990, and was the first Albanian ever to graduate from New York's Columbia University. He was a whirlwind of gregarious energy, and could have done well anywhere. But he'd chosen here.

'Albania is still white sand,' he said. 'There's such possibility.'

We were sitting in the capital of a European country whose central bank was running, in 2003, a billboard campaign announcing AND NOW, FOR THE FIRST TIME IN ALBANIA . . . VISA CARD.

'Sure, there are problems,' said Gazmend. 'The cars – all those Mercs in Europe's poorest city? Okay, the older ones were stolen in Germany, or driven here by Italians who'd claim the insurance, but police are cracking down – drive a nice car in Tirana now, you'd better have the papers. The institutions are becoming less corrupt. When you consider what this country has gone through, what's happening is amazing. In 1990 we were amazed to learn that Hoxha's wife had twenty pairs of shoes. We couldn't imagine such wealth. That's where we've started from. Things really are happening here.'

Tirana was, as even the most ebullient Tiranese reminded us, an oasis of relative prosperity in a country which still rivalled Moldova for bottom place of most European statistical analyses, other than those pertaining to unlicensed gun ownership. I didn't doubt that there were dodgy parts of Albania, but there are dodgy parts of everywhere – nobody judged Britain by Middlesbrough on Friday night. I didn't have time to visit the bandit country of Albania's north, or the reputedly gorgeous beaches of the south, but in my limited ventures beyond Tirana I again failed to find the Albania I'd imagined. The mountain fortress of Kruja could have been transplanted from Italy's Amalfi coast. The seaside resort of Durres, from where ships loaded with refugees left for Italy during the – really very recent – bad times, was crowded with sunbathing daytrippers, the beach's bunkers converted from coastal defence positions into gaily decorated ice-cream parlours. The Italian coast was visible through the shimmering heat, but all the people hiring pedal boats were bringing them back.

What startled us most were the colours. When the press shipped out of Tirana in 1999, it looked like a huge London council estate with some self-important government buildings. Tirana still had the self-important government buildings: the impressively ugly blue glass pyramid mausoleum erected to house Hoxha's remains, which was now a disco; the dreary National History Museum, redeemed by the splendid socialist realist mosaic along its front. But every other building that faced a main street had been painted in lurid hues – yellow, green, pink, purple, black, orange, red, blue and silver – arranged in exuberant stripes, checks, polkadots and zigzags. Tirana looked like it had been assembled from gigantic liquorice allsorts, and the effect was to make walking down any road a strangely joyous experience, the gleeful impudence of the colours an omnipresent affirmation of life's possibilities.

When I asked Tiranese what had transformed their city from a violent cesspit to such a vibrant, charmingly weird place, the answer, whether delivered with an amused smirk, a manic nod, or a roll of the eyes, was always one word: 'Edi'. 'Edi' was Edi Rama, Tirana's mayor, and its principal topic of conversation. A conceptual artist who had spent much of his adult life in Paris, Edi had run for office as an independent in 2000, aged thirty-six, and won a thumping mandate from an electorate weary of the sloth, stupidity and corruption of Albania's established parties. Tiranese talked of Edi as a colony of ants would talk of the bunger detonated in their nest. It had been Edi, marshalling Tirana's art students, who'd painted the city; Edi who'd bulldozed the illegal bars, brothels and casinos which had clogged Tirana's now-verdant parks; Edi who'd planted thousands of trees.

'Edi's a character,' said his namesake, Edi Muka. Muka was the director of the 2003 Tirana Biennale. He bought us coffee at the cafe outside his gallery, across the road from Rinia Park, a shady green haven from the sunshine. 'You never know what he's going to say, or do, or wear next. Rinia Park was a shanty town two years ago – full of illegal kiosks and bars. Edi had them flattened, and now it's beautiful.'

'Edi's a strange guy,' said Nora Kushti, of the UN's Development Program for Albania, 'but you have to be, I think.'

'I like Edi,' said Eni, a language student visiting home in a break from her studies in Paris. We met her in Quo Vadis, a bar across the street from Hoxha's villa, in the area of Tirana known as Block. Once off-limits to all but Albania's communist elite, Block was now as pleasant a cafe district as might be found anywhere in Europe, marred only by clumsily aspirational bar names: Yahoo!, Lucky Strike, Cowboy Pub Manhattan.

'He has made things better,' says Dorian, at the same table in Quo Vadis. 'But the contracts seem to go to the same people.'

'Edi needs medical help,' chimed in Artur, a lecturer. 'He has a touch of the dictator about him.'

In person, Edi did not disappoint. A couple of the legends that surrounded him were confirmed as truth as soon as we arrived at his offices. There was the surreal redecoration of City Hall, now touched with the arch post-modernism of an Ian Schrager hotel, every wall painted as brightly as the rest of Tirana, one immense chandelier replaced by a vast hanging of garlic cloves. There were Edi's staff, who looked like they'd been recruited by going to Block one Friday night and hiring a dozen of the most beautiful women available (which, it would be remiss to omit, was saying something: Edi's campaign against Tirana's potholes must have saved thousands of distracted male pedestrians, ourselves possibly included, from undignified plunges into sewers).

Edi greeted us from behind a wooden desk in the middle of a marble floor, which was inlaid with a mayoral seal of his own design. Behind him flew Albania's national flag – the splayed, double-headed eagle on a blood-red background, which looked unfortunately like roadkill – and the flag of the European Union, a universal Albanian desire. The walls were covered in a sepia panorama of 1930s Tirana, divided by green marble pillars. The green and gold ceiling looked like it might have been looted from Uday Hussein's bathroom.

'I decorated this myself,' explained Edi, unnecessarily.

Edi was wearing blue tartan trousers and an iridescent blue shirt, an outfit which looked particularly extraordinary on this six-and-a-half-foot bear of a man, covered with thick black hair everywhere except his head. I made some remark about his height.

'I used to play basketball for Albania,' he said.

I asked if he'd been any good.

'No,' he replied. 'Just very tall.'

Edi seemed tired. He had just returned from a festival in Kosovo – where, to the delight of Albania's television news programs, he'd made a guest appearance with an Albanian hip hop group, Westside Family. He spoke English very slowly, in a guttural drawl which sounded like an idling tank.

'The painting,' he began, 'was because Tirana was in need of change and hope. After years of chaos, people had lost hope. Also, it is not too much of a strain on our finances. My budget is nothing point something.'

Almost as if worried that this sounded too prosaic, Edi attempted the first of many ambitious metaphors. 'It's like you're on a boat cruising past a desert island, and you see a fire – someone's making a signal. This is not exactly like *Robinson Crusoe*, though . . .'

Edi paused, sensing that the allegory was getting away from him. His head disappeared into his huge, hairy hands until he wrestled his thought to the ground. 'Those fires,' he decided, suddenly remaking eye contact, 'said "Don't leave without me". Ours are telling people not to get on the boat.' The smile at the conclusion of this Cantona-esque flourish was one of triumph mixed with relief.

'Anyway,' he continued, invigorated, 'the colours are all my personal choice. I didn't want different neighbourhoods lighting different fires. The colours were intended as a shock. People were used to sleeping after they woke up – their surroundings were grey, and unchanging. There was resistance, but people got used to it, and the poorest country in Europe became like a Montmartre cafe, with everyone discussing colours. It was very strange.'

I asked if there'd been any consultation with the residents of the buildings.

'No,' he smiled. 'I couldn't go around knocking on doors. People would have said things about my mother. The point is that I try to be independent from the past. Our crises here are all linked to the past – psychologically, both our big parties are either linked with communism, or Balkan totalitarianism.'

Not everyone in Tirana was a fan of Edi. He had recently been the subject of a government investigation into allegations of corruption.

'That's not all,' he said, grinning mirthlessly. 'My opponents also say I'm the contact of al-Qaeda in Albania, I'm chief of a money-laundering racket, I used to sleep with my mother, I'm homo-sexual – which is a big offence here – I'm on drugs . . .'

I told Edi we'd met people who thought him not far removed from the lineage of Balkan despots himself, and who believed he had an eye on loftier, if perhaps more modestly decorated, offices.

'No,' said Edi. 'It's not an honour to be a national politician. I like being mayor. I'd never be mayor in a normal country. It would be boring and depressing. In a normal city, what difference can you make? Here, small projects can have an enormous effect, like launch-ing a computer virus. This job is like adventure, like madness, like art.'

With Tirana as a blank canvas, I suggested.

'That,' he corrected, 'would be a pretentious thing to say. It's more like conceptual art. This is not Albanian politics. Albanian politics is about escaping the truth through a mixed salad of words. I don't have the chances to prepare any mixed salads. But I am tragically optimistic about this city.'

As we were leaving, I told him that I'd been pleasantly surprised by Tirana.

'You know,' he said, as my hand disappeared into his furry fist, 'journalists come here all the time and tell me that. And then they write shit. I am terrified of you people. Terrified.'

After my article ran, I posted a copy to Edi. The email he returned compressed some umbrage at my description of his office into the subject header ('Uday's fucking bathroom style'), but said much about the pride of Albanians, and their pain at what the world thought of them. 'You got beyond all my (un)expectations!' wrote Edi. 'Thanking you for your watercolour!'

I felt like I'd asked an ugly chick to the prom.

It must be a hoot, to get to dream a country up from scratch. I wouldn't have traded the life I'd led in Australia and the UK for the same years in Albania, under the repression of Hoxha and the shambles that succeeded him, but I felt envious of Albanians – the young and clever ones, at least. Walking through Block, I was bailed up by someone trying to interest me in his services as a translator. I declined, but we chatted a bit, and he gave me a business card. It was made from transparent plastic, bore a design of a red palm print, and the word MJAFT!.

'You should call these guys,' the chap said. 'They're interesting.'

I called Mjaft!, explained who I was, and agreed to meet who or whatever they were in a cafe.

Mjaft! manifested itself as two men in their early twenties: Erion Veliaj and Arbi Mazniku. Mjaft!, they explained, was Albanian for Enough!, and also the name of the civil activist movement they had founded three months previously. In that short time, they'd caused a considerable stir, which was the idea.

'Albania's greatest problem,' said Erion, 'is apathy, people not giving a shit.'

Erion had grown up in Tirana, attended university in America, and had worked for NGOs in dozens of countries before coming home. Erion was acutely aware of, and depressed by, his country's reputation.

'The worst thing is that people here have started to believe it,' he said. 'They read foreign newspapers, they see reports on Italian TV, they start to believe that we are all gangsters, and that we're all doomed.'

Mjaft! had raised money from local businesses and western governments, and were inspired by the tactics of fellow youthful Balkan agitators Otpor! in Serbia, who'd played a significant role in bringing down Milosevic. Mjaft! were campaigning against Albania's chronic ills – corruption, organised crime, unreliable water, erratic electricity, the traditional blood feuds which condemned rural families to avenge slights against their ancestors with murderous violence. Mjaft! had staged a bogus criminal street fair in Tirana, pretending to offer weapons, drugs and forged visas; they received several genuine inquiries.

Erion and Arbi were terrifyingly bright, and I suspected that if I visited Albania twenty years hence, I might find myself addressing one of them as Prime Minister. Both could have walked into the offices of any NGO in the world and been hired on the spot. They must have had grounds for optimism.

'Albania's problem,' said Arbi, 'is that too many smart people are leaving. All my friends left after school, and I'm the only one who came back. To me, it was a choice between leading a comfortable, mediocre life in Canada or somewhere, and staying here and struggling for a future.'

'Besides which,' added Erion, 'this is really good fun.'

In a bookstall in Tirana, I bought a glossy volume entitled *Forty Years of Socialist Albania*. It had been published in 1984, appropriately enough, by Hoxha's Communist Party of Albania, and was one of those sumptuous propaganda tracts produced by Eastern bloc governments to promote subversive jealousy in the West. One glimpse of rosy-cheeked peasants beaming at their new tractors, the theory seemed to be, and we'd be ploughing the gaudy rubble of our shopping malls into the fields of collective farms, and cheerfully denouncing our neighbours as class enemies to a hearty chorus of 'The Internationale'. Of all the gale force nonsense contained in *Forty Years of Socialist Albania*, I was entranced by one paragraph in particular:

> Our people have become the masters of their fate, and now are building and protecting a new life without oppressors and oppressed, without enslaving treaties imposed by foreigners, without misery. They rise a step higher with each passing year. All this has been achieved through a fierce class struggle, overcoming the backwardness inherited from the past with an iron will, foiling the plots of internal and external enemies and coping with the difficulties of growth.

The party hack who penned this paragraph must have known they were writing the most fearful rubbish, but the irony that he or she may yet be proved right, if in circumstances they'd have found incredible, was richly appealing. In less than twenty years, Albania had gone from being a concentration camp to a free-fire zone to somewhere I fancied returning on holiday – and, more importantly, where people like Edi and Gazmend and Erion and Arbi wanted to stay. It was possibly the most maddening mystery of our time. Why were some places able to rebuild, regenerate, rise above violence and retribution, even when almost nobody outside their borders cared about them? And why did others sulk and fester and fight despite bottomless international concern, indulgence and expense?

6

It was the first Friday after the election. It was, therefore, the first Muslim holy day passing in the knowledge that the voters of Israel had handed the reins of their skittish state to Ariel Sharon, probably the primary hate figure of the entire Arab world. That afternoon in Ramallah, I was learning three things, clearly and briskly. One, that predictions that Palestinian reaction to a Sharon victory would be more than a collective shrug were accurate: around me, the weekly post-prayers riot at the Israeli army position based in Ramallah's City Inn Hotel was escalating into something resembling a full-scale battle. Two, that for all the sneering criticisms regularly made of the accuracy of war movies, those films are spot on with their re-creation of the noise of a ricocheting bullet: that shrill twang, redolent of a snapping banjo string, sounds the same if you're watching a western in an air-conditioned cinema, or crouching behind a worryingly low brick fence on the forecourt of a grocery store. And three, that the vague ambitions, which I'd nurtured up until precisely that point, of becoming a proper, grown-up war correspondent – insouciantly filing grave dispatches from the frontline, amassing shelves of awards and breaking the hearts of the impressionable – were as deluded as those which I'd harboured, until bizarrely late into my teens, of one day coming in as a swashbuckling middle-order biffer for Australia. When I'd encountered more or less organised violence before, in Bosnia, Croatia, Afghanistan and one or two other places, it had been something I could contemplate from a reasonably safe distance, or which loomed only as a vague threat: a flak-jacketed drive through bandit country, or a rifle barrel in one ear while some semi-uniformed goon pretended they could read anything in my passport.

At that moment, however, I – or, at least, the crowd of Palestinians among whom I was cowering – was being shot at properly, by people who, if they weren't trying to hurt us, weren't trying terribly hard not to, and it was just plain frightening. Every zip, fizz and thwack of bullet splitting air and striking brickwork punctuated the truth that the merest fluke of physics could alter my life, or end it, and there was, until it let up long enough for me to run, nothing I could do about it. I really couldn't do this for a living, and I can neither quite understand, nor overstate my admiration for, the people who can.

I'd gone to Ramallah looking for trouble. Myself and photographer Paul Donohue were doing a feature about young folk in Israel and the Palestinian territories for the *Face* magazine, and we'd been advised that a dust-up at City Inn was a regular fixture – we'd even heard that the Israeli soldiers respected one hillock overlooking their position as bleachers seating, and tended not to shoot at the people who sat there to watch the fun. We wanted to rub some grit into the gloss which constituted the *Face*'s usual bill of fare, and we'd been wandering among the back of the crowd, well back from the bolder souls at the front who were slinging rocks at the Israeli barricades and dancing between the clouds of tear gas that the Israelis fired back. It all felt rather jolly, one of those quaintly violent folk traditions that people all over the world inflict on themselves – like a rodeo, or a palio, or chasing rolling cheeses down a hill.

Then, from somewhere behind us, came the unmistakable sound of Kalashnikov fire – it's not as loud as the untutored might expect, resembling more than anything the amplified twisting of a roll of bubble wrap. 'Hamas,' hissed someone, and most of the crowd began gingerly walking and skipping backwards, as everyone now under-stood that this wasn't just a riot anymore, but a firefight between two well-armed militaries, and that several hundred of us were standing in the middle of it. Tanks emerged from behind the Israeli fortifications. A couple of Palestinian men in the retreating crowd drew pistols and loosed a few rounds towards the Israelis, though they'd have done more damage to the Israeli fortifications if they'd thrown their guns rather than firing them. The Israelis responded with the sense of proportion for which they had become famous, firing rubber-coated bullets into the crowd, and live rounds over it; a couple of people went down, and were dragged away. I looked to the locals for guidance. The ones nearest us ducked behind the low fence on the grocery store fore-court, so that's what we did, too.

Despite the shooting, most of the crowd did their best to put up a show of cool, dignified retreat, even as more among them fell yelling, or were borne limply through the throng, carried by blood-soaked shirtsleeves and trouser cuffs. The only things going in the other direction, other than occasional pointless pistol bullets, were Palestinian ambulances, whose crews put on a formidable display of heroics.

I elected to stay put until everyone else reckoned it was safe to move, on the obviously sensible grounds that they understood these things better than I did, and on the frankly craven grounds that I liked my chances better as part of a group than as a single, if swiftly moving, target. When the shooting from the Israelis dwindled to the occasional speculative round, we all jogged back up the steep street, then over the dip at the top of it, out of the Israelis' line of sight. As Paul and I caught our breath, a kid, maybe twelve or thirteen years old, gleaming smile, muddy face, grazed elbows, slingshot in pocket, a Palestinian Huck Finn, said we should follow him.

He took us to an apartment block further down the road. The ground floor car park had been turned into a makeshift field hospital. The afternoon's casualties lay on stretchers between the cars, attended by the ambulance nurses, in their tightly pinned veils and Red Crescent bibs, and doctors in white lab coats. The medic in charge, Dr Hassan Basharat, estimated that today's score was nine collected by rubber-coated bullets, ten stricken by tear gas inhalation, and two wounded by live rounds, one seriously.

'Amazingly,' he said, in impeccable English, 'nobody's dead. Not yet, anyway.'

The injured were all men, said Dr Basharat, mostly between eighteen and twenty-five, which was no great surprise. I've long thought – well, since about my twenty-sixth birthday – that the world would be a calmer place if all males could be compelled to spend those years of their lives hitting rocks with picks on Greenland. I asked Dr Basharat if he thought these young blokes really believed they were engaged in a revolutionary national struggle, or whether this might be just the Palestinian equivalent of surfing waves too big, or driving cars too fast, or drinking too much and starting fights in kebab shops.

'Partly that,' he said. 'But really, what's going on out there is a reflection of the political situation. Those are the parameters I work within. When there's trouble between leaders, there's trouble here. When there's not, there isn't.'

As he spoke, a middle-aged man in a brown suit, clutching his hip where his trousers were staining red, was being helped to a stretcher.

'You'd better make that ten by rubber-coated bullets,' sighed Dr Basharat, nodding at my notebook, and went back to work.

My journey to Ramallah had begun with a phone call from London. I had commissions from the *Face* and the *Australian* to come up with features from Israel and the Palestinian Territories during Israel's election week. I also had daunting instructions from both that the pieces be free of the usual eye-glazing trading of grievances that dominates reporting of the region. Trawling websites looking for plausible angles, I'd happened across the Popular Art Centre in El-Bireh, a municipality adjacent to Ramallah. The site was written in English, so I guessed someone at the Popular Art Centre might speak it (my Arabic, sadly, has never progressed beyond whimpering 'Sahafi' – 'journalist' – while attempting to project an air of benign haplessness). I called the number on the website. Someone there did speak English, but the accent it was spoken in came as a surprise.

'G'day,' answered a male voice. As a greeting from a Palestinian institution, I could only have been more startled by a hearty 'Shalom!'. Sensing my bemusement, the owner of the voice explained himself. His name was Nick Rowe, he was from Darwin, he'd been living in Ramallah the last nine months, and he was the Popular Art Centre's activities director. He explained what the PAC did. Funded by various international NGOs, the PAC staff travelled all over Palestine, instructing children in dance and physical education. In their building in El-Bireh, they ran yoga and Shaolin classes, as well as operating a cafe, a cinema and a dance studio. Nick gave me directions, saying I should ask any taxi driver in Ramallah for the Al-Ain Mosque; the PAC building was across the street.

Getting to Ramallah from Jerusalem was, as Nick had warned me, difficult, and annoying. Under normal circumstances – if that phrase had ever held much meaning in this part of the world – there would be no way of telling where Jerusalem ended and Ramallah began. The urban sprawl of this part of the West Bank was as solid as it was dusty, and there was no obvious break in the jerry-built build-up to indicate that I'd left Israel proper and arrived in the jurisdiction of the Palestinian Authority. So, as far as helping me understand where in the world I was, I suppose I should have been grateful for the huge Israeli checkpoint, and its sandbags and soldiers and armoured vehicles and billowing Israeli flag, which blocked the highway that connected the two cities.

While the checkpoint was useful for helping visitors get their bearings, it was useless as a security measure. Every vehicle travelling to or from Ramallah was driving around it, joining a slow-moving conga line of cars, trucks and buses on a tortuous route of narrow, rutted, suspension-mangling side streets, before returning to the highway on the other side of the Israeli post. The Israeli troops scoping the street through their rifle sights weren't stopping anyone or anything from travelling between Jerusalem and Ramallah: the armies of Syria and Iraq could have been invading Israel by taxi for all that the soldiers under the Star of David would have known about it. The only reason for the checkpoint was as a humiliation designed to remind the

West Bank's Palestinian population who was in charge. The rest of the passengers in the minibus I'd caught from Jerusalem were so resigned to the inconvenience that not a single complaint was audible above the wailing radio.

Ramallah – Arabic for 'Mountain of God' – had never been regarded as a must-see for the Middle Eastern tourist, but it had been getting an especially lousy press in the months before I arrived. In October 2000, Ramallah had provided a definitive image of the new Palestinian intifada when one of its young men was photographed howling triumphantly from the window of a Palestinian police station, his outstretched hands stained crimson with the blood of the two Israeli soldiers he'd just helped beat to death. Israel had responded with customary severity, destroying the police station with helicopter-launched missiles. The wreckage was near the car park where the minibuses which had struggled up from Jerusalem decanted their seasick passengers.

At the Popular Art Centre, Nick made me coffee, and recounted his remarkable life story. At thirty-two, he'd already performed with the Sydney Dance Company, the Australian Ballet, the Finnish National Ballet and the Royal New Zealand Ballet. As part of the Nomad Dance Theatre, he'd followed the terpsichorean muse to such unlikely habitats as the Philippines, Pakistan, Turkey and Bosnia-Herzegovina. He'd fetched up in Palestine nine months previously, before the intifada had erupted. He seemed a serious sort, but retained an Australian's hesitation to sound too serious.

'I got tired of the, uh, decadence of being a ballet dancer,' he said. 'I wanted to do something constructive.'

He'd picked a difficult city to do it in. After the lynching of the Israeli reservists, he'd spent three days hunkered down in the PAC office, terrified that the wrath of the mob might be vented upon any passing foreigner. He was once sniped at while on the roof of the PAC, probably by a trigger-happy zealot in the Israeli settlement of Psagot, which glowered at Ramallah from a hilltop. Despite these handicaps, Nick had got the cinema running at a profit – among the films playing in election week were *The Perfect Storm* and *High Fidelity*. Nick explained that they kept episodes of *Friends* in reserve for when people couldn't leave because of incoming fire from Psagot.

I was interested in the PAC's school visits. I hoped that going along on one of these might make a change from the usual dynamic of Middle Eastern reportage, in which a serve of primeval griping from one side would be returned, with wearying predictability, with ancient grudge from the other. My previous visits to the Holy Land had left me an adherent of the a-plague-on-both-their-houses creed articulated so succinctly by Sir Ronald Storrs, a British governor of Jerusalem in the 1920s. When asked where his sympathies lay in the conflict between Arab and Jew, he'd declared, 'I am not for either, but for both. Two hours of Arab grievances drive me into the synagogue, while after an intense course of Zionist propaganda, I am prepared to embrace Islam.' Nick, I sensed, had more partisan views, but he told me that if I returned in a few days, I could come along for the ride.

I headed back to Jerusalem to spend some time getting vexed by the arrogance and paranoia of Israelis before I got too much into being irritated by the self-pity and intransigence of Palestinians. It was what Sir Ronald would have wanted.

In Jerusalem, Paul and I went hunting for suitably hip interview subjects among the kids on the pedestrian arcade of Ben Yehuda Street. The cafés and restaurants on Ben Yehuda were the centre of what passed for nightlife in Jerusalem, and a favourite target of Palestinian suicide bombers. Within a short walk were several cafés and restaurants which had, in recent years, been turned into abattoirs.

Ben Yehuda was nonetheless crowded, and our notebooks and cameras had the same effect that a big pot of free money would in most other cities. Everybody had opinions that they were mercilessly keen to share, and the quickest to spot us was Jason, an eighteen-year-old student from New York who was in Israel studying at a Jewish religious school, or yeshiva.

'I was happy Sharon won the election,' said Jason, though upon further examination he seemed even happier that Ehud Barak, Sharon's predecessor, had lost. Jason talked quickly – so quickly that in the time it took me to say 'Well, hang on a second,' he was three sweeping generalisations and half a dozen rhetorical questions ahead. Jason believed that Barak was intent on giving Israel away, that the country was promised to the Jews in the Bible, so there, that at any rate Israel had won it fair and square in the 1948 War of Independence, that the present violence was all the Arabs' fault and that any coexistence between Arab and Jew was impossible. I thanked Jason for filling my cranky Zionist stereotype quota, and half a second later found myself speaking to Yonit, a twenty-year-old Azerbaijani who'd been twitching with annoyance at Jason's sermonising.

'I was for Barak,' she said. 'I think the Palestinians have a right to a country of their own, just as we do. For 2000 years, this was their land and our land, then we started with all this Zionism bullshit. We Jews are not the chosen people. I think we're the people that have been punished the most, and that's made us a fucked-up bunch with really big egos. Sharon goes to Temple Mount, Palestinians get frightened and retaliate . . . where does it stop? People shouldn't be dying for this. Israel is my country, and this city is my home. But it's a city that is important to all religions – Judaism, Christianity and Islam. All should have equal access.'

After a couple of hours popping the vox, I scored it roughly a two-to-one win to the Jasonites over the Yonitniks, with Jason's American-born compatriots the most hardline – maybe Azerbaijanis, and others with experience of occupation, could summon more sympathy for the Palestinians. There was consensus on one subject: business – and business was terrible. The proprietor of Mr T's Disposals offered a 35 per cent discount before I even asked about his I GOT STONED IN GAZA T-shirts. In an Italian restaurant on Yosef Rivlin Street, the waitress brought a complimentary dessert with my bill. When I asked what I'd done to deserve it, she replied, 'Turned up.'

Jerusalem's Old City was a desolate contrast to my previous visit, just seven months earlier. At the Church of the Holy Sepulchre, the querulous queues of cross-lugging pilgrims were gone; the only people visiting were a platoon of Ukrainian soldiers on UN deployment.

Many shops in the Christian Quarter were closed. Those in the Jewish Quarter gave the impression of staying open only to keep up appearances. The Palestinian shopkeepers in the Muslim Quarter still touted their incongruous wares of Jewish and Christian religious tat and Israeli army T-shirts, but could hardly be bothered looking up from their backgammon as I walked past.

'It's hopeless,' said one. 'I've had to borrow money from my father and my brother to feed my family. You come here as a friend, you'll have no problems with Arabs – do you have a problem now? Of course not. Sharon, all the Jews, they don't want peace. Do you see Arafat going to the Western Wall?'

There wasn't much goodwill to all men in evidence in the Jewish Quarter, either. I met Nataniel, a yeshiva student, sweeping his forecourt. Nataniel, born in Johannesburg, had come to Israel nine years previously.

'Things have got worse since Sharon's visit in September,' he said. 'The aggression of Arabs towards Jews has been terrible – bad words in the streets, telling us Hezbollah is coming to kill us, other antisemitic stuff.'

I asked what he'd thought of Sharon's walkabout at the time.

'I remember it,' said Nataniel. 'The helicopters woke me up. I didn't think much would come of it, but the Arabs lost their nut. It's just their barbaric nationalism. I live around Arabs, and they're so mean to each other. The other day, I saw a boy of about eleven beating a boy of about nine years old with a broom. I saw some other Arab kids cutting up a mouse they'd caught with a knife . . . What kind of people are these?'

Children, I suggested. Badly behaved and cruel children, but neither quality was peculiar to Arab infants. As tactfully as I could, I asked Nataniel whether he felt that Jews, of all people, should have a better understanding than most of where such crass generalisations can lead a country. He proceeded in some-of-my-best-friends mode.

'I have Arab neighbours I have good relationships with,' he said. 'I buy my food from an Arab grocer. He lets me buy groceries on credit. I don't think he gives credit to Arabs.'

I felt that Nataniel found this observation unnecessarily funny, and took my leave. There is a psychological phenomenon called Jerusalem Syndrome, a religious psychosis induced by a visit to the city's holy sites. I thought perhaps research should be done into a similar affliction, Jerusalem Fatigue, a chronic weariness which afflicts journalists who've spent too long wandering Jerusalem's alleyways in search of the most rudimentary commonsense. I went, as I often do when stressed, to the nearest bookshop, in this case the Pomerantz bookshop, which nestled in the clean, post-1967 stone that defined the Jewish Quarter. A sign on the counter thanked visitors for 'showing your support' at 'this trying time'.

'We're down to about 60 per cent of normal trade,' said Max, the shopkeeper, his Australian drawl unsoftened by twenty-three years' residence in Israel. 'It's only thanks to yeshiva students buying religious stuff that we're open at all.'

I asked Max if he reckoned there would ever be an end to this, or whether the Israelis and the Palestinians were, like two men bound to each other by handcuffs they couldn't find the keys to, doomed to each other.

'I think there will be a solution,' he decided, 'maybe in another fifty or a hundred years. But I'm an optimist.'

In a sane world, it would take forty-five minutes to drive from Ramallah to the Al-Fawar refugee camp. It took us – myself, Nick from the Popular Art Centre, photographer Lee Jenkins and several dancers from the world-renowned Al-Fanoun troupe, who rehearsed at the PAC – three hours. Our rented minibus had Palestinian licence plates. Israeli army checkpoints at every entrance to the main highway turned us back. Instead, we took to the bumpy back roads which criss-crossed the rust-coloured hills of Judea, the distinguishing features of which included robed shepherds steering their flocks, Israeli patrols, wandering donkeys, and a covering of litter, as if God, not content with the perplexities he had already visited upon the region, had upended his bin over it as well. Even on the remotest roads, there were more obstacles – barricades of earth bulldozed into place by Jewish settlers in order to obstruct the comings and goings of the Palestinians whose land they were squatting on. At one of them, three Palestinian men were struggling to tote an old woman in a wheelchair over a muddy berm.

Al-Fawar, like most Palestinian conurbations called refugee camps, didn't look like a refugee camp – the buildings were made of concrete, not canvas, the roads were paved, if haphazardly. It looked like an unfashionable outlying suburb of Hell. Al-Fawar had existed since 1948 – there are towns in the commuter belt around London with shorter histories. The appellation 'refugee camp' was clearly, as far as the locals were concerned, a signifier of something. I asked Faisa, the head teacher of the school we'd come to visit, what. She didn't quite answer the question.

'This is not a good place to live,' she said, something I had no trouble believing, especially as Israeli fighter jets made low passes overhead, drowning out conversation. 'There's no running water, no telephones, no reliable electricity. People live ten to a room – one room which has to be kitchen, bathroom, bedroom, everything.'

'The streets are damaged,' added Zohoun, a volunteer teacher at the school. 'There's rubbish everywhere. It's unhealthy. We have no land. We have only the place we live, and that isn't the same thing. Jews live in Palestine, but I don't – and I'm Palestinian. If you lived here, you'd fight.'

Faisa had lived in Al-Fawar her whole life, but refused to regard it as where she was from. 'My family,' she explained, 'is from Beit Jibrin, a village near Hebron. My parents left there after the war in 1948, and I was born here in 1949. I think Beit Jibrin is used to train Israeli soldiers now. I've never been there, but it is my home. Every day, I hope it is the day I can go back. My country is a beautiful country. My parents showed me pictures.'

Faisa was of the second generation of Palestinians who consider themselves refugees. The Palestinian tendency towards young parenthood meant that the refugee mentality, that combination of bitterness and wistfulness, had recently been taken up by a fourth generation.

'I've always lived here,' said thirteen-year-old Mohammed, one of Faisa's students. 'But this isn't my home. My family also came from Beit Jibrin in 1948, and after the war they helped build the first camp here. We will go home again when God allows it.'

God, I thought but didn't say, didn't seem to regard it as a priority. And, not that I imagined my earnest desire to please my editors was keeping Him awake nights either, He hadn't been much help with my original assignment to depict the denizens of His Holy Land as something other than predictably, trenchantly, mutually resentful and hostile. Almost nothing in my notebook read like hope, fresh thinking, or sense. I'd think of this moment a couple of years later, when the editor of an American magazine dismissed my suggestion of a return visit to Israel and Palestine with the sort of contemptuous snort that would normally be provoked in such circumstances by the proposal of an extensive critical reappraisal of German rock'n'roll. 'What,' he asked, 'is the fucking point of spending money to send you to the Middle East? Is anyone gonna say anything I haven't read a million times already?'

It wouldn't have aided my case to reply that at Al-Fawar, someone had said something that surprised me, but only insofar as it had managed to make a thoroughly dispiriting day even worse. When the kids at the school finished with the games and dances organised by the PAC volunteers, they waited beneath the watchful eyes of their veiled mothers to have their faces painted. The most frequent request was for the Pokemon character Pikachu, whose fans were so numerous that we ran out of yellow paint, and had to improvise with green. Close behind in numbers were nascent nationalists who asked to be daubed in the red, white, green and black of the Palestinian flag.

One other design was also popular – a plain white face, flecked with black to resemble an Arab keffiyeh scarf. So I asked one grinning imp, no more than ten years old, as I applied the colours to his face, what he called it.

'Hezbollah,' he said.

7

BEIRUT, LEBANON
DECEMBER 2001

In between the tumbledown high-rises, underneath the cat's cradles of jerry-rigged television cables, the streets of south Beirut resembled a ghost train ride commissioned to terrify American policy makers. A statue of Iran's late spiritual leader, Ayatollah Khomeini, glowered over a hedge. Posters of Iran's current spiritual leader, Ayatollah Khameini, billowed from streetlamps. Shop windows were decorated with portraits of the man whose organisation ran the neighbourhood: the black-turbanned Sayyed Hassan Nasrallah, secretary-general of Hezbollah.

There was a time when organising a meeting with Hezbollah would have necessitated weeks of negotiation in Middle Eastern bazaars, being hustled blindfold to meetings with bearded swashbucklers holed up amid stacks of rifles in sandbagged basements. It would have been an appealingly romantic prospect, so long as there was an attendant guarantee that I wasn't going to end up chained to a radiator and spending the rest of the decade picturing the begonia on my kitchen windowsill engulfing the flat. However, such shenanigans had been rendered redundant by technology. Not long after September 11 2001, thinking Islamic militancy a topic that merited further exploration, I'd emailed Hezbollah via their website and said I'd like to visit.

A few weeks after September 11, the US State Department reissued its list of twenty-eight 'Designated Foreign Terrorist Organisations', including Hezbollah among such unsavoury company as al-Qaeda, the Basque separatist group ETA and Hamas. Of the twenty-two men on the FBI's list of Most Wanted Terrorists, three – Ali Atwa, Hasan Izz-Al-Din and Imad Fayez Mugniyah – were described as members of Hezbollah. Each had $25 million on his head.

After September 11, America declaring you a terrorist at that moment – certainly as America seemed to see it – was the equivalent of the sheriff striding through the swinging doors of the saloon and inviting the chaps in black hats to draw. I wondered how it felt, knowing that in the most powerful offices of the most powerful nation on earth, very angry people were planning to freeze your finances, disrupt your communications and perhaps, even, dispatch awesome military force to destroy you. I also wondered what those likely to find themselves on the receiving end of America's wrath might have to say for themselves. Scanning the State Department's hit list for likely subjects, I'd written off al-Qaeda as too difficult to get hold of, what with one thing and another, and settled on the second-most famous name: Hezbollah.

In twenty years of existence, Hezbollah, the Arabic name of the Iranian-backed Party of God, had become a brand as intractably associated with terrorism in the western popular imagination as Coca-Cola had with cola. Hezbollah's name was a key that sprang open a bank of news memories: pistols waved from the cockpit of a hijacked airliner; a hole in the ground that was once a US marines barracks; the wreckage of an American embassy blocking a Beirut street; weekly, then monthly, then yearly updates of the plight of kidnap victims.

They were initially hesitant about meeting me, but after a couple of weeks of email exchanges, assented. 'Hi Andrew,' said a message on 3 October, 'now things have changed and we are ready to receive you.' I dismissed as unworthy the thought that they'd spent the time renovating the cellar and looking for the handcuffs.

At Hezbollah's Central Information Office, located above a bakery, I was met by Hussein Naboulsi, who'd been fielding my email enquiries. At thirty-five, he was already a veteran of the movement, having worked within Hezbollah in some capacity since it coalesced following Israel's 1982 invasion of Lebanon. He began with an apology for not offering refreshments – it was Ramadan, so everyone was observing a daylight fast. He was intrigued to hear that I'd been to New York since September 11 – he'd lived there himself for a while. When I described Ground Zero, he shook his head. 'Terrible,' he said. 'Incredible.' I braced myself for the 'But . . .' and the litany of American perfidy which was, depressingly frequently, accompanying half-hearted condemnations of September 11 from the western left. It didn't come. 'Terrible,' said Hussein again. 'Incredible.'

Hussein explained that he wanted me to see what Hezbollah really did, or at least the part of what they did that they were happy for journalists to see. My request to visit the disputed Shebaa Farms region in southern Lebanon, where sporadic fighting continued between Hezbollah and Israeli forces, received a dismissive look from Hussein. My request to meet one of Hezbollah's $25 million men provoked delighted, incredulous laughter. The trio were accused by the USA of the 1985 hijacking of TWA flight 847, in which one passenger was killed. Like the suicide bombings of the American embassy and US marine barracks in the early eighties, which killed hundreds, and the kidnappings of Associated Press correspondent Terry Anderson and others, including John McCarthy, Brian Keenan and Terry Waite – all of which America blamed on Hezbollah – the TWA hijacking was a subject Hussein didn't care to discuss.

'We had no presence then,' said Hussein. 'There was a civil war. Everyone had a gun. Anyone could have kidnapped a journalist.'

I'd arrived in Beirut on the tenth anniversary of Terry Anderson's release. In an interview in that morning's edition of Lebanon's English-language newspaper, the *Daily Star*, Anderson described the people who'd held him for nearly seven years as Hezbollah members, and I imagined that he'd got to know them pretty well, if only to pass the time.

'We have no connection with what happened in the past,' reiterated Hussein, when I mentioned the article. I guessed that 'the past', as far as Hezbollah were concerned, was any period of time in which something happened that they didn't feel happy talking about.

'We are,' insisted Hussein, 'the most civilised party in the world.'

I started to laugh, and didn't catch myself quickly enough.

'Seriously,' Hussein continued. 'If we were a party with no honour or dignity, a party which practised violence, nobody would give us their vote. You can't make people love you. Love comes from work on the ground.'

Hezbollah's campaign to convince me of their essentially compassionate nature began with the Al-Jarha establishment. Al-Jarha was a refuge for Hezbollah's wounded veterans, and for civilians permanently injured by Lebanon's interminable internecine wars. Men in wheelchairs or on crutches, blind or deaf or missing limbs, built furniture and carved woodcuts, which were sold to raise money for the hospice. Their best-selling items were wooden sculptures of Hezbollah's logo: a rifle clutched in a fist sprouting from the middle letters of Hezbollah's name.

I was introduced to Abu Ali, who had been blinded in an operation against Israeli troops in 1986. He was weaving baskets and, despite his loss of sight, was teaching others to do so. Before he was wounded, he told me, he'd been preparing to go to university to study mathematics, but he had no regrets.

'It was an honour for me to be a resistance fighter,' he said, 'and an honour to be injured.'

Mohammed Abbas Younis told me how, since recovering from a shocking leg wound, he had been applying his training as an architect to adapt the homes of disabled Hezbollah veterans. One of those who'd benefited from Mohammed's work, Ali Haydar, had lost his right arm ten years earlier, but was quick to assure me that this had not stopped him becoming the scourge of Al-Jarha's billiard table. Like everyone at Al-Jarha, Ali was perplexed by America's characterisation of Hezbollah as devious enemies of civilisation.

'I fought Israel because they took our land,' he said. 'That's all we did. And now you see what is implied about us by America.'

The other men in the room, all missing various bits, offered gently indignant assent. They asked if I would not have done the same if my country had been invaded. I didn't know what to say. The two countries I thought of as home – Australia, where I grew up, and Britain, where I live – were islands, and unlikely targets for invasion (it hadn't happened to Britain since 1066, or to Australia since 1788). Both countries also had professional armed forces probably capable of seeing off anyone who fancied their chances. If either ever got to the point where it was relying on my martial expertise, I'd reckon the game was pretty much up. The men in Al-Jarha, confronted with the fact that their country had been invaded, had reacted with what can only be described as courage, and had paid for the liberation of their country – Israel had finally ended its frequently brutal occupation of Lebanon in May 2000 – with their health. I could respect their bravery, and their sacrifice. I admired the care Hezbollah took of their veterans – Al-Jarha was an impressive facility, offering classes in computing, art, languages and calligraphy. I just wasn't sure I was buying the sales pitch that Hezbollah were a Salvation Army armed with rifles and rockets instead of trombones and tambourines.

That said, there certainly was more to Hezbollah than the dimly remembered headlines had led me to think. Eight members of Hezbollah sat in Lebanon's 128-seat parliament. Aside from Al-Jarha, Hezbollah owned or funded several other hospitals, including the enormous Al Rassoul Al Aazam hospital in Beirut, as well as schools, sports clubs, cultural societies, construction companies, agricultural cooperatives and charities. Back in the Central Information Office, neatly bound annuals chronicled the doings of all these enterprises, as well as listing Hezbollah's military operations, rounding up each year's martyrs, and compiling media commentary on Hezbollah's doings. Some of this coverage was less than impartial, drawn as it was from Hezbollah's weekly newspaper (*Al-Ahid*), Hezbollah's television channel (Al-Manar) and Hezbollah's radio station (Al-Nour).

Al-Nour – the name translated as 'the Light' – was housed in a labyrinthine basement. The underground location had been a necessity of wartime, to protect the station from Israeli air raids, but Al-Nour didn't feel like a bastion of revolutionary desperados. The walls were freshly painted, the furniture was polished, the staff – many of whom were women, which was pointed out to me twice before I'd mentioned it – were courteous. In the office of the general manager, Youseff Al-Zein, a shelf was stacked with awards from Arab broadcasting associations.

'We're here to support the resistance,' said Youseff, 'but we have all kinds of programs – for women, for children. And we have exclusive rights to the Lebanese football league.'

As was the case with most Hezbollah members, it was difficult to keep Youseff's conversation from spiralling into a prolonged monologue outlining Israel's serial malfeasances, and America's complicity in same. For an organisation who wouldn't talk about what happened in their own country as recently as the early eighties, Hezbollah had a remarkable enthusiasm for discussing what happened in the country next door in 1967 and 1948. They seemed to assume that, as a representative of the western media, I would be naturally inclined to the Israeli point of view, and/or the dupe of some ghastly Jewish conspiracy to deprive me of the information that, for example, Israel's Christian Phalangist allies had slaughtered hundreds of Palestinians in Beirut's Sabra and Chatila refugee camps in 1982, or that Israeli artillery had killed 106 civilians sheltering in a UN base at Qana, in southern Lebanon, in 1996. I tried to deflect him with a question about Al-Nour's musical policy.

'We like European classical composers,' said Youseff. 'We play Beethoven, and Mozart. But we mostly play revolutionary songs recorded in the current period. These are songs related to the resistance of the occupation of our land, and are targeted to provoke and inspire the people.'

I asked if I could hear some of these, and was shown to an impressively equipped studio. The three songs the engineers chose for me had no discernible Arabic musical influence. Instead, they borrowed heavily from 1980s synthesiser pop. 'Hezbollah's Song' resembled a Norwegian Eurovision Song Contest entry. 'Hezbollah Are Victorious' sounded like a cross between a military march and, ironically, 'The Lebanon' – the Human League's unforgettably asinine commentary on Hezbollah's homeland. 'The Resistance is the Honour of Lebanon' suggested a disco version of the 'Knights of the Round Table' singa-long from *Monty Python and the Holy Grail*.

They also played a longer piece – a twenty-minute musical drama-tisation of a 1996 Hezbollah action in which an Israeli patrol near Marjayoun was struck by two roadside bombs, killing four Israeli troops. The accompaniment was samples of Vangelis instrumentals. The narration was provided by the guerilla who'd run the operation, his voice distorted to prevent recognition. A gruesome verity was added by the genuine screams and oaths of injured and terrified Israeli soldiers – Hezbollah, keen propagandists, were at least as diligent as the Pentagon about recording their actions. A few days later, Hussein sent one of his colleagues to a market to buy me a video called *Heroic Epics: Major Operations of the Islamic Resistance*, which contained footage of Hezbollah operations shot by their own frontline camera-men. The video's cover was emblazoned with Arabic writing and pictures of explosions. (I have never been so happy to get through customs at Heathrow without being stopped.)

Hezbollah's television station, Al-Manar – 'the Beacon' – was housed in a sparkling new white building. An armed guard dressed in black stood at the gate. The entrance was draped with coloured streamers in honour of Ramadan. While my bag was searched in the marble lobby, I watched the monitor showing Al-Manar's current output: footage of fighting between Israelis and Palestinians set to techno music. When the pictures changed to shots of maimed Palestinian children, the music shifted to gentle Arabic pop. The screen then faded to a commercial break, advertising products local and foreign – including, startlingly, the Kraft-owned, European chocolate brand Milka and the Proctor & Gamble-owned British washing powder Ariel. I wondered if anyone was trying to sell Israelis a cleaning product called Yasser.

Al-Manar, like Al-Nour, was a conspicuously professional enterprise. The station broadcast via satellite to the whole world, aside from Aust-ralia and South-East Asia, and they were working on those. Al-Manar was especially proud of its news department, with correspondents in nearly a dozen countries. I asked the chairman of Al-Manar's board of directors, Nayef Krayem, if Al-Manar put any kind of spin on its news.

'No,' he said. 'We broadcast what Hamas says, what Arafat says, what the Israelis say, what America says. Our reporting is objective.'

The biggest Middle East news story just before I arrived had been notably barbarous attacks by Hamas. Two suicide bombers and a car bomb had detonated in and around the bars, shops and cafés of Ben Yehuda Street in Jerusalem. The following day, a suicide bomber had blown up a bus in Haifa. The combined death toll was reckoned at twenty-six. Hundreds were wounded. I started asking how Al-Manar had covered this, but Nayef immediately objected to my use of the term 'suicide bomber'.

'Those were martyrs' operations,' he said.

When you call someone a martyr, I responded, you're implying that they're a hero.

'Of course,' he said.

I thought this was nuts, and said so. The dead and injured were shoppers, commuters, kids out having a drink – all those killed on Ben Yehuda Street had been aged between fourteen and twenty-one. Had Hamas dispatched its kamikazes to Ben Yehuda on a different Saturday night, I – or any other visitor – might have been among the victims, as might have been Israelis who supported Palestinian statehood, Israeli citizens who happened to be Arabs, or Palestinians who worked there . . . and none of that mattered, anyway, because they all had the same right not to die like that as the most demented Rabbi Meir Kahane-loving Zionist crackpot. Only the most hapless moral idiot could see this as anything other than murder. Everyone from Hezbollah had been at pains to state their objections to the attacks on America a few weeks previously. I asked Nayef to point out the ethical difference, because I wasn't sure I could see it. Did Al-Manar accord bin-Laden's hijackers the same reverence?

'That did not occur in occupied territories,' said Nayef, 'so they are not considered martyrs. Hezbollah is against what happened in America.'

The Hezbollah press statement issued on September 16 wasn't an endorsement of September 11, but it wasn't the most thunderous condemnation. 'We are sorry,' the concluding paragraph read, 'for any innocent people who are killed anywhere in the world. The Lebanese, who have suffered repeated Zionist massacres in Qana and elsewhere, massacres that the US administration refused to condemn at the UN Security Council, are familiar with the pain and suffering of those who lost their loved ones in bitter events.' I wondered how Al-Manar's obituary for bin-Laden would go – whether, if he died waging jihad against the Great Satan, Al-Manar would shroud him in the same soft-focus hagiography it did those who doled out vigilante capital punishment for the crime of being Israeli.

'No,' said Nayef. 'Osama bin-Laden is not a hero. He won't be a martyr.'

I asked Nayef how safe he felt at work. America certainly regarded Hezbollah as an enemy, possibly one with whom it had scores to settle. Al-Manar's tall, white headquarters was probably the easiest target in Beirut. It was only a few weeks since an American missile had demolished the Al-Jazeera bureau in Kabul, and a little over two years since NATO had whacked Radio Television Serbia in Belgrade. If the US or the Israeli air force ever came calling, Nayef's office would be one of the first things to go (and, in the summer of 2006, it was).

'We have another base ready in case that happens,' said Nayef.

I explained that this wasn't really what I was concerned about.

'Ah,' said Nayef. 'Well, if I was killed here, then I would be a martyr.'

As I left Al-Manar's offices, they were broadcasting a cookery show.

'We're not the Taliban,' said Abdullah Kassir. Kassir, a forty-three-year-old father of seven, was a member of Hezbollah's central board, and a deputy in Lebanon's parliament. He was once, he confirmed, active in Hezbollah's resistance, but wouldn't go into detail.

'We don't deny our Islamic way of thinking,' he continued, 'but we don't want to make it compulsory. We are happy for Lebanon to be a democracy.'

Beirut was being rebuilt and redeveloped at an astonishing pace. In another decade, give or take further war, its downtown and seafront could look more like Seattle or Boston than Damascus or Tehran. Beirut's malls already contained all the familiar signifiers of international capitalism, except spoilt students protesting against international capitalism.

'Well, my children will never eat at McDonald's,' he laughed. 'In our society, unfortunately, there is a tendency to imitate America and the West in general.'

Was he annoyed about being called a terrorist by America?

'No,' he said. 'Even before September 11, they've always categorised countries and organisations, but never based on facts. They are not the people to categorise the world. They supported terrorism in El Salvador as they support Israeli terrorism now. Hezbollah have never acted as terrorists. We formed to resist terrorism – if it wasn't for Israeli terrorism, Hezbollah wouldn't exist.'

Israel's ultimate responsibility for Hezbollah's creation – and Israel's ultimate responsibility for a lot more besides – was echoed by Hezbollah's deputy secretary-general, Sheikh Naim Qassem. My translator, Ghada, and I had travelled to previous appointments in taxis, or in a weather-beaten Volvo driven by one of Hussein's colleagues, but for this one Hezbollah put on a bit of a production, leading us from the Central Information Office to a hidden garage improvised from girders and blankets. Here, besuited men with earpieces ushered us into a black Mercedes with tinted windows. On arrival at our destination, more besuited men with earpieces searched our bags, and made photocopies of my press card. We were then directed to a waiting room, where we waited, and waited, while a silent sentry watched us waiting. After we'd waited so long that I started to imagine that, in the outside world, diplomatic efforts were being made to secure my release, another besuited man with an earpiece appeared, apologised for the delay, and led us to Sheikh Qassem's office.

Sheikh Qassem was the only Hezbollah member I met who didn't wear western clothes, though the shoes beneath his robes were smart leather loafers. He looked older than his forty-nine years, but was an affable sort whose grey beard split frequently into a shining white smile. I started by asking him if anything had changed for Hezbollah since September 11.

'No,' he said. 'Because conditions here didn't change. We are still suffering the same problems – there are still Israelis in Shebaa Farms, there are still Lebanese detainees in their jails, we still have Palestinian refugees here in Lebanon, Israeli planes are still flying in Lebanese airspace and the Israeli navy are still sailing in Lebanese waters.'

What did he think, as an avowed enemy of America, when he saw the planes hit the buildings?

'Like the whole world,' he said, 'I was surprised. It was clearly an act against American interests, but because innocent civilians were killed, we issued a declaration expressing our point of view.'

I asked one of those questions you have to ask, even though you don't expect an answer: whether Hezbollah had ever cooperated with, or contacted, anybody involved with al-Qaeda.

'We have no communication with them,' said the sheikh. 'We are only interested in what is happening here.'

Again not expecting an answer, I asked if Hezbollah cooperated with Hamas.

This time, Sheikh Qassem's response was startlingly candid. 'We support their way of operating,' he said. 'We consider that they are right, but their geographic region is different to ours. There is limited cooperation, as conditions permit.'

Heart-warming, I thought, to see Shi'a and Sunni getting along so swimmingly. What kind of cooperation?

'Those,' he said, 'are details we don't speak about.'

Other details Sheikh Qassem wouldn't speak about were the three alleged Hezbollah members on the FBI's list, the four Israelis captured by Hezbollah in October 2000 and either dead or still prisoner, or any of the bombings, hijackings and kidnappings during Lebanon's civil war that were attributed to Hezbollah. So I asked if he could at least tell me what he thought, himself, of these events at the time.

'I don't remember these details,' he said. 'These are part of happenings here that were very complicated.'

Sheikh Qassem, like so many parties to so many conflicts, reminded me of a football manager – one who possesses total recall of every decision that has gone against his team, but always seems to have been looking the other way, perhaps distracted by a seagull, when one of his own players elbows an opponent. The reluctance to accept responsibility is invariably matched by an eagerness to award it, and Sheikh Qassem was unstoppably forthcoming on the subjects of American and Israeli perfidy. I asked him if he was bothered by Hezbollah's inclusion on the US State Department's list of terror organisations.

'No,' he said. 'For many years, the United States has been describing Hezbollah as terrorists. This is not the first time they have issued such a list.'

Things were different now, I said. I didn't think they were just calling people names anymore. Was he not worried that Hezbollah could suffer the same fate as the Taliban?

'No,' he repeated. 'America's blackmail, it has no effect on us. Our destiny is to continue as a resistance. No one can stop us from taking back our land.'

But the occupiers were gone, pretty much, and it was difficult to believe that Hezbollah's ambitions went no further. When I'd interviewed Abdullah Kassir, he'd sat next to a Hezbollah flag which had Jerusalem's Dome of the Rock embroidered on a corner of it. Al-Manar's station identification clip showed Hezbollah guerillas on one side of the screen, and Jerusalem's Al-Aqsa Mosque on the other. The symbolism wasn't subtle.

'We don't agree,' said Sheikh Qassem, 'with a Jewish state, because it is on the land of another people. The Israelis came from different parts of the world to take the place of others. The presence of the Israeli state is unjust. The world is imposing Israel by force.'

Why would the world do that?

'America is trying to control this region through something which causes fear to everyone else.'

I wasn't keen to pursue this angle – the idea that history is a chaos of happenstance and improvisation is not popular in the Middle East, where belief in some grand, malign plot is universal, and I didn't want to get mired in another conspirazoid lecture. So I told Sheikh Qassem that many people in the West, myself included, found things they could admire about the Islamic world – its respect for its elders, its hospitality to visitors. Was there anything he believed commendable or enviable about the West?

'What is good in the world is welcome here,' he said. 'We use the internet, we use new technology – we'll use anything we can against Israel. We don't agree with everything given to us, but we don't deny everything, either. We have our principles, and we base our judgements on them.'

So, I said, briefly relieved, Americans shouldn't think the Arab world hates them.

'No, that's right,' he said, beaming. 'Arabs do hate America, and Hezbollah hates America. This is because of their policies in this region, because of their support for Israel. When confronted with these facts, we don't have time to look for positive things.'

Hezbollah were keen for me to see the south of Lebanon, the scene of their greatest victory – Hezbollah's mythic status throughout the Arab world, the reason that children in Palestinian refugee camps regarded their fighters as rock stars, derived from their uniqueness as the only Arab force to have beaten Israel on the battlefield. The south was also, Hezbollah officials told me, very beautiful, though they worried that the weather in the hills might come as a shock after the Mediterranean mildness of Beirut. 'You'll need to wrap up,' said Hussein. 'Is that the only jacket you brought?'

Hezbollah arranged a lift for myself and Ghada. We headed down the coast, stopping for coffee on the waterfront in Sidon, one of the most important cities of the Phoenician Empire, which had apparently been quite a place in about the fifth century BC. It seemed to have been downhill ever since. In Nabitiyeh, Hezbollah's green and gold flag flew from a monument in the city square, and from dozens of windows and roofs. At Hezbollah's local office, I was introduced to Hassan Abu Hani, who'd been deputised to show me and Ghada around. He was a cameraman – one of those who made Hezbollah's home movies – but was disappointingly reluctant to talk about his work.

Nabitiyeh was also adorned with portraits of the young men who had fallen in Hezbollah's war with Israel. The first place Hassan took us was to meet the mother of two of them. Hajjeh Im Hassan Sabbah lived with her husband and four daughters in a large modern house. The walls of the living room were bare but for two portraits each of her two dead children, Hassan and Ali. They were killed exactly three years apart, on 5 February 1987 and 1990. Both were twenty-one.

'I used to ask Hassan,' she said, smiling at the thought of her wayward son as mothers do, 'why not get married? Why not lead a normal life? But he hoped that God would choose him for this since he was thirteen years old. He always wanted to become a martyr.'

It is not unusual for thireen-year-old boys to dream of becoming soldiers, even in countries at peace; at that age, before completely accepting my lack of hand–eye coordination and inability to get out of bed in the mornings, I wanted to fly F-111s for the Royal Australian Air Force. All countries revere their war dead. But the most perplexing aspect of Hezbollah, and one or two like-minded outfits, was not just that they thought death preferable to figuring out a way to get on with neighbours, but that they pursued it with a craving that verged on the ecstatic.

'I have another son,' said Hajjeh Sabbah. 'He's thirty-three now, but if they ask for him, they can take him. Me too, if they want.'

South of Nabitiyeh, tiny Lebanon suddenly offered expanses of barren space. The Mercedes that Hezbollah had wrangled for us wound between hills crested by historic ruins of varying vintages, from the twelfth century Beaufort castle, built by the Crusaders and used by the Israelis during the occupation, to the positions that the Israelis had built more recently. The gloomy hulk of Beaufort was holding up okay, but the chances of the Israeli posts being admired nine hundred years hence looked slim. Hassan took us to two of them, Al-Bourj and Dabsheh. Both were abstract sculptures of shattered concrete and twisted metal, the only upright remnant of either the flagpoles, which now flew Hezbollah's banner. Hezbollah blew up Al-Bourj after the Israelis withdrew, but the larger Dabsheh base was deliberately destroyed by Israel's own air force – to the considerable amusement, Hassan told me, of watching locals. This was the only time all afternoon that Hassan's beard creased into a smile.

Al-Bourj and Dabsheh, like all former Israeli bases in the area, had billboards alongside them, erected by Hezbollah (ISLAMIC RESISTANCE, read the credit at the bottom, OFFICE OF MILITARY INFORMATION). These offered, in Arabic and English, histories of the encampments, along with details of troop strength, weaponry, the number of Hezbollah operations waged against them (242 in fifteen eventful years, in Dabsheh's case) and the Israeli casualties these caused (in these two bases alone, according to the billboards, Hezbollah's attacks killed forty-three and injured seventy-five, the vast majority at Dabsheh, which lost forty-one men; Hassan confirmed that he'd carried his camera on some of these raids). The billboards also noted, in a somewhat gloating tone, the DATE OF IGNOMINOUS (sic) DEPARTURE (23 May 2000 for Al-Bourj, 24 May 2000 for Dabsheh). The more of these we passed, the more the day started to feel like a coach tour of the sort that roam old battlefields in Europe and America. Back in Beirut the following day, I told Hussein that he should buy a green and gold minibus, paint HEZBOLLAH TOURS on the side and advertise in travel magazines – thrillseeking backpackers would queue around the block.

Our next stop was the prison in Khiam, a little over a stone's throw – a measure of distance which had a more literal resonance than usual in these parts – from the Israeli border. The sickly yellow fort was built in the 1930s, when Lebanon was still a French possession, but it became infamous during the eighties and nineties as a prison run by Israel's local collaborators, the South Lebanon Army. Some of those held in Khiam, invariably without trial, were Hezbollah guerillas. Others were relatives of Hezbollah guerillas, or otherwise uninvolved locals who didn't fancy cooperating with the SLA. Eighteen months since the last prisoners were freed, the wire and watchtowers remained profoundly forbidding.

Since the Israelis had withdrawn and the SLA had stopped answering to its name, Hezbollah had been turning Khiam into a shrine. Plastic signs recalled the horrors that had occurred with a clarity that transcended clumsy translation: A ROOM FOR INVESTIGATION AND TORTURING BY ELECTRICITY; The HALL OF TORTURING: BURYING–KICKING–BEATING–APPLYING ELECTRICITY–POURING HOT WATER–PLACING A DOG BESIDE. The names of two men, Ali Abdullah Hamza and Hussein Ali Fayyad, were mounted next to the pylon to which both had been tied, then tortured to death.

Ghada and I were shepherded around by Ali Darwich, a twenty-six-year-old Hezbollah veteran from whom a palpable sadness radiated. He'd been brought to Khiam as a fifteen-year-old in 1990, captured by the SLA after being wounded while taking part in a Hezbollah operation. He was held for three years, much of that time in darkness in a cell so tiny there had barely been room for him and his five cellmates to lie down at once. He showed me into one such hovel, and clanged the door shut behind me. Given Hezbollah's track record with journalists and arbitrary imprisonment, I was unable to resist banging on the inside of the door and asking them to let me out before Terry Waite felt obliged to make another visit to Lebanon. Outside, I heard Ghada translate and, to my relief, laughter.

Ali had been tortured in Khiam, and had ugly scars on his neck and hands to prove it – sometimes electric shocks, he said, other times they'd just hacked at his flesh with blades. Ali recalled returning to Khiam on 23 May 2000, when the SLA guards, fearing reprisals, had bolted over the border with their Israeli paymasters. I asked how it had felt to come back.

'Glorious,' he said, quietly. 'But it was much better than it had been in my time – things changed after the Red Cross came here in 1995. I couldn't believe the prisoners had mattresses.'

In the yard in which Ali had been permitted ten minutes of exercise and sunlight beneath a chicken wire ceiling every twenty days – most of which he'd usually spent, he said, trying to open his eyes properly after nearly three weeks without light – I asked how he'd coped.

'We are,' he said, 'inspired by God to be patient.'

Hezbollah had opened a souvenir shop at Khiam, selling

Hezbollah videos, flags, keyrings, baseball caps, stickers of Ayatollah Khomeini, handicrafts made by disabled veterans, and a board game, modelled on snakes and ladders, in which you lost places for landing on squares showing a boy throwing a stone at a cat, and advanced when you landed on an image of the same boy heaving a rock at an Israeli soldier – you won by being the first to get your counter to the Dome of the Rock in Jerusalem. Caught between my desire for some truly sensational souvenirs, and reluctance to contribute to the coffers of an organisation whose motives and methods I had a number of difficulties with, I hesitated. Ali, perhaps sensing my discomfort, nodded at the shopkeeper, who packed a selection of items, and presented them with a smile, holding one hand over his heart: a terrorist showbag.

Outside the shop, there hung a poster bearing pictures of four Israelis. I'd read about them before I'd left for Lebanon: Sergeant Adi Avitan, Staff Sergeant Benny Avraham and Staff Sergeant Omer Souad – the three Israeli soldiers captured by Hezbollah in October 2000, all officially regarded as dead by Israel – and Elhanan Tannenbaum, taken by Hezbollah at around the same time. Israel claimed he was kidnapped while on private business in Switzerland, Hezbollah said he was a Mossad agent who'd been in Lebanon on a false Belgian passport. Ghada translated the Arabic text under the portraits. 'Wait for us,' she read, 'who knows when you can expect us?' Hezbollah's sense of humour was possibly an acquired taste. I asked Hassan if he knew where the prisoners were.

'No,' he shrugged, then muttered that nobody ever asked about Lebanese detainees held by Israel, a typical piece of Middle Eastern responsibility ping-pong. I assured Hassan that if I was ever in a position to ask the relevant Israeli officials about his imprisoned countryfolk I would, but seeing as how it was his organisation who had captured the men on the poster, I was asking him. He shrugged again.

From Khiam, we drove to the fortified border that separated Lebanon from Israel. I walked behind Hassan down the dirt track which led from the road to the outermost of the wire fences, careful to plant my feet in his bootprints – much of southern Lebanon was still an Israeli minefield. The limits of the Israeli town of Metulla were maybe 40 metres of fortifications from where we were standing, and in the Israeli army observation post behind the wire, I could see soldiers raising their binoculars and levelling their rifles. I pulled back the hood I'd raised against the cold breeze, hoping to be recognised as foreign and harmless down the telescopic sights that were scrutinising us.

On the Israeli side of the frontier, a white sedan pulled up. From the back seat, someone waved. I waved back. Hassan kept his hands in his pockets, and a tiny opportunity to improve relations between Arab and Jew was lost forever. Such things were possible, though, however incredible it might have seemed, there and then. If you knew where to look, you could find different sides of Abraham's family getting on just fine.

8

'I heard a huge bang,' said Hedi. 'I didn't know what to think.'

Hedi was a shy, walnut-faced man in late middle-age. He was very lucky to be alive. On 11 April 2002, he'd been at work as usual at the La Ghriba Synagogue on the Tunisian island of Djerba. At around ten o'clock that morning, a lorry stacked with cooking gas cylinders had drawn up in the narrow cobbled street between the synagogue and its boarding house, and exploded.

'The windows blew in,' continued Hedi. 'I didn't know what was going on.'

The blast had been more incendiary than destructive. It had done only superficial damage to the synagogue and the boarding house, scorching the whitewashed walls and causing minor harm to La Ghriba's blue and gold interior. Repairs had been completed swiftly and, three months later, it was only possible to see the effects of the explosion if they were pointed out.

'Fire poured into the place,' he remembered. 'I could hear lots of screaming.'

At the moment the truck erupted, a coachload of German tourists had been walking towards La Ghriba. Eleven of them were killed instantly, and three later died of their injuries. Also burned to death were a French tourist, three local workmen, and the driver of the truck. Hedi couldn't find the words to describe the scene in the immediate aftermath of the fireball, and I couldn't blame him.

'I ran to another door,' said Hedi, 'further away from the fire, and that's how I got out.'

La Ghriba and Hedi had survived a suicide attack perpetrated by a Tunisian-born resident of Lyon called Nizar Ben Mohammed Nast Nawar. He had been claimed as a martyr by al-Qaeda.

'I couldn't believe it was an attack,' said Hedi. 'When I was told it was deliberate, I was shocked. I couldn't imagine something like that could happen here.'

Hedi's job was to protect La Ghriba's virtue by passing hats, scarves and skirts to visitors who'd dressed for Djerba's scorching summer weather, rather than the proprieties of a house of worship. As we talked, he was struggling gently to fold a polka-dotted shawl around a reluctant Jewish boy whose embroidered yarmulke did not, apparently, make up for his bare shoulders. Hedi smiled as he eventually got the garish wrap fastened over the kid's singlet. He said he never thought of quitting after the bombing. He liked La Ghriba, he liked the job, and he liked the people he worked with.

'Everybody on Djerba was shocked,' he said. 'We've always lived and worked together here.'

Hedi's full name was Hedi Hadj Messaoud. The doorman of this Jewish holy place was an Arab, and a devout Muslim. On Djerba, that's how things were.

And that's why I'd come, dispatched by the *Independent on Sunday*, along with photographer David Sandison, to try to figure out what was so special about this place – a place whose people, despite believing in different versions of the same God, apparently felt no obligation to murder, oppress, terrorise, tease or even dislike each other. I mean, what if it caught on?

Jews had lived on Djerba since 586 BC, arriving as part of the exodus from the Holy Land that followed the destruction of Jerusalem's First Temple by the Babylonian King Nebuchadnezzar; the first synagogue on the La Ghriba site was built around then. The present chairman of La Ghriba was a combative sixty-one-year-old wine merchant called Perez

Trabelsi. Perched on a bench inside La Ghriba, Trabelsi confirmed that it was going to take more than the anger of fanatics to persuade Djerba's Jews to leave now.

'You have to understand,' he said, 'that when a lot of Jews left here for Israel and France in the 1960s, it wasn't because they were scared, but because there were no jobs here – tourism didn't start on Djerba until the 1970s. My sister and brother went to Israel, but I decided to stay, because I could earn enough as a businessman. Nobody has even talked about going because of this attack. We are more secure here than Jews in most other countries.'

I asked Trabelsi if, aside from the attack on La Ghriba, he could recall any anti-Jewish feeling on Djerba – any beatings, any name-calling, any vandalism of the kind that had recently been disfiguring synagogues in Europe.

'Nothing,' he said, shaking his head vigorously. 'Sometimes children tease each other, but children do that everywhere. President Ben Ali always emphasises that Tunisia is a country for all people, and all cultures.'

The unprompted testament to Tunisia's long-serving president, Zine El Abidine Ben Ali, wasn't the last I heard from Djerba's Jews. Ali had run Tunisia since 1987, and was usually returned to office in the kind of election where the incumbent gets 99 per cent of the vote. Perhaps he really was a sagacious and popular leader – I'd seen his portrait in shops and cafes, and been assured that there was no legal compulsion for this. Since the attack on La Ghriba, the Tunisian government had paid to have a ten-foot-high concrete wall, white-washed in keeping with La Ghriba's architecture, built around the synagogue compound. They'd also closed the street between the synagogue and the boarding house to all vehicles, and posted a round-the-clock armed police guard. Back in Tunis, Ben Ali had sacked his minister of the interior and chief of national security.

'We have total confidence,' declared Perez, 'in the measures the government has taken to protect us.'

Perhaps this was the case. And perhaps the Jewish community leaders I spoke to had been given some of their lines in advance.

Tunisia wasn't the kind of country where you could just turn up and commit journalism. On arrival at Tunis airport, Sandison and I had been met, to our bemusement, by an official from Tunisia's Ministry for External Communication. She'd taken us for a drink at a seaside restaurant and told us about the shock felt by all Tunisians at the attack on La Ghriba, about the happy coexistence on Djerba, and that the main Jewish neighbourhood on the island, Hara Kebira, was 'not a ghetto' – a curious choice of phrase, given that I hadn't suggested, or even considered, that it might be.

On reaching Djerba, we'd hired a translator, a local languages teacher called Taofik, but he wasn't our only company. The first morning we visited La Ghriba, we were approached by a grinning, balding man with a folder under one arm and the oleaginous manner of someone trying to sell something. He'd been hovering around a reporter from the *Wall Street Journal*, and I was preparing my well-practised list of annoying questions with which to deter Middle Eastern rug-pushers ('Do you have any that fly?' and so forth) when he said something that surprised me.

'You,' he said, 'are Mr Andrew Mueller, of *Independent on Sunday* newspaper.'

An excellent guess, I told him.

'And you,' he said, turning to David, 'are Mr David Sandison, also of *Independent on Sunday* newspaper.'

You're good, I said. You should have your own show.

'I am,' he said, touching his chest, 'a completely unaffiliated translator. I have no connections with the government.'

Clearly, Tunisia's intelligence services had put one of their best chaps on my case. The completely unaffiliated translator, who I'll call Al-Clouseau, pressed his folder into my hand. It was full of government press releases.

'Yes,' Al-Clouseau acknowledged. 'But I am completely unaffiliated translator. I have come from Tunis to work for you, and there will be no charge.'

A masterly cover: the somehow psychic volunteer translator willing to fly across the country at his own expense to help foreign journalists. We ignored him as far as possible during our stay, but he showed up everywhere we went, at one point even swimming half a lap behind Sandison in the hotel pool. And, everywhere we went, there would always be a moment at which some or other grandee of Djerba's Jewish community would approach me, with Al-Clouseau following close behind, and deliver a variation on the following speech: 'I would like to extend our thanks to the president of the Tunisian Republic, for granting us our rights and allowing us to lead normal lives. Djerba is an island of peace and coexistence. I would also like to thank the local authorities who helped us establish our education system so that we may all work towards the betterment of Tunisia. It's our country.'

This example was delivered, with only slightly laboured sincerity, by another constant companion during our time on Djerba, the president of the Jewish community, Youssif Ouzan. The weird thing was that the longer I spent with Djerba's Jews, the more I believed that the claims of cross-community harmony were true. By the time I left Djerba, the only reason I was at all suspicious was the hapless oversell of Al-Clouseau. In fairness to Al-Clouseau, I went everywhere I wanted to go on Djerba, and met everyone I wanted to meet. And I guessed I could understand why the Tunisian government was trying a little too hard. Djerba had a tourist business to resuscitate, 30,000 hotel beds to fill back up. At the vast resort hotel Sandison and I had been booked into, the wing containing our rooms was entirely deserted, except for us and – in the suite between Sandison's and mine – Al-Clouseau.

Djerba was a rugged little island, connected to the mainland by a narrow, winding road bridge. Its towns were quiet, basking in the sun as languidly as cats on a hot balcony, the whitewash with blue trim favoured by most Djerban householders an echo of the sand and water that surrounded them. The beautiful beaches aside, Djerba's landscape was unprepossessing, resembling a Mars that had unaccountably sprouted date palms and olive trees. The only grass interrupting the red sand was on the golf course.

Djerba's recorded history went back a long way – the foundations of that bridge were laid by the Romans – but it had only been in the last thirty years, since the advent of mass tourism, that it had really joined the modern world. Almost all of the island's 20,000 people had some connection to the travel industry. The island had its own international airport, and one corner of Djerba's coastline had been annexed by a district of vast hotel complexes. These had proved most popular with German package holidaymakers – but, since the attack on La Ghriba, Djerba's deckchairs were conspicuously naked of pre-emptive towels, with grim consequences for Djerba's economy.

In the leatherware and souvenir shops of Houmt Souk, Djerba's biggest town, opinions of the La Ghriba attack didn't vary according to the faith of the person expressing them. In Place Mokhtar Ben Attia, where some competitive souls engaged in fierce domino matches while spectators slurped fresh orange juice, I got talking to two old friends, Yahuda Bchiri, a Jewish shopkeeper, and Ben Jemiaa Charfedinne, an Arab schoolteacher.

'The bomb at La Ghriba,' said Charfedinne, 'hurt Arabs to the marrow. This kind of thing does not serve peace. It does not serve us. If that bomber was still alive, if you put him in this square, it would be a race between Jews and Arabs to tear him to pieces first.'

'But you mustn't overdramatise this,' said Bchiri. 'It was a strike against the Tunisian state, not just the Jews. If it were against the Jews, he'd have done it on a Saturday, when the synagogue would be full of Jews praying. He picked his time to make sure it would kill tourists.'

It may just have been that he wasn't very bright. Since the logistical and symbolic masterstroke of 9/11, none of al-Qaeda's overseas operations had been noteworthy for their brilliance. In attacking a synagogue on the wrong day, Nizar Nawar would have been well up to the standard of hapless would-be shoe-bomber Richard Reid, who tried to detonate his explosives in full view of his fellow aeroplane passengers – a terrorist so transcendentally dim that if he'd been sent to blow up a bus rather than an aircraft he would, to resuscitate an ancient anti-IRA joke, have burned his beard on the exhaust pipe.

This was, I was starting to think, the major flaw with the War on Terror. It had become commonplace to portray our enemies as evil geniuses, plotting from inside hollowed-out volcanoes, possibly while stroking white cats and tapping their fingertips together. What if, I was wondering, our enemies weren't as cunning as our governments and media kept claiming on their behalf, but just . . . thick? Not so much al-Qaeda as al-Qa'eystone? What if our war, such as it was, wasn't with terror, but utter fuckwittery? And if it was, how did we win it?

On the Saturday night, Youssif Ouzan took us to the heart of his community, the district of Hara Kebira, just as it was coming alive again after sundown on the Jewish Sabbath.

'Jews here are very conservative,' he explained. 'That's why you haven't seen any of us outside today. On the Sabbath, we don't work, don't drive cars. We don't even use the telephone.'

The Jews filling the cafés Ouzan showed us were only distinguishable as such by the yarmulkes on the heads of the men. Aside from the headgear, the look was standard Mediterranean casual. I told Youssif that I'd been vaguely expecting the frock coats, hats and beards that distinguished orthodox neighbourhoods in Jerusalem. They'd be no less impractical in a Tunisian summer than in an Israeli one.

'We don't like the word "orthodox",' he said. 'We are just very religious, in coherence with our faith.'

He wasn't kidding – the thousand-odd Jews on Djerba worshipped at their choice of eleven synagogues. What Djerba's Jews did have in common with the ultra-orthodox of their co-religionists in Israel was an exemption, at their request, from the military service which was compulsory for their fellow citizens. Otherwise, Youssif insisted, they were Tunisians. He showed me his Tunisian identity card, which made no mention of his religion. When I asked the admittedly crass question of whether he considered himself principally a Tunisian or a Jew, he admonished me with a wagged finger.

'Why should there be a difference?' he asked. 'My religion is Jewish, my nationality is Tunisian. There's no conflict.'

As we walked further, Youssif pointed out houses where Jews lived next door to Muslims, and shops where Muslims employed Jews. The only line never crossed, Youssif says, was marriage. Three years previously, there had been a scandal when a Jewish man had fallen in love with a Muslim woman – neither his family nor hers approved, and he eventually left the island, alone. A friend of Youssif's explained how, on the Saturdays when Djerba's Jews were observantly idle, Arab bakers delivered fresh bread for their Sabbath meals. While talking to an Arab shopkeeper, in Djerba's hybrid dialect of Arabic, French and Hebrew, it was Youssif who ended some conversational speculation with the common Arabic expression 'Insh'allah'. Not only was Hara Kebira not a Jewish ghetto, it was barely even a Jewish enclave – there was more of a separatist siege mentality in Brooklyn.

Coexistence was learned early. Jewish parents had the option of a wholly Jewish education for their children, but most of Djerba's Jewish kids went to the same schools as their Muslim friends, and attended to their religious and Hebrew studies in separate extra lessons. We visited a couple of Djerba's Jewish schools. At the school for girls, I asked two teachers, Katia Bietan and Mary Elia, how their students had been affected by the La Ghriba bombing, whether it had caused any of them to express feelings of vulnerability about being part of the last major Jewish community in an Arab country. Katia and Mary reacted like this was one of the sillier things they'd ever heard.

'The children never really asked about the attack,' said Katia. 'They certainly didn't seem frightened.'

'My great-grandfather lived here,' added Mary. 'We will always live here.'

The voices of experience on Djerba sounded just as content and comfortable as the voices of innocence. David and I were summoned for lunch one day at the handsome home of well-loved local musician Jakob Bchiri. He showed me his Tunisian identity card, giving his date of birth as 5 February 1912.

'Though I am sure,' he said, 'I can remember my mother telling me I was born after the First World War.'

Either way, Bchiri was nearly twice the age of the Republic of Tunisia, which had been founded in 1957, having won independence from France a year earlier.

'The Jews who left Djerba to go to Israel,' he said, 'didn't go because they were scared. They went for the jobs – like Arabs who go to France for work now. Those of us who already had a bit of money stayed, and are now quite wealthy. I think the people who went just weren't patient enough.'

Bchiri's singing was in demand at Muslim and Jewish weddings and festivals – he'd played for the pilgrims who journeyed to La Ghriba for the annual Lag B'Omer celebration every year since 1931. He'd toured Austria, France and Israel, and recorded many albums. When he picked up his ten-string oud and sang for us, his croaky speaking voice gave way to a passionate baritone, and his ninety-year-old (or eighty-four-year-old) fingers danced around the fretboard with the speed and skill of a man seventy (or sixty-four) years younger.

Bchiri's wife of fifty-eight years, a radiantly mischievous seventy-seven-year-old called Qhomsana, served us a fabulous lunch of spicy Djerban fish, over which Jakob told equally extraordinary stories. He agreed that the La Ghriba bombing was a freak occurrence, at total odds with the day-to-day reality of Djerba, but he did remember one other, earlier, attempt to intimidate the island's Jews.

'In 1943,' he said, 'the Germans came ashore for one day. They wanted 50 kilograms of gold, or they'd burn Hara Kebira. We knew what they were doing to Jews in Europe. We were very frightened.'

I asked what they'd done.

'We gave them 47 kilograms, which was all we could find. They said they'd come back for the rest. But the British army got here first.'

And since then?

'I've never felt any reason to leave. I thank God for what I have here. I love my island.'

On a few days' acquaintance, I was starting to feel similar stirrings for Djerba. There were many reasons for this: its starlit nights, its cluttered antique stores, the fish market in Houmt Souk, where I had my purchases cooked to melting perfection as soon as I'd paid for them. The reason I really warmed to the place, however, took a while to come into focus – and it took, as it often does, someone else to point it out.

On the Monday night I was on Djerba, an Israeli F-16 fired a missile into a residential neighbourhood of Gaza City. The strike killed Hamas commander Salah Shahada, a prolific murderer. It also killed fourteen Palestinian civilians, including nine children. It was a grotesque collective capital punishment, and the subsequent world-wide outrage was not placated by Ariel Sharon describing the carnage, with his customary tact, as 'a great success'. The following morning, I was fossicking in the jewellery stores of Houmt Souk – silversmithery is a centuries-old tradition among Djerba's Jews. I got talking to a shopkeeper called Hai Haddad. He sold his own work – Jewish religious artefacts, exquisite bracelets and necklaces, and representations of Djerba's favourite totem, the Hand of Fatima, believed by Jews and Muslims alike to keep the Evil Eye looking elsewhere. Fatima was Mohammed's daughter, the mother of the Imams Hasan and Hussein. Hai Haddad's Hands of Fatima linked that heritage to his with a Star of David engraved in the middle of them. While I looked for one I liked, Haddad asked why I'd come to Djerba when everyone else had stopped.

I absent-mindedly muttered that it had seemed like it would be an interesting and unusual place to visit.

'Why?' he asked.

Er, well, I mumbled, Jews and Muslims living together in what was either peace or a thoroughly convincing facsimile of it, that kind of thing.

'You're looking at this the wrong way,' he said.

I asked what he meant.

'It's Europe,' he said, 'that has the history of antisemitism, not the Arab world. I lived in London in the seventies, and I'm much safer here. Jews and Arabs are cousins, and most Arabs realise this.'

I mentioned the Israeli attack on Gaza, the awful footage of Arab children killed by a Jewish pilot which was being shown on BBC, CNN – and, with no doubt slightly less nuanced commentary, on

Al-Jazeera and Hezbollah's Al-Manar. Would any of that make life difficult for him?

'Nope,' he said. 'Look, I'm not saying there is never bad feeling here, but the mentality of the Tunisian people, and the Djerban people especially, is that there is no reason why what happened in Israel, or anywhere else, should affect us.'

It would be nice, I said, if more people could see it like that.

'That's why you're writing the wrong story,' he said. 'What you should write is: everywhere else, everyone else, is crazy. Djerba is normal.'

I hung the Hand of Fatima I bought from Hai Haddad from a book-shelf in my lounge room. The silver has corroded, because I'm too lazy to polish it, and so it doesn't glimmer as brightly as it did, but I like having it there, because I like what it represents. Even if I was entirely wrong about Djerba, even if I was the victim of a colossal PR stunt, shunted round a Potemkin imitation of concord, the inhabitants of which set about each other with axe handles the second my plane was airborne, it doesn't matter. The Hand of Fatima waves to remind me that, if left to their own devices, untormented by big ideas, unburd-ened with dramatic solutions, and permitted and encouraged to deploy commonsense and common courtesy, people can and will get along.

The thing I love most about London, the uproariously diverse city I live in, is that it demonstrates this, all day every day, better than any other place in the world. That it continued to do so subsequent to the most revolting provocation – after it suffered its own La Ghriba – didn't surprise me at all, despite the determination of some its citizens to miss the point entirely.

9

'Are you okay?'

It was the most phoned, emailed and texted question of the day. On the morning of Thursday 7 July, it was the question that woke me up. A friend, hearing that there'd been an explosion at Liverpool Street station, and knowing I live about a twenty-minute walk away, called a bit after nine am – when, like any self-respecting freelance journalist, I was still asleep. When I focused on the television, it was reporting four explosions, casualties, and was still running with the early explanation that some sort of power surge was responsible.

Like most Londoners, I had little difficulty imagining a catastrophic unravelling of the Underground's fraying infrastructure. Weeks of my life had been wasted sitting in stationary carriages, wondering why Moscow's Metro cost two turnips a ride, and worked, and why one of the world's most expensive transit systems, in one of the world's richest cities, didn't. Like most Londoners, though, I'd also assumed that my city would be whacked by Islamist terrorists one day, so absorbing the eventual revelation that four suicide bombers were responsible did not strain the powers of comprehension.

London was obviously a target, though not for the reasons that became conventional wisdom in ensuing days. London was no longer the capital of the world, but it remained, more than any other city, the heart of the world. Everyone knew about it. Everyone had an idea of it. Everyone, which is to say anyone who mattered much, went there at some point – Osama bin-Laden, certainly the inspiration if not the author of these bombings, was reportedly a supporter of Arsenal Football Club. A hefty percentage of the world's population would be able to name a friend, relative, colleague or acquaintance who made, or had made, their home in London.

So, if you were a malevolent crackpot determined to bomb a city to make a point, however deranged or obtuse, it made sense to bomb London, on the grounds that more people would care. Mohamed Sidique Khan, Hassib Mir Hussain, Shehzad Tanweer and Germain Lindsay, the four young idiots who'd blown up three tube trains and a bus, killing fifty-two people and maiming and traumatising hundreds more, understood this much.

As the scale of what had occurred on 7 July became clear, I hoped two things. First, I hoped everyone I cared about was all right, and they were, though I later discovered that a woman I'd met at a party a few weeks before had been injured in one of the Tube bombs, and that one survivor of the mangled double-decker in Tavistock Square was a former colleague of a friend in Melbourne. Second, and much less importantly, I hoped that this – obviously, surely – insane, inexcusable murder of random civilians would finally silence the 'root causes' chorus which had attended every Islamist outrage from September 11 onwards. The words varied, but it was essentially the same song, the one about Palestine, oil, Iraq, Israel and how, whenever anything like this happened, it was 'our' own fault for inciting Muslim anger.

This hope was dashed fairly rapidly. One response was at least bleakly amusing. Gerry Adams offered condolences to the city his organisation had bombed on dozens of occasions, which felt like getting a Christmas card from an ex-girlfriend who'd cut up all your suits before she moved out. That same afternoon, while most Londoners were working through checklists of friends and family, punching telephone numbers with crossed fingers, and emergency workers were labouring at their unimaginably horrific task in the tunnels, George Galloway MP took the floor of the House of Commons. The former Member for Glasgow Kelvin had been expelled from the Labour Party for his characteristically vituperative opposition to the invasion of Iraq. At the general election a couple of months earlier, he'd run under the banner of a new party, Respect, and sensationally lifted from Labour the East London constituency of Bethnal Green and Bow. Galloway started his speech deceptively well.

'I condemn the act that was committed this morning,' he said. 'I have no need to speculate about its authorship. It is absolutely clear that Islamist extremists, inspired by the al-Qaeda world outlook, are responsible. I condemn it utterly, as a despicable act committed against working people on their way to work, without warning, on tubes and buses. Let there be no equivocation: the primary responsibility for this morning's bloodshed lies with the perpetrators of those acts.'

Dern tootin', George. But then . . .

'However . . .'

'However' was the 'One-two-three-four!' of the Root Causes Chorus. Galloway had got to it from 'Let there be no equivocation' in fourteen words flat, and then he was away. Invasion of Iraq. Occupation of Afghanistan. Abu Ghraib. Destruction of Palestinian homes. The Israeli security fence. Palestinian children shot by Israeli snipers. Guantanamo Bay. This massacre of London commuters, said Galloway, 'Did not come out of a clear blue sky, any more than those monstrous mosquitoes that struck the twin towers and other buildings in the United States.' The not-out-of-a-clear-blue-sky motif was a poor choice of phrase, especially for an orator of Galloway's skill – a clear blue sky was literally what those hijacked aircraft had come out of, on that September morning, and all before Iraq had been invaded, Afghanistan occupied, Abu Ghraib revealed, Israel's fence built and Guantanamo Bay converted into an absurd Caribbean gulag. (I felt that the idea that bin-Laden's hijackers were motivated by anguish about Palestine was rather too dependent on the implicit assumption that, if Israel had withdrawn to its 1967 borders on 10 September 2001, then al-Qaeda would have called the whole thing off.)

Galloway wasn't alone in blaming the victims while their remains were being scraped off the tracks. Dozens of dazzlingly silly newspaper think-pieces swiftly suggested that we'd brought it on ourselves. Tariq Ali, as ever an instant answer to the question of how long a career can be wrung from a knack for being wrong about almost everything, kicked off a piece in the following morning's *Guardian* by noting – correctly, if somewhat pedantically – that we didn't yet know precisely who had attacked London, or why. 'But it is safe to assume,' he continued in the very next sentence, 'that the cause of these bombs is the unstinting support given by New Labour and its prime minister to the US wars in Afghanistan and Iraq.' Even by Ali's formidable standards, this was splendid stuff. Start by arguing that we didn't know who did it, continue by explaining why they did it, and conclude that in any case, it was all Tony Blair's fault. Nowhere did Ali concede that the 'cause of these bombs' might have been the four men, as capable of moral choices as any adult human, who built the devices and carried them onto trains and a bus.

The rest of the usual suspects were not far behind. John Pilger penned an article in the *New Statesman* baldly describing the attacks as 'Blair's bombs', an apparently inevitable consequence of 'his and Bush's illegal, unprovoked and blood-soaked adventure in the Middle East'. It always struck me as peculiar that people who pushed this line never considered its inverse logical upshot – if ostensibly retaliatory violence is always really the doing of the victim of the violence, then surely Hamas, not Ariel Sharon, were to blame for the Israeli occupation of Palestinian territory, and Iraq's insurgents, not the US Marines, were culpable for the demolition of Fallujah, and the Blitz was all Winston Churchill's fault. 'Were it not for his [Blair's] epic irresponsibility,' Pilger pilgered, 'the Londoners who died in the Tube and on the number 30 bus almost certainly would be alive today.' Pilger used not a single one of the 1641 words he wrote on the subject to apportion a whit of blame to messrs Khan, Hussain, Tanweer and Lindsay – whose deliberate detonation of explosives aboard rush hour public transport had, I felt, contributed in some small way to the body count. Pilger didn't even mention their names.

Robert Fisk is an incomparably brave reporter, but he occasionally gives the impression of having spent too much time in the Middle Eastern sun without a hat on. His analysis of 7 July in *The Independent* went close to accomplishing the unprecedented feat of making Tariq Ali and John Pilger sound sensible. Again, despite the lack of any formal statement from the bombers – for all we knew for certain at this point, they might have been fervently in favour of reintroducing the back-foot no-ball rule – Fisk was confident as to their motives. 'They are trying to get public opinion to force Blair to withdraw from Iraq, from his alliance with the United States, and from his adherence to Bush's policies in the Middle East.' He approvingly noted Osama bin-Laden's rhetorical question 'Why do we [al-Qaeda] not attack Sweden?', apparently forgetting, as bin-Laden had apparently forgotten himself, that Swedish troops were part of the effort to encourage civilisation in Afghanistan and peace in Kosovo.

The deeply weird conclusion of Fisk's contribution said a great deal, I thought, about the Root Causes Chorus. He recalled that on September 11 2001, he'd been on a plane bound for the United States, which was instructed to return to the UK. 'The aircraft purser and I,' Fisk reminisced, 'toured the cabins to see if we could identify any suspicious passengers. I found about a dozen, of course, totally innocent men who had brown eyes or long beards or who looked at me with "hostility". And sure enough, in just a few seconds, Osama bin-Laden turned nice, liberal, friendly Robert into an anti-Arab racist.' Fisk, to his minor credit, did not pretend to be speaking for anyone but himself. Had I been a brown-eyed, bearded type on a plane that day – or, I'd like to think, been myself and sitting next to such a chap, perhaps engaging in idle speculation as to the peril posed by the inflight meal – and been confronted by some self-appointed vigilante, I'd have been tempted to do a sight more than 'look at' him with 'hostility'. On the last day of that innocent era in which aeroplane passengers were issued with metal cutlery, someone making such crass assumptions based on appearance might well have got my fork up his nose.

Such was the Root Causes Chorus, though. It refused to consider that Arabs, and Muslims, were individual people, as opposed to a seething, undifferentiated mass of rage. It insisted that Muslims were incapable of acting independently, for better or worse, and that they reacted only to our provocations, usually in extreme fashion. The Root Causes Chorus regarded Muslims, implicitly, as animals: don't tease them, don't goad them, treat them nice or they'll bite.

A Palestinian who is tired, who has a headache, who is going home with heavy shopping, and who is being buggered about by some snotty uniformed Israeli teenager at a checkpoint, who momentarily loses his temper and bounces a tin of beans off the soldier's helmet, has reacted in a human and forgivable way. The 7 July bombers, like all other terrorists, had meetings, discussed plans, approved some, rejected others, slept on it, and decided that random mass murder still seemed a good idea.

Two weeks after 7 July, four more men thought so. Fortunately, they turned out to be inept as well as stupid. On the morning of Thursday 21 July, I was, like any self-respecting freelance journalist, watching the cricket on television – the first day of the first Test of that summer's extraordinary Ashes series. The coverage was interrupted by a news flash. Four more explosions, it said, the same pattern as before: three tubes and a bus. The bus, said the newsreader, was a number 26, on Hackney Road in East London. I think I tried to drink coffee through one ear. My flat is in a building on a street just off Hackney Road in East London. The 26 is the bus that gets me home from the South Bank or Covent Garden. The frontline in the early twenty-first century's war had moved to my doorstep – almost literally, as I discovered when I went outside and found police officers spooling blue and white tape across the end of my street.

'It's at the bottom of Hackney Road,' said one, 'near the junction with Old Street. You know, in between Browns and the Olde Axe.'

A couple of hundred metres away, around a slight curve, out of sight. I wondered whether it said more about him or me that he'd used two strip clubs as reference points.

'If you've got the news on in your flat,' he said, 'you know more than we do. Doesn't seem to have been a very big bang. Didn't detonate properly, or something. I don't think anyone's hurt. Few windows broken, though.'

Television crews were setting up amid the small, strangely quiet, crowd of onlookers. The journalists couldn't see any more than the rest of us, and had no better idea what was happening, but set purposefully about interviewing people who knew exactly as little as they did. It was a perfect post-modern moment. I was standing at the epicentre of the biggest story in the world, on a spot being watched on millions of screens in dozens of countries, and my best chance of finding out what was happening was going back to my flat and switching the news on. When I got upstairs, I noticed an email from a friend in America, who'd stayed at my place the previous year.

'Quick!' Sarah had written. 'Go stand next to the NBC camera and wave!'

I made and fielded all the same calls, emails and texts I had a fortnight before. The gallows humour set in with unseemly, but reassuring, haste. As the Australian batting withered before a startlingly vicious England bowling attack at Lord's, I emailed an English friend. 'In the interests of public safety and out of respect for common decency,' I wrote, actually worrying rather more for the safety of my countrymen being treated as fairground targets by Harmison, Hoggard, Flintoff and Jones, 'this match should be abandoned immediately.' 'Nonsense,' my friend replied. 'If we let terror disrupt our way of life, then they will have beaten us.' A couple of hours later, as Glenn McGrath calmly uprooted England's top order, Sean wrote back. 'We should call it off at once,' he'd decided, 'out of respect for all the people who aren't dead.'

Three days before 7 July, I'd had dinner with a friend, a journalist who had extensively researched British Islamist fundamentalism. I'd asked him what, in particular, his contacts in British intelligence were worried about. British citizens, he'd replied. First-generation children of model, hard-working immigrants. Muslims, obviously, most probably of Pakistani rather than Indian or Bangladeshi descent. More likely from the north of England – Leeds or Bradford – than London. No criminal record, no known propensity for extremism, from prosperous, relatively secular families. Educated, male, aged between twenty and thirty-five. I'd remarked that, given that he'd just described himself almost precisely, he was lucky he hadn't been interned on the spot, and then asked him what these people – these uncannily accurately anticipated but, for another seventy-two hours, still hypothetical bogeymen – were so bothered about.

He'd mentioned the obvious – Palestine, Iraq, Afghanistan. But he also mentioned a couple of things which surprised me. Bosnia, he said, had been a hugely radicalising catalyst. I could understand that inasmuch as it had made me pretty angry as well – a preventable genocide being allowed in 1990s Europe – but most Bosniaks were as devout Muslims as most Britons are devout Hare Krishnas, and didn't the infidel west get some credit for sending the planes in eventually? Not really, my mate said, before saying something which struck me as completely unbelievable, and despair-inducing. The Salman Rushdie fatwa, he said. It was still a big deal for a lot of Muslims. It still hurt them that it wasn't taken more seriously. Which is to say that people who'd called for the murder of an author of a book none of them had read were upset that they were regarded as ridiculous.

The Rushdie fatwa – the 1989 death sentence passed on Rushdie by the Ayatollah Khomeini – is the unarguable rebuke to the Root Causes Chorus. A mentality that can believe that it is remotely excusable, or anything other than howling-at-the-moon barmy, to regard the writing of a book – any book – as a crime, never mind a capital offence, is not one that can or should be reasoned with. The fatwa demonstrated that modern Islamist fundamentalism is driven by its own deranged logic. If there wasn't – for example – the invasion of an Arab country to use as an excuse for punitive violence, a novel would do. It may be that Ali, Pilger and Fisk were right to argue that the invasion of Iraq had inspired the crime committed by Khan, Hussain, Tanweer and Lindsay. But not even Ali, Pilger or Fisk could seriously believe that if Iraq had not been invaded, London would never have felt the dumb fury of Islamist terrorists. It already had. Salman Rushdie lived in London. The fatwa was an act of terrorism.

On 10 July 2005, a forty-eight-year-old Pakistani called Kamal Butt, in Britain visiting relatives in Nottingham, was beaten to death in the street by a local gang who taunted him with sneers of 'Taliban' as they murdered him. It may have been that the rage of the mob was fuelled by the slaughter in London, but they didn't kill Kamal Butt because of that, any more than Khan, Hussain, Tanweer and Lindsay killed fifty-two people because that statue of Saddam Hussein was yanked from its plinth. They all did what they did for the same reason – that they are, or were, ignorant, malevolent, irredeemable scum, the 'root causes' of whose anger should no more concern anyone than the reasons for the yappings of a rabid dog.

Aside from anything else, if the bombers and would-be bombers of London in July 2005 really had been protesting the invasion of Iraq, then the mandate they could claim for their actions from the people whose opinion mattered most – Iraqis – was doubtful. The invasion of Iraq may have been the first war in history where it was – and, for a while, it really was – easier to find people who opposed it in the capitals of the aggressors than in the capital of the victim.

10

It was a Middle Eastern remake of *The Cannonball Run*. At the customs house on Jordan's side of the border with Iraq, a cast of eccentrics, swashbucklers and out-and-out buffoons were preparing to make the sprint across the desert to Baghdad. The difference between *The Cannonball Run* and the journey we were attempting was that when Burt Reynolds said 'bandits', he meant tobacco-chewing highway patrolmen. Today, 'bandits' would mean bandits – several vehicles bearing aid workers and journalists to the Iraqi capital had been robbed, or sniped at. We debated whether we were better off wearing our flak jackets – hot, uncomfortable, like having a dinner service stuffed under your shirt – or stacking them against the doors of the vehicles. We applied red and silver masking tape to the trucks declaring 'TV', universal war-zone shorthand for 'Press, please don't shoot'. I'd never been convinced of the wisdom of this tactic; you might as well put a sign in the window announcing OCCUPANTS HAVE CASH, EXPENSIVE EQUIPMENT, NO GUNS, AND ARE OUT-OF-SHAPE MILQUE-TOASTS INCAPABLE OF HANDLING THEMSELVES IN A SCRAP.

We'd already been driving since midnight, leaving Amman to make the border by daybreak, allowing plenty of time for the six-hour hurtle to Baghdad; nobody wanted to be on Iraq's roads after dark. There were five people in our white GMC SUV. There was an implacable Jordanian driver, whose name I'd never quite caught, who'd staved off sleep on the overnight run from Amman by watching, on a dashboard-mounted monitor, DVDs of belly dancers; I'd been less mesmerised by the undulating houris on the screen than I had by the needle on the speedometer, flickering against 160 kilometres an hour on a single-lane desert road illuminated only by the lights of oncoming trucks. There was aid worker Faoud Hikmat, veteran of the deepest hellholes on Earth, now working for the British NGO Merlin, who'd been kind enough to offer me and my colleagues a lift. There was photographer Damian Bird, travelling with me on assignment for the *Face*. There was Robert Young Pelton, the adventurer chiefly famous for his cult travel guide *The World's Most Dangerous Places*, sort of a *Let's Go* for countries no sane person would go to. And, attached to the spare wheel mount on the rear of the vehicle, the trip mascot: a large yellow Teletubby, purchased in Amman the day before, and solemnly christened La-La Hussein Al-Tikriti. 'Strap him in tight,' Faoud instructed Robert. 'We don't want the brains behind the operation falling overboard.'

We were travelling in a convoy of six burly GMCs – the vehicles and their drivers had been doing the Amman–Baghdad run for years, while Iraq's air routes had been closed by international embargos. Among those preparing to ride with us in the other trucks were a news crew from France, distinguished by their freshly pressed beige utility vests. We had journalists from Japan, identifiable by the painstakingly laminated Jordanian press IDs strung round their necks, and by that luminous cluelessness that the Japanese radiate when outside their own unfathomable country. There was a carload of weirdly tall Swedes whose motivation we never discerned, another NGO vehicle, and a delegation from a mid-western American church group. Two of them had never left the United States before, and none of them had any idea what they were doing.

'Say,' asked one of them. 'Have you been to Baghdad before?'

I had, I confirmed, under its previous management.

'Do you know what the hospital is called?'

I said I thought it was possible there was more than one. It was a big city.

'Huh. We thought we might be able to help them out.'

I asked how.

'Uh . . . well, we thought we'd go see what they need.'

I supposed it was possible that post-war Iraq was suffering some sort of moron shortage. But these hapless saps, with a truckload of medicine and matching T-shirts printed at the Kinko's in Dead Elk, or wherever they were from, had come a long way, and meant well. It seemed churlish to suggest that few Iraqi doctors were likely to be yearning for a visit from a gaggle of knock-kneed inbreds from the First Church of Idiot.

On the Iraqi side of the border was a queue of vehicles which seemed bewilderingly long – we were, after all, despite George W. Bush's triumphal Action Man impression on the deck of the USS *Abraham Lincoln* the day before, trying to get into a war zone. But it was a war zone which for many people was nonetheless a home they'd not been able to visit for years, and/or a rare business opportunity. Many cars were weighed down with so much merchandise that the tops of their tyres were disappearing into the wheel arches; one Chevrolet had two washing machines lashed to its roof. At the end of the line were the two stone arches I remembered from my previous trip across this border in 2000. Between them, the enormous mosaic portrait of Saddam Hussein, in the regalia of a Bedouin chieftain, had been indelicately refurbished: riddled with bullets, spattered with whitewash, covered in Arabic graffiti, little of which I suspected was arguing that he was really a great guy who'd made the trains run on time.

Two sunglassed American special forces soldiers sauntered down the line, politely telling waiting press, aid workers, returnees, carpetbaggers and Jesus junkies that we were welcome to take pictures of anything except them. 'We,' they explained, 'are very much not here, if you get our drift.' On spotting Robert, the shorter soldier, who wore a Mexicana moustache, did a double take.

'You're the *Dangerous Places* guy, right?' said the soldier. 'I met you in Afghanistan while you were with General Dostum.'

Robert had a knack for cultivating peculiar company. He'd spent the war in Afghanistan as a guest of General Rashid Dostum, the Uzbek warlord. Robert asked the soldiers if they were enjoying Iraq.

'More fun than Afghanistan,' grinned the clean-shaven one. 'This stuff's pretty boring, though – trying to help the Iraqis get their customs post working again.'

I expressed mild surprise that the Americans were working with Iraqis already.

'Hell,' said the one with the moustache, 'it's their country. We just gave it back to them.'

This, of course, was the press release version of what this war was, eventually, supposed to have been about. In Britain in particular, an exasperated government had finally sold Operation Iraqi Freedom as a moral crusade to topple a repulsive dictator and liberate his long-suffering subjects. This tack had enabled Bush, Blair – and, performing his usual sterling work banging the coconuts together, John Howard – to abandon a case based on terrorist links nobody could prove and weapons nobody could find, and clamber to the high ground while insinuating that anyone who disagreed with them was a card-carrying member of Saddam's moustachekateers, rather than a concerned citizen wondering why we were spending skipfuls of our money to attack a country that hadn't done anything much to us.

I'd marched and written against the war. I thought that while Saddam Hussein's regime was overdue for removal, there were smarter ways of doing it, whether by subversion or assassination. I couldn't see the necessity for a war which would kill so many – Iraqis in and out of uniform, and coalition troops – who didn't deserve to die. I was nigh hysterical with irritation at the ridiculous whoppers peddled by our governments, whose propaganda campaign would have insulted the intelligence of cheese, or even evangelists from Nebraska. It was hard to pick an absolute low point, but for my money it was a toss-up between the Downing Street dossier, which turned out to be a thesis downloaded by some hapless press office lackey – the 'Sir, the dog ate my casus belli' approach to manufacturing consent – and the lurid promise that Saddam Hussein owned a hideous arsenal of inter-continental megadeath, fuses fizzing, 'ready to launch in forty-five minutes'. How did we know it was forty-five minutes, not thirty-seven or fifty-three? More to the point, what were they waiting for? If I ran my own heavily armed, oil-rich despotry, when I said 'launch', I'd mean go, already. What were we supposed to imagine was the scenario when Saddam Hussein lifted the gold phone in his platinum-lined bunker and ordered his forces to DefCon One? 'Yes, Mr President Field Marshal Anointed One Glorious Leader Direct Descendant of the Prophet, peace be upon him, thank you for your instruction to smite the infidel with God's holy fire, we'll get right on it after we've had a cup of coffee and watched *Frasier*.' Not since the pickled ear of Captain Jenkins was passed around the House of Commons in 1738 had Britain gone to war on a more preposterous pretext.

That said, by the time tanks rolled across Iraq's borders, I was almost as exasperated with the anti-war protestors I'd been marching alongside. The anti-war argument, I'd thought, should have been about means, not ends. No sensible person could dispute the desirability of regime change. I just thought that invading an entire country seemed a klutzy way to get one guy out of his job. On my previous visit to Baghdad, I'd been startled, perhaps more than I should have been, by the ubiquity of western popular culture. Iraq wasn't Afghanistan or North Korea. It could surely have been subtly subverted, by sending Starbucks and Slipknot, rather than the 1st Armoured Division (the Soviet Union was destroyed less by nuclear deterrence than it was by the fact that nobody wanted to listen to Russian rock'n'roll). Failing that, I had difficulty faulting the strategy suggested by a British officer I'd met in Kabul earlier in 2003, who was unenthused about his imminent deployment to Basra: 'I can't believe,' he said, 'that there's never a moment at which we're 90 per cent sure he's in one of three or four buildings. Fuck, blow 'em all up. They don't have any air defences. They wouldn't see it coming. Anyone else we cleaned up in those buildings wouldn't be any great loss.'

Inside Iraq, we stopped to fill the car with petrol, feeding it directly from one of the brightly painted tankers servicing traffic to Baghdad.

The robed chap wielding the pump settled at $US8 for 100 litres, making petrol substantially cheaper than the bottled water other merchants were touting. I asked Faoud what the drive would be like. 'Boring for five hours,' he replied. 'Wrong kind of interesting for one. The desert will be desert. Once we cross the Euphrates, from Ramadi onwards, that's a rough neighbourhood, apparently.'

The road from the border was unrelentingly straight dual carriage-way. The only memorable landmark was a recent addition to the land-scape: a Syrian bus which had been parked on a bridge at the moment an American missile had hit. We'd heard about this incident, among the first of the war's many confirmed damages to the proverbial collateral. The bus had been struck by a wave of shrapnel and flame, which had shattered the glass, and dented and warped the metal. Five passengers had been reported killed.

As we neared the Euphrates, the driver switched off his DVD player. We piled our flak jackets against the doors. There was a lot of traffic on the road now, and some of it looked unpromising. One car pulled up alongside ours, feinting an overtaking manoeuvre, before falling back, unable to keep up, which suited me: the four men inside wore keffiyehs over their faces, and were dandling Kalashnikovs on their laps.

The six trucks in our convoy were travelling ever-closer together. There were no radio links between the vehicles, but the drivers communicated in a semaphore of shrugs, eyebrow wrinkles and the limited hand gestures you can make while clinging to a steering wheel like it's a trapeze and you've just noticed one of the circus lions asleep on the safety net.

It was Faoud who saw the roadblock first. Two men, toting rifles, had placed rocks and sand across the highway, and were holding a length of rope as a barrier. They were a way off when we spotted them – on a road this straight and this flat, their loose grasp of the basics of camouflage suggested that they were new to whatever it was they thought they were doing. At the speed we were travelling, we had to make a decision quickly. Were they the bandits we knew had been robbing vehicles along here? Were they the public-spirited vigilantes who, we'd heard, were policing the road to prevent miscreants from preying on foreigners? Our drivers didn't stop to ask. In two rows of three, wing-mirror to wing-mirror, our SUVs ran the roadblock at full tilt. Through the rear window, after we roared through, I could see the two men, now covered in dust, yelling and waving their rifles – although that, mercifully, was all they were doing with them.

Barely two minutes later, we passed, heading in the other direction, an American armoured column, more than a dozen Abrams tanks and Bradley Fighting Vehicles.

'Man,' giggled Robert. 'Those two poor bastards back there think they're having a bad day *now*.'

In Baghdad, we found lodgings in a genial fleapit around the corner from the better-appointed Al-Hamra Hotel, which was teeming with hacks and NGO types wilting under the weight of laminated ID badges. We were still within staggering distance of the Al-Hamra's bar, and it was only US$30 a night for a four-room suite. The staff's commitment to their guests' safety also impressed us – at night, the family who owned the hotel slept in the lobby, with rifles and grenade-launchers under their camp beds.

We hired a driver/translator from among the men looking for business outside the Al-Hamra. Amar sold himself on his excellent English and air-conditioned yellow Chevrolet. I asked him to take us to Rashid Street, the heart of downtown Baghdad, for breakfast in a fruit juice bar. I'd fallen in love with these places in 2000: gaudy cafés with tiled, mirrored interiors, piles of fresh fruit stacked in the windows, rows of blenders, surfaces painted and staff dressed in colours matching the merchandise: bananas, oranges, kiwifruit, pineapples and pomegranates.

Rashid Street wasn't the vibrant shopping district I remembered. Most shops, and most juice bars, were closed. The rubbish hadn't been collected for a couple of months. There were no cars on a street which had once been so congested that I suspected that places in the traffic jam were passed from father to son. The few people present were talkative, which wasn't surprising – they had a lot to talk about – and generally optimistic, which was surprising. The views of the shopkeepers who fed us tea and cakes could be summarised thus: the hell with Saddam Hussein; thank you, America, for removing him; please fix everything you broke, and bugger off. Complaints about the present state of affairs were also unvarying: absence of security, electricity, hot water and telephones, the removal of all the everyday miracles of modern urban life. One man showed me a receipt for the US$25,000 in taxes his company had paid the previous October. 'Where is it?' he demanded. 'What has happened to my money?' I told him that bafflement regarding the end use of one's taxes was not unique to Iraq. Some of mine, I explained, had recently been spent on bombing his city, for reasons which remained unclear to me.

Also on Rashid Street were a couple of previously unimaginable displays of independent political thought – the New Iraq Progressive Movement Party were selling a newspaper, and the Workers Communist Party of Iraq had set up a labour exchange on the footpath. If this looked like good news, it was balanced by less heartening omens: stalls selling postcards of the Ayatollah Khomeini, and Hezbollah secretary-general Sayyed Hassan Nasrallah. And, in the juice bar we decided on, the chaps behind the counter, having noted our cameras, directed us around the corner.

In an avenue off Rashid Street, an incongruously clean blue and white blanket lay on the dirty footpath. A grey hand protruded from underneath it. A thief, someone said, shot earlier that morning, though nobody in the curious crowd who gathered around us was clear whether he'd died in the heat of pursuit or the cold blood of summary execution. It would be ludicrous to suggest that arbitrary death had not been a feature of life in Baghdad under Saddam Hussein, but this pathetic tragedy seemed to encapsulate everything that was wrong with post-war Iraq – all the usual rules of life had been suspended. There were no laws to deter the thief from contemplating his crime. There were no police to call when he was observed in the act. There was no judicial process to try him. There wasn't even anyone willing to collect the corpse. Not far away, on Jamhuriya Street, we met our first American soldiers, men from the 27th Infantry, guarding a bank. We told them what we'd found.

'I think someone's dealing with that kind of stuff,' said one. 'Not sure who, though. But basically the rule is that if we don't kill 'em ourselves, we can't pick 'em up.'

All over Baghdad, the American soldiers looked as perplexed as people who'd togged up for a fancy dress party and gone to the wrong address. Like every American position in Baghdad, the 27th Infantry's position outside the Al-Salehya bank was a mixture of sentry post, talking shop, freak show and sitting duck. Although the crowd of Iraqis around the knee-high barbed wire that delineated the perimeter seemed affable, it was impossible, when seeing the street as the soldiers did, to forget that any overlooking window could secrete a sniper, any passing motorcyclist could toss a grenade, any truck could explode.

Some Iraqi children joked with the soldiers, one capering rapscallion maintaining a spirited, if annoying, chorus of 'USA! USA! George Bush very good!'. An impeccably mannered grey-haired gent in a suit asked, in perfect English, when he'd be able to withdraw his money. ('Sir,' sighed the sergeant, 'I wish I could help you.') Most people just stood and stared – the reality of American soldiers in downtown Baghdad still only slightly less bizarre than the idea of invasion by six-headed green men from Saturn. Out of earshot of the soldiers, some hostile muttering was discernible.

'Fucking assholes,' spluttered one man, with commendable grasp of the colloquial. 'They destroyed my country. If I had a gun I'd shoot them.'

Nice, I said, to meet the only unarmed man in Baghdad.

'I swear,' he said, unnecessarily. 'Fucking assholes.'

Would he rather have Saddam back?

'Fucking asshole.'

No pleasing some people.

At the compound which included the Sheraton and Palestine hotels, where most of the press who'd covered the war had stayed, the entrances were sealed with barbed wire and guarded by Abrams tanks. The security was impenetrable, unless you looked like you were in no way Iraqi, in which case you were waved in with smiles from the soldiers. The tanks belonged to Charlie Company, 3rd Battalion, 69th Armored Regiment. Each tank had a nickname, beginning with the company identification C, painted on the barrel. One crew had made a real effort, with a striped, appropriately coloured, *Courtesy Of The Red, White & Blue*. This was a homage to the post-September 11th Toby Keith ballad whose fist-pumping middle eight, which promised to insert a boot into the posterior of anyone possessing the temerity to mess with the US of A, seemed to have mutated from sentimental, populist anthem into American foreign policy. Another tank crew, obviously *Beavis & Butthead* fans, had plumped for *Cornholio*. Outside the Palestine, Robert and I got talking to the crew of the Abrams named *Camel Tow*; they said, not sounding entirely convinced themselves, that the name had seemed funnier at the time.

Lieutenant Temple, *Camel Tow*'s commander, guessed that C Company had killed at least 130 'fedayeen' on the way up from Kuwait. While an excited correspondent from Fox News rooted around inside the tank – probably trying to start it, so he could invade Syria – I observed that Lieutenant Temple sounded like he'd rather enjoyed his ride to Baghdad. He didn't disagree.

'It was pretty awesome,' said Lieutenant Temple. 'We're a tank crew, so this was the Super Bowl for us. Kind of sad, though. This was probably the first and last tank battle of the twenty-first century. We're not going to fight wars like this anymore.'

At the wire fencing the hotels off from Firdus Square, the barrel of another Abrams squinted across to the plinth from which the famous statue of Saddam had been hauled down before a crowd of several hundred hysterical foreign journalists and several bemused Iraqis. I spoke to a couple of the locals peering over the barricade. One young man, who introduced himself as Sadil and told me his father was a sports reporter, was upset.

'The whole world,' he said, 'is laughing at my people.'

I doubted that, I said. Whether people were for or against the war, they were generally sympathetic to the folks on the receiving end.

'No,' he insisted. 'You laugh.'

His problem may have been the soldier at the far end of the check-point, an unimpressive specimen several sizes too small for his uniform, regarding the people he'd conquered through spectacles with lenses that looked as if they'd been sawn off the bottom of Coke bottles. It must have been hard for Iraqis, who I knew to be proud people, to think 'Did we get our butts kicked by that?' The discussion began to involve several, then a dozen, then dozens of Iraqis, then American soldiers as well. Though animated, it was jovial, remin-iscent of rival cricket fans ragging each other during a drinks break. Adding to the cacophony, a demonstration arrived in the square, bearing the Kurdish flag and some regrettably mistranslated banners deploring Saddam Hussein's 'Comical bombing'. A group of five musicians, clad in black, set up in the middle of the roundabout and struck up a mournful tune on two violins, a cello, a clarinet and a mandolin.

The American soldier closest to the Abrams addressed the chatter-ing crowd.

'People!' he yelled, at parade-ground volume. 'Could you all please can it for a few minutes so we can enjoy the music?'

They did, and we did, and the Kurds seemed genuinely touched by the subsequent applause. An inspired piece of improvised diplomacy – a quality in short supply elsewhere in Baghdad.

We figured we couldn't leave Baghdad without going looting. Everyone else was at it, and most seemed to be having better luck than the guy we'd found under the blanket. Amar drove us to the wreckage of the Ministry of Information.

There was an Iraqi policeman on duty when we arrived, recognis-able by his Iraqi eagle belt buckle. He told us that, rather than run around the ruins chasing looters, he was waiting for them to cart stuff out of the building, ordering them to stack it in the room he was guarding, then instructing them to piss off, or words to that effect; he patted the pistol in his belt. We, however, were welcome to look around.

There wasn't much left, let alone much worth pinching. Most rooms had been burned. The ones the arsonists hadn't got to were ankle deep in the detritus of decades of bureaucracy. I found some impressive-looking folders and gave them to Amar for translation, briefly nurturing dreams of an award-winning scoop – a fortuitously unincinerated letter of the sort that other lucky hacks had found, perhaps reading 'Dear Saddam, let's fly planes into New York, love Osama. PS, kisses to George Galloway.'

'Invoices for carpets,' said Amar, tossing one out the window into the street. 'Job applications,' he said of another, which followed it down three storeys onto the footpath.

Robert had just discovered a cupboard full of Iraqi licence plates, with which he hoped to confuse California Highway Patrol officers back home, when we heard gunfire. As we made our way tentatively downstairs to see what the excitement was about, two Iraqi boys barrelled into us. They exhibited the extremes of the spectrum of fear – the younger one, wearing an Iraqi football shirt, was gripped by giggles, while his friend was pale, and looked on the verge of crapping himself. Outside, an American Humvee had drawn up. The soldiers had dismounted, and had two looters up against a wall, both looking properly terrified as the soldiers screamed at them down the barrels of their rifles. The sergeant in charge was not in a hearts and minds mood.

'Goddamn,' he shouted, at nobody in particular, pulling out his Discman earphones. 'I'm TIRED of this FUCKING PLACE and I'm TIRED of these FUCKING PEOPLE.'

The soldiers kept yelling, and jabbing their rifles towards the trembling looters. I thought two things: one, that I really didn't want to get involved in this; two, that I didn't want to watch anyone get shot, either. Myself, Robert, Damian and Amar edged uncertainly into the gap between the Americans and the Iraqis.

Afternoon, chaps, I stammered. Can we help?

'Do you guys have an Arabic speaker?' barked the sergeant. The soldiers, to my relief, lowered their guns.

I indicated Amar.

'Thank Christ,' said the sergeant. 'Right. Tell this guy here' – he pointed at one of the looters – 'that if I see him here one more time I'm going to give him three more fucking gaps in his fucking front teeth to match the one he's already got.'

Amar, a decorous soul, provided what I suspected was a somewhat bowdlerised translation. As he did so, two more American soldiers arrived, clutching by the collar the policeman we'd met earlier.

'This asshole,' announced one of the soldiers to the sergeant, 'had a gun.'

I think he's allowed one, I said. He's a cop.

'He's a what?' asked one of the soldiers.

I indicated the belt buckle, and explained that he'd been trying to hinder the looters, not help them.

'Are you sure he's supposed to have a gun?' asked the soldier.

I thought he was permitted a sidearm, but I wasn't sure. It wasn't like I was serving in the occupying army or anything. Eventually, Amar negotiated a settlement whereby the policeman surrendered his pistol in return for a name he could contact about getting it back, the looters went home and promised never to return, and the Americans accepted with handshakes Amar's best wishes for themselves and their families. The man was wasted as a taxi driver.

'It's hard,' said one soldier as the squad prepared to move. 'I've met good people here. I just don't understand why they're doing this to their own country. Everywhere we go, they're smashing, stealing, burning. We've put out three fires today, and while we do it, they shoot over our heads.'

It was pretty weird, I agreed, but maybe just what came of having no freedom at all, and then more than they knew what to do with. They'd need time to find their range, so to speak. In the meantime, it seemed incredible that America's post-war planning hadn't advanced as far as the manufacture of a few English/Arabic PLEASE KEEP OUT signs.

'Maybe,' he sighed. 'All I really want is to get out of here. Which I guess is one thing we've all got in common, right?'

A few days later, back at the tank position outside the Palestine Hotel on Firdus Square, I pointed out the graffiti on the famous vacant plinth to an American soldier. In large red letters, it read JOB DONNE [sic] GO HOME.

'Yep,' said the soldier.

What we couldn't figure out – other than the boring, obvious stuff, like what the war had been about – was who we'd been fighting against. This invasion of Iraq, much like Operation Desert Storm in 1991, didn't look like a war at all – more a peremptory thrashing, the military equivalent of Real Madrid belting forty goals past a team of ten-year-olds with a cross-eyed keeper. I asked Amar where his country's army had gone, and he took us to meet some of them.

The deserters and their families were camping in what had been a club for Iraqi air force officers, and was now a wreck; in the rubble, I found panels from British-made missiles. The deserters were happy to talk, if only to relieve the monotony. Mithrak was twenty-nine, and wore a bandage around his head.

'Shrapnel,' he explained, 'but it's not too bad.'

He was from Sadr City, the Baghdad slum known until recently as Saddam City. He was no longer able to afford his rent, so he was eking out a living by selling pipes pulled from the wreckage of the officers' club. Marwan, his friend, was twenty, and also from Sadr City. He'd been stationed near Basra, manning an observation position when the British came over the horizon. I asked him how long he'd stayed at his post.

'About thirty seconds,' he smiled. 'I'm not crazy. The British have good tanks and good soldiers. I didn't want to fight.'

Our chat was punctuated by sporadic heavy-calibre gunfire, probably American, coming from somewhere or other, directed at somewhere or other else; in Baghdad, it was often hard to tell. Its rhythm became more purposeful, like a morse code message tapped with greater urgency as the boat went down. It got louder, possibly closer.

'You should probably go,' said Marwan.

We asked Amar to show us more of the fierce Iraqi war machine we'd overcome. He took us to what he said was the headquarters of

Iraq's air force. This complex, the reception hall of which was crested by an immense sculpted profile of Saddam Hussein, was curiously large for a country which, to judge by the efforts it had made to defend itself, didn't have an air force. The ancient MiG mounted on a plinth beside the gate may have been the most airworthy machine the Iraqis had.

Like most other regime-related buildings in Baghdad, the office blocks had been ventilated by missiles, then lustily ransacked by looters. In a neat metaphor for Iraq's shift in its priorities of worship, someone had left a vast oil-on-canvas portrait of Saddam Hussein draped over a windowsill – they'd only stolen the frame. To my annoyance, Robert spotted the painting first, leaving me to make do with a pair of air force berets which I found in an upstairs room and which I thought would make a cool engagement present for a couple of friends in London.

If any of us harboured doubts that the pre-war tales of Iraq's fearsome weapons stockpile had been the most fabulous crock of nonsense, they were dispelled by poking around the offices. On one floor, each room was devoted to one of Iraq's potential enemies. There was a Turkey room, a Saudi Arabia room, an Iran room, an Israel room. The walls of each were covered with maps of the corresponding country, red stickers indicating potential targets. Around these maps, rather touchingly, were pictures of fighter aircraft, cut out of the back issues of *Jane's Defence Weekly* that littered the floors. The Iraqi defence establishment which, we'd been told, was plotting to lay us waste in forty-five minutes, had in fact been making collages. If I imagined the Iraqi officers making 'Zoom! Kapow!' noises as they stuck the pictures up, it was kind of heartbreaking. A wall was covered with a lovingly painted artwork of all the things the Iraqi air force hadn't had: fighter planes, AWACS aircraft, satellites.

Our contemplation of this sorry spectacle was interrupted by shooting from outside. We picked our way down the shattered staircases. The view that confronted us wasn't encouraging – a terrified Iraqi looter bolting towards us while, about 30 metres behind him, an American soldier, his rifle levelled, yelled at him to stop. Robert and I waved our hands in the air and shouted placatory expletives at the soldier. He lowered his rifle, and one Iraqi survived to loot another day.

The soldier's colleagues were ordering another party of looters to unload the stolen furniture they'd stacked on their truck. I asked the soldier what would happen next.

'We'll drive off,' he sighed, 'and they'll come back and pick it up anyway. We can't be everywhere.'

We thought we should look into Baghdad's new boom industry, the procurement and retail of stolen goods. We asked Amar where all this stuff was being sold.

'A place called New Baghdad,' he said. 'But it's a bad area. Many Ali Baba.'

'Ali Baba' was the Iraqi slang for 'thief'. Amar's point was a fair one: if he lost his car, he lost his livelihood. We agreed that we'd visit New Baghdad on the condition that the second he decided to leave, we'd go.

If *Mad Max* had included a jumble sale scene, it would have looked like New Baghdad. Along the footpaths, people sold computers, filing cabinets, kidney machines, guns – Robert was quoted US$350 for a Beretta pistol, though his foreignness and perturbing eagerness may have skewed the price upwards – and clean Iraqi passports, bright green and spangled with Saddam's portrait in gold, fresh out of boxes lifted from the Ministry of the Interior. We purchased our citizenship for 10,000 dinars, about seven American dollars each.

Few foreigners were visiting New Baghdad, and a crowd quickly gathered around us. What was most interesting about the crowd was what it didn't do. Robert, Damian and I were, respectively, an American, a Briton and an Australian – a tempting representation of the three nations who'd led the charge to attack the country we were visiting. Between us, we carried three foreign passports, half a dozen cameras, and five figures of US dollars in cash. If any of this mob stuck a gun in our necks and told us to hand it all over, it wasn't like calling the cops was going to do us much good. When a few people started gesturing at Robert and Damian's cameras, I thought things were going badly wrong. When one wiry, wired young man in a New Jersey Devils hockey shirt pushed aggressively through the crowd and seized me meaningfully by the shoulder, I was absolutely convinced they were. Then I absorbed what he was saying.

'Ali Baba,' he gibbered. 'You understand? Ali Baba. Bad people. They know you here. Bad people coming. Ali Baba. Get out. Go.'

In the Thieves' Market, the thieves were telling us to look out for thieves. If I consider how a team of blundering Arab journalists might fare in London immediately after Britain had been invaded by a coalition of Iraq, Syria and Egypt, I'm grateful enough that nobody in Baghdad even tried to tar and feather us and chase us to the city limits at pitchfork-point. For our delivery from robbery by a man who couldn't profit from his generosity – possibly quite the opposite, if the incoming Ali Babas figured out who'd sprung their prey – the handshake I left him with, heartfelt though it was, seemed pitifully inadequate. But, in the immeasurably brief time it took to decide to follow his advice as fast as Amar's car could carve up the traffic, it was all there was time for.

Whatever the reason for Baghdad's anarchy, it wasn't a lack of people offering to run the place. More than eighty new political parties had set up shop since Saddam's defeat, and were thrashing out manifestos, holding press conferences, opening headquarters in any government buildings that still had four walls and a roof. Robert and I were thinking of running for office ourselves, reasoning that we had Iraqi passports, knew where to buy guns, and that there were several less plausible candidates than La-La Hussein Al-Tikriti running around. An electoral strategy was coming into focus. Judging by the rhetoric of every representative of every party who'd bent our ear in the Al-Hamra's bar, the freedom, democracy and security vote was going to be split at least eighty ways.

'If the La-La Party ran,' reasoned Robert, 'on a platform of oppression, corruption and larceny, we could clean up.'

We decided to visit one of the new parties. We picked on the

Assyrian Democratic Movement, on the grounds that we'd never heard of them, and that we admired their chutzpah in commandeering a barracks which had belonged to Saddam's fedayeen militia. The vast portrait of Saddam by the gate had been whitewashed over, except for about a foot at the top. The first thing the ADM were going to need to buy if their State Department funding came through was a longer ladder.

The ADM headquarters was patrolled by the ADM's own militia, one of whom turned out to be a plasterer from Chicago ('I wanted to do something for my grandfather's people,' he explained). Inside, the walls had been redecorated with gaudy murals of ancient Assyria – a civilisation which, if these illustrations were accurate, had been constructed principally from Mardi Gras floats, many of which featured winged bulls with human heads. The ADM's spokesman, Shmael Benyamin, gave us some cool purple lapel badges. These, he explained, bore the standard of King Sargon the Great, who'd founded an Assyrian empire twenty-four centuries before the birth of Christ. Today's Assyrians, Benyamin said, were a nation of 1.2 million Aramaic-speaking Christians from the north of Iraq. For the last few decades, they'd been getting at least as severe a kicking as the Kurds without attracting half the attention. Saddam Hussein, said Benyamin, had destroyed 200 Assyrian villages.

I asked him what the Assyrians wanted now.

'Freedom and democracy for Iraq,' said Benyamin. 'And security.'

Just like everyone else. So far, Iraqis had freedom, if arguably too much, democracy only inasmuch as there was little impediment to anyone saying what they damn well pleased, and security as long as a gun was to hand. When we looked around for who might be willing or able to impose order, we didn't find anyone who'd have figured prominently on George W. Bush's cast list.

We went to a visit a hospital with Jonathan Kaplan, a full-time battlefield surgeon whose part-time job was making people who merely write for a living feel pitifully inadequate (his two volumes of memoir, *The Dressing Station* and *Contact Wounds*, are works of exemplary reportage).

Jonathan told us that Islamist groups were already appearing at hospitals, harassing male doctors who attempted to treat women. We arrived at the Ibn Al-Baladi paediatric hospital in Sadr City at a perfectly symbolic moment. The picture of Saddam at the entrance was being replaced with a portrait of Ayatollah Mohammed Sadeq Al-Sadr – the popular Shi'a cleric assassinated by Saddam's agents in Najaf in 1999, and after whom Saddam City had recently been renamed (Al-Sadr's son, Muqtada, was not yet infamous as an insurgent commander). The group which had commissioned this portrait – the men shifting the painting gave me the names Al-Hawza, Al-Noor and Al-several-other-things, which suggested this outfit was only just up and running – had been at work elsewhere. By the hospital's gate, they'd sprayed over graffiti reading US PLEASE STAY and THANK YOU MR BUSH.

Once the portrait of Al-Sadr had been fastened into place, I asked the bloke who looked most in charge – something that, where militant Shi'a groups are concerned, can usually be judged by beard length – what his people wanted.

'Freedom and democracy for Iraq,' said the cleric. 'And security.'

I wanted all those things for Iraq as well. I mean, I want all those things for everywhere, but when I'd left Baghdad in 2000, I'd wanted them for Iraq more than I wanted them for pretty much anywhere else not already thus blessed. I wanted them especially for Odai, a twenty-year-old antique shop assistant who'd been the only person prepared to tell me what life under Saddam Hussein was really like, about the fog of fear through which all human interchange in Iraq was conducted. By telling me what he'd told me, he effectively put the power of life and death over him and his family in my hands – a reflection of his desperation rather than my own innate saintliness.

Odai was now twenty-three, and owned the antiques store, which he'd inherited upon the death of his father. Since we'd last met, he'd got married and had a son. He sent out for a fabulous lunch of the Baghdad specialty *mazgouf* – a fish slit open, turned inside out and slowly roasted in front of an open fire (broadly similar things used to happen to people who spoke of Saddam Hussein as Odai spoke of him to me). Odai had closed his shop during the war, and protected his stock from the looting by hiding it in his home, and the houses of friends. He'd reopened four days previously, and seemed nervous. I asked if he had a gun. He winced, and opened a cupboard. It contained a gold- and silver-plated Uzi, an absurd weapon that would have got laughed off the set of a Snoop Dogg video on the grounds of gauche, graceless blingingness.

Where the hell, I marvelled, had he found it?

'In the market,' said Odai, regarding it glumly. 'I think it was stolen from Uday Hussein's house. I don't even know if it works. I would never fire it.'

I asked how business had been.

'Not great,' said Odai. 'Some American soldiers come in, wanting Saddam watches, which I don't have. Some people try to sell things stolen from the museums, which I won't buy.'

And life in general?

'I was happy in the first moments when I knew Saddam was gone,' says Odai. 'But now I'm miserable again, because it's not turning out like we hoped.'

On the street outside the shop was possibly the most damning illustration of the extent of the post-war chaos. In Baghdad of all places, capital of a country which owned the world's third-largest oil reserves, there was a queue, at least a hundred cars long, for the petrol station. A futures market had been improvised around it. People who'd bought petrol carried surplus down the queue, selling it on at a markup which increased the further back they went.

Odai and I negotiated a deal for an enamelled Kurdish plate for my then-girlfriend, Roni, and an HMV portable gramophone for myself. The model was of an age that suggested it might have come to Baghdad with the British in the 1920s; I was taking it home.

'Next time you come,' said Odai, 'maybe things will be working again. I don't understand how it is that America can bring hundreds of tanks all the way to Iraq, but no generators.'

I found similar exasperation among other Iraqis. A Baghdad journalist I'd met in 2000, now exiled in Sweden, had asked me to check on some friends of hers, a family who lived in an apartment in the Salhiya complex of identikit apartment blocks. The first time I'd come to Baghdad, many of these had been draped in banner portraits of Saddam Hussein several storeys tall. They were gone now. Being a dictator is like being a rock star. When you're hot, you're worshipped by millions, showered with wealth, your every statement commands headlines and even people who don't love you pretend they do so as not to appear out of step. As Saddam Hussein or Marilyn Manson could confirm, fashion can desert as quickly as it embraces. One moment you're on posters and billboards, the next you're a wretched figure who nobody sane cares about, with the possible exception, in both cases, of journalists with overdeveloped senses of irony.

I didn't record my friend's friends' real names in my original article for the *Face*, and I won't do it here, because of the way they stiffened with agitation when I reached for my notebook – living in a police state will do that to people. The mother, who I'll call Rana, lived with her three daughters, who I'll disguise as Hala, twenty-five, Zeinab, twenty, and Anna, eight. They'd left Baghdad during the air campaign, and had returned a few days before my visit. When I asked how they felt about American soldiers on their streets, Rana's reply was startling.

'I'm surprised,' she said. 'I thought we would win.'

I asked her if she was serious.

'Yes,' she confirmed. 'I thought we would defend our country. We have a brave army.'

Her eldest daughter, Hala, rolled her eyes.

'We didn't have good leadership,' she said gently. 'We had a bad regime here.'

Hala was in the final year of an engineering course. 'But,' she said sadly, 'the university is closed. And everything has been stolen. It's supposed to open next week, but I don't think I can go. Even if there was transport, it's not safe to travel, especially for girls.'

I asked what they'd been doing all day.

'Nothing,' said Hala. 'We can't go out, except sometimes to buy food. There are no telephones, so we can't call friends. No radio, no television. It is very boring.'

Hala asked me, wistfully, about London. She explained that she'd been born in Bath while her parents were living there in the seventies, and was waiting for the British to reopen their embassy so she could find out if she was entitled to a British passport. It seemed that even British bombs couldn't destroy the ingrained Anglophilia of Iraq's middle classes. This phenomenon dated from a previous occupation. On 8 March 1917, Lieutenant General Stanley Maude, commander of the Anglo-Indian Army of the Tigris, proclaimed that 'Our armies do not come into your cities and lands as conquerors or enemies but as liberators'. Eighty-six years we'd been freeing Iraq, and we still couldn't get it right.

If there was one sight, and one site, that encapsulated the interweaving storylines of immediately post-war Baghdad – the furies of America's bombing, the city's subsequent efforts to eat itself alive, the perverse optimistic stoicism of its people – it was the ruined communications complex which included the Saddam International Tower, and the Al-Mamoun telephone exchange. The tower, a futurist hallucination resembling an immense hypodermic needle, had survived an obvious attempt to topple it: holes had been punched in its base by American cruise missiles, components of which were scattered like metal confetti.

The seven-storey telephone exchange was as complete a wreck as a building can be while still being more or less recognisable as a building. It had been bombed, looted and burned: its metal frame had warped in the fire. Inside, on the ground floor, in what looked like a scene from one of those after-the-blast films which were all the rage in the 1980s, four smartly dressed men sat around a table, drinking coffee. They stood as we approached, bid us join them in excellent English, and explained that they were telephone engineers.

'This is where we work,' smiled the oldest of them, who sported a silver moustache and a white golf shirt.

Okay, I said.

'It is true,' he conceded, 'that there is no work for us at present. However, one day, Insh'allah, there will be work. So we will wait.'

'We have,' said one of his colleagues, in dapper smart casual rig of blue chinos and a button-down work shirt, 'tidied up as best we could.'

He indicated the bent, dented filing cabinets and half-melted furniture they'd arranged in the rubble. My immediate thought was that they'd all gone mad. The more they talked, though, as I waited for the coffee they'd sent for, the clearer it became that the opposite was the case. They were trying, with a dogged earnestness that still knots my ventricles when I recall it, to stay sane.

'You must understand,' said silver moustache, 'that it's unbearable for us to sit around our houses, with our women and children, unable to provide. So, every day, we get up as normal, and we get dressed, and we come to work.'

'But,' said button-down shirt, 'we have not had any wages for two months, so it is difficult.'

They would not hear of me paying for the coffee.

On our last afternoon, Amar drove Robert and me to a Hussein family palace complex on the banks of the Tigris. It consisted of one huge pseudo-Roman villa, with Saddam's silhouette emblazoned on the brickwork at several points, surrounded by several smaller palaces, which looked modest by comparison, and grotesque by any reasonable standards. The smaller buildings had all been bombed, the main one left curiously untouched – though a crater in the garden suggested that one cruise missile might not have lived up to the promises in the brochure. Looters had taken everything portable, and made heroic attempts at a couple of things that weren't. As we walked into one upstairs room in the main palace, we were hit, with the force of a thump in the solar plexus, by the aroma of rotting human. When Amar asked a couple of passing scavengers who the dead guy was, they explained that he'd perished in an ambitious effort to liberate a room-sized chandelier.

All that was left was stuff nobody wanted – schoolbooks belonging to junior members of Saddam's family, chunks of a broken fake Ming vase, which I scooped up to give to friends as novelty paperweights. One wall of the main building was covered with an inlaid marble mosaic portrait of the entire Hussein clan, suggesting the title sequence for the least funny sitcom of all time.

I asked Amar if this was the first time he'd visited the Husseins at home, and he laughed, but the more we explored, marvelling at the ornate detail in the ceilings, and the ghastly brown marble bathrooms, the more Amar's mood darkened. Amar had been a limitless source of good cheer during our stay, and I sensed that anger was not an emotion he was easy with. I decided to ditch the mutually mocking banter that had characterised our working relationship. Outside, on the balcony overlooking the river, I asked him if he was really okay with being here.

'This is crazy,' he said quietly. 'I have not one metre of my own in Iraq. I'm thirty-four years old, and I live with my wife and two daughters and five of her family in three rooms. He has all this, and how many more palaces besides? Why does he need all this?'

It clearly wasn't enough. One of the villas in the compound was missing a roof not because it had been attacked, but because it was still being built.

'Do you know,' asked Amar, 'where I could find the pilot who bombed this place? I would like to kiss him.'

We drove out of Baghdad at the same demented speed we'd driven in, our convoy of SUVs weaving between cars carrying rifle-toting, sunglassed, keffiyeh-swaddled bandits like a school of blundering whales trying to outrun pirhanas, our driver so terrified he didn't relax enough to switch on the belly dancer DVDs until we were past Ramadi and into the desert. 'Dangerous,' he said, exhaling heavily as he pointed us towards the Jordanian border, 'now finished.'

If only Iraq had been able to say the same. At that early stage, though, I was surprised by how sanguine a lot of Iraqis seemed, and doubly surprised by how hopeful that made me feel. Maybe, I thought, invading this place hadn't been such a bad idea after all. Maybe it would work out, even if America and Britain, swatting aside the options of diplomacy and inspections, had done the wrong thing and done it too early. It might be better than doing the right thing too late.

11

Illustrations of how not to deal with international crises didn't come starker. In July 1995, the rabble of drunk hillbillies which traded as the Bosnian Serb army, under the command of General Ratko Mladic, came to Srebrenica. At the time, the town was allegedly a UN Safe Area, guarded by a battalion of Dutch troops. Thousands of Bosnian Muslims, who'd fled Bosnian Serb army pogroms elsewhere in Bosnia, had gathered in the Srebrenica enclave, naively assuming that when the UN, and the military strength at its disposal, called something a Safe Area, it meant the area might be, uh, *safe*.

By the time of my visit, nearly nine years later, a thousand or so of those trusting souls had been buried beneath green headstones in the new memorial cemetery at Potocari, a hamlet just outside Srebrenica. There was room in the memorial grounds for another 7000 corpses, due to be interred as soon as their names were confirmed – a task that had dragged on almost a decade because Mladic's goons had removed identifying material from their victims before executing them.

Opposite the cemetery was the decaying battery factory in which the Dutch battalion had established their headquarters, and to which thousands of terrified people had come seeking the protection of the international community. The graffiti left by the Dutch soldiers who'd sat on their rifles and watched the massacre occur was still there – childish drawings of tanks, planes and heavy-breasted winged vixens, accompanied by misspelt, disobliging remarks about Bosnian women. The sketch of Donald Duck in a United Nations Protection

Force (UNPROFOR) beret was apposite, though it would have been more so if it had depicted Mickey Mouse.

I'd arrived in Potocari with the convoy bearing the UN's High Representative in Bosnia-Herzegovina, Paddy Ashdown. Ashdown, known formally in the UK as Lord Ashdown of Norton-sub-Hamdon, and universally in Bosnia as 'Padi', was a former leader of the Liberal Democrats in Britain, and was now, to all intents and purposes, King of Bosnia. As high representative, he could close newspapers, freeze bank accounts, overturn court verdicts and sack government officials, up to and including any of Bosnia's three presidents and three prime ministers. As high representative, equally, he didn't really have to do anything, and it's hard to imagine that anyone outside Bosnia would have cared much if he'd spent his term with his feet up on the drinks trolley. He'd thrown himself into the role, however, with a passion and energy that startled and inspired most Bosniaks I asked. Jonathan Dimbleby, the veteran ITN reporter, who was also following Paddy's progress, told me that Chris Patten had been like this during his tenure as the last British governor of Hong Kong, working all hours, going everywhere, meeting as many people as he could. 'I believe,' said Dimbleby, with what seemed an approving smile, 'the expression is "gone native".'

I'd wanted to meet Paddy – everybody, at his insistence, called him Paddy – to see if there was still a place for such a role, effectively that of an old-school imperial viceroy, a hangover from the period which bequeathed such phrases as 'gone native'.

Paddy had come to Potocari to meet with members of the Srebrenica Memorial Foundation's executive board, and with survivors of the massacre. These women – and they were all, for the depressingly fundamental reason that all the men were dead, women – had told their stories before, but they told them again to Paddy, about the mass of frightened, starving, reeking humanity that had cowered there, hoping that the west would protect them, about the people who died and women who gave birth as they waited, about the rapes, beatings and murders committed by the Bosnian Serb army, about the husbands, brothers, sons and fathers loaded onto trucks and buses, or marched into the forests, and never seen again. Nearly a decade on, there was no hint of resignation or acceptance in these women. They were, still, suffused with incoherent rage, marooned forever in the moment at which their lives as they knew them had ended. Tears twinkled in the corners of the high representative's eyes.

The King of Bosnia's palace, the office of the high representative, was a whiteish seven-storey block on the south bank of Sarajevo's Miljacka River. When I arrived, Paddy was giving an interview to a journalist from a newspaper in Mostar. He greeted her, and her translator, in reasonably proficient Bosnian, which impressed me instantly. It's a tricky language, and despite several visits to Bosnia – the first witnessing the lifting of the siege of Bihac by Croatia's brutal rout of the Krajina Serbs in 1995, most recently for a friend's wedding in Sarajevo in 2003 – my proficiency in it had never proceeded much further than ordering coffee or beer in the reasonable certainty that I'd receive coffee or beer, and not directions to platform three or a smack in the mouth.

When Paddy returned to English, he yammered at the journalist about Bosnia with a careening enthusiasm, often tearing off at a new tangent before anyone else present had worked out where they were, never mind where he was going; I would later learn that walking anywhere with Paddy left one with much the same feeling. He made frequent recourse to metaphors, feeling his way through them to be sure they made it across the language gap without anything dropping off. Bosnia, Paddy explained, had been a mortally wounded patient, but it was recovering, progressing from intensive care to crutches to the walking stick which the high representative was providing. Or maybe, Paddy offered, Bosnia was like a computer. The high representative could build the hardware – judiciary, police, the institutions of a functional state – but changing the software, the mindset of the people, was more difficult.

'This is within our reach,' he said to the journalist, 'but not within our grasp. Does that make sense?'

The journalist nodded. She asked if he was optimistic.

'You have to be to do this job,' he laughed, 'as you have to be to lead the Liberal Democrats in Britain. Yes, I'm very optimistic about Bosnia.'

It would, of course, be surprising if someone in Paddy's position answered that question with, 'Are you crazy? This broken-down jerkwater swamp is holding a one-way ticket to hell on a sled, baby, and if I were you I'd keep my savings in a sock and a pistol under my pillow.' As the journalist would have known, however, Paddy had made an unusually solid show of his faith, buying a holiday/retirement home in Bosnia, by a lake in Jablanica. Maybe this should be a condition of all international community nation-building appointments.

The question was: why was Paddy optimistic? There were any number of reasons not to be. When surveying the view from his office, it was still impossible to miss, between the refurbished yellow cube of the Holiday Inn and the rebuilt mirrored pillars of the UNIS towers, the hulking wreck of the Bosnian parliament building, a favourite target of the Bosnian Serb army during the siege it had laid to Sarajevo between 1992 and 1995. Nearly a decade after the Serbian marauders were scattered by criminally overdue NATO air strikes, I couldn't walk two Sarajevo blocks without noticing the war's effects on the architecture, and any equally cursory survey of Bosnia's politics induced the same depressing nostalgia. Both of Bosnia's constituent parts – the Bosniak/Croat Federation and the largely Serb Republika Srpska – were dominated by parties selling ethnicity as ideology. Crime and corruption were accepted as resignedly by Bosnians as rain was by the British. Two of the chief architects of Bosnia's torment – Bosnian Serb president Radovan Karadzic, and his attack dog, General Mladic – continued to evade capture, despite US$5 million on the head of each.

'Think of how far you've come,' Ashdown urged the journalist.

She asked, finally, about Ashdown's fondness, which had caused some bemusement in Bosnia, for long trips around the country, to meet people, to hang out, often staying with locals in their houses – or, as had been the case with refugees, their tents. He didn't have to do it – or anything else, come to that. He wasn't running for anything.

'I need to know,' he said, 'how my decisions affect their lives. It's my style. I'm leaving Sarajevo this afternoon, in fact.'

We headed out of Sarajevo in a convoy of three vehicles. Leading the way was a black armoured BMW sedan, carrying Paddy, his wife Jane, their driver and a bodyguard from Paddy's Close Protection Unit (CPU). Behind them was a four-wheel drive carrying its driver, a spare driver, and two more CPU men. The CPU were plainclothes Royal Military Police. They were linked to each other via earpieces and discreetly armed with pistols, with more serious hardware stashed in the vehicles. Bringing up the rear in an unarmoured, unarmed – journalism promotes a healthily humble perspective of your importance in the scheme of things – four-wheel drive were a driver called Nisad, a saturnine and charming office of the high representative spokesman called Vedran, myself, and photographer Dave Thomson. It was only Dave's second time back in Sarajevo after being medivaced out in the early stages of the siege, having collected an arseful of Serbian shrapnel.

We drove east out of Sarajevo, across the Inter-Entity Boundary Line (IEBL), the squiggle on the map which divided the Federation from Republika Srpska. The view from the road was wild and thrilling: brooding mountains, dense forests, lonely farmhouses, circling eagles.

'Those caves,' said Vedran. 'Anyone could be hiding in there.'

I asked if he was thinking of anyone in particular.

'That,' grinned Vedran, 'is the five-million-dollar question.'

We arrived in Zvornik as the sun was setting. Zvornik sat on the Drina River, and we could look across the water into Serbia, and see one of the grim absurdities in which the Balkans specialised. In Zvornik, which before the war had a majority Muslim population, the mosques had been destroyed as the town's Muslims fled the ethnic cleansers of the Bosnian Serb army. Over the river in Mali Zvornik, inside Serbia, the local mosque was never touched, at least not back then – in another grim absurdity, the Mali Zvornik mosque had had its windows broken just a couple of weeks before, in a wave of anti-Muslim violence that had swept Serbia following anti-Serb pogroms in Kosovo.

From Zvornik, we headed into the hills, to a village called Krizevici. Everything in Krizevici was new, or being built, the muddy roads lined with grey cement frames cradling walls of orange brick; all of Krizevici's original buildings had been destroyed in 1992 by Serbian militias. At the highest point of Krizevici, a white mosque, the base of its minaret ringed by green lights which glowed against the gathering gloom like flying saucers searching for a landing pad, was a subtly defiant monument to the failure of an ambition of ethnic and religious purity. A detachment of local police awaited us. Paddy greeted them, then asked them to return to their base. Vedran explained that Paddy always did this, and that it was a constant source of bewilderment to Bosnian officials, who seemed unable to understand why a man would turn down police escorts if he was entitled to them.

Our convoy stopped at the house belonging to the Hrustanovic family. The large home was planted in a generous yard which contained a wooden lodge for a dozen or so goats. Salih Hrustanovic, the head of the household and the Ashdowns' host for tonight, had led the return of Muslims to Krizevici. He reckoned that about half the pre-war population had come home. As our party picked its way down the slippery track to Krizevici's youth centre, where Paddy was due to speak to local teenagers, we stopped to talk to a couple of returnees, a middle-aged woman and her elderly mother, who were living in a wooden lean-to while a new house was built on the site of the one they'd lost. There wasn't much need to ask where the men of their family were, but Paddy did, and again struggled to keep his eyes dry as the women unspooled another belief-beggaring story of murder, theft, exile and return.

'If it had been my family,' Paddy said as we continued on our way, 'I don't think I could have come back.'

At the youth centre, an audience of fifty or so adolescents had been coralled into a classroom. Paddy started with a wilfully provocative question: how many of them wanted to leave Bosnia? There was an awkward pause, then one hand – the class joker, I suspected. 'Come on,' said Paddy, 'don't be shy.' About thirty more hands went up. It was one of the major difficulties of reinvigorating failing states in a world of increasingly mobile populations: when setting about the long, difficult process of fixing a broken country, how could you stop its brightest people, the ones you were going to need most, from thinking, 'Bugger this for a box of soldiers, life's too short,' and moving to a place where hot water came out of the taps, and the chances of their families being slaughtered on the whim of some deranged despot were relatively slim?

Paddy told the kids he was going to talk for a bit, and then ask them to name one thing that he could do, as high representative, that might persuade them to stay. What followed was rather a joy: watching a politician who didn't have to do it trying to engage an audience. He told them how he'd grown up in Northern Ireland, of mixed religious parentage – 'Paddy' is a nickname that was first bestowed upon Jeremy Ashdown when he went to school in England. He told them how he'd returned to Northern Ireland as a Royal Marines officer, and watched his own people burn each other out of their houses. 'After thirty-four years,' he said, 'not one of them has come home. A million Bosnians have. You have freedom of movement, you've had elections without violence. It may not look like it to you, but what has happened here is a miracle.'

The kids launched a barrage of questions, in English and Bosnian; Paddy scribbled notes. All their questions were framed in terms of what the international community was going to do to fix things. Given that the same international community had done nothing much useful for nearly four years while Bosnia's Muslims were put to the sword, it was hard to say whether the faith these kids still had in a benevolent, cooperating world was reason to hug them or slap them. Paddy did something nearly as startling as either: told them the truth. Since the war here, there had been Kosovo, East Timor, Afghanistan, Iraq. The international community wasn't interested in Bosnia anymore. The job of rebuilding Bosnia would have to be done by Bosnians.

At the end, after promising to report back on a couple of more mundane matters – when Krizevici would get a regular bus service, for example – Paddy asked his big question. 'What's one thing I could do,' he said, 'that would encourage you all to stay here?'

'Use your powers more,' urged a blond boy in the front row. 'Abolish the nationalist parties.'

'I can't do that unless they do something illegal,' said Paddy, though he looked faintly wistful. 'But anyway, it's not my job to abolish political parties. It's yours. By voting for other people. Or standing for office yourselves.'

The room was a sea of energised grins by this point, the audience talking excitedly among themselves as well as calling out suggestions to Paddy.

'Any more ideas?' asked Paddy, wrapping things up. 'One thing I could do to keep you all in Bosnia.'

'Go into politics,' said someone, to sustained applause.

The following day, we paid our visit to Srebrenica, and took a long detour into the nearby mountains to a village called Bucinovici. Bucinovici had been destroyed in the summer of 1995 – every house burned, every male inhabitant killed but one. The Bosnian Serb army thugs who did this would have had to march uphill for hours, along rough tracks – and Bosnian summers are hot. There are many less determined bigots, rapists and murderers who would have got halfway up and thought, 'Can we really be bothered? Can't we just stay home and, I dunno, lynch all the redheads or something?' To ruin a village as remote as Bucinovici, you really have to hate the people who live in it.

Bucinovici's lone surviving male, Hasib Bucinovici, had come home a few years previously. The women had followed him. These widows, mothers, daughters and sisters of Srebrenica's dead were putting their village back together, brick by brick. After we said our goodbyes to these extraordinarily determined people, I joined Paddy in his armoured BMW for the drive back to Sarajevo. It was strangely quiet inside the car, its heavy doors and reinforced windows blocking out the sound of its own engine along with any surrounding static; even on Bosnia's rugged roads, it felt like we were gliding. I mentioned the kid from the night before, the one who'd suggested that Paddy run for office. Paddy had reacted to that, once the clapping had subsided, with another lapse into honesty. He'd wondered aloud if his very presence didn't give Bosnia's people license to keep voting for the kind of boneheads who think the irrelevant happenstance of your parentage is the basis for a manifesto. Bosnia's voters might complacently reason that if the cranky nationalist politicians didn't play nicely, the high representative could send everyone to bed without pudding.

'People want us to stay,' said Paddy. 'Seventy per cent want us here forever, 60 per cent want me to do more with my power, not less. But when does your presence help put a country back on its feet, and when does it create dependence?'

The first time I went to Sarajevo, in March 1996, to write a story about the astonishingly fecund rock'n'roll scene which had developed under the siege, I'd been struck by how many homes and bars displayed portraits of Tito, the (Croat) dictator who ruled the then-Yugoslavia from 1945 until his death in 1980. In 2004, his face was even more common in Sarajevo: on coffee mugs, T-shirts, and on a huge banner, strung across the city's main drag, protesting plans to rename Ulica Marsala Tita – Marshal Tito Street – after Bosnia's late wartime president, Alija Izetbegovic. Off the road to Sarajevo airport – the highway once infamous as Sniper Alley – a new bar called 'Tito' was decorated with Tito memorabilia. This was partly a manifestation of the ironic sense of humour that prevails in Sarajevo, but not entirely. There were reasons why Tito's rule, undemocratic though it was, was warmly remembered in Bosnia – secularism, tolerance, an absence of genocidal rednecks firing cannons from the hills. I wondered how concerned Paddy was about a similar personality cult evolving around his own benign dictatorship. The 'Padi' handle that the Bosniak press had awarded him was an unmistakable echo of the four-letter name of the former Yugoslav leader. In Bucinovici, one house we'd stopped in had a framed picture of Paddy on the wall, where they might once have had one of Tito.

'You've got to be worried about that,' Paddy nodded. 'But it isn't me, it isn't Paddy Ashdown.'

I doubted that. On previous visits, I'd detected little of the same reverence, which verged on pop star-style fandom, for Paddy's predecessors.

'Remember where this country has come from,' continued Paddy. 'I sometimes describe my job as falling between two opposing statements. My Bosnian friends say look, we had the Greeks, we had the Romans, we had the Turks, we had the Hapsburgs. You're the new Hapsburgs – tell us what to do, and we'll do it. The other side is my international friends, who say, for goodness' sake, we fought their war for them – a lie, incidentally – and we spent massive amounts of our treasure on them, why isn't Bosnia Switzerland already? We've forgotten how long it takes to build peace after war.'

It must be frustrating, I thought, having all the high representative's theoretical power and being continually confronted with problems that couldn't be fixed with a wave of a hand or a bang on a table.

'I do feel frustrated sometimes,' he agreed, 'and I'm not very good at dealing with it. When you walk into somebody's room, and all they want is a tractor. Or all they want is for someone to connect the house to electricity. Or all they want is a cow, for God's sake. And it really matters to them. And they look at me and they say "You're the most powerful man in the country, you can do it. Give me this thing." And I can't respond to that. There's this look of half-puzzlement, half-wonderment, as if to say, "I don't understand. You can do anything here. Why can't you give me a cow?"'

There was a reason, as Paddy knew, and knew that I knew, why that family in Bucinovici had his picture on their wall. When Paddy's entourage had made the drive up to the village a couple of years previously, that family had been the people who'd told him that what they needed most was a cow, and Paddy had provided one, paid for out of his own pocket. We'd trooped to its shed to see it. It had looked very well, not at all like the baggy-kneed heifers wandering most Bosnian paddocks; in my admittedly inexpert judgement, it seemed a pretty flash cow. So did the calf it had since produced. Paddy's gift had come from a good place, but it was a pretty old-school piece of patronage, the emperor scattering sovereigns from his chariot.

'That was a private thing,' he said. 'Obviously, you can't do that for everybody. The hard fact is the international community is withdrawing from this place. Money is getting less. But you can never explain to people, when they say, "You know Tony Blair. You've met President Bush. You went to The Hague and took on Mr Milosevic. Now you're here with all the power in the world, and you can't solve my problem, which is some slate for my roof." That's the difficult thing. You feel a terrific sense of guilt, and a little bit of shame, in not being able to do these things.'

I was glad he'd mentioned shame. It seemed to me to be not just a motivating factor for Paddy, but also for the international community's continuing involvement in Bosnia. The shame was justified: the same international community had fiddled while Bosnia burned for nearly four years. I felt the same myself, every time I visited. In 1993, while backpacking aimlessly in Eastern Europe, I'd thought of heading for Sarajevo, and trying to report, or somehow make a difference, as a lot of people my age, if more confident and much braver, had done. I didn't get to Bosnia until 1995, and that was by accident – a magazine sent me to cover a rock festival in Croatia, which was cancelled when Croatia's military began its onslaught against the country's Serbian enclave. With my original assignment overtaken by events, I'd hitched a ride on an aid convoy and gone to the war instead. That first trip to Sarajevo in March 1996, to write about rock bands – something I was pretty sure I could do, having spent most of the nineties writing for British music magazines – was undertaken at my own expense, as a sort of penance.

Paddy had come to Sarajevo earlier than I had, but was still kicking himself that it had taken him so long.

'I arrived in 1992,' he said. 'There was quite a dull period after the election in the UK, and someone said, "You're interested in conflict, go and take a look." I don't think I could have pointed to Sarajevo on a map, but I packed my things, and hitched a lift from Zagreb. I was fascinated, instantly – it's that thing about places where tectonic plates meet, and in Sarajevo there was that great mix of religions and ethnicities and cultures. The Brits were always fascinated with the North-West Frontier in Pakistan, for example. I felt an immense attachment to the ordinary people – not the politicians. The ordinary people here I find unbelievably brave, and mischievous, and roguish. I'm an Irishman, and there's quite a lot of the character of my own country about them.'

At Paddy's last Prime Minister's Questions before stepping down as leader of the Liberal Democrats, Tony Blair, a serial enthusiast of post-imperial nation-building, had saluted Paddy's long campaign for western military intervention in the Balkans. On Bosnia and Kosovo, said the prime minister, Paddy was 'well ahead of the rest of us, and right long before the rest of us'.

'I used to get called the Member for Sarajevo,' recalled Paddy, and he didn't seem displeased with the epithet. 'Very early in 1992, when I started taking up the cause, I used to get called a warmonger – and Labour used to shout that quite as loud as the Tories. It struck me that this war was a bit like the Spanish Civil War – ordinary people understood it better than their leaders. People wanted to report it, or deliver aid. You'd drive over the Dinaric Alps and you'd find this broken-down truck from Little Piddlington-in-the-Mire, where they'd raised some money.'

That always seemed the weird thing. A non-state army was besieging a European capital, blazing away at its civilian population, and western governments acted like they couldn't figure out who the bad guys were.

'The idea of intervention had become foreign to us. We had a sort of historic view of the Balkans, that it always happened there.'

That the whole of the Balkans, as Bismarck had it, wasn't worth the bones of a single Pomeranian grenadier.

'Precisely. I had a very precise example of that in '93 or '94, when I went to see [then UK foreign secretary] Douglas Hurd and said, we have to intervene. Douglas, a man for whom, until then, I had a reasonable degree of respect, said, "It's the Balkans, they've always fought each other. There's nothing we can do. Build a firebreak around it and let it burn itself out, is the best policy." I said, "Douglas, that's nonsense. If there's a people who have always killed each other, it's we Europeans. How can you deny the Balkans access to the European ideal which has brought us peace?" Historians will treat us very harshly for what we failed to do. If there's an ideal that fires modern Europe, it's this idea of tolerance and multi-ethnicity. And there was arguably one operating model of that in Europe – Sarajevo. And we did nothing to preserve it.'

In shops in Sarajevo now, you could buy coffee mugs that boasted of that tradition of plurality. Adorned with pictures of the city's churches, mosques and synagogues, they were captioned 'Europski Jerusalem' – European Jerusalem. I bought one, but hoped it wasn't tempting fate.

As our convoy prowled the mountain roads back to Sarajevo, the conversation turned to the efforts to capture Radovan Karadzic, the former Bosnian Serb leader, and bring him to justice.

'It's vitally important,' said Paddy. 'He is the boil that has to be lanced.'

I asked Paddy when he'd last seen Karadzic.

'Around '93, '94,' he said. 'I thought it was my duty, when I first came to this country, not to listen to just one side. I went to see Karadzic because he asked me to. I have to say, he fooled me. I was really ignorant, knew nothing of the Balkans, but the first four or five hours we talked – having dinner with him and his wife, discussing philosophy and poetry – I listened to him, and I believed him. I didn't realise that he was only the first of many Balkan leaders I'd meet who have the capacity to lie, completely straight-faced, to your face. It didn't take me long to realise what he was – until the next day, in fact, when I visited some of his death camps.'

Paddy also met Mladic, and Milosevic. I asked Paddy whether he'd ever got any sense of what drove these people, assuming their overarching ambition was something other than being reviled as war criminals. It's often the simple questions that people avoid asking the powerful, for fear of appearing unsophisticated. But there's always a place for the purposefully simplistic query: 'Dude, seriously, what do you think you're doing?'

'I don't know,' said Paddy, still apparently vexed. 'Did I see the murderous glint in Karadzic's eyes, or Mladic's eyes? Absolutely not. It's a complete nightmare to me still. I travelled through this area in 1992 – not in the company of Karadzic, but with his written permission, and I never knew what was going on, except when I visited the death camps around Prijedor. Did I see Mladic as someone who could have done what he did at Srebrenica? No.'

Paddy still had to deal, regularly, with people sympathetic to Karadzic, Mladic and their cause, such as it was. He had flexed the high representative's legal muscle against them, freezing the bank accounts of Karadzic's family, and dismissing several Bosnian Serb politicians from office. In April 2003, in a case straight out of the only-in-the-Balkans file, Mirko Sarovic, the Serb member of Bosnia's three-man presidency, had resigned before Paddy sacked him for complicity in a plan to smuggle military aircraft parts from Serbia to Iraq. Later, in 2004, Paddy fired another sixty Bosnian Serb officials for helping Karadzic evade capture – including Dragan Kalinic, the speaker of Bosnia's parliament, and interior minister Zoran Djeric.

'They react in all sorts of ways,' said Paddy. 'I have a rule that if I am going to get rid of someone, I tell them personally before I tell the press. I don't have to, but I do. The practice of firing thunderbolts from Olympus and taking everyone by surprise is not a good one. I had to get rid of one of the heads of one of the organisations that looks after Bosnia's forests, because he was manifestly involved in organised crime. He was very charming about it. He said, "I understand what you've done, and I understand why you've done it, and I do hope we meet in the forests of Bosnia sometime."'

Those same forests were, as Paddy told this story, looming close around the road, and even through armoured glass looked suddenly like an ideal hiding place for any number of time-biding enemies.

'I'm not sure about that last statement,' Paddy laughed, 'but he said it in a cheerful way, and I took it at face value.'

Even as we spoke, Paddy was presumably aware that, within hours, NATO forces would make yet another attempt to seize Karadzic, in his wartime stronghold of Pale. I didn't find out until I returned to London, and got an email from a friend in Sarajevo, reporting an explosion in the hills. 'They went after Special K again,' wrote my friend, and then, referring to several previous attempts to land him, 'Latest result: SFOR 0, Karadzic 4. Ho hum.'

For a torturously, stupidly long time, Bosnia was no sort of example of thoughtful diplomacy or intelligent peacekeeping. However, as Paddy was spending his days persuading doubtful Bosniaks, what had been achieved in the eight years since the Dayton Accords ended the war was astonishing. Less than a decade after it might have served as a punishment block for Hell, Bosnia was peaceful, and more or less functional. The relationship between the internationals and the locals was broadly cooperative and friendly, which is to say that while there were reasons why Paddy travelled in a vehicle with doors that took two hands to close, it would have come as a considerable surprise if anyone had taken a serious shot at at him. The circumstances and motives of the west's intervention in Bosnia had not been comparable to the rhyme and reason advanced for the invasions of Afghanistan and Iraq, but surely many of the problems of nation-building were constant. I asked Paddy what we'd learned here. He reacted, for the only time during the trip, like a politician.

'I don't want to comment from thousands of miles away,' he said. 'One of the lessons I learned as a politician – the thing that brought me here in the first place – is that you should always go and see for yourself.'

Fair enough, I said. But he must have known I'd ask.

'Well, okay,' he conceded. 'I think there are some lessons – broad, broad lessons. One, start with a plan – a clear idea of what you want to do. Two, what you want to do first is the rule of law. It took six years to get to that here. We ought not to make that mistake again. Three, be tough at the start, then you can become less tough later on. Four, peacekeeping is measured in decades, not weeks. What Kipling called "the savage wars of peace" – a very good phrase – requires as much energy, as much will, as much intelligence and as much resource as fighting the short, sharp wars we've become so good at.'

He was, presumably, concerned about the legalities of these Kiplingesque enterprises.

'Absolutely,' Paddy replied. 'That great line of John Donne, "No man is an island", is elevated, in our interdependent world, from a moral precept to a code for survival. We can be threatened by what happens in other countries. If you have instability in the Balkans, you have refugees, and criminality in our cities. If you have terrorist states in the Middle East, you know the consequences. The idea upon which the UN charter was based, which is the absolute sovereignty of states, has had to be adapted. In recognising the reality that we had to do it, we should have applied ourselves to establishing some rules as to how we should do it.'

Paddy spoke not just from the experience of running a peace-keeping and nation-building operation from the top, but from the experience of – to re-embrace Kipling – toting the white man's burden with a rifle, as a Royal Marines and/or Special Boat Service commando in Borneo, Northern Ireland and the Persian Gulf.

'It has changed hugely,' he said. 'I think we learned very painfully. This is the most difficult soldiering there is. It requires a higher degree of discipline than red hot battle. It requires huge political knowledge and sensitivity on the part of commanders. And we ought to get skilled at it. Most of the armies of the world are still trained in total war – but this is the kind of war we're going to do from now on.'

Twelve months earlier, I'd watched Paddy's successors in British khaki waging exactly this sort of modern warfare, where success is measured in how many people you don't kill, how much you don't destroy.

12

Of Kabul's vast repertoire of picturesque rubble, the Darulaman Palace was the most spectacular. It was built in the 1920s, during the reign of King Amanullah. Amanullah was still in his twenties when he inherited the throne, after his father, King Habibullah, was murdered on a hunting trip in 1919; despite the involvement of assassins, this was one of the more orderly transfers of power in Afghan history. Darulaman Palace was spattered with bulletholes, as tragic as acne on a handsome face, its forecourt littered with fragments of masonry which had been blasted off it as various factions had used the building for shelter and/or target practice during the civil wars of the 1990s.

It was a melancholy sight, the more so if one was given to contemplating omens. 'Darulaman' translates as 'Abode of Peace', and Amanullah had been a moderniser. Inspired by Muslim reformers Mustafa Kemal Ataturk in Turkey and Reza Shah in Iran, Amanullah instituted an elected assembly, abolished Islamic dress codes for women, adopted a constitution which enshrined the rights of the individual, tried to ease religion away from the centre of public life, and sought to establish relationships with the outside world – a program which read like a wish-list for the western intervention I'd come to Kabul to see. It hadn't worked out too well for Amanullah. A rebellion by conservative tribesmen forced him into exile in 1929, and he spent most of the rest of his life in Switzerland. That he lived to a pensionable age despite having tried to govern Afghanistan may have been some consolation.

I'd arrived at the palace with British and German soldiers serving with the International Security Assistance Force (ISAF) in Kabul. While photographer Damian Bird was wandering inside the ruin, gathering images for our feature for *Esquire* magazine, I waited outside with our British military media liaison, Squadron Leader Mark Whitty. A young Afghan in a dapper two-tone salwar kamiz, hair smartly combed, rode up on a bicycle and bid us good afternoon. He dismounted, and produced a crumpled piece of paper from the folds of his outfit.

'Please,' he explained. 'You will help with my English.'

The scrap of paper was a carefully handwritten list of common phrases and expressions.

'Please,' he said. 'What do these mean?'

Squadron Leader Whitty and I struggled with an explanation for 'Don't let the grass grow under your feet'.

'It means don't be lazy,' said Whitty. 'Don't rest on your laur . . . well, that's a whole other can of . . . look, never mind. It means to get on with things.'

'I see,' the kid nodded. 'What about "You're getting . . . warm"?'

This was harder than it looked. Judging by our new friend's baffled expression after we'd thrashed hopelessly at a definition for a few minutes, we hadn't got warm at all. It was like playing Pictionary without a pencil.

'Okay,' said the kid, moving us along to the next one on his list. 'What about "My watch is broken"?'

Whitty looked at me; I shrugged. He looked back towards the palace, as if searching for a surreptitious camera being held by giggling squaddies. He composed himself and delivered a verdict.

'My bet,' he finally announced, 'is that it means your watch is broken.'

'I see,' said the young man. 'Thank you for your help.' He folded his precious piece of paper, shook our hands, bowed, remounted his bicycle, and rode back down the hill to the barely habitable ruin of a suburb where he lived, doubtless to work further on his colloquial English and dream of the future it might bring him.

'It's different, this place, isn't it?' said Squadron Leader Whitty.

Kabul certainly was different, though not necessarily in the way Whitty meant. Measured against my recollections of the city during the barmy reign of the Taliban, it had undergone dramatic changes, and only someone as metaphorically or literally one-eyed as Taliban leader Mullah Omar would deny that they were for the better. The theoretical guarantor that these changes would be permanent improvements, rather than temporary reprieves, were the foreign soldiers patrolling Kabul's filthy streets. This was a frontline in what Kipling, and Paddy Ashdown, had called a 'savage war of peace' – a war which, at the time, the khaki-clad interlopers appeared to be winning handily.

The British soldiers at Camp Souter were making themselves at home. The original factory buildings had been converted into offices, shops, a gym and a canteen. Two accommodation blocks and a guardroom had been added. These had been erected by Afghan contractors, who'd then used the money they'd made, and expertise they'd acquired, to tender for work on other building projects. This seemed a sensible means of jump-starting Kabul's moribund legal economy – there was barely anything in the city that didn't require repairs, though I felt sorry for the wretches employed to sweep Kabul's streets, a task as awesomely futile as attempting to drain the Pacific with an egg whisk. Camp Souter was also doing its bit for the souvenir trade, with a few lucky rug-sellers and DVD bootleggers invited to set up shop inside the base.

Camp Souter's canteen was crowded with soldiers of all the militaries contributing to the multinational International Security Assistance Force (ISAF) – word had got around that the food served at the British base was superior to that provided by the cooks of other armies, and I would later contemplate the truth of this when sitting down with German soldiers to a meal of what looked, and tasted, like boot soles boiled in ditchwater. There were also some Americans, plainclothed but for a few accoutrements of military gear, and sporting ostentatious beards. I asked Squadron Leader Whitty who they were.

'Don't ask,' he replied.

Damian and I had come to Camp Souter to join a patrol with a platoon of the Royal Anglian Regiment, a routine wander around Kabul intended to fly the flag, reassure the locals, and perhaps acquire intelligence. At the pre-patrol briefing, this was translated by the platoon's commander, Lieutenant Martyn Cook, as 'Win the trust and support of the population of Police District 9 in order to promote ISAF and the Transitional Authority'. The official line was that this shouldn't be too hard. One ISAF poll had returned the finding that 98 per cent of the population of Kabul was glad of the international force's presence. I wasn't sure this should be taken as much of an indication of anything. The Afghans' diligently observed tradition of courtesy to visitors was not conducive to scientific measurement of opinion. Kabul was the kind of place where, if you asked for directions, a local would feel obliged to give you some even if they had no idea where you wanted to go; this had already resulted in a couple of entertaining mystery tours. More to the point, even ISAF officers were willing to agree that in Afghanistan of all places, 2 per cent of people wishing you'd clear off was more than a handful.

District 9, the objective of that day's patrol, covered an area of Kabul dominated by rickety Russian-built apartments, and a mud-brick suburb called Koly Zamam Khan. The noticeboard in the briefing room warned: 'Russian flats remain hostile – high threat of suicide bomber or IED [Improvised Explosive Device]'. Damian and I were lent flak jackets, which made me feel, as they always do, like a turtle standing on its hind legs, and acutely paranoid about being shot in the head.

There were nine soldiers on the patrol, in three vehicles – two Land Rovers, and one roofless vehicle with a mounted gun. Only the soldiers driving this fearsome-looking bit of kit were permitted the desert warrior get-up of helmets, dark goggles and keffiyeh scarves over the lower halves of their faces. For the troops who'd have to get out and walk the streets, the order was berets rather than helmets, with a strict ban on sunglasses. The combined message was clear: we're nice guys, we're here to help, but don't push your luck. As we headed out of

Camp Souter, I noticed the sign on the gate, delineating five possible levels of alert: low, medium, high, imminent, emergency. Today, whoever decided these things had pointed the arrow at 'medium'. On a scale of 'low' equalling a slow Tuesday in Bury St Edmunds – the sleepy Suffolk burg where the Royal Anglians had their regimental head-quarters – and 'emergency' approximating the climactic scenes of *Zulu*, I was happy enough with that.

The soldiers huddled in the Land Rover looked, and were, shock-ingly young, and had been in Afghanistan for a week. They were impressively focused, though. At their age, I was disdaining the opportunity of a free university education in favour of loafing and trying to scratch a living as a rock journalist; they'd voyaged halfway around the world to fix a busted country. Having been told that the person sharing their ride had seen something of Afghanistan under the Taliban, they didn't miss the chance, asking questions, taking shaky notes as I answered, and airily referring to dense texts on Central Asian history which I solemnly pretended I'd also read.

When we dismounted at the Russian flats, we were immediately surrounded by hordes of grinning, filthy children, who followed us everywhere we went, importuning for money ('Baksheesh!') or choco-late ('Cacao!') or just emitting the whoops of delight and bang-bang noises that armed, uniformed men always elicit in small boys. As they set off on their beats, each trailed by flocks of kids, the soldiers looked like birthday clowns who'd shown up in the wrong costume. Harmless and happy though the children looked, Lieutenant Cook explained that they often caused the most difficulty. Small boys in Kabul, like small boys everywhere, played with toy guns. Small boys in Kabul, unlike small boys everywhere, were therefore in danger of falling victim to misunderstandings.

'There was an ISAF program,' said Lieutenant Cook, ruffling the hair of the urchins huddling around him, 'to get the kids to trade in toy weapons for notebooks and pens. But they had to call it off.'

I asked why.

'They started approaching patrols with real guns and unexploded ordnance.'

The patrol proceeded to the edge of the district of flats, between a disused fountain full of stagnant, olive-coloured water and a row of shops improvised from sheets of tin. We reached the point at which the vehicles were due to pick us up, opposite a barracks belonging to the budding Afghan National Army, a detachment of which was parading up the street. It was a curious sight. No soldier looks more splendid than the bearded Afghan mujahideen in robes and turban, Kalashnikov slung carelessly over a shoulder. The same men in the mismatched uniforms of Afghanistan's new defence force presented a less impressive spectacle, these once insouciant warriors transfixed with concentration at trying, and wretchedly failing, to march in step, their combined footfalls sounding like one of Keith Moon's more exuberant solos.

'Good grief, no,' said Lieutenant Cook.

Not to worry, I started to say, it may not be Sandhurst in there, but they'll get the hang of things, then realised he wasn't worried about the Afghans' deportment. Cook had spotted his own vehicles, driving up the street behind the Afghan soldiers to collect us, and presenting watching civilians with a contrast perhaps unflattering to the local army. 'Turn around at once,' radioed Lieutenant Cook to the driver of the lead vehicle, 'and get out of sight. It's their parade, we're not to upstage them.' As the three Land Rovers executed a balletically graceful about-turn and vanished, Lieutenant Cook crossed the street in search of his Afghan counterpart, and congratulated him fulsomely on his troops' turnout.

We rolled on to Koly Zamam Khan, a one-stop illustration of how much needed to be done in Kabul. The unpaved streets were sodden with sewage. The police operated out of a barely furnished station whose most sophisticated equipment was that used to brew the tea they provided us. Lieutenant Cook, looking for foundations upon which to build bridges, congratulated the captain on the station's carefully tended flowerbed. This elicited the response that ISAF troops were 'always welcome' in the captain's district. After further discussion, it was clear that the captain needed all the help he could get. He had thirty police for a district whose population he estimated at

65,000. He said there was a lot of thieving and violence, as well as Taliban and al-Qaeda fugitives at large. Outside the station, the soldiers were mobbed by more children. They attempted conversation in the local language from their laminated sheets of everyday phrases, provoking general hysterics.

The idea of British soldiers behaving with tact and sensitivity would startle anyone who has only encountered them in Essex nightclubs, but Camp Souter had embraced an ethic of political correctness that would make the town halls of left-wing London councils look like something out of *Animal House*. During the time I spent with the ISAF soldiers, Kabul's Shi'a population were celebrating Ashura – the commemoration of the martyrdom of Imam Hussein, grandson of Mohammed, at Karbala, Iraq in AD 680. Shi'a Muslims often observe Ashura with spirited masochism, beating their chests and flailing at their own flesh with an instrument called a *zanjeer* – a chain with small blades fixed to the end. Given the Taliban's ruthless suppression of the Shi'a, Ashura was going to be a big deal this year, and signs on Camp Souter's noticeboards offered stern advice about appropriate behaviour while it was occurring: don't smoke in public, don't play loud music, don't 'display any overt cheerfulness', don't take photographs.

There had been much speculation among the soldiers about whether it might be possible to watch the Ashura celebrations. On the premise that one doesn't get if one doesn't ask, we rode with a joint detachment of British and German officers, accompanied by soldiers from the Royal Anglians, to a mosque frequented by Kabul's ethnic Hazara population. The Hazaras had suffered dreadfully under the Taliban, terrorised, persecuted and forced to worship in secret. They were turning out in numbers today.

Squadron Leader Whitty asked a passing scamp to fetch someone in a position of authority. A grey-bearded man emerged from the mosque and introduced himself. Through the patrol's Afghan translator, Whitty explained that we very much wanted to come in and see the celebrations.

'Please,' replied the old man. 'It is because of you we can have these celebrations.'

He grasped Whitty gently by the elbow and began to usher him inside.

'Hang on,' said Whitty. 'I haven't finished. We won't be able to take our boots off, and we'll have to bring our guns in – those are our orders, I'm afraid. If that's a problem, say the word, and we'll go.'

'Absolutely no problem,' translated the translator.

We filed around the edge of the large, square central room of the mosque. On the floor, two or three hundred young men, bare-chested or in T-shirts with the backs cut out, sat cross-legged in rectangular formations, chanting and keeping time with hearty slaps on their chests. In the gap between the facing rows, they took turns, singly or in pairs, to sashay on their knees from one end to the other while flogging their own backs viciously with the zanjeers, raising a red mist of blood. Among the British squaddies, a desire to show the folks back home something extraordinary inevitably overcame the standing orders. One soldier gingerly produced a camera from inside his tunic, gestured towards the old man who'd invited us in, and composed the nervous, hopeful facial expression universally recognised as meaning 'Is this okay with you chaps, or am I about to get hung off a lamppost?' The old man raised two thumbs, and with a synchronicity that years of parade ground drill couldn't have taught, the entire patrol whisked their cameras out and began blazing away at the flagellators, who hammed it up furiously, redoubling their rhythm and grinning manically at every lens.

There was a time when invading armies measured their success by the size of the heap of native skulls they piled up behind the mess hall. The soldiers serving with ISAF were charged with stockpiling more metaphorical, and hence more nebulous, portions of the human anatomy: hearts and minds. ISAF had set up something called a Civilian Military Cooperation (CIMIC) branch. This was run largely by earnest, enthusiastic soldiers from an assortment of European militaries, and operated out of a warehouse complex. This was officially named, with a disappointing lack of poetry, Camp Warehouse, and unofficially named, by British soldiers often bemused by their continental counterparts, EuroDisney.

At Camp Warehouse, a Dutch colonel with a tremendous waxpointed handlebar moustache, of the sort not seen on British officers since the battle of Omdurman, frowned over a map of Kabul. He explained that he was working on such mundane essentials as roads, irrigation and garbage disposal. I couldn't help but imagine the residual Taliban bitching in some mud-walled hut, trading crescendos of self-righteous rhetoric climaxing in, 'Well, all right, but aside from roads, irrigation, garbage disposal, hospitals, fire stations, steps on the hill paths and education, what has the International Security Assistance Force ever done for us?' The colonel fretted about money. 'I'm only here six months,' he said, and the moustache furled downwards. 'I'm going to spend four of those waiting for my funding.'

I joined a CIMIC patrol of Swedish, Finnish and British soldiers. We spent a day meeting with Afghan grandees and administrators, noting concerns, drinking tea. The tone was always friendly. When Lieutenant Savela, of the Finnish army, asked a village representative called a Wakil whether the patrol's Land Rovers would be safe on the busy street outside, the Wakil smiled and replied, 'You're okay, but the Russians couldn't have parked here.' One officer in the new Afghan army invited the patrol to his home for tea, even allowing his teenage daughters to join the conversation, on condition that they were not photographed. When considered alongside the fact that the girls were permitted to leave their faces uncovered, this marked the Afghan officer as a bit of a hippy, by local standards.

The CIMIC soldiers and I passed around photos of our homes, friends and families. The picture of my father in uniform – he was, at the time, a Lieutenant General in the Australian army – received nods of approval and exaggerated salutes from the men. They were less sure about the picture of my girlfriend, Roni, photographed at a party in a gold cocktail dress, though I couldn't tell what perturbed them most – Roni's bare shoulders, or the fact that she wasn't the same colour as me. The women of the house liked that one, though, giggling and whispering and passing it back and forth, asking me excited questions I couldn't begin to answer about Roni's hair and makeup, before returning it, remarking, correctly, that Roni was very beautiful. I wondered if any of these girls would ever be allowed to go out and have something as simple and marvellous as an unchaperoned good time.

Neither gender in the house knew what to say to one Swedish officer on the patrol, Lieutenant Brehmer – Cecilia Brehmer. I couldn't think what presence would seem as alien in my living room as a woman in uniform – slinging a rifle, and with strawberry blonde hair billowing from an uncovered head – did in the home of a Kabul family, except possibly an actual alien. Later, when the patrol dismounted amid the ruins and improvised market stalls of one of Kabul's main streets, Lieutenant Brehmer was surrounded by a crowd of several dozen gawping men – unthreatening, but also almost entirely silent, literally dumbstruck. She smiled, waved and nodded. 'It's like being a film star,' she said, and I noticed that the British soldiers, who occasionally muttered about the naivete of their less experienced comrades, had adopted the role of bouncers, forming a discreet perimeter at the edge of the crowd and clearing a path back to the vehicles, just in case.

'That's the difference between us and them,' said one of the British soldiers as we returned to Camp Warehouse. 'We've been doing this a few centuries longer.'

The following afternoon, I watched Kipling's ghost accompany a British army medical team as it discharged the 'Fill full the mouth of famine/And bid the sickness cease' measures of the white man's burden. The medical team was running a clinic for Afghan police, and the scene was irresistibly evocative: a kindly British medical officer, Lieutenant Colonel Menzies of the Royal Army Medical Corps, dispensing medicines to native soldiers. Lt Col Menzies was aware of the precedent. He carried in his wallet an East India Company one rupee coin, dated 1840, which very likely arrived in Kabul with the doomed army of General Elphinstone, Britain's first, disastrous, attempt to impose influence on Afghanistan.

The police officers' complaints were, as Menzies had expected, trivial.

'To be honest,' he said, 'I think a lot of them just come because we're here. Nobody has taken much interest in their wellbeing before.'

The translator relayed tales of inflamed throats, aching legs, mouth sores caused by chewing tobacco and, surprisingly given Afghanistan's conservatism regarding such matters, the symptoms of one man who said that his daily quart of vodka was making him ill. Lt Col Menzies gave him a mild lecture on the dangers of his habit. I wondered whether a more appropriate response mightn't be to congratulate him on his resourcefulness in finding the stuff. Everyone in British uniform knew, though, that this wasn't really about throats or knees, but those elusive hearts and minds. And everyone in British uniform knew, better than most, that hearts can be broken, and minds can be lost. Everyone in British uniform most certainly remembered that when their fore-bears were deployed on the streets of Northern Ireland in 1968, the Catholic population brought out tea and biscuits.

'At this stage,' said Lt Col Menzies, 'it's about continuity of treat-ment. There's no point in coming in, making promises, getting every-one's hopes up and then vanishing overnight.'

He was talking about a police sergeant with high blood pressure. But he could have been talking about Afghanistan.

Flying out of Kabul airport was as disconcertingly shambolic as flying into it. In Kabul, of all places, the X-ray machines weren't working, and pre-flight security inspection of hold baggage consisted of a woman randomly poking rucksacks and suitcases. A nervous flyer at the best of times, I attempted, with limited success, to overcome the thought that the passengers queueing behind me looked like a casting call for the FBI's 'Most Wanted Terrorists' poster. The ancient Boeing on the tarmac, sprayed in the blue and white livery of Ariana Airlines, had written on its fuselage 'A gift to the people and government of Afghanistan from the people and government of India', translating approximately as 'Not even Indians will take their chances in this whimpering bucket of bolts anymore, but if you silly buggers want it, knock yourselves out'. I sat in a middle row, and spent the flight to Dubai convinced that every next second would be the one at which the prayers of the passengers, surely all that was keeping the winged jalopy airborne, would prove insufficient, and I'd be plummeting to an end as messy as that suffered by any number of previous foreign efforts to make sense of Afghanistan.

Inevitably, the descent and touchdown were so smooth that I didn't notice we'd started our approach until I took my fists out of eyes long enough to look across the aircraft, out the window, and see Dubai's gleaming terminals. The sparkling citadels of the developed world were welcome and welcoming, and I wondered if Kabul would ever look anything like that. How could you possibly build a democratic, prosperous nation out of nothing at all, especially when outside powers kept interfering?

13

KINMEN AND TAIPEI, TAIWAN
APRIL 2005

It was quiet at the observation point at Mashan, but it had probably been quiet on the western front in 1913, and pretty slow along the German–Polish border circa 1938. In the early twenty-first century, most fantasies of apocalypse involved bearded crazies detonating a nuclear suitcase at Grand Central Station, or turning smallpox loose on the London Underground. We'd pretty much forgotten about the prospect of an old-fashioned superpower punch-up. I'd travelled to this tourist lookout, in a refurbished bunker on the north-east tip of Kinmen Island, to see where World War III might start. Kinmen belonged to Taiwan. Taiwan, officially, belonged to China – a claim that Beijing had been asserting with increasing belligerence.

From where I stood, it was less than two kilometres to the coast of China. If the current was with me, and I wasn't mistaken for a Taiwanese frogman by sentries on the opposite coast, I could have swum to China faster than I could have flown back to Taiwan's capital, Taipei. I'd been spending some time there trying to understand how the Taiwanese had turned a place which was recognised by almost nobody as a sovereign state, and largely unblessed by natural resources, into an economic powerhouse and stable democracy, in less than six decades of precarious existence. Inside the tourist lookout, the guns this bunker once housed had been replaced with coin-operated binoculars, ominously similar to submarine periscopes – a still-operational Taiwanese military observation post perched on the grassy slope that led down to the water.

There wasn't much moving on the deceptively calm strait between China and its reluctant island province – a couple of fishing boats, a tourist craft from the other side. With the binoculars, I could see the flag of the People's Republic of China fluttering from the stern of the boat, a pretty guide delivering her commentary, and a deckload of Chinese daytrippers waving. The Chinese boat crept as close to Kinmen's shoreline as it dared. A Taiwanese man next to me made a rifle-pointing gesture, said 'Boom boom!', laughed, and waved back.

If Kinmen didn't belong to Taiwan, Taiwan's extraordinary modern history would never have happened. In October 1949, 10,000 Chinese People's Liberation Army troops stormed ashore at Kuningtou, on Kinmen's north-west coast. They were pursuing the forces of the nationalist government of General Chiang Kai-Shek, who were in the final stages of losing the Chinese civil war to Mao Zedong's People's Liberation Army, and retreating to Taiwan with ambitions of regrouping before retaking the mainland.

The Kuningtou assault was a disaster for the communists. Half the invasion force were killed, the rest captured. This pivotal clash was commemorated at Kuningtou by a museum whose tone was unmistakably, if understandably, gloating. The museum's star exhibit was the Jeep in which Chiang Kai-Shek rode to review his victorious troops. The Jeep was American-supplied, as were the M5A1 tanks in the painting of the parade that lined a wall of the museum, as was Taiwan's continuing ability to defend itself. Reassuring as a security guarantee from Washington doubtless was, it wasn't enough for Kinmen, whose landscape was punctuated with appeals to still higher powers – statues of dragon deities, draped in coloured capes, and a temple honouring one of the commanders at Kuningtou, Colonel Li Kuang Chien, who, after his death on the battlefield, had been promoted to General, and God.

At Kuningtou, the nationalists won a battle and lost a war, the communists lost a battle and won a war. Both were sore losers. Chiang Kai-Shek never got China back, but he kept Taiwan, and officially insisted, until his death in 1975, that his Kuomintang party were the legitimate government of China (Taiwan's stamps and passports still bore the nomenclature Republic of China, and Taiwan's constitution retained quaint clauses pertaining to quirks of regional governments in Mongolia and Tibet). The communists who took China off Chiang never regained Taiwan, but had been equally tenacious in insisting that, one day, they would.

China bombed Kinmen throughout the 1950s, most famously in 1958, when 450,000 Chinese shells hit Kinmen in forty-four days. The assault continued until the late 1970s, China firing shells containing propaganda leaflets between the hours of 7 pm and midnight on alternate days, an unlikely hearts and minds gambit. ('Well, they've knocked our house down again, but tractor production in Guangzhou is up 10 per cent, and Mao is the red sun in the heart of every worker. I'm convinced.') With a pragmatism and enterprise that said much about Taiwan, the immense heaps of spent ordnance resulting from this demented psy-ops campaign were still being recycled into Kinmen's most famous souvenirs: the cutlery manufactured by the Chin Ho Li knife factory.

Kinmen was a mix of island paradise and military bulwark. There were beautiful old houses whose elegantly curved roofs were decorated with intricate pictures of dragons, and there were fortress-style entrances to military installations. The tracks leading to the inviting beaches were planted with signs warning of landmines; on one beach, a recent art project had bequeathed a replica of one of the immense loud-speakers with which Kinmen used to taunt China with tales of Taiwan's progress.

The roundabouts through which islanders zipped on their motor scooters had concrete observation posts, painted in wholly useless jungle camouflage, in the middle of them. Kinmen's botanic gardens were full of old tanks and artillery, eternally manned by life-size model soldiers. The real soldiers guarding Kinmen's active military bases did sentry duty in pairs, one always wearing a gas mask, just in case. Kinmen wasn't without a sense of humour, though. A restaurant was decorated with Maoiana: communist posters and PLA uniforms. Mao beamed from the menu, which you'd think would put most Taiwanese off their lunch. I wondered if the owner had ever thought of franchising his idea, perhaps opening a Vladimir Putin pizzeria in Grozny, or a Slobodan's burger bar in Sarajevo.

Kinmen's local government was presided over by Magistrate Juh-Feng Lee, whose bearing suggested a distinguishing regional informality. Every official I'd met in Taipei wore sharp suits and circulation-suppressing ties. Magistrate Lee sauntered into our meeting in slacks and a golf shirt. To my surprise, his attire wasn't all he was relaxed about.

'Yes, people worry about war,' he said. 'But what can you do?'

In keeping with Taiwanese tradition, Magistrate Lee presented me with his business card, and my entire baggage allowance in gifts, including a coffee-table book of Kinmen photos, and a presentation box containing two bottles of the infamous 58 per cent proof local firewater, which I'd probably drink as well if I lived on Kinmen and spent much time thinking about what China might have pointed at it.

'It depends what sort of war it would be,' Magistrate Lee mused. 'If it was a transitional war, Kinmen would be the frontline. But if they really want to attack, they'll go straight to Taipei.' This was a prospect that Magistrate Lee seemed oddly – or perhaps diplomatically – ambivalent about. 'Our first priority,' he said, 'is no war. We'd surrender rather than fight, to preserve lives and property. A lot of European countries have done so in the past.'

This was true, though it was a struggle to find elderly French people whose chests swelled with pride as they said, 'Yes, when we heard the Germans were coming, we fixed the rooms so they were just like they'd left them in 1918, and hid in the cellar.' Magistrate Lee reminded me of the Hong Kong market stallholders I'd interviewed on the eve of the handover, back in 1997. When I'd asked if they were bothered at the prospect of being ruled by the Chinese, they'd looked at me like I was mad and answered, 'I am Chinese.'

'And we're Chinese and Taiwanese,' said Magistrate Lee. 'This has never been a problem before, but now politicians in Taiwan are trying to cut those ties for their own purposes.'

This was oddly un-strident talk, I thought, for a man running one of the world's most volatile flashpoints. Driving around Kinmen, I'd seen the Taiwanese propaganda posters erected during the long years of Chinese bombardment, for the edification of binocular-wielding PLA soldiers across the water. Magistrate Lee sounded like he might have been in favour of replacing these with banners reading, 'Go ahead, see if we care.'

'We're a global village now,' he said. 'Kinmen belongs to the world. So it doesn't really matter.'

Back in Taipei, attitudes among those in charge were more rigid. In 2000, Taiwan's presidential election had been won by Chen Shui-Bian, of the pro-independence Democratic Progressive Party. China had been sulking ever since. In March 2005, China passed an 'anti-secession' law, awarding itself the right to use what it whimsically described as 'non-peaceful' means to prevent a declaration of independence by Taiwan. While I was in Taipei, China invited the leadership of the Kuomintang – the party descended from Chiang's nationalists – to visit Beijing for the first time since 1949. The Kuomintang were even offered China's supreme diplomatic gift: pandas. This may have appeared a gesture of rapprochement, but given that the Kuomintang were no longer in power – they'd ruled Taiwan for fifty-one years until losing the 2000 election – China's invitation was actually a pretty tacky divide-and-conquer manoeuvre.

The first Taiwanese official I met harboured no illusions about where confrontation between superpowers could lead. Ming-Min Peng, senior adviser to President Chen, lost his left arm in an American bombing raid on Japan in 1944. He recuperated at the home of his brother, a doctor, who lived a few miles outside Nagasaki.

'I remember this huge, metallic noise,' he said of 9 August 1945. 'Like a hammer hitting the Earth. And I remember the big, black mushroom. We had no idea what it was.'

Eighty-one-year-old Peng had lived the modern history of Taiwan. When he was born, in 1923, Taiwan was halfway through a period as a Japanese colony which had begun with China's defeat in the Sino–Japanese war of 1895. Peng remembered the Japanese as 'ruthless, but efficient'. They trod heavily on any notion of Chinese or Taiwanese ethnic identity, made the Japanese language compulsory – it was the first language Peng learnt – and dealt mercilessly with dissent. The Japanese also built roads, railways, harbours and the handsome presidential building in which Peng worked. After World War II, Taiwan was returned to China.

'We'd grown up believing we were Chinese,' said Peng, 'but then we found we weren't as Chinese as we thought. The Chinese administration in Taiwan was backward, incompetent, hopeless beyond description. We started to think we might be different.'

Taiwan remained a dictatorship under Chiang Kai-Shek until the general's death in 1975. By that time, Peng was an exile. Peng had at one point risen high enough in Chiang's estimation to be sent to New York as part of Taiwan's delegation to the UN – Taiwan only lost its UN seat to the Peoples' Republic in 1971 – but in 1964 he and some of his students issued a pro-democracy manifesto. Peng was sent to military prison, then placed under house arrest. He escaped Taiwan in 1970, and lived for twenty-two years in Sweden and America. He returned to Taiwan in 1992, and ran for president in 1995 as the candidate for the Democratic Progressive Party. He lost, but the DPP won power in 2000, and narrowly retained it in 2004, despite – or because of – a bizarre attempt to assassinate President Chen Shui-Bian, who was apparently shot as his motorcade travelled through the city of Tainan (KMT politicians claimed the shooting was staged, and refused to address Chen as President). Now, Peng was an unabashed advocate of Taiwanese independence, down to the tiny green silhouettes of Taiwan mounted on the frames of his glasses, and still utterly tireless. He'd arrived for our meeting off an overnight flight from Johannesburg. His unpacked suitcase sat next to his desk.

'If we're not a state,' he wondered, 'what are we? When surveys were done ten or fifteen years ago, and people were asked if they were Chinese or Taiwanese or both, most said Chinese or both. Now, nearly

70 per cent say they're Taiwanese. Taiwanese identity is quite established. The "one China" idea is dead.'

The Chinese talked, as they did of Hong Kong, about 'one China, two systems' . . .

'I know,' said Peng. 'They say they wouldn't send a single soldier, and that nothing would change, so what's the point? What's their interest? Satisfying racial vanity.'

I asked Peng what he thought, then, when he contemplated Taiwan's mighty, covetous neighbour.

'I think,' he smiled, 'they're not crazy enough.'

There was a pause.

'I hope,' he said, 'they're not crazy enough.'

When I met Peng, I'd only been in Taiwan a few days, but had already formed the view that Taiwan may have made itself too tempting a prize. The scale of what Taiwan had accomplished, in just six post-war decades and under extremely straitened circumstances, was astonishing. In 1952, 42 per cent of Taiwanese were illiterate. Fifty years later, nearly 60 per cent of Taiwanese went to university. (Tellingly, the illustration on Taiwan's 1000-dollar note was four schoolchildren studying a globe, though it wasn't apparent whether they were learning their foreign capitals or plotting Chinese missile trajectories.) Taiwan's 23 million diligent, dogged and courteous people had built the seventeenth-biggest economy in the world, and accrued the third-largest foreign reserves. Their tiny island boasted six domestic airlines, trains you could set your watch by and, in the shape of Taipei 101, the world's tallest building. And they'd made their transition from military dictatorship to pluralist democracy without getting any blood on the carpet. For a country that didn't formally exist in the eyes of most of the world, this was decent going.

Having visited many broken-down, violent dumps where everybody insisted that The Struggle superseded all other considerations, like picking up the rubbish and teaching kids to read, and invariably blamed someone else for all their problems, I fell hopelessly in love with the place. Were I a George Soros-style billionaire eccentric, I'd establish a program under which the world's nationalist crazies, idiot warlords and dingbat terrorists would be sent to Taiwan, to see what can be accomplished when people stick the grievance schtick on the back-burner, put in a day's work and behave in a civilised manner.

Taiwan was a place of endemic seemliness. Railway inspectors bowed to the carriage before asking for tickets. At the baseball match I went to, the teams lined up at the end of the game and bowed to their own fans, to those of their rivals, and were applauded by both sides of the stadium. When Taipei's garbage trucks reversed, instead of the bullying beep emitted by most such vehicles, they played ringtoneish versions of Beethoven's *Fur Elise* – and that was the only ringtone I heard. Though the Taiwanese were enthusiastic mobile phone users, they'd figured out what no western commuter seemed able to comprehend – that you can set them to vibrate silently, and that you don't have to yell into them to be heard. In several of Taipei's spotless, air-conditioned subway stations – whose escalators, warned digital signs, MOVE FAST, AT 39 METRES PER MINUTE – the halls had framed paintings hanging on the walls. The first time I saw these, I stood thunderstruck. I wasn't marvelling at the quality of the pictures, though some were pretty good, but imagining what would happen if anyone hung original artworks in Leicester Square tube station in London.

The only time Taiwanese were ever discourteous was when they mounted the 10 million motor scooters at large on Taiwan – almost one for every two Taiwanese. They rode these everywhere – on roads, along footpaths, through shopping malls, between the tables of outdoor food stalls. It was like being caught in a swarm of giant metal mosquitos, any one of which could break your leg with a single sting. I wondered if it was actually some sort of national defence initiative, maintaining Taiwan's security by ensuring that most of any invading Chinese army would be knocked down before they got across the street.

Given that cross-strait relations had degenerated as far as they had, it wasn't surprising that Taiwan had created an entire government department devoted to dealing with them. The Mainland Affairs Council was chaired by Joseph Wu, a funny man who, I suspected, needed his sense of humour.

'It's a very exciting job,' he grinned. 'I only get three or four hours sleep a night.'

I asked if his job was essentially about avoiding war.

'Yes,' he said. 'That's one of my responsibilities. War would be detrimental to Taiwan, and disastrous for China as well.'

I wondered what he feared most: a strong, confident China asserting itself, or a collapsing China looking for a nationalist rallying point.

'A strong China,' he smiled, 'is probably not a 100 per cent blessing. A chaotic one would be a disaster. China's a very uncertain entity. It's still highly authoritarian, but its economic development has got to the stage where you would expect urban intellectuals to demand more freedom.'

I told Wu he could stop me as soon as he thought I was sounding crazy, but there seemed an obvious fix. Why couldn't he suggest that China acknowledge that it had been a long time, things had changed, and ask them to sign a treaty and let Taiwan get on with it? The Chinese government would look like nice guys – a novelty they might enjoy – and would need worry no longer about jeopardising a valuable trading relationship (Taiwan, according to Wu, had US$70 billion invested in China). Why wouldn't China give Taiwan up?

'They've made it a national issue,' said Wu, 'so any Chinese leader who suggested it would be overthrown. Also, some departments of China's government need Taiwan as a problem – like the military, so they've got reason to buy more submarines, more missiles.'

When China stated, as China often did, that the international community did not recognise Taiwan, they were being somewhat parsimonious with the truth. In the lobby of Taiwan's foreign ministry, I counted twenty-five flags – the flags of the twenty-five nations which had chosen to have full diplomatic relations with Taiwan rather than China (you couldn't attempt both, lest Beijing fling its rice pudding off its high chair). Life at ambassador rank in the Taiwanese diplomatic service must have been unbearably nerve-racking, as they contemplated the choices of postings: palm-fronded paradises (Tuvalu, St Vincent & Grenadines, Marshall Islands), dangerous hellholes (Liberia, Chad, Burkina Faso), or both (Haiti, Solomon Islands).

'We're doing our best,' said Taiwan's foreign minister, Tan Sun Chen, when I asked him if he was trying to persuade more countries to recognise Taiwan. 'As a sovereign country, we have the right to do that. We want as many friends as possible.'

Many other countries, even if they officially regarded Taiwan as a rogue province of China, did exchange some sort of envoy with Taiwan – few could afford not to. Taiwan maintained a network of de facto embassies around the world, called things like the Taipei Economic and Cultural Representative Office, and these were reciprocated by such gently hypocritical presences as an American Institute and the British Trade and Cultural Office. These were better than nothing, but Taiwan's weird semi-status nonetheless meant that, for a foreign minister, Chen didn't get out much.

'No,' he confirmed. 'I did accompany our president to the Vatican for the funeral of Pope John Paul II [the Holy See was alone in Europe in recognising Taiwan]. But even when I'm trying to attend the funeral of a great person, China tried to impose pressure on the Italian government not to give us visas to enter the country.'

Everybody I met in Taiwanese officialdom told similar stories of Chinese pettiness. I collected them in a designated section of my notepad. The best, from a strong field, was the one about Yang Chih-Yuan, a thirteen-year-old high school student from Taipei county. A painting he'd done, called 'Dreaming About Peace', won an international poster competition, and was chosen by UNESCO to be a United Nations postage stamp. However, forty-eight hours after his victory was announced, UNESCO informed him that the design had been rejected. It had been noticed that his design contained a small Taiwanese flag, and Beijing officialdom weren't having it. (Taiwan's post office did the proper thing, and put it on a stamp themselves.)

My second favourite was related by Freddy Lin, singer with Taiwan's biggest speed metal band, Chthonic. Freddy told me the sorry tale of Punk God, a Chinese group who'd come to play at the 'Say Yes to Taiwan' festival, which Freddy organised every February (even Taiwan's black-clad, mascara-smeared, life-is-a-meaningless-vale-of-tears Gothic rock types were surreally industrious). The hapless Punk God, seeking to return the hospitality of their Taiwanese hosts, had made statements in support of human rights and independence in Taiwan. On their way back to China, Punk God's members phoned some friends and family from Bangkok airport, who told them not to come home. Police had visited their houses and taken their computers, and said they'd be back. Punk God were now refugees in Sweden.

Freddy took me to a bar decorated like an opium den. Ah, I thought, here at last was the degenerate demimonde lurking beneath Taipei's orderly surface. He ordered us apple juice. We were joined by three friends of his: Doris Yeh, who also played in Chthonic, and Mika Wu and KK Yeh, from the band Nipples.

The name of Freddy's annual festival, 'Say Yes to Taiwan', suggested an explicitly nationalist outlook, as did the date on which it was held – 28 February, the anniversary of the 1947 uprising against the then Kuomintang government which had been ruthlessly crushed, leaving as many as 30,000 dead. Discussion of the revolt, usually known as '228' on Taiwan, had been banned by Chiang Kai-Shek for years, but it was acquiring resonance among younger, independence-minded Taiwanese. There was a museum commemorating it, and 28 February was now a holiday. Among the demands of the rebels in 1947 had been free elections, which Taiwan now had, and independence, which Taiwan still didn't.

'We don't write political things in lyrics,' said Freddy. 'It's too deep.'

'Also,' said KK, 'if we think about these things, we get very angry, and we don't want that in our songs. My band cares only about beauty.'

'China is totally foreign to us,' continued Freddy. 'The Japanese would be closer to how we think. We find it easier to talk to them – like an Australian would find it easier to talk to British people than Americans. If we deal with Chinese people at all, we often get people from Hong Kong to act as translators. Not because we don't understand the Chinese language, but because we don't understand the Chinese.'

Both Chthonic and Nipples had been approached to play concerts in China, and both had been refused permission. Both, it seemed, were on a blacklist. There, I thought, was everything one needed to know about totalitarianism. Somewhere, a grown person was being paid money to decide that rock bands called Chthonic and Nipples represented an intolerable threat to the stability of his society.

For a place living with the threat of war, Taiwan felt remarkably like Denmark with humidity, or Denmark with humidity and some endearing cultural hiccups. The seaside suburb of Danshui could have been any beach resort, except that the ice-cream sellers also sold alarming seafood, meaning that the promenade bustled with people nonchalantly chewing on what appeared to be science fiction monsters. A great many people wore T-shirts bearing slogans which seemed to have resulted, almost appropriately, from games of Chinese Whispers. I collected these, as well: TEL BOY WAS SPORTS ON A GAME; NOBODY CAN CATCH A GALLOP; HANG TEN COOL ROCKING; I WAS BORN ON BEGIN PLANET; TO BE HANG TEN IS TO BE COOL; HAPPY WAVES RIDE WORTHY NOTHING STEP UP.

And all foreign television is weird, but Taiwanese television was especially foreign, and especially weird. Several channels broadcast nothing but muttering monks. Frequent infomercials extolled the virtues of 'Staying Power' tablets, illustrating this local Viagra with curiously coy sex scenes – I was tempted to call the toll-free number to suggest that Taiwan's men might find the pills unnecessary if they tried taking their boxers off. Late at night, several channels offered reserved and unconvincing striptease, in which arhythmic young women got about as undressed as the Iranian beach volleyball team. Taiwan really wasn't Thailand.

In the two weeks I spent in Taiwan, the only overt indications that it perched on a potential frontline were the military presence on Kinmen, and the F-16s of Taiwan's air force, which made frequent passes over the coastal cities of Taichung and Tainan – judging by the fact that I was the only person who looked up when these roared across the sky, this was a regular occurence. There was tension, however, and the degree to which it was usually repressed was best illustrated by the colossal riot which farewelled the Kuomintang delegation on its historic trip to the mainland. Three and a half thousand Taiwanese cops and soldiers clashed with several thousand demonstraters armed with bottles, fireworks, slingshots, sticks, eggs, rocks and, in one clip highlighted by Taipei's excitable newscasters, a samurai sword. Astonishingly, nobody was killed, and only nine people wound up in hospital, suggesting that the Taiwanese riot fairly politely, as well.

The night before, I'd visited the offices of Joanna Lei, one of the KMT legislators preparing to make the trip.

'A lot of the problem,' she said, 'is economics.'

Lei unfurled some maps, and explained the importance of the oilfields around the Tiaoyutai islands – which were claimed by Taiwan, China and Japan. She seemed less worried about the likelihood of war with China than most Taiwanese, possibly because, as she pointed out, the war that gave birth to the modern Taiwan never officially stopped.

'There was no treaty after the civil war,' she said. 'We – the Kuomintang – are officially still at war with the communists. But I'm an optimist. Taiwan has lived with this since 1949, and under those conditions built a remarkable country, and there's no reason why we can't continue to excel.'

I could think of one. The large, bellicose tyranny next door – which, despite her party's official state of hostility with it, she was about to visit.

'We realise,' she smiled, 'that at this point there is little prospect of us regaining China through military means. Look, all China asks is that we don't declare independence. That's their non-starter. Our nonstarter should be war. Then you figure out how to build a relationship.'

This made sense. But was there time?

'Five years,' said I-Chung Lai, director of Foreign Policy Studies at the Taiwan Thinktank. That, he thought, might be all Taiwan had left.

'Hu Jintao,' he elaborated, 'is likely to remain in power until about 2012. He won't jeopardise the Olympics in 2008, but there's four years after that to define his leadership. Militarily, economically, diplomatically, it would take China about two years to recover from war. So, 2010, I think.'

When I walked Taipei's teeming streets, it was difficult to imagine warheads crashing into the buildings, or paratroopers tumbling from the skies. Taipei looked, in many respects, like any prosperous, orderly First World city: picturing war here was like picturing war in Toronto, or Oslo. Such a thing seemed even less plausible when I visited the National Revolutionary Martyrs' Shrine, the memorial complex commemorating the battles already fought by the Republic of China, from the days when Chiang Kai-Shek dominated Asia, to the decades in which, like a losing player in a game of Risk clinging to one last territory and plotting an unlikely comeback, he continued to insist that his word was law as far away as Lhasa. It wasn't the history that made a future war seem such a fantastic concept, but the present. The complex was manned by soldiers in Ruritanian uniforms and brightly polished chrome helmets, whose boot heels were fitted with clappers to make their marching sound more dramatic. Their changing of the guard, involving much stamping and rifle-twirling, was about as warlike, and almost as camp, as a Village People tribute act.

Back in London, I visited the Chinese embassy, to ask them if they were serious – and, more to the point, why they were serious. Zhang Lirong, the embassy press counsellor, began by noting that Taiwan's authorities could also descend to spite: they'd just bounced the Chinese news agency Xinhua out of Taiwan. I reminded him that this was in retaliation for Beijing blocking the websites of Taiwanese newspapers. I also asked if he was sure, given who he worked for, that he wanted to get into an argument about press freedom. Lirong regarded me with a displeasure that I feared might burn eye-sized holes in my suit. I pushed on. What, I asked, would be wrong with permitting bygones to be bygones, shaking hands, wishing the sovereign state of Taiwan good luck, and buying them something nice for their new embassy in Beijing?

'The "one China" idea is in the interests of the Chinese people,' said Lirong, like he was reading it off something, 'and that includes the

Taiwanese people. We are one country, and have no reason to be two.'

It had been a while since Taiwan was part of China in any practical sense – since 1895, in fact, when Japan took it. Ireland had been part of Britain more recently than that, but nobody in London wanted it back. I didn't know any Russians who burned with desire to see Kyrgyzstan or Turkmenistan reincorporated within the Kremlin's remit. Things change, sometimes for the better.

'Taiwan and China,' he reiterated, 'have been one country for centuries. Think about the Malvinas. Ninety-nine per cent of people would say they belong to Argentina.'

I couldn't believe my ears – or imagine a more idiotic argument. I was pretty sure that roughly that percentage of people who actually lived on the Falklands would say they belonged to Britain. And call me a wishy-washy democrat, but I thought their opinion counted for rather a lot.

'Well,' he said, miffed, 'some people there might say they belong to Argentina.'

Would he care to name one?

'Well,' he harumphed, 'this is different, anyway, because it's a dispute within one country. The anti-secession law makes it clear. Only if Taiwan declares independence, or in the event of external interference, will non-peaceful means be considered.'

There was another solution, which I reckoned would leave everybody happy, and which could have been an immense boon to any nation willing to see the sense of it. At stake was the future of 23 million hard-working, educated, creative, courteous, law-abiding people who'd built an economic colossus out of nothing. The offer that should have been made by some forward-looking government with spare real estate was this: China could have Taiwan. We'd take the Taiwanese.

Among their many other achievements, the Taiwanese were successfully playing two superpowers against each other. As another unrecognised republic was discovering, playing a collapsing behemoth against a confused new nation was a trickier proposition.

14

At moments of international crisis, the refrain that invariably bursts forth from what still passes for the left is that nothing should be done without the imprimatur of the United Nations. These people, who believe that any international intervention is doomed and illegitimate if the UN has not bestowed its approval, have never tried to get the UN to do something simple.

In 2005, the easiest way into Abkhazia, a restive patch of Black Sea coast with aspirations of statehood, was the flight that the UN's Observer Mission In Georgia – UNOMIG – operated between Georgia's capital, Tbilisi, and the capital of the breakaway Republic of Abkhazia, Sukhum. For a fare of US$140, the UN would permit approved applicants, including such eminences as journalists research-ing obtuse travelogues, to ride along. Organising this should have necessitated no more than four emails: one from me expressing an interest, one from them saying yes and providing some times, one from me picking a flight and proferring thanks for their help, one from them assuring me that it was no trouble, that they were looking forward to having me on board, relax and enjoy your trip, please ensure that your table is stowed for takeoff and landing, and so forth.

The reality was a correspondence which, if printed and bound, would be thicker than the W.B. Yeats/Maud Gonne letters. I stopped counting the emails when they cleared triple figures. There were forms that had to be filled in, then faxed to numbers that turned out not to exist. There were assurances I needed to give, in very specific forms of words which had to be precisely honed. There was the invocation of an entity called MovCon, which I came to think of as a reeking troglodyte putrefying in a slimy dungeon cell, from between the mildew-encrusted bars of which it would spit the entrails of raw goats, which would be scrutinised by timorous UN officials for indication of whether the request to travel had been granted.

To my disappointment, when I arrived at UNOMIG's headquarters, atop one of Tbilisi's many dishearteningly steep hills, MovCon – or, at least, the terranean representative thereof – turned out to be a jovial UN bureaucrat from Thailand. After accepting my dollars, he called up on his computer some pictures of the aircraft I'd be riding on. It was almost enough to induce me to ask for my money back, and start walking in the direction of Abkhazia.

The ancient Russian-built Tupolev twin-prop lifted off from Tbilisi at a quarter past dawn, engines whining like a pair of bronchitis sufferers holding a chin-ups contest. From the outside, the plane looked like the black paint spelling the words UNITED NATIONS was all that was holding its dingy white fuselage together. The view from inside wasn't much more encouraging. In testament to the aircraft's antiquity, the in-flight safety card, in which I took intimate interest, had a hammer and sickle emblazoned across the top of it.

We touched down forty-five minutes later at a Georgian military base near Senaki, its runway an immense grey mosaic of concrete slabs being slowly separated by the vigorous weeds pushing between them. A tiny white terminal building flew a UN flag. After just enough time for some coffee which tasted like it might have been tapped from a petrol tank, passengers for Sukhum were directed towards our conveyance, a Russian-built Mi-8 helicopter.

I'd seen Mi-8s in two other places, neither a reassuring precedent. There were Mi-8 hulks in the piles of aircraft wreckage gathered by the runways at Kabul airport. There were Mi-8s inside the Chernobyl Exclusion Zone, in the melancholy paddock which served as a grave-yard for all the irredeemably irradiated vehicles which laboured to clean up the 1986 meltdown of Reactor Number 4. In both these places, the Mi-8 had looked about right: it wasn't flying, and nobody within earshot was seriously suggesting that it was going to. Any Mi-8 looked like an Amsterdam houseboat to which some optimistic loon, possibly just home from an evening in the red light district's Rockink Bongz cafe, had decided to affix a rotor. Up close, it seemed astonishing that the Mi-8 ever got off the drawing board, never mind the ground. The ride turned out to be smooth, if circuitous. Ever since a UN helicopter was shot down over Abkhazia in October 2001, with the loss of all aboard, UN aircrews had understandably tried to spend as little time as possible in Abkhazian airspace. From Senaki, we flew so far out into the Black Sea that I briefly imagined that the pilot fancied a weekend in Istanbul, or had nodded off, before banking late, and descending steeply, into Sukhum.

There weren't any formalities at Sukhum's Dranda Airport. There wasn't much of anything. The only other aircraft were a couple of ageing Aeroflot jets, which looked like they hadn't been airborne since Brezhnev was in office, and another Mi-8, painted in the red, green and white livery of the Abkhazian government. Stray dogs slept by the runway. Inside the terminal, a bored guard didn't ask for my passport. Outside, there was none of the usual airport scenery – no buses, no taxis, no little men in ill-fitting pseudo-military outfits holding up the names of conference delegates – just three UN vehicles meeting the flight.

The road from the airport was cracking concrete, unmarked but for dollops of dung deposited by wandering cattle. There was no traffic, until we got onto the bigger road leading to Sukhum, and then what little there was represented the standard mix of post-communist Eastern Europe: backfiring Volgas and Ladas transporting those too thick or too honest to be successful in the new order, and gleaming BMWs, Audis and Mercedes-Benzes driven by those who'd been quicker to notice which way the wind was blowing, and trim their sails accordingly.

Something looked familiar to me, but not from any meanderings in the former East. It was something from further back than that, which may have been why it took a while to figure out exactly what it was. I eventually realised that I was thinking of childhood road trips in the old country.

The trees, I exclaimed. They were Australian.

'Yes,' confirmed the Abkhazian UN driver. 'They are eucalyptus.'

Dozens of them lined the road – immense, magnificent creatures, bark gathered in tangled tresses around their bases, branches drooping low. They must have been there for decades.

'Since the middle of nineteenth century,' explained the driver. 'There used to be much water, and many mosquitos in Sukhum, and malaria. The water was soaked up by the eucalyptus. Mosquitos go.'

The driver had been born in Russia, but had lived in Sukhum nearly all his life.

'Used to be nice,' he said, glumly. 'Before the war. Before the war, an apartment in Sukhum cost more than an apartment in Moscow.'

And now?

'Sukhum,' he said, even more glumly, 'much cheaper.'

UNOMIG's base was in a compound which had grown up around an old beachfront hotel, the Aitar. My decision to stay at the Aitar was more to do with budget than security: the UN charged its guests just five dollars a night. The accommodation was basic, but not uncomfortable. In a tempting metaphor for the gulf between promise and delivery of so many UN missions, the toilet had a padded seat, but didn't flush.

My first appointment in Abkhazia was fittingly absurd: the foreign ministry, of a country with no diplomatic recognition, to be issued with my visa, by its officially non-existent government. Abkhazia's foreign ministry was, almost by definition, a punchline, an equivalent to the Swiss admiralty or the Dutch mountain rescue service. The security guard brightened upon my approach. I may have been his only passing trade in weeks. It would have felt churlish to deny him the satisfaction of meticulously filling in every detail of an entirely unnecessary form granting me permission to enter the dusty, echoing building.

I'd met Abkhazia's deputy foreign minister, Maxim Gunjia, a few months previously in The Hague, at the annual wing-ding of the

Unrecognised Nations and Peoples Organisation (UNPO), a sort of un-UN for countries which, if one imagined the United Nations as a nightclub, would be rebuffed with a firm 'Your name's not down, you're not coming in.' In between chronicling the cases of such fantastical entities as Tartarstan, Buryatia, Cabinda, Nagaland, Circassia, Assyria and Mapuche, I'd agreed with Maxim that permission to visit Abkhazia – and possibly even some sort of ambassadorship – could be organised if I brought something that would confirm the claims I'd made on behalf of Australian winemakers.

Maxim whooped when I presented the bottle. He placed it in a cabinet in his office, next to an odd-shaped white felt hat.

'A gift,' he smiled, 'from the president of South Ossetia.'

Another unrecognised country. The same head of non-state, Maxim explained, had also given the ministry the wooden plate which hung in the lobby, next to a rug presented by a delegation from Nagorno-Karabakh, the unruly slice of the Caucasus which had been fighting to establish the world's least spellable nation. Abkhazia's only friends were other breakaway republics who nobody else wanted to speak to.

Maxim was twenty-nine, but looked younger. His impish face was crowned with an unruly mop-top. He kept a tie thrown over his coat-rack, to be donned in the event of an unavoidable meeting with a grown-up. His computer emitted bumptious pop music, almost loud enough to cause perceptible billowing in the small Abkhazian flag next to it. Abkhazia's flag was similar in layout to that of the United States. It was dominated by seven stripes – four green, three white, reflecting Abkhazia's Christian and Islamic religious heritage. The panel in the top left corner was red, and contained an open white hand which appeared to be juggling seven small white stars, one for each province of Abkhazia, arranged in a crescent.

'It was designed by a neighbour of mine,' yelled Maxim over the jackhammer techno thundering from his computer's speakers. 'His name was Valery Gamgia. He died during the war.'

I was about to shout back some fatuous observation to the effect that adopting his design was a generous homage to a martyr, but fortunately Maxim finished his sentence first.

'He had a heart attack,' bellowed Maxim.

Abkhazia's 1992–93 war with Georgia was as hideous as it was obscure. With the world's attention mesmerised by the contemporaneous slaughter in the former Yugoslavia – a country of which most people had heard – several Caucasian conflagrations raged disregarded. Abkhazia won its war with Georgia, insofar as Georgia's rule no longer ran on Abkhazian soil in any practical sense – there were no Georgian police or soldiers in Abkhazia, business was conducted in Russian roubles rather than Georgian lari, conversations were held in Russian and Abkhaz rather than Georgian. Abkhazia had its own judiciary, and its own military.

Abkazhia paid a terrible price for these trappings of statehood. As many as 10,000 Abkhazians had died, out of a population Maxim estimated at 250,000, and most of Abkhazia's ethnic Georgians – up to 300,000 people – had fled. Abkhazia was left isolated, tense and uneasily dependent on Russia, whose soldiers were ostentatiously visible in Sukhum, and whose passports were becoming popular among Abkhazia's people – the reasoning being that Georgia might be slower to attack Russian citizens than Abkhazian nonentities. In Georgia, inevitably, they saw it differently. Back in Tbilisi, I'd dined with a Georgian government adviser who'd argued that Abkhazia, and other tetchy Georgian provinces South Ossetia and Adjaria, were treacherous Russian proxies, helping Moscow to destabilise Georgia.

'It's not true,' sighed Maxim, as he showed me around downtown Sukhum. Sukhum was dominated by the same colours as Abkhazia's flag – the green of the palm trees and eucalypts, the white of the handsome, battered buildings along the beachfront. A few Turkish ships loaded at dilapidated wharves. 'It's not as if the Russians like us,' continued Maxim. 'I have a Russian passport, because it's the only way I can travel, but every time I cross the border between here and Russia, the treatment is terrible. I feel raped.'

We reached a humpbacked bridge with white iron railings.

'The war started here,' said Maxim. 'The Georgians came with tanks and helicopters and cannons. Our commander had a pistol, and the rest of our soldiers . . . they weren't even soldiers. They had one Kalashnikov for every three men.'

I asked Maxim if he'd fought.

'I wanted to,' said Maxim. 'But I was only sixteen, so they wouldn't let me. But I went to the front lines anyway, carrying ammunition and helping with the wounded.'

I sensed that everyone else's indifference hurt almost as much as his own memories. Abkhazia's Institute of Language, Literature and History, Maxim told me, was torched by Georgians in 1992, the same year that the Bosnian Serb army announced their genocidal intent towards Bosnia-Herzegovina by burning the National Library in Sarajevo. The latter attack had been headline news. Sukhum suffered its tragedy unnoticed. Maxim showed me statues of Abkhazian heroes – poets, patriots – which had been beheaded or otherwise vandalised by Georgian troops.

Despite working for a government which had an annual budget of only US$50 million, just 600 employees, and no recognition from the outside world, Maxim was optimistic, as the young often are in places where everything is up for grabs. He introduced me to a friend of his, Nadir, who'd spent ten years living in New Zealand, but returned to Abkhazia to take his chances.

'In New Zealand,' said Nadir, 'everything has been finished. There's so much to play for here.'

'Is Abkhazia nicer than New Zealand?' asked Maxim.

'Much,' said Nadir. 'The poorest Abkhazian lives better than the wealthiest New Zealander.'

While I looked forward to repeating this exchange to Kiwi friends in London, I thought Nadir's claim a bit of a stretch – but, that said, Sukhum wasn't anyone's idea of a war-torn heck-hole. The only indication that anything was amiss was the Russian military presence. The Russian soldiers were based in beachside dachas which had once served as holiday homes for Red Army soldiers. The compound was haunted by mosaic portraits of Lenin, and manned by lackadaisacal sentries. They never bothered the holidaymakers in swimming costumes who sauntered through the barracks, and when they bothered me, their hearts weren't in it.

'Passport,' said one soldier, as I negotiated a turnstile. 'Want see your passport.'

I told him he couldn't. I wasn't trying to start a fight. I simply couldn't be bothered fishing it out of my money belt.

'Okay,' he croaked, and waved me through.

The duties of the Russian soldiers consisted of lounging next to their vehicles, nodding their heads to American hip hop booming from their stereos, and chatting up passing women. And, I imagined, offering hourly prayers of thanks that they were here, not Chechnya.

It wasn't necessary to compare Sukhum with Grozny to find it pleasant. Sukhum looked positively tropical. The trees were in riotous health, overpowering Sukhum's war-damaged buildings and the disused seafront railway line. Sukhum felt tropical, as well, wilting in a clammy heat. Sukhum sounded tropical, too, a voluble cicada population chirruping a permanent tinnitus.

Though Sukhum possessed the appearance of the lush, raffish capital of a Latin American banana republic, a tatty paradise of rum, salsa and Cohibas, it wasn't just the Russian soldiers that made it impossible to forget where I really was. All Abkhazians whose job involved dealing with the public, or at least with me, took their cues on customer service from Russia. Shopkeepers and restaurant staff reacted to the merest request for assistance like it was the twenty-seventh time I'd yelled at them that morning to clean up their room.

Sukhum's beaches were unlikely to impress anyone who grew up near Waikiki or Manly, but the Russian tourists crowding them didn't mind the cement-coloured sand, the litter, or the fact that it was possible to discern, squinting across the water, the line that delineated the cool grey of the Black Sea from the deeply unappetising brown of Sukhum's pollution. Otherwise, the place was doing its best to be a normal seaside resort. There were open-air bars, blaring strident Russian pop bad enough to make any sane person wish that the hyperbolic adjective 'deafening' was literally true. There were restaurants on terraces overlooking the water, a couple of which weren't bad – which would explain the popularity of Sukhum with tourists from Russia, a country which is to cuisine what Sudan is to the giant slalom. There were stalls selling the perplexingly hideous souvenirs common to such places from Blackpool to Barbados, with particular emphasis on fabulously hideous animals constructed from seashells and indelicately applied glue. I bought a couple of fridge magnets which, I suspected, had parted company with a consignment created for sale on the Cote d'Azur. They depicted a pristine resort of gabled waterfront walkways, gleaming white hotels, brilliant seagulls and cavorting dolphins. The black and gold sticker beneath this vision, claiming that this was 'Abkhazia', looked like it had been pasted on rather subsequent to the magnets' manufacture.

Raul Khadjimba, Abkhazia's vice-president, worked in a sparsely decorated, but refreshingly air-conditioned, office. By his desk sat a bank of six white telephones, whose antiquity could be divined from the fact that when they rang, they actually rang, in a way that no telephone in the western world had since about 1986. Khadjimba had previously been Abkhazia's defence minister, deputy prime minister, prime minister, and head of its security services – he was a one-man war cabinet. He'd been a close ally of Vladislav Ardzinba, Abkhazia's wartime leader and first president, and during the long stretches in which Ardzinba had been too ill to carry out his duties, Khadjimba had served as de facto head of his de facto state. Like the rest of Abkhazia's officialdom, he compromised with the climate, and wore a short-sleeved white shirt, with no tie. The informality ended there: he was resolutely sombre, every question answered with a blinkless gaze down his long nose.

'Why not us?' he wondered, when I asked why Abkhazia's independence was worth fighting for. 'When the Soviet Union collapsed, there was freedom for many nations – the Baltic states, Armenia, Azerbaijan, Georgia. All these countries became more independent, while we became less independent.'

Khadjimba couldn't understand why the freedom that had been offered to so many former peoples of the former Soviet Union had not been extended to his.

'It's about the peculiarities of the people,' he said. 'Whatever the Georgians say, Abkhazians and Georgians are brothers – all people of the world are brothers. But an Englishman would never call himself American. We are different people, with different histories, different languages, different customs.'

You could say the same, I observed, of the English, the Scots and the Welsh, who managed to rub along within one country, working off residual tensions with sporting fixtures and occasional name-calling.

'The example of Scotland is good,' he allowed, 'but in Great Britain, you find Northern Ireland. Any problems there?'

This was as close as he got to a joke.

'It's funny,' he said, though he clearly thought otherwise, 'when people call the Abkhazian leadership separatists. Whatever post I hold, I just express the people's will, but nobody gives us a chance. But we can develop. Look at Switzerland – it only exists because of banks. We don't have that opportunity, but we can compete with Switzerland in terms of beauty. After the collapse of the USSR, there is no industrial production here, so everything is very beautiful.'

It seemed a good moment to mention the eucalypts.

'They are wonderful,' he intoned, still talking like he'd just received news of the death of a pet rabbit. There was a pause, during which his face fell further, as if it had struck him that he might have trouble selling the hutch. 'But,' he mourned, 'we do not have kangaroos. I think they would do well here.'

Khadjimba was, in his dour fashion, optimistic – sort of a goth cheerleader. Abkhazia's president, Sergei Bagapsh, was jollier, but no less frustrated. Bagapsh had become president earlier in 2005, following a disputed election. Khadjimba, now his deputy, had been his rival. The first count had declared Khadjimba the winner, but a subsequent Supreme Court ruling found in favour of Bagapsh, at which point Khadjimba's supporters stormed the building, as a result of which the Supreme Court changed its mind. With Abkhazia on the verge of the ludicrous travesty of civil war over a country which didn't exist, Bagapsh and Khadjimba had mercifully agreed to run as a national unity ticket in a new election. They won 90 per cent of the vote.

Bagapsh was recently back from a visit to Moscow.

'It wasn't treated as a state visit, no,' he said wistfully. 'But I was treated as president of a country in which 80 per cent of the population are Russian citizens.'

I asked if it wasn't kind of weird for a people who prided themselves on their independence to be signing up for passports from a country which wasn't famous for its tolerance of uppity minorities.

'Small nations are always concerned about being assimilated,' he agreed, 'but Russia helped us when we were in trouble. Russian troops stand on the Abkhazian–Georgian border. Russian tourists and businesspeople come here. Russians died here in the war.'

Bagapsh was also happy to talk about the gum trees, about which he knew an almost disturbing amount. I felt we were getting on well enough that I could ask one mildly impudent question. Give me one good reason, I said, why anyone should care whether you guys ever get to compete in the Olympics.

'Excellent question!' he boomed. 'The Abkhazian people are friendly and peaceful. Many people from other countries have visited here, and they know this. Leaders of top world governments used to rest here. They, too, learned that we are peaceful and hospitable. But we do not like our enemies.'

Maxim's boss was Abkhazia's minister for foreign affairs, Sergei Shamba. His office had books about art on the shelves, abstract paintings and tapestries on the walls. These may have been attempts to compensate for the cheerless view out of his window, of buildings gutted during the fighting more than a decade ago and still awaiting repair. Though I'd thought Raul Khadjimba was heavy going, Shamba made him seem like Robin Williams after several sugary espressos. I was certain I noticed the translator's eyelids struggling to stay apart. I knew for sure I was having the same difficulty, and I was surprised Shamba didn't fall asleep himself.

Shamba was excruciating to listen to, but when I read my notes that night, over a bottle of cheekily atrocious Abkhazian wine, there were, in between my doodles of Shamba being assaulted by men armed with shovels, some useful insights.

'Our independence,' he droned, 'is a long-term objective. It will require tolerance and effort from us. We have to demonstrate that we are capable of creating a modern democratic state. Our recent change of power was complicated, but it was done within the framework of a democratic constitution, not any sort of Rose Revolution, as they had in Georgia.' Shamba offered a barely discernible smirk with this barb.

'The history of humanity,' he said, 'shows that borders change. I know we're called a de facto state, but the most important thing is that the state is recognised by our own society.'

Shamba was right about this. All nationalities are a collective whim. When enough people in a reasonably concentrated space decide that they are something, it's usually impossible to persuade them otherwise, even – or especially – by threat of destruction. The Middle East at the beginning of the twentieth century was as fractious as the Middle East at the beginning of the twenty-first, but back then nobody called themselves Israeli or Palestinian. Abkhazian nationality had a longer history than Israeli or Palestinian nationality, and the Abkhazians weren't about to be talked out of it.

I went to meet one of the people responsible for keeping the Georgians on the other side of the Inguri River. Deputy Defence Minister Garry Kupalba worked in an office block near the UN compound. Shirtless Abkhazian conscripts sweated through callisthenics exercises in the courtyard. He talked me through a brisk history of the war.

'Armed hostility began against our nation on 14 August 1992,' he said. 'Our people were not armed, and we had heavy military equipment thrown against us, but many people had hunting weapons, and our patriotic people united and mobilised themselves to stop the oppression by our Georgian enemy.'

I suspected he'd spun this yarn before. However, the image of a plucky people's militia, armed only with blunderbusses hitherto employed to keep the rabbits down, seeing off a fearsomely tooled-up malevolent invader, while universally appealing, is rarely the full story. In the early stages of the war, the Abkhazians had done as well as you'd expect a disorganised, under-equipped force facing the army of an angry state to do – that is, badly. Abkhazia's eventual victory was achieved with the assistance of some dubious customers. The Russian military joined in, as did a poetically named outfit called the Confederation of Mountain Peoples of the Caucasus, an amalgamation of Islamist hillbillies from the region's more ornery corners, notably Chechnya. There had been a clamour of reports of vengeful crimes against ethnically Georgian civilians. Human Rights Watch had declared both sides responsible for 'gross violations of international humanitarian law'.

'Our army didn't begin until 10 October 1992,' continued Kupalba, in moving-swiftly-along mode. 'That was the day our Ministry of Defence and general staff HQ were created. I became a major. I served on the Gumista front, named after the river.'

I asked when he felt like he'd won.

'There were several attempts to relieve Sukhum,' he said, and I wondered how the Georgians residing in the city at the time would have felt about the 'relieve'. 'There were attacking operations on 5 January 1993, and on 16 to 17 March and 17 September. The last operations in September led to the enemy being driven back beyond the boundaries of our republic.'

And also, according to any number of reports, to large numbers of people being murdered, raped and displaced for being Georgian. Which wasn't to say that things just as bad hadn't happened to people for being Abkhazian. Did the ends justify the means?

'Both sides suffered great losses,' he said. 'But we had to free our motherland.'

I set forth to see what Kupalba had fought for. Abkhazia was so small that almost any of it could be reached in a daytrip. Drivers were easily found among Sukhum's ranks of unemployed young men, although it was a source of persistent frustration that I never mastered the Abkhazian for 'Please proceed in a more temperate fashion'. I found, however, that if sufficient passion was invested in the delivery of the

English expression 'For Christ's sake slow down, you maniac, you'll get us all killed!', it was readily, if reluctantly, understood.

My guides could scarcely have been better qualified. Professor Viacheslav 'Slava' Chirikba, an Abkhazian who now lived in the Netherlands, and Professor George Hewitt, an English professor who was married to a local, had between them written a fair percentage of the available literature on Abkhazia. I'd asked Slava, who had also been a member of the Abkhaz delegation to the post-war peace negotiations in Geneva, if Abkhazia had a place, or totem, which Abkhazians thought of as a spiritual or historical heart, a Gallipoli, a Liberty Bell. He'd mentioned a place called Lykhny. This was about forty minutes north of Sukhum, which would have been twenty minutes by normal standards of Abkhazian driving, but we instructed the pilot of the seatbelt-free Lada I'd hired to experiment with sanity.

At Lykhny, there was a sprawling memorial to the dead of the 1992–93 war. It consisted of several large reliefs carved from white stone, planted in a field in front of a small chapel. The reliefs were magnificent – understated throwbacks to the socialist statuary that must have dominated Soviet Abkhazia's public spaces. One depicted soldiers brandishing Kalashnikovs, another a cavalryman astride a rearing horse, another a mourning family. At the head of these was a giant figure of a man, his body shrouded in a cloak, his bearded visage topped by a Soviet-style forage cap. Though I'd have been surprised to learn that it was the artist's intention, the resemblance to Laibach's vocalist Milan Fras was uncanny.

At a headstone bearing portraits of two men, Slava pointed at the one on the left, a bearded fellow in camouflage fatigues, who looked like a still image from *All Quiet on the Western Front*. His name was recorded as Mushni Khvartskia, 1955–1992.

'He was one of my best friends,' explained Slava. 'He was an archaeologist, but when the war started he became a military commander, very brave and successful. He led hit-and-run raids on the Georgians.'

We trudged across a paddock to the Palace of Culture, a semi-derelict Soviet building monstrous in its nondescriptitude. The doors that hadn't been stolen were open, so George and Slava and I wandered in, surprising stray dogs and a couple of furtively smoking youths. The lobby was dominated by collages of black and white portraits: on one wall, victims of the 1992–93 war, on the other the dead of World War II, which took a severe toll on the Abkhaz, as it did on all Soviet peoples. I was photographing the photographs when Slava called excitedly from the top of a dogshit-strewn staircase.

'Come and look at this,' he said.

George and I proceeded carefully upstairs to a landing, which looked up at a colossal painting stretching along an entire wall, perhaps 15 metres long and 3 metres high. From left to right, it chronicled the history of Abkhazia.

'That's the coming of Christianity,' said Slava, pointing at a golden-bearded figure emptying holy water over a loinclothed pagan. 'So that's probably Saint Andrew.'

The next panel was consumed by a battle scene, presided over by a regal cove on a horse. Behind him, an archer brandished a scarlet banner bearing the same open hand motif that appeared on Abkhazia's present-day flag. The bloke in the crown was an eighth-century king called Leon II, explained Slava. In the foreground, Leon's knights were dealing some hapless mob a fearful smiting. Judging by the next panels, this may have been as good as it got for Abkhazia. There followed scenes of unrelenting woe. In one, a white horse bled to death against a backdrop of ragged refugees queuing for boats.

'The 1870s,' said George. 'After the Caucasian War. Thousands of Abkhazians left for Turkey.'

I squinted towards the top of the picture. The ship whose sails were furled into the clouds on the horizon was flying a Turkish flag.

'The horse is dying,' continued Slava, 'because his owner has shot him before leaving Abkhazia.'

He pointed at a distraught figure weeping against a tree, pistol dangling by his side. 'You see also,' he said, waving towards a woman weeping over a pale infant, 'the mother mourning her baby. There is a famous poem about her, which is now a popular folk song.'

I could figure out the last panel unguided: Red Army cavalry planting their flag in Abkhazia's reluctant soil. In the bottom right of the mural, a bouquet of pink flowers bloomed above a signature: Gamgia, the flag designer, Maxim's late neighbour. This painting was a national treasure, a chronicle of Abkhazia by their own Betsy Ross, yet it was hanging unprotected in wrecked building, ripped and tattered, covered in dust and bird crap. It was one thing, and not an uncommon thing, to found a nation on some notion of martyrdom. It was something else entirely to martyr the very artwork that best expressed it.

'There's an Abkhazian joke,' grinned Slava. 'From Soviet times. The Russians launch a lunar mission. So, the first two Cosmonauts land on the Moon. When they get there, to their surprise, they find an Abkhazian. They ask him: "What are you doing here?" He replies: "I heard there was a funeral on."'

The seafront road into Gagra was, for any visiting Australian, the most discombobulating in Abkhazia, and possibly the northern hemisphere. It was lined by colonnades of the fattest gum trees I'd ever seen. Vice-president Khadjimba's baleful contemplation of importing kangaroos made even more sense, especially after another hair-greying dice with Abkhazian roads. It would work for Australia, humanely relieving my homeland of a plentiful pest, and the leaping creatures might have a calming effect on Abkhazian motoring, by introducing a dangerously random element to Abkhazian traffic. Abkhazia's cows moved, as cows do, slowly and predictably, and so weren't much of an impediment, and dogs and cats weren't considered worth slowing down for. Giant reds vaulting randomly into the road might promote a life-preserving circumspection, I'd mused, as our Lada careened on two wheels around a truck whose driver threw an abrupt U-turn on a blind corner.

Along Gagra's beachfront, there were indications of a recovering tourist infrastructure: more horrible souvenirs, and cafés offering the opportunity to have one's eardrums burst by dreadful Russian pop bellowing from speakers which might have been salvaged from some Soviet sonic warfare project. There was also a depressing animal attraction, consisting of four small cages, containing a comatose fox, mangy raccoons, a clearly crazed pacing bear, and two baboons, though they might have been taking time out from their day jobs as driving instructors. Near this dismal gulag for quadrupeds, a couple of touts had a leopard cub in a carry-cage, and were offering photos with it for a few roubles a time. When they produced the animal for prospective customers, the leopard revealed itself to be nudging adult-hood, and understandably irate. It was some consolation that the day it deducted one of its handlers a few fingers was probably not far off.

On the way back from Gagra, we stopped in Pitsunda, once a prestigious Soviet resort, now a slightly less prestigious holiday camp. The hotels were, in their melancholy way, masterpieces of Soviet futurism, chessboards in their lobbies, hexagonal lookout pods on their roofs. These offered views over another litter-strewn beach. It was neither the first place, nor the first time, that I'd contemplated land that the people upon it had pledged that they would die for, and wondered why, if they loved it that much, they didn't keep it tidy.

I arrived at the foreign ministry one morning to find Maxim and his staff assembling chairs. He was glad of the distraction, and took me for brunch in the ministry's canteen. He wouldn't hear of my con-tributing, and I remarked upon the difficulty I'd had paying for anything if an Abkhazian who knew me was close enough to hear my wallet opening.

'That's how we are,' said Maxim. 'The saying is "If you pay, you win". We have a code of conduct. It's called *apsuara*.' He spelled it out as I wrote it down. 'It means something like "hospitality". It means we respect elders, we stand when someone enters a room, things like this. It's also about how to drink, how to behave at the table.'

I asked if it was anything like the Kanun of Lek, the – in fairness, largely unheeded – bible of Albanian folk wisdom that contained colourful clauses pertaining to the conduct of blood feuds, the circum-stances in which it was permissible to shoot the wife, etcetera.

'No,' said Maxim. 'It's mostly just about being polite to guests.'

A nation founded on a belief in getting one's round in was, I thought, to be encouraged. But did Maxim honestly think it could work?

'Yes,' he said. 'I know there is much to do here. But we get the chance to build everything our ancestors dreamed of, to build the country the way we want it.'

How much of a triumph would that be, though, if nobody recognised it? If a flag was hoisted and nobody saluted it, was it really flying?

'Look,' said Maxim, 'it's fun visiting places as a diplomat from an unrecognised country, it really is. I've been to the Ukraine, Poland, Bulgaria, Holland, and I have fun, I tease them. They don't want to invite me as deputy foreign minister now, but they will. One day, they will.'

A tiny country, about which the world knew and cared little, huddled among great powers with intermittently predatory tendencies. It couldn't possibly work. Could it?

15

I had no idea when I'd arrived in Luxembourg. In the process of boarding the morning train in Amsterdam, changing in Brussels, and disembarking in Luxembourg City, there were no border formalities, no interest taken in my passport or luggage. The Schengen Agreement, under which several European states had pretty much ceased bothering to police their borders, had affected continental travel in much the same way as the introduction of the euro, making it more convenient, but less fun.

I used to like going to European countries and wondering who the bearded blokes on the banknotes were. I enjoy accumulating stamps on the pages of my passport – something I'm only able to do because my passport is Australian. My compensation for having to stand in Europe's glacial non-citizens queues has always been the envy of the photographers I've travelled with, who get waved through without collecting stamps from such evocative ports of arrival as Berlin-Tegel, Amsterdam-Schiphol, Nice-Cote d'Azur, Wien-Schwechat, Brussels-Luchthaven, Paris-Charles de Gaulle, Paris Nord. Also, rather charmingly, EU passport stamps include a cartoon of an aeroplane if you've arrived by air, a car if you've come by road or a puffing locomotive if you've travelled on Eurostar. These details are important. They make travel feel, as it should, more like an adventure than a commute.

In one day, I'd travelled across three countries, and it felt of no greater consequence than getting a tube from one side of London to the other. But maybe this was how the world should work.

Maybe tiny, tedious Luxembourg was something other countries should aspire to.

Luxembourg had its own government, its own flag, its own anthem, its own military, its own royalty, its own seat at the UN. Before joining the euro, it had its own currency. But it was preposterously small, only 2586 square kilometres. If Luxembourg was an American state, its size would be mocked by Rhode Islanders. You could fit it into Great Britain a hundred times. You could lose it in Tasmania.

It was, arguably, unfair to pick on Luxembourg. It wasn't alone in Europe in assuming the trappings of sovereignty despite barely having sufficient territory to unfurl the flag without flicking the neighbours on the head. I could have gone to Leichtenstein, but I'd no idea where it was, or even if that was how it was spelled, and I'd be exaggerating if I suggested I cared. I could have gone to San Marino, except that I'd already tried, on a day off while working on a story in more or less the right region of Italy, and hadn't been able to find it.

I'd never been to Luxembourg. I couldn't name one figure from its history, or any of its living citizens. The only things I knew about Luxembourg were that it was the title of a lesser track from Elvis Costello's *Trust*, and was mentioned in a song by The Smiths. But I thought Luxembourg might represent a way forward. It seemed probable that the reason I knew so little of Luxembourg were that it had caused few people any trouble.

From a distance, Luxembourgeois nationalism seemed commendably low-key. Where other countries named their capitals after revolutionary leaders (Washington) or religions (Islamabad), Luxembourg's capital was named after itself: the equivalent of a place called Germany City or Australia Town, a failure of imagination and/or sign of chronic modesty only equalled by Brazil's Brasilia.

Luxembourg's flag was similarly diffident. Many small countries seek to compensate for their irrelevance by flying banners suggesting something designed by a spotty fifteen-year-old for his computer game fiefdom. The flag saluted by the inconsequential French possession of

St Pierre and Miquelon, for example, looks like every inhabitant of those disregarded Atlantic islands was determined to have a say in its design. Luxembourg's flag was the same as the Netherlands' – red, white and blue horizontal bars – aside from a barely perceptible lightening of the blue. This must have been the result of one of the least fervid meetings in the history of nation-building.

'Chaps, we need a flag to raise above our redoubtable new state, a standard which will flutter proudly alongside the banners of the great nations. Any ideas?'

'The clog-wearers next door just got a consignment from a cheap contractor they're trying out, and one of the colours is a bit wrong, so they'll let us have them at cost.'

'Right then.'

Luxembourg's national anthem, 'Ons Heemecht' ('Our Homeland'), was even more self-effacing. It made few grand claims for the country, even implicitly acknowledged the hilarious fluke that is Luxembourg's existence. Its last verse was a prayer to whichever benign, if eccentric, mystical potentate blessed this miniscule realm with the dignity and security of statehood. The pertinent lines translate as 'O thou above whose powerful hand/Makes states or lays them low/Protect this Luxembourger land/From foreign yoke and woe.' The message of 'Ons Heemecht' is 'Look, we're no trouble. Seriously, you'll hardly notice we're here. If you have to invade somebody, try France.'

I spent my first day in Luxembourg being a tourist. This is never a good way to understand what a country is really like. It is, however, a perfect means of appreciating a country's perception of its visitors' expectations. What would Luxembourg assume I had come to see?

I climbed aboard a deserted double-decker tourist bus. My fare included headphones which, when plugged into seat-side jacks, provided crackly automated commentary, maddeningly intercut with one bland but insistent pop song, called 'Someone By My Side'. The effect was like struggling to tune in to a DJ who not only talked over the music, but only owned one record. I ended up spending most waking hours in Luxembourg, and possibly many sleeping hours, humming the tune. Intrigued despite myself, I ran the lyrics, branded as they were deep into my reluctant consciousness, through Google. I discovered that 'Someone By My Side' was the work of a Luxembourg group called T42 – not after the Soviet tank, but pronounced, excruciatingly, 'Tea For Two'. I suspected them of owning shares in the bus company, or some severely compromising photographs of its directors.

It didn't take long for the flaw in the automated commentary to become apparent – it only worked if the bus proceeded at exactly the same speed every trip. But the traffic was bad, and we were quickly out of sync. If the commentary was to be believed, the Luxembourg Philharmonic Orchestra rehearsed halfway across a bridge, and former Luxembourgeois prime minister Robert Schuman was born in a rubbish skip behind an office block.

This miscalibration of sight and sound wouldn't be a problem on a tour of London, Paris or Rome. Nobody needs to be told that they're looking at Big Ben, the Arc de Triomphe, or the Coliseum. But in Luxembourg, I didn't know what anything was. The bus company could at least have had some fun with it: 'The trees along this boulevard are actually a cunningly disguised missile system, and when we've planted twenty more, we're going to bomb Belgium'; 'In this court building, custody cases are settled, according to ancient Luxembourgeois law, by the divorcing husband and wife hurling live ducks at each other'.

The bus ambled past some large outdoor contemporary sculptures, which looked like planes that had missed the airport. The commentary introduced us to some banks – banks! – and the Kirchberg hospital, by which point I was tempted to ask the driver if said establishment had wards dedicated to the care of patients dying of boredom. We saw the European Court of Justice, the Court of Auditors, and did two laps round the Quartier Euro, presumably in case I'd slept through the construction site for the new European Investment Bank building the first time.

In between T42's warbling, and a commentary of entrancing irrelevance to the view, the headphones imparted a potted history of

Luxembourg. The country started as a castle, built on the site of modern-day Luxembourg City in 963. For the next few centuries, Luxembourg was independent, and influential. Luxembourgeois monarchs were also kings of Bohemia, Germany and Hungary. Between 1308 and 1437, the House of Luxembourg provided four Holy Roman Emperors. This made as much sense as whoever happened to be Mayor of Ougadougou announcing that they were in charge of Africa, but nobody minded. After the House of Luxembourg ran out of male heirs, the tiny territory spent the next few centuries being shunted among the great European powers. It was ruled by Spain, then France, then Spain again, then Austria, then France again, suggesting that Luxembourg was never exactly seized, just sort of nicked when the owner wasn't looking, and then pinched back a few decades later when they noticed it was gone. We drove past another bank.

The 1814–15 Congress of Vienna decided to call Luxembourg a Grand Duchy, and gave it to King William I of the Netherlands. He passed it on to two further Williams who succeeded him, despite Luxembourg attaining theoretical political autonomy through the Treaty of Vienna in 1839. There was briefly some excitement in 1867, when France decided it was their turn again, but the issue was resolved by the Treaty of London, at which everyone promised to respect Luxembourg's neutrality and independence. In 1890, Luxembourg was granted to its current heads of state, the House of Nassau. We drove past another bank.

Luxembourg reminded neighbouring Germany of its neutrality before the outbreak of both world wars, and on both occasions was listened to as diligently as a badger colony emphasising its non-combatant status to a bulldozer. The experiences cured Luxembourg of its enthusiasm for neutrality, and they'd since signed up to NATO, the EU, and anybody else who'd have them.

The bus stopped outside another bank. I disembarked, slightly the wiser about how this place had survived the storms of centuries, and wondering if it might be possible to make more of the world like this: amiable, if dull, wealthy (in 2004 Luxembourg had the second-highest

GDP per capita on Earth) and resolutely unwarlike (landlocked Luxembourg had no need of a navy, didn't bother with an air force, and maintained an army of 430 troops – less than many US civil war re-enactment societies).

In search of enlightenment, I dropped in on Professor Gilbert Trausch. Professor Trausch was the world's foremost authority on the little-discussed subject of Luxembourgeois history. He had taught at the Sorbonne, and served as a prime ministerial counsellor. His house was obviously the habitat of a veteran academic, every wall lined with bookshelves. He accepted my mystification as regards the existence of his country with gentle humour.

'Luxembourg is very small,' he agreed. 'But its influence is greater than its size. It has always been very active in the EU, for example, and Luxembourgers are very proud of that.'

This was true – and, for a resident of Britain, odd. In Luxembourg, the flag of the EU was flown almost as prolifically as the flag of Luxembourg – not just from official buildings, but in shops and restaurants. In Britain, it was probable that more people felt allegiance to the swastika.

'Well,' smiled Professor Trausch, 'Luxembourg has always rather suffered from German–French tensions, which may be why we welcome the EU. The first EU plan was drawn up by Pierre Werner, one of our prime ministers. Luxembourg doesn't have any policy based on power – that would obviously be absurd.'

I asked Professor Trausch if he'd ever seen *The Mouse That Roared*, the 1959 Peter Sellers vehicle about an obscure European principality – the Duchy of Grand Fenwick – which accidentally acquires a super-weapon, and with it, the balance of global power. He hadn't, but the idea tickled him.

'I remember,' he says, 'about thirty years ago, a minister from another European country asking if it would be a catastrophe if there was no longer a Luxembourg at all.'

So how did we get here? How did Luxembourg's 468,571 citizens end up with their own country, when so many other deserving peoples had been less fortunate? Was it just a question of setting up shop huddled among greater powers, and hoping nobody noticed?

'A definition of nationality,' said Professor Trausch, 'cannot just be about numbers.'

That was true. Luxembourg wasn't the least populous nation in the world. Out of the 191 countries recognised by the United Nations at this time, Luxembourg finished 161st in terms of population. Given a long winter plagued by power cuts, accompanied by air-drops of oysters and Marvin Gaye albums, Luxembourg was within reach of overhauling Djibouti to crack the top 160. So if it's not just numbers, what else do you need?

'Territory,' said Trausch, 'which we have, even if we don't have much. A language of one's own, which we developed – though it is, in reality, a German dialect. Luxembourgers, between themselves, speak Luxembourgish, what we call Letzebuergesch, which is important. It seems to be becoming more difficult to keep together communities speaking different languages within one state. You see troubles in Belgium, Canada, even in Switzerland.'

Language couldn't be that crucial. The peoples of Yugoslavia mostly spoke more or less one language, and the language which had once been called Serbo-Croatian had become known as Serbian, Croatian or Bosnian, depending on who you were talking to.

'Quite,' said Trausch. 'Which is why you also need a collective memory, based on history. You can't have a nation if you have no sense of a past. You need a historiography, which is often based on very rudimentary things. In France, everyone knows about Napoleon. Maybe not much, but they know something.'

The country I came from had its Anzacs, its convicts, its Ned Kelly, its Bradman. The country I lived in had more to choose from – and a population often shockingly ignorant of all of it – but most Britons could have told you something about Churchill, Henry VIII, The Beatles. They'd be less than the whole story, but a useful framework of shared assumptions. What did a Luxembourger think of when he thought of Luxembourg? I was guessing it wasn't the Smiths song.

'There was a poll,' said Trausch. 'The Luxembourger most people knew was Grand-Duchess Charlotte. She led the government-in-exile during World War II, and is the symbol of resistance.'

Charlotte's name now adorned the Grand Duchess Charlotte Bridge, the tallest and most terrifying of the tall, terrifying spans that linked Luxembourg's Old City to its outer districts.

'The third thing,' said Trausch, 'is willingness of the people to accept sacrifices for the survival of the community. You cannot be a nation without solidarity. During World War II, the Nazis tried to Germanise Luxembourgers. The people refused. Hundreds were shot, and thousands sent to concentration camps. They clung very strongly to their country.'

Reminders of Luxembourg's scourings by war were never far away (in Luxembourg, nothing was). Near Trausch's house was a street named after General Pershing, commander of American forces in Europe during World War I. The boulevard along one side of the Old City's fortifications bore the name of Franklin Roosevelt, and there was a Boulevard General Patton (Patton was buried at Hamm, just outside Luxembourg City).

How secure could a tiny, practically unarmed country with practically unpoliced borders feel?

'Well,' pondered Trausch, 'our economy has been booming, so we had to ask for a workforce. Every morning, 105,000 people cross the border to work. The time will come when Luxembourgers become a minority in Luxembourg. Then, there may be difficulties. Our national motto is "Mir welle bleiwe, wat mir sin", which translates as "We want to remain what we are".'

Trausch was quick to emphasise that Luxembourg was showing no inclination to embrace the populist racism of the sort which had become visible in France, the Netherlands and Austria.

'A xenophobe is simply a stupid man,' observed Trausch, accurately. 'But this is important. I was recently asked by a newspaper if I thought there would still be a Luxembourg in a hundred years.'

A question which in itself bespoke a certain insecurity.

'Indeed,' he nodded. 'I said yes, but it will be a different Luxembourg. People are afraid, and fear is a bad counsellor.'

* * *

Evenings in Luxembourg were slowish. Entertainment options revolved around restaurants which were expensive and empty – the relationship between those two adjectives had eluded the restaurateurs. At 7.30 on a Friday night, the place was absolutely stiff. There were only the windows of closed shops to gaze into, and these seemed calculated to contribute to an atmosphere of bureaucratic stolidity. In the window of one bookshop by the Old City's main square, Place d'Armes, the same space that would, anywhere else, be occupied by garish displays touting the new John Grisham, contained piles of Luxembourg's Code Penal, Code Civil and Commercial Law. Posters which, in other cities, scream of forthcoming musical attractions, seemed to verge on embarassment, and with good reason: the bill of fare for Luxembourgeois gig-goers included a Led Zeppelin tribute act called Physical Graffiti, AC/DC impersonators High Voltage, and Vonda Shephard, an American caterwauler chiefly infamous for braying the theme from *Ally McBeal*. Getting invaded by Germany a couple of times a century was doubtless tiresome in many respects, but it must have relieved the monotony. Could a civilised country at the heart of early twenty-first-century Europe really be this dull?

'Yes,' said Josee Hansen. Hansen was an arts reporter for a local newspaper, who dodged the tumbleweed to meet me for a drink. 'The problem is that everybody is too rich. You leave school at eighteen knowing what you're going to do, you've got a job for life in banks or in government, and by the time you're thirty all you're worried about is your third car or second kitchen.'

I'd wanted to meet Hansen because I'd been interested in how Luxembourg's national identity might be expressed by its artists. My two frames of reference, Australia and Britain, boasted authors, painters, comedians, musicians and poets struggling to distil something of their nations' essence. Was there, I asked, a Luxembourgeois Les Murray, a Martin Amis of the Moselle?

'Difficult,' decided Hansen. 'Mostly, artists hate Luxembourg. They tend to ignore it. Have you heard of Michel Majerus?'

I hadn't. Hansen explained that he was a Luxembourg-born pop artist, who died in November 2002, aged thirty-five, when the Luxair plane he was travelling on crashed on approach to Luxembourg's Findel Airport.

'He hated Luxembourg,' Hansen said. 'He wouldn't even speak to Luxembourg's newspapers. He lived in Berlin, and pretended to be German.'

Well, both Britain and Australia had stirred the muses of non-native artists. Were there any resonant observations of Luxembourg by artistic titans from the outside world?

'Henry Miller,' giggled Hansen, 'said he'd rather die poor in Paris than live rich in Luxembourg. It caused a big scandal at the time.'

Endearing though this self-deprecation was, I wondered if there were aspects of Luxembourgness that made Luxembourgers' hearts swell at the thought of all things Luxembourgian.

'We're proud of our languages,' she decided. 'Everyone here speaks four or five. We're proud of our tolerance. Most people who live here aren't from here, but trouble is unusual. And we've never started a war.'

Hansen saw my riposte – that the only European power against whom you'd rate Luxembourg's chances would be Legoland – coming from a way off.

'I suppose,' she conceded, 'our options would be limited.'

I was starting to think there might be something in this, of trying to work towards a world in which states were forced to sublimate their competitive urges in rank impotence. And then I realised that few peoples possess the necessary diffidence, modesty or, perhaps, sense of the absurd. I learned this by going to the football. Luxembourg were playing Russia in a World Cup qualifier. The Josy Barthel Stadium – named for Luxembourg's sole Olympic gold medallist, who won the mens' 1500 metres in Helsinki in 1952 – was far from sold out, but it was actually kind of weird that there was anyone there at all, including Luxembourg's team.

Being a Luxembourg supporter, or player, was an occupation only for those whose devotion was metastasising into insanity. Since the national team's foundation in 1908, Luxembourg had accrued a record of failure almost impressive in its consistency. They had finished bottom of their group in every World Cup qualifying campaign they had embarked upon. In recent years, they had been tonked by such superpowers as Estonia, Latvia, Bosnia-Herzegovina and the Faroe Islands. Luxembourg's finest hour of modern times occurred in November 2002, when they managed a nil-all draw with the Cape Verde Islands, which I wasn't sure had eleven people living on them, and may have had to make up the numbers with potted palms and the governor's dog.

Despite the fact that victory over Russia looked, on paper, as likely as the stadium levitating, there were not only a few thousand in the stands, but a devoted cheer squad of forty or fifty behind one of the goals. According to the banner they'd hung along the fence, they were the M-Block Ultras, and according to all appearances they were completely crazy. The motivation of the coachloads of Russian fans was equally difficult to fathom. Why would anyone drive so far to watch what was going to be either the sporting equivalent of a seal-clubbing expedition, or your country's most humiliating reverse since losing an entire fleet to the Japanese in 1905?

Luxembourg did rather better than I – and, I suspect, they – expected. Russia had given their best players the night off, and Luxembourg initially looked like they were going to make Russia regret it. Luxembourg didn't resort to the usual defensive tactics of out-gunned football teams – hoofing the ball into the car park every time they gained possession, reacting to every touch from an opponent like they'd been shot in the kneecap – and at half-time it was 0–0, and I reckoned Luxembourg had had the best of it. The M-Block Ultras agreed, spending the break capering delightedly to a symphony of air horns.

The Ultras were silenced ten minutes into the second half when Dmitri Sychev scored for Russia. There was a sense of a dam bursting. Andrei Arshavin banged in a second, and Sychev scored again. Luxembourg did win a corner, and suppressed what must have been an overwhelming urge to embark on a victory lap. In the melee that followed, a scuffed shot headed goalward, only to be cleared off the line by a Russian defender. Judging by the thunderclap of air horns from behind the goal, the M-Block Ultras thought this worth half a goal, at least.

With a few minutes left, Sychev completed his hat-trick, and the M-Block Ultras began furling their flags. The horns were heard just once more, when Luxembourg's shaven-headed number nine found himself unmarked, on the receiving end of a decent cross, two metres from goal. It was a chance that most blindfolded drunks with one foot in a dustbin would have put away, but the number nine contrived to miss it. It was a fitting end to a poor night for the hapless forward. The more I'd seen of him, the more I'd suspected that his presence on the pitch might have had something to do with the half-time raffle at the previous match. Still, for a country as small as Luxembourg, getting spanked 4–0 by Russia was no disgrace. Getting spanked 4–0 by Liechtenstein was a disgrace, however – and that's exactly what happened to Luxembourg a couple of nights after I left.

Luxembourg was self-effacing, quietly industrious, inoffensive and almost painfully reasonable, and I returned to London with exactly zero desire to ever go there again. Once home, I packed to travel for the fourth time to a place that was Luxembourg's opposite in almost every respect. The peaceful, prosperous, free and civilised world is a nice place to live. But I wouldn't want to visit it.

16

WEST BANK, PALESTINE
DECEMBER 2004–JANUARY 2005

Yasser Arafat had been dead forty days, but nobody looked ready to let him go. Thousands had come to the Muqataa – the battered beige fortress in which he'd spent his last years, besieged by the Israeli army – to mark the end of the official period of mourning. A modest, glass-walled mausoleum had been erected on the spot where he'd been buried the day of his unruly funeral. The grave was covered in flowers and posters of the late chairman of the PLO and president of the Palestinian National Authority, and guarded by soldiers sporting Palestinian flag sashes over their khaki. A sombre, smartly dressed crowd shuffled around it. The people I followed out of the Muqataa courtyard and into the carport-like structure over Arafat's tomb were either unusually bereft at Arafat's passing – or averse to joining him, wherever he'd gone. Outside, mourners amid the mob were venting their bereavement through the idiotic means, aggravatingly common throughout the Islamic world, of firing clips of bullets skywards, playing Russian roulette with gravity – the ultimate test, perhaps, of the goodness of God's will. Any that came down among the crowd outside could well have necessitated another memorial service for anyone they happened to hit on the head.

My attendance at Arafat's lively wake had begun the same way as my previous visit to Ramallah, nearly four years earlier – with a call from Jerusalem to Nick Rowe, the Australian-born ballet dancer resident in Ramallah. From my room in the audaciously named Jerusalem Hotel, a short walk from the Old City's Damascus Gate,

I asked Nick if the drill was the same – the minibus from Jerusalem, that ridiculous detour around the Israeli checkpoint.

'No, it's much worse now,' said Nick. 'The Israelis have built a huge checkpoint at Qalandia. The bus will take you to that, then you'll have to walk through and get a taxi.'

Qalandia was, as Nick had promised, a huge Israeli checkpoint. No vehicles could pass through, meaning that passengers had to dismount and walk around the checkpoint – nobody cared who was going to Ramallah. Those leaving Ramallah to head into Israel queued to have their belongings searched by Israeli soldiers. I walked across and found a cab.

I was planning to spend a month in the Occupied Territories. I wanted to figure out why this conflict, of all early twenty-first century conflicts, transfixed so many outside observers – and why so many of those outside observers adopted such obdurately doctrinaire positions. There was something about this particular squabble that turned otherwise reasonable people into the conversational equivalent of loaded mousetraps.

On the flight to Tel Aviv, I'd reviewed my opinions. I believed that Israel had a right to exist, although I'd have preferred that it did its existing within its 1967 borders. I believed that Israelis – and, self-interestedly, people visiting Israel – were entitled to ride on buses, and sit in cafes, without feeling an icy clutch upon their innards every time someone pitched up wearing an unseasonably heavy coat. I believed that Israel had every right to defend itself from bombers willing to destroy themselves, and anyone in the vicinity, on the promise of the eternal – although, surely, eventually tiresomely maladroit – services of seventy-two virgins.

But I also knew my checked-in luggage contained a flak jacket, and I knew I hadn't packed it because I was scared of the Palestinians.

Ramallah was much as I remembered it, chaotic but agreeable, distinguished by the hyperactive courtesy of the locals. A taxi driver, noticing me polishing my glasses on my shirt, pulled over and fussed in his glove compartment for a handkerchief, which he insisted I kept. Cafe owners brought complimentary coffee after I'd polished off my falafels. Even the guy on the main street, selling pendants with portraits of Arafat, Osama bin-Laden and the late Hamas figurehead Sheikh Yassin, offered me a discount.

Nick had got married since I'd last visited. He and his Palestinian wife, Maysoun, were expecting their first child, and Nick was completing his PhD thesis on the evolution of dance in traumatised communities. He still believed that art could communicate suffering to an indifferent world, and transport the wretched beyond their pain. He worked with theatre and musical groups, and was making a film, a Palestinian *Lord of the Flies*, with a cast of kids from Ramallah's Arab Evangelical Christian School. The parallel with Golding's novel was appreciable – since the present intifada had started, Ramallah had been isolated partly or totally by Israeli barricades, incursions and curfews. Nick drove me to the home of Iyad and Tina Rafidi – the Evangelical School's headmaster and English teacher respectively. I wanted them to tell me how claustrophobic Ramallah's situation really was.

'My son Ziad is ten,' said Tina. 'He's never been to Jerusalem or Bethlehem. Yazan, who is five, thinks that if we went to Jericho, we'd have to go in an aeroplane.' It was like meeting Londoners who lived in Walthamstow and were banned from the West End, Chelsea and Greenwich.

In March 2002, when Israeli forces stormed Ramallah, the Rafidis' world temporarily became even smaller. They were trapped inside their house for three weeks, listening to bullets hitting their walls as the Israelis battered Arafat's nearby redoubt. 'Then the Israelis raided us,' said Iyad. The soldiers used Iyad as a human shield, forcing him at gunpoint into each of his rooms first, lest they contain booby traps or gunmen. 'But they didn't kill me,' said Iyad. 'And they didn't beat me. So my children didn't have to see that – and a lot of Palestinian children *have* had to see that. Ramallah is luxurious, really, compared to other cities.'

Iyad was being sarcastic, to say nothing of supernaturally philosophical about the gratutious damage to his home and terrorising of his family. But a lot of the time, it was hard to believe that Ramallah was all that bad. There was no shortage of anything. There was plenty of fun to be had – Ramallah boasted at least two world-class restaurants, any number of excellent cafes, and some surprisingly rocking bars. I was sure life was hard for poor people, but that's always a lousy way of taking the measure of a place – life sucks for poor people anywhere. There was even a tourist trade – a couple of shops sold Palestinian flag scarves, Yasser Arafat friendship bracelets, and representations of Handala, a widely beloved Palestinian cartoon character. Handala, a creation of the brave and brilliant Palestinian artist Naji al-Ali – shot dead in London in 1987, by persons still unknown – was a barefoot, raggedy-trousered ten-year-old boy, always drawn in rear view, the legend being that he wouldn't turn around or grow up until his people went home.

The reminders that Ramallah wasn't just another bustling, cheerful Arab metropolis, like Marrakech or Amman, were all the more jarring for their incongruity. One afternoon, my contemplation of embroidered cushion covers was interrupted by boots crashing on the street outside, interspersed with shouts of 'Allah Akbar!' From the shop doorway, I beheld a parade of a dozen men in black and khaki jumpsuits and balaclavas, green bandanas wrapped around their heads, green capes draped over their shoulders, armed with rifles and truncheons. I asked the shopkeeper what gave.

'Hamas,' he said.

Nobody else paid them any attention. They were, I guessed, the local equivalent of Hare Krishnas.

Just when a visitor could almost find themselves starting to wonder what so many of these people were so angry about, the Israelis could be relied upon to provide a jolt of perspective – literally so, in my case. Leaving Ramallah one night, I'd negotiated the Qalandia checkpoint and was looking for a ride back to Jerusalem. I'd found the right minibus, and was climbing aboard when I felt a sharp shove in my right side. It was a hefty, painful whack even by the standards of Arab queueing, and I reacted instinctively, asking the blundering shape in the dark, as I turned around, what the fuck it thought it was doing.

I found myself facing an Israeli soldier. He looked at me, startled, but decided I wasn't his problem. He peered into the minibus for a few seconds, took a couple of steps backward and yelled at three Palestinian guys standing by the front passenger door. They yelled back. The soldier seized one of them by the throat and pinned him to the bus, which shut him up, but inspired his two friends to yell even louder. The soldier released his grip, and raised his rifle. He cocked it theatrically, with an emphatic click-clack, and jabbed the barrel towards the faces of the three men, all the while screaming hoarsely. For a few seconds that felt like an hour, I thought I was about to witness something hideous, or at any rate something more hideous than armed intimidation of unarmed civilians. As forcefully as I dared, I asked the soldier what his trouble was. He ignored me, and continued yelling at the three Palestinians, who continued yelling at him, more loudly than I would at someone pointing a gun between my eyes. Other Palestinians, who'd already been sitting on the bus, dismounted in silence, and wandered off in search of alternative transport.

After more yelling and gun-waving, the Israeli soldier, believing his point made or unmakeable, thundered back towards his base through the Palestinian vehicles parked outside Qalandia. He kicked the door of a yellow Mercedes taxi, hard enough to leave a dent, and yelled at the driver, who responded with the universally recognised facial expression for 'Huh?'. The soldier stopped at another minibus, yanked open the driver's door, hauled a man roughly out of the vehicle and yelled at him, before shoving him back against the minibus with a metallic thud. He then stalked off into the night, yelling and jabbing his gun.

I'm not very good with violence, or the threat of it. Trivial though this incident was in the local context – any Palestinian who read this would wonder why I even bothered to record it – it made me angry, sad, almost overwhelmingly nauseous. I couldn't imagine how I'd react to having someone barge into my own country and kick in my own door and force me, with a gun in my back, to search my own home, to a soundtrack of the cries of my own children. I found another minibus, and rode back to Jerusalem, shaking slightly. I tried to see it from the soldier's point of view. A charitable assessment might conclude that he was a frightened young man, his nerves frayed by having to do a dangerous job in hostile territory. A less sympathetic view – one to which, as I lifted my shirt and noticed the purple, rifle-butt-shaped welt on my ribcage, I was inclined to subscribe – might have held that he was an arrogant, bullying prick who should mind his fucking manners.

Of all the annoying aspects of the Arab–Israeli conflict, the most enraging was that every party to it knew how it was going to end, if it ever was. Israel would withdraw to its 1967 borders, other than the defensively important Golan Heights – if the Syrians didn't like that, well, they should have fought harder. Israel's West Bank settlements would have to go, unless the settlers were happy to pay the taxes, and obey the laws, of the state of Palestine, which would exist in the West Bank and Gaza – and which would make its capital in East Jerusalem.

Canvassing the views of Palestinians in the Arab Quarter of Jerusalem's Old City was only as difficult as ambling past any souvenir shop. The intifada had been slow death for these businesses. It would be an exaggeration to say that Zaim, the sixteen-year-old proprietor of Al-Rahman Souvenirs on Al-Wad Street, actually bundled me into his premises, but it would be true to say that I've seen less aggressive methods employed by London club bouncers ejecting disorderly drunks.

Zaim sold keffiyeh scarves, kitschy pictures of the Dome of the Rock, and tatty trinkets aimed at Christian and Jewish customers, including ceramic wall-hangings reading SHALOM, Y'ALL!.

'We have no problem with nice people who come here,' explained Zaim. 'Muslims, Christians or Jews. The trouble is, nobody's coming here. For five years, since intifada started, nobody comes here.'

I told Zaim about my visit in 2000, to write that *Sunday Times* travel feature, which had been as well-timed as, say, standing on the steps of Rome's Forum in AD78 to announce your belief that Pompeii would be next year's happening destination.

'The year 2000,' whispered Zaim wistfully. 'If every year since had been like 2000, man, I'd be a millionaire.'

We were joined by Zaim's friend, a twenty-year-old called Ahmed. Ahmed wanted to study engineering, preferably in Europe. He asked me many questions, few of them bearing much relevance to their predecessor. It was a like having three conversations at once. He asked how he could get a visa to study in the UK, whether James Bond was a real person, and whether or not I was aware that suicide bombings against Israelis were, in fact, the work of Israel's own government. I'd spent a lot of time in the Middle East since I first backpacked around the region in 1993, so I was better at dealing with this kind of thing than I once was. Back then, when ludicrous conspiracies intruded on otherwise pleasant conversations, with the congruity of the Loch Ness monster emerging from one's cornflakes, I used to sneeze coffee all over my shirt. Now, I just nodded.

'The Jews,' elaborated Ahmed, 'do not want peace. So they create this image of war.'

The difficulty with this theory, I suggested, was that there was rarely a shortage of Palestinians willing to take the rap for this Zionist subterfuge. Many of them, indeed, seemed quite keen to sing to it.

'Yes,' conceded Ahmed. 'That is true. Well, maybe not all the bombings are by Israel.'

The shopkeepers of the Arab Quarter could perhaps have revitalised their fortunes by offering, to busy or budget-conscious people without time or money to travel widely in the Middle East, a convenient sample of the fathomless depths of paranoia, resentment and overwhelming charm possessed by the region's people. I pulled up in front of the perfume stall of Yousef al-Khattab when I noticed the signs plastered on the front. These looked an unlikely sales pitch: THE UNITED STATES CONGRESS IS AN OCCUPIED JEWISH TERRITORY; DOES FREEDOM OF SPEECH JUSTIFY JEWISH OCCUPATION OF ARAB LANDS?; IF YOU BELIEVE THE LIES YOUR JEWISH ENTITY-CERTIFIED GUIDE IS TELLING YOU, THEN I HAVE A BRIDGE IN BROOKLYN AND OCEANFRONT PROPERTY IN LAS VEGAS TO SELL YOU; and, below a warning that US DOLLARS ARE NOT WELCOMED HERE, the words HAPPY SEPTEMBER 11.

In a city whose economy, such as it was, depended largely on tourists, many of whom were American and/or Jewish, it couldn't have been good for trade.

'I get the finger a lot,' admitted Yousef. 'And the Jewish police pull the signs down. But I put them back up.'

Yousef, I couldn't help noticing, had an American accent. If I was guessing, I'd have said New York.

'That's right,' he grinned, and told me his bizarre life story. Yousef was born and raised Josef Cohen, an ultra-orthodox New York Jew. He and his family made Aliyah – Hebrew for migrating to Israel – in 1998, acquiring Israeli citizenship, and lived on Jewish settlements in Gaza. After discussing matters theological with Arabs over the internet, the zealous Jewish pilgrim had a rethink, and converted to Islam in 2000. Clearly a man who believed that if something was worth doing, it was worth doing to extremes, Cohen now went by the name al-Khattab, had a beard like a black hedge, two wives (his first, a Moroccan Jew, converted with him, his second was a Palestinian Muslim), and a spectacular grudge against the people from whom he was descended.

The Israelis, I ventured, must love him.

'Not exactly,' he said, and showed me his Israeli identity card. He'd sat for the photo wearing a red keffiyeh and a scowl.

'I chose the outfit,' he explained unnecessarily, 'to piss them off.'

Talking to Yousef was a disorienting experience, a bit like flicking channels between a whimsical sitcom – on the assumption that Yousef won't read this, I'll say *Seinfeld* – and an al-Qaeda propaganda broadcast. Just when I thought we'd located common ground in a shared love of satirical newspaper the *Onion*, he said, 'But I've stopped reading it, because they were mocking the prophets, especially brother Jesus, and I think that kind of crosses a line.' As I warmed to the fact that he tempered his holy fervour with wry humour – he broke off our chat at one point to pray, saying, 'It's an extra credit prayer, this, but it won't take long' – he trotted out opinions which, to borrow his phrase, kind of crossed a line.

'Hitler did some terrible things,' he said, unprompted, 'but he understood the Jews. Read *Mein Kampf*. I had a picture of him on my website, with a caption saying "Why not focus on the good things he did?".'

Yousef found this funnier than I did. When he stopped chuckling, he said, sadly, 'But my website is down again. It is always being hacked.'

I didn't need to ask who Yousef held responsible for this. Yousef thought the Jews ran everything. So avid was his belief in Jewish control over banks, the media, America and even the imminent Palestinian elections, that his decision to abandon his people seemed weirder the longer he raved. Why walk out on a winning side?

Yousef laughed at the question, but didn't answer. He was a severe case, certainly, but as such a stark illustration of the distance, geographical and philosophical, which some people – actually, as you scanned any given newspaper on any given day of the early twenty-first century, quite a lot of people – would travel in order to have something to be righteously upset about.

I found a translator in Ramallah, who I'll call Rana. She was excellent company, smart and sarcastic, though vexed by my failure to unequiv-ocally embrace the idea that nothing that was wrong with Palestine was the fault of Palestinians. Rana had grown up in Canada, and had an outsider's overcompensating ardour. She also had a Canadian passport, which meant she could cross the Israeli checkpoints most Palestinians couldn't. On Christmas Day, she met me in Jerusalem, and we took a taxi to Hebron. It wasn't the most obvious Christmas des-tination in the neighbourhood, but I figured that Bethlehem would be heaving, and besides which, Hebron seemed somehow more appropriate. The guy whose birth people were celebrating in Bethlehem had tried to sell this region on a vision of what it could be. The chap buried in Hebron – Abraham – was the one whose family had started most of the trouble that had plagued everyone here, and by extension the rest of us, ever since.

Where we got out of the taxi, Hebron was busy, noisy, even jolly, approximately one person in five shaking my hand and welcoming me personally. But the closer we ventured to the centre of Hebron, the quieter it became. The heart of Hebron was once a classic Arab souk, hundreds of shops huddled along concrete alleys leading to Abraham's eternal repository, the Tomb of the Patriarchs. But the market was as dead as Abraham, everything shut, and not just because it was Christmas – the shopkeepers had moved out when Jewish settlers, and the Israeli soldiers guarding them, had moved in. The settlers had asserted their claim on Hebron with a peculiar campaign of vandalism. Many of the green shutters on the abandoned Arab shops were gloatingly daubed with the Star of David. Above the alleyways, chicken wire, hung by the Palestinians before they gave up and moved out, sagged with the rocks, bricks and household rubbish that the settlers in the overhanging apartments had tossed into the streets to persuade the Arabs to hasten their departure.

After walking past dozens of locked green doors, Rana and I found two open shops, on opposite sides of the street, where the alley widened slightly. Both, with an optimism that verged on the psychotic, were catering for Hebron's barely existent tourist trade, selling embroidered dresses and purses, and keffiyehs. I asked one of the shopkeepers how business was.

'Terrible,' was his unsurprising answer.

Before the intifada started, he recalled, the market was profitable and friendly – Hebron's Jewish settlers used to shop there, as did Jewish pilgrims walking through to Abraham's tomb. Now, he had days when he didn't meet a single customer.

'I make enough to get by,' he shrugged, 'but only just.'

Rana and I emerged from the shop to find a six-man Israeli patrol picking its way up the street. The soldiers swept their rifles back and forth, up and down, then gathered in a corner. They conferred quietly, cocked their weapons loudly, and took up positions covering the stretch of alleyway. One soldier scampered across the road and withdrew behind a pillar a few feet from where I was standing. I bade him good morning, and asked if there was a problem.

'No,' he said. 'Go ahead.'

He shouldered his rifle and pointed it along the street down which we intended to walk. I explained that his unit's posture was not filling me with confidence.

'Just routine,' he said. 'Don't worry. Say, where are you from?'

Australia, I told him.

'Man,' he said, without lowering his gun, 'I'd love to go there.'

I looked at Rana. She shrugged. We set off. The soldiers followed us, walking then crouching then walking, always keeping their rifles raised.

'This is ridiculous,' observed Rana, correctly.

We stopped. So did the soldiers. I told the one who seemed to be in charge that he was spoiling our walk.

'You're spoiling our patrol,' he grinned.

We decided to leave them to it, and headed back the other way.

'Just once,' said Rana, 'I'd like to ask one of these guys what the hell he thinks he's doing, stalking around my country pointing guns at people.'

We walked out of the empty market to the area of Hebron that was now a Jewish settler enclave, demarcated by barbed wire, barricades and checkpoints.

'The nerve of these people,' continued Rana. 'The nerve. Just once, I'd like one of them to explain to me what they think they're doing.'

On the other side of an abandoned Arab petrol station which was now a Jewish settler's chicken run, a sandbagged sentry post was manned by a lone Israeli soldier. He looked, I dared Rana, friendly enough.

'Where are you from?' Rana asked him. A common complaint among Palestinians was that the soldiers who demanded their documents often did so in accents that suggested they weren't long off the plane from Azerbaijan or Ethiopia.

'Near Tel Aviv,' replied the soldier. He was an annoyingly handsome sort, who could have stepped out of David Rubinger's iconic photo of IDF soldiers gazing at the newly seized Western Wall in Jerusalem in June 1967.

'Where are you really from?' pressed Rana.

'I'm really from near Tel Aviv,' he smiled. 'My mother is from Haifa, my father is from Mexico.'

'What are you doing here?' asked Rana, forcefully. It was a brusquer approach than I usually took with men equipped with guns and the power of arrest, but the soldier just shrugged. 'I don't really think I should be here,' he said. 'I don't think the IDF should be occupying the Territories.'

It wasn't the answer Rana was expecting.

'I'm kind of a left-wing radical,' he elaborated.

Rana was incredulous. 'You're a left-wing radical?' she asked.

'Yeah,' he said. 'Not just in terms of here, but internationally.'

'But,' said Rana, 'you're occupying my country. That doesn't sound very left-wing to me.'

A fair point, I thought.

'You could refuse,' Rana suggested.

And another. There was an Israeli organisation, Yesh Gvul, which represented Israeli conscripts who declined to serve on Palestinian territory.

'I've thought about that,' he said. 'But it's difficult. There's the man, then there's the country, and I have a responsibility. And if I'm not here, someone else has to be, and I don't want to feel like I'm responsible for that guy.'

I asked the soldier if Hebron was dangerous.

'Kind of,' he said. 'Hamas are big here, and they have a very sophisticated set-up. It's not as bad as Gaza – that's a death trap, for Israelis *and* Palestinians. But Hebron is worse than the north – up there, you know who and where and why Hezbollah are.'

'You shouldn't be here,' said Rana.

'Look,' said the soldier, discerning that Rana's wish that he was elsewhere was not born of sympathy, 'you think this is my idea of fun? There's 3000 of us here, guarding 700 crazy people who think God told them to come to a city where nobody wants them. I've seen friends killed, friends hurt. I'm nineteen years old. Do you think I wouldn't rather be chasing girls in Tel Aviv nightclubs?'

He nodded down the road, up which a couple of his comrades were coming to join him. 'Anyway,' he said, 'we do talk a lot among ourselves, but we don't agree about everything. So I think you guys should be on your way. Nice to meet you both. Good luck.'

Rana and I wandered off. It wasn't the conversation she'd been expecting. The flutter of optimism that briefly tickled me didn't last. A couple of middle-aged Palestinian women smiled as we crossed their path. Rana struck up conversation.

'They said,' Rana translated, 'that when they go shopping, the settlers throw rocks at them.'

The settlers. It was difficult, reading coverage of the Middle East, to avoid the conclusion that they were, by and large, a sack of belligerent, obstinate fruitcakes. Any theoretical parallel for their behaviour quickly collapsed beneath the weight of its own preposterousness. If the East Timorese, having won independence, started encouraging their people to build homes in West Timor, we'd suspect LSD in the water supply. If Kosovo, when independence came, announced an intention to help itself to choice hilltops in Serbia, the international community would suggest, forcibly, that they pull their heads in. It seemed a no-brainer. The Israelis had a homeland. Why didn't these Israelis live in it?

I spent an afternoon in Efrat, a settlement south of Jerusalem. I'd got in touch with one of Efrat's 7500 residents, a young man I'll call Brian, after reading a defence of himself and his kind that he'd posted on a website. Brian was from London. He'd made aliyah four years previously. After first making his home in Jerusalem, he'd moved to Efrat with his Israeli wife.

'I'm sort of a logical Zionist,' he said, over an excellent hamburger at an Efrat fast-food concern. 'So I had some ideological reasons for coming here, but it is, really, mostly about quality of life.'

When we reached the street where he lived, I could see what he meant. It was quiet, and orderly – basically, as Brian said, 'Ramsay Street in Judea.' The view from his lounge room was fabulous, the hills of the West Bank like a scrunched-up desert-coloured rug, with Jerusalem glinting on the horizon. The apartment was huge.

'And cheap,' admitted Brian, 'and safe. I got my windows broken by suicide bombings twice in Jerusalem.'

Efrat was protected from such attacks by a checkpoint at its entrance. Residents took turns staffing the post, or bought themselves out of duty by contributing to its upkeep. I asked Brian what would have happened if I'd strolled up unaccompanied.

'You'd have been let in,' he said, 'if the guard was awake.'

And if I was of duskier appearance?

'You'd be stopped,' he said guiltily. 'They'd ask what you were doing.'

And if I happened to be Palestinian and I replied that it was my country and I'd go where I damn well pleased in it?

'I know it sounds bad,' he said, 'but you'd be seen as a security threat. Terrorists don't have "I am a terrorist" tattooed on their fore-heads.'

Efrat was, Brian stressed, not a neighbourhood of fanatics. Most people, he said, weren't serious Yahweh-pesterers, and most people didn't own guns – and most of the ones who did, noted Brian, were Americans. None of which altered the fact that they'd built their suburban idyll on someone else's land.

'Efrat is new,' protested Brian. 'It was founded in 1982. There were never Palestinians living here. I'd feel incredibly uncomfortable if that had been the case.'

I asked how he felt about settlers who had no such qualms – the ones in Hebron, for example.

'If they weren't there,' he said, 'then the IDF wouldn't be there, and then I don't think any Jews would be able to go there. So I support them for that reason.' He sighed. 'Look,' he said, 'I'd like to be able to walk the streets of Ramallah. I'd like to go shopping in Gaza. I go shopping in the Old City of Jerusalem, in the Arab Quarter, not in a here-we-are-this-is-ours way, but to show that it's normal, or that it should be.'

But weren't the settlers part of what was making the place un-normal? By which I meant, I guessed, that Belgians were able to spend weekends in Amsterdam whenever they liked, but it mightn't be the case if Belgians were squatting on spare bits of the Netherlands – to say nothing of sending Belgian troops to protect their settlements, and building roads to them that the Dutch weren't allowed use.

'I recognise,' he said, 'that I live outside the state of Israel. But there was never a place called Palestine. There's this idea that we invaded a sovereign state called Palestine.'

The problem, I thought, was that rightly or wrongly, that's exactly how it was perceived by the people who now regarded themselves as Palestinians.

'I know,' he said. 'And I'm not averse to a Palestinian state. Not because they're historically entitled, but because it seems the most realistic chance for peace.'

There, then, was the question. Would he live in a town inside a Palestinian state? Would he show his Israeli passport to Palestinian customs guards to get home?

'If –' began Brian, then stopped. He considered the view from his window. Brian's love of the land was palpable, but tainted with the torment of infidelity. 'If we're talking about peace,' he decided, 'and I mean peace, not armistice or ceasefire, yes, I'd be fine with that. Though a lot of people here might not be.'

I joined him at the window. I noticed a half-built house in the foreground, another home for people who already had a home, going up on the land of a people who didn't. The builders appeared to be Palestinian.

'They are Palestinian,' said Brian. 'When I walk past, they wave and say they're building it for their children. They say they're coming home one day.'

In the meantime, the Palestinians waited.

I still didn't understand the settlers. Brian was a decent guy, who had no desire to oppress anybody. But he had two perfectly pleasant homelands already – Britain and Israel. In a world full of people damned to just one dismal, frightening swamp of a place, some of whom were hardly a million miles from Efrat, pitching camp on a third country seemed greedy. That said, I didn't understand the settlers' opposite numbers, either – those Palestinians who still, two and three generations since 1948, called themselves refugees. But I tried.

Rana took me to the Dheisheh refugee camp near Bethlehem. I was surprised we got that far. At the Israeli checkpoint on the outskirts of Bethlehem, Rana bridled at the sign the Israelis had put up, reading HAPPY HOLIDAYS & HAPPY NEW YEAR.

'Honestly,' she said. 'The nerve . . .'

As we queued to present our passports, I reminded her that I didn't want to spend the day being interrogated. She didn't listen.

'Hey,' she said to the conscript scrutinising our documents. 'Would you let Jesus through?'

The soldier ignored her.

'Seriously,' she continued, 'what would Jesus think of what you were doing here?'

If he was paying attention to this particular checkpoint, I hoped Jesus would remind the soldier pretty vigorously of the stuff about turning the other cheek.

'Really,' said Rana, 'do you think Jesus would like your check-point?'

My prayers, it seemed, were being heard.

'Just go,' said the soldier.

'The *nerve*,' said Rana again as we walked through.

In Bethlehem, Rana made a call, and a car appeared. People making calls and cars appearing is a common means of travel when impersonating a foreign correspondent in the Middle East; you have to forget everything you were ever taught about accepting lifts from strangers. We stopped to pick up a sunglassed, silver-haired cove with a game-show host's grin. He told me his name, but as he also gave his occupation as 'retired terrorist', I'd better call him something else: Mahmoud will serve as suitably generic.

The 11,000 residents of Dheisheh lived in half a square kilometre. Inside the gate, I was shown into a building which housed a cultural centre full of kids playing computer games, a craft shop, a restaurant, and . . . a guesthouse. It was an absurdity that defied simile. I had to be satisfied with the knowledge that next time I tried to express the self-defeating, self-perpetuating daftness of something, I could liken it to opening a guesthouse in a refugee camp.

Still, it was a useful conversation-starter. I wanted to know why Palestinians insisted on referring to themselves as refugees, when what they meant was that their parents, or grandparents, or great-grandparents were refugees. I wanted to understand why they revelled in this victim status. The shop, I could applaud – it was producing beautiful work that could be sold without reliance on the dubious cachet of where it came from. But encouraging people to holiday in Dheisheh's misery seemed grotesque, especially when I imagined the lemon-sucking, professionally indignant foreign fretters the hotelier must have been subjecting Dheisheh's people to, as if they hadn't suffered enough.

Mahmoud walked us upstairs to the restaurant. The stairwell's walls were covered with paintings telling Dheisheh's story. The camp was established in 1948, to house Arabs who'd fled villages around Jerusalem and Hebron during Israel's War of Independence. In the decades since, canvas had evolved to caravans to concrete. Dheisheh's people were regularly arrested, injured and killed in clashes with the Israelis. Photos of Dheisheh's young men being cuffed and blindfolded were a signature motif of the decor, along with Naji al-Ali's mournful observer Handala.

Mahmoud ordered us coffees. I asked him if he'd care to elaborate on the 'retired terrorist' thing.

'They arrested me six times,' he said. 'I didn't admit anything then. Why should I now?'

Mahmoud worked on the committee that helped run Dheisheh. 'Each house here,' he said, 'has a story about jail, martyrs, injury, sacrifice.'

I didn't doubt it. What I didn't get, I explained, was the insistence on clinging to refugee status through succeeding generations. I'd met people in refugee camps in the Balkans, Pakistan and Afghanistan. They weren't proud of where they lived. As a general rule, if they couldn't go home – which was usually actually their home, not their grandfather's – they wanted to go somewhere else. I even knew Palestinians who'd taken a pragmatic view. I mentioned a driver I'd employed in Amman who'd grown up in a West Bank

refugee camp. I'd asked him why he'd left. He'd regarded me as
if I'd announced that I was Montezuma II, last Emperor of the
Aztecs, and wished to be taken to Mount Popocatepetl, and replied,
'Because it's a terrible, dangerous place, and Amman is really
nice.'

'It's important to maintain refugee identity,' said Mahmoud, 'to
keep the issue alive.'

But at what cost, I was asking, when a friend of Mahmoud's joined
us, with a high five and a hug for him, and a handshake for me.

'Another old terrorist,' smirked Mahmoud.

'I can't imagine,' said Mahmoud's friend, 'that anyone would want
to forget about it. I'm from a village three kilometres from here, in
what is now Israel. My grandfather owned a thousand square metres.
I just want some of it back. Not all. Just enough to live. I don't want
to drive the Israelis into the sea. What's wrong with wanting our
children to live like theirs?'

Nothing, I said. I just wasn't sure how encouraging someone to see
themselves as a victim from birth would make that more likely.
Supposing, I said, my parents still considered themselves convicts –
and certain of my mother's side of the family, at least, had had little say
in their relocation to Australia – and supposing they'd raised me as a
convict. Wouldn't that seem weird?

'Aha!' whooped Mahmoud. 'Australian? You are an Israeli! The
Aborigines are the Palestinians!'

Sensing that I was unlikely to recover from that, I called for
the bill. Mahmoud and his friend refused to let me pay.

On a page in one of my notebooks, I doodled Middle Eastern peace
plans. Given the extreme unlikelihood of anything I thought being
taken seriously, I felt I had a licence to roam beyond the usual vernacular of borders, security, refugees and all the other issues which, after
a few weeks in the Holy Land, were having the same effect upon me
as a hypnotist's backwards count from ten.

These were what I came up with.

1)   The world pays China to dispatch an invasion force big enough to make the scrap interesting, but not big enough to actually win or anything, giving the Israelis and Palestinians a common enemy that neither of them had any already established grudge against.

2)   The world's unbelievers mount a new Crusade, with the aim of converting everyone in the Middle East to atheism. The trouble being that my fellow heathens are too disorganised, and too polite – nobody's baths are ever ruined by someone buzzing their doorbell and asking if they've been saved from the risible, meretricious, cretinising fraud of organised religion.

3)   A mad meteorologist, ideally attended by a bikini-clad assistant and a chimpanzee in a top hat, be commissioned to envelop the region in fire, floodwater or locusts, in order to remind Jew, Christian and Muslim of the essential triviality of human squabbles. It said much about the collective narcissism engendered by their conflict that not a single Israeli or Palestinian that I encountered initiated a conversation about the tsunami which, during my visit, washed 230,000 people into the Indian Ocean.

4)   The Palestinians get properly organised and stop being so silly, and the Israelis cease acting like jerks. This plan I immediately discounted as obviously insane.

5)   The rest of the world ignores the place, in the same way that a parent on a road trip might tune out the squabbling pre-teens in the back seat in the hope that they'll shut up if nobody's paying attention. It wasn't like anyone here had any oil.

6)   The Palestinians hold elections every week, thereby ensuring that the place was always full of observers, peaceniks and journalists, thereby ensuring all parties played nicely.

The Palestinians were, in fact, holding an election the last week I was on the West Bank, and the Palestinians to whom I'd mentioned this last plan quite liked it. The Israelis had scaled down their patrols and backed off at their checkpoints, and every hotel and restaurant in Ramallah was stuffed to the gunwales. I was agreeing on the brilliance of this scheme with a hotel receptionist when I felt an urgent tug on my sleeve. It was Rana.

'For the love of God,' she said, 'go now. It's too late for me, but save yourself.'

When I'd hired Rana, she'd told me she'd be unable to work a couple of days on my schedule, as she was required to accompany a bus tour of the West Bank by something called the Women's International Peace Movement. My heart broke a little at the thought of the acronym that would have transpired had they called themselves the Women's International Movement for Peace. I'd asked if I could tag along, and Rana had agreed. That day had dawned, but I sensed from Rana's expression, which had something of Brando as Kurtz about it, that the previous evening's meet-and-greet had not gone swimmingly.

'Oh, they're wonderful,' she grimaced.

The aim of the bus tour, as I understood it, was to support the women of Palestine during the election, and promote democracy. It had been sponsored by Suzanne Mubarak, wife of noted feminist and democrat President Hosni Mubarak of Egypt. The delegates included: Gertrude Mongella, president of the African Union parliament; Anne-Marie Lizin, president of the Belgian Senate; Flora MacDonald, former Canadian foreign minister; Ruth-Gaby Vermot, a Swiss MP; James 'Chip' Carter, son of former US president Jimmy Carter, who was also on the West Bank for the election; and Lauren Booth, journalist and sister-in-law of Tony Blair. With the exceptions of Lauren and Rana, every single person on the bus had a demeanour of ostentatious seriousness; indeed, I was prepared to believe that a couple of them had never found anything amusing.

The minibus was equipped with a microphone. I sensed that the chances of it being used for a rowdy singalong of 'The Irish Rover' were slender, and in this suspicion I was proved correct. The delegates took turns to make impassioned speeches outlining their immense regard for each other, and reiterating the opinions which they knew every other delegate already agreed with.

'This,' said one of them, 'is the first mission of its type ever undertaken. This is very important.'

I did a poor job of disguising a snigger as a cough. Rana's heel made abrupt contact with my instep.

'If I lived here,' declared President Carter's son at the end of a litany of Israeli calumny, 'I'd probably be in Hamas.'

This sounded like a monstrously stupid thing to say – why endorse Hamas, as opposed to one of the reasonable Palestinian democrats? – but then I figured that if I'd lived in America while his dad had been president, I'd probably be in the Republican Party, the National Rifle Association and the Branch Davidians, so maybe he had a point.

Our first stop was in Qalqilya. Geographically, Qalqilya was the apex of Israeli paranoia, the westernmost promontory of the hostile Arab continent that surrounded Israel – Qalqilya's city limits were just 12 kilometres from the Mediterranean. The Israelis had all but sealed off the town. The security 'fence' – which, here, was soaring concrete slabs punctuated by watchtowers – encircled Qalqilya. The only road in and out was at the mercy of a gate operated by the Israelis. On one order, Qalqilya and its people could be utterly confined.

We stopped by a stretch of fence built through what had been a marketplace. The concrete was slathered with graffiti – Palestinian flags, brisk suggestions that the Israelis should give some thought to taking it down. It was depressing, as barriers between people are. It was also, I thought, the greatest gift the Israelis could have given the Palestinians. This wall would not have long withstood the international outrage if Palestine's militant groups foreswore terrorism against Israel's people and, instead, every day sent one of their volunteers for death to the wall to make a short speech in favour of freedom before flicking their switch and adding themselves, and only themselves, to the decorations already daubed upon it. It would be gruesome, certainly, but it might shore up Hamas's somewhat unmade case that they were more interested in building a nation than killing Jews.

We descended upon Qalqilya's governor, Mustafa Almalki. Pinned behind his desk by a phalanx falling over each other to agree with him even more vehemently than he agreed with himself, he had the look of a movie star whose security detail had deserted as the autograph-hunting mob broached the velvet rope. As his staff served coffee, he tried to make his points – that 600 shops in Qalqilya had closed since the wall went up, that the Israelis had confiscated a bunch of land and twenty wells in erecting it, that more and more Qalqilyans were giving up and leaving, that his town was being choked to death – but had to yell to be heard over people agreeing with him. So he started barking the usual boilerplate, threatening a war against Israel lasting a century, and so on, which calmed everybody down.

Gertrude Mongella loudly insisted on observing correct protocol. 'Correct protocol' apparently necessitated her making a long, soporific speech. 'As leader of this delegation,' she intoned, 'I have a responsibility to brief you on our mission.' Governor Almalki now wore the expression of a man who wished that his first act upon assuming office had been to install a trapdoor in his office floor. President Mongella ploughed into an excruciating oration extolling solidarity with Palestinian women – we were yet to meet one – and complaining that, in a global perspective, women were left out of the decision-making process. On today's example, it was no wonder. With the rest of the delegation nodding solemnly, and your correspondent and Governor Almalki's staff nodding off, President Mongella embarked on what felt like a complete history of the African continent from the dawn of time to that very afternoon, stressing that everything that was wrong with the place was the fault of somebody other than Africans. 'Africa,' she concluded, 'is totally committed to the Palestinian cause.' It was nice to know that Africa's otherwise chronically querulous, fractious, tribal and sectarian peoples agreed about something.

A question-and-answer session was proposed. An argument developed over whether it was proper to do this before absolutely everyone in the delegation had introduced themselves – introduced themselves, that was, to their fellow junketeers, who already knew them, and to the Palestinians present, who I was reasonably certain couldn't have cared less. As a sideshow, one of the delegation started on Governor

Almalki about how few women worked for him. Eventually, Flora MacDonald, the former Canadian foreign minister, rose majestically above the quacking rabble.

'I have seen,' she wittered, 'as I have travelled, that where peace has been achieved, women have been involved.'

Behind her, the sisterhood appeared on the verge of coming to blows. Governor Almalki did his best, honouring women as sisters of fighters, mothers of martyrs, Rocks of Gibraltar, Charges of the Light Brigade, and so forth. Jimmy Carter's kid picked that moment to ask if everyone agreed with him that George W. Bush was the biggest terrorist in the world. This provoked uproar – not at the fatuity of the statement, but at the fact that, as an owner of testicles, he was not officially a member of the delegation, and was therefore not permitted to ask questions, so there.

With friends like these, I muttered to Rana.

'Shut up,' she said, and kicked me again.

After several months of further indignant discussion, we adjourned to a restaurant. The food, as always in Palestinian restaurants, was tremendous. Lauren, Rana and I occupied a table as far away from everyone else as it was possible to be while remaining technically on the West Bank.

'They mean well,' said Lauren.

Back on the bus, there was singing – the standard we-shall-overcome anthems. By the roadside, stray dogs collapsed with their paws over their ears. A Palestinian chap riding with us, who had been retained as a fixer, took a turn. He announced the title in Arabic.

'It's a traditional love song,' explained Rana. 'Very beautiful song.'

He lowed in a rich baritone. He was getting into his stride when a couple of Arabic-speaking members of the delegation yelled at him to stop. The ripples of outrage that spread up the bus and back down again eventually drowned him out.

'They said the song was anti-feminist,' sighed Rana.

We passed a Bedouin encampment.

'And these,' said someone balefully, 'are people who've lost their homes.'

The Bedouin are nomads. They live in tents.

At Deir Sharaf checkpoint en route to Nablus there were queues of Palestinians, despite Israel's promises to open it for the election. There'd been a confrontation the night before between an IDF unit and the local Al-Aqsa Martyrs' Brigades, leaving one Israeli soldier dead and three injured, and the Israelis' enthusiasm for Palestinian freedom of movement had dwindled. Palestinians stood in lines of dozens, corralled beneath a tin-roofed construction glared over by a watchtower.

'Tch,' said someone on the bus, 'it's just like Nazi Germany.'

There was general agreement. I fought the temptation to jab someone in the ear with my pen and loudly remind all present that, unpleasant though this was, it wasn't anything like Nazi Germany, and nor would it be until the Israelis started doing to the Palestinians what at least one of the countries sending guns and money to the Palestinians' alleged allies had threatened to do to Israel. Anyone who makes this fatheaded comparison contributes nothing useful to the discussion, and implicitly asserts that the gas chambers were an incidental detail of Nazi rule. I banged my head slowly against the back of the chair in front.

In Nablus, everyone gathered in a room and made speeches at each other. After a couple of hours of this, it was decided that we had a few minutes free to go and see Nablus. We hit the market, where traders sold spices from beneath stone arches upholstered with posters of dead fighters and suicide bombers. As a slogan on a war memorial, I thought 'Never Forgive, Never Forget' was sulky, but made up in honesty what it lacked in decorum. A youth with a grenade-launcher stalked across the Old City square.

On the bus back to Ramallah, there were more speeches, mostly to do with empowerment of Palestinian women. I asked Rana, the one Palestinian woman we'd spent any significant amount of time with, if she felt empowered.

'Shut up,' she said, and kicked me again.

We passed more Israeli checkpoints on the way home, all of them less open than promised. At each one, Jimmy Carter's son called his dad from his mobile to inform him of the transgression. Eventually, he handed his phone to Rana.

'Hey,' he said. 'Can you talk to my dad?'

'Er,' said Rana. 'Hello, Mr President . . .'

While we waited at the last checkpoint, an altercation erupted alongside the bus. A middle-aged Palestinian taxi driver had incurred the displeasure of three Israeli soldiers. What the source of the dispute was I knew not, but as his open boot manifestly did not contain a crate of Kalashnikovs, there was no excuse for the behaviour of the soldiers, who yelled at him, shoved him around and brandished their guns.

'I'm not an animal,' the driver roared back at them. 'If you want to talk to me, talk to me.'

It was, by some distance, the most sense I'd heard all day. The WIPM tour was scheduled for a second instalment the following morning. I told Rana I couldn't face it.

'Quitter,' she said. 'If you turn on CNN tomorrow and see that a busload of peace activists has been destroyed by a suicide bomber, you'll know what's happened, right?'

'It just doesn't seem that complicated,' said Sani Meo. 'Israel returns to the 1967 borders, and we reach some sort of settlement about the refugees. Everything else is just a waste of time, money and life.'

Meo was the publisher of *This Week In Palestine*, an English-language what's on guide to the Occupied Territories. The January 2005 issue – despite the title, it was a monthly – contained an article on the Greek Orthodox community in the Holy Land, a few ruminations on the election, pieces on the arts, profiles of local personalities, comprehensive restaurant, cinema, theatre and music listings, as well as the reason I'd invited myself to Meo's office – a fabulously sarcastic open letter to journalists who'd descended on the West Bank for the election. He especially recommended Abu Dis: 'Trust me,' he wrote, 'when I say that you won't have to wait long to take a great shot of an old woman or a schoolboy climbing through the cracks of the monstrous wall. You might just break the heart of an old southern baptist lady from Arkansas. On the brighter side, think of the Pulitzer award.'

I asked Meo why so few Palestinians realised how thoroughly patronised they were by the outside world – by Arab governments who saw them mostly as a convenient stick with which to poke Israel, and by the western left who found them a convenient focus of self-righteous self-hatred.

'I am sick and tired of sympathy,' he muttered. 'I want something done. You know, I got a call this morning from an Israeli woman who was angry about this month's cover.'

It was a representation of Palestine, showing the West Bank and Gaza as coloured patches linked by straining threads.

'She was upset that it didn't show Israel. So I told her I was pretty upset about the occupation.'

Meo commuted to his office in Ramallah every day from his home in Jerusalem. What should have been an 8-kilometre drive each way was, thanks to closures and checkpoints, a daily round trip of more than 80 kilometres.

'There is a strategy,' he said. 'They want to subjugate, depress, and harass us, so we'll settle for anything. But I think we actually underestimate our effect on them.'

The reverse, I thought, was also true. Few Israelis or Palestinians understood how scared each was of the other.

'But our little magazine is progressing,' he said. 'It pays for itself. We're amazed, really.'

Sani had established *This Week in Palestine* six years earlier. It now employed nine people.

'We weren't supposed to be political,' he said. 'We wanted to be cultural, musical. But everything here is political.'

By way of illustrating this point, a crackle of gunfire interrupted us. It was coming from the street outside – Ramallah's main road – in the middle of a weekday afternoon. You might, I said, give thought to an editorial on gun safety.

'No,' he said. 'That's something falling down. We can distinguish these things.'

I appreciated his efforts at reassurance, but I was pretty sure it was gunfire.

'I don't think so.'

There was another volley, longer, louder and closer.

'No, you're right,' he sighed. 'That's shooting.'

We were a few floors up. We – gingerly – approached the window overlooking the street. There were a group of young men brandishing pictures of Mahmoud Abbas – who had, as everyone expected, won the presidential election, the results of which had been announced that day – and their rifles. As they shouted, and shot skywards, a couple of foreign news crews filmed them. This, I said to Sani, is where it gets difficult to sympathise. If people wandered the main drag firing an automatic weapon in the air in any reasonably civilised city, they'd get a police sniper's bullet between the eyes in seconds, and properly so. These guys weren't doing that because they were under occupation. They were doing it because they were idiots – and this was the image that Palestinians kept presenting to the world, as opposed to that of, say, urbane, witty, hard-working magazine publishers.

'Who said we were perfect?' he asked.

Lots of people, I told him. Many insisted on confusing the Palestinians' suffering with inherent nobility, and were willing to excuse them the most rudimentary standards of behaviour. Like, for example, the commonsense of not discharging weapons in public.

'Yeah,' said Sani. 'I know. People think everything we do is legitimate. Which it isn't.'

Later that night, I was walking back to the flat I was staying in, just down the hill from Ramallah's main square, where four marble lions mounted guard on a pyramid-shaped metal scaffold. At the top of the road, I encountered three young men, keffiyehs around their heads, great grins splitting their beards, portraits of Mahmoud Abbas on their T-shirts, rifles in their hands.

'Hey friend!' yelled one of them. 'Welcome in Ramallah!'

I reciprocated the hug as little as I felt I could.

'Welcome in Palestine!'

Two of his mates hoisted their guns skywards and let fly. I winced. They did it again, adding to the din of celebratory gunfire being raised by Mahmoud Abbas fans all around Ramallah. I very badly wanted to be back in the flat, or under any solid roof, but I was curious, and I'd had a few drinks. I asked if they spoke English.

'I do,' said one. 'I am Ahmed.'

Here's the thing, I said. CNN, the BBC, they're going to do maybe thirty seconds on the announcement of the election results. What do you reckon is going to be the picture? Irritated, tired, drunk, I provided my own answer: it'll be you silly bastards, I said, or someone like you, waving guns around and yelling. Did they want the world to feel relaxed about welcoming them to the family of nations, or not? Could they grasp the idea that acting peaceably might be a precursor to, you know, peace?

'My friend,' said Ahmed, 'we are just very happy.'

And he opened fire at the heavens again. Once you started fighting for your own country, it seemed, it was tough to know when to stop. And not just here.

17

MITROVICA, PRISTINA, PRIZREN AND PREKAZ, KOSOVO
OCTOBER 2004

In February 2000, Mitrovica, lodged like an impacted tooth in the top of Kosovo, had been described by the American diplomat Richard Holbrooke as 'the most dangerous city in Europe'. In the shake-out of populations that followed the 1999 war, the Ibar River, which flowed through Mitrovica, had become Kosovo's principal ethnic faultline, dividing the Serbs on the north side of the city from the Albanians on the south. Seven months before I visited, as if worried that another continental conurbation may have had designs on its title, the most dangerous city in Europe had erupted again. After three Albanian children drowned in the Ibar, in uncertain circumstances – it was claimed that they had been chased into the water by Serbs – Albanians and Serbs clashed at the bridge that crossed the river. In the ensuing violence, at least six people had been killed and dozens injured, including several foreign soldiers serving with the multinational Kosovo Force (KFOR).

I rode to Mitrovica from Pristina with a French army reservist. Lieutenant Pierre Mergerlin alternated stints of military service with stretches of freebooting travel – he'd been backpacking in Australia the previous year. He located the collection of AC/DC on the iPod he'd plugged into his Land Rover's stereo, turned the volume up, and put his foot down. After lunch at the French barracks in Mitrovica, which led me to conclude that Mergerlin's comrades had done something to grievously affront the caterers, I was taken on a tour of the town. This was only possible after baroque negotiation with the two translators the soldiers were forced to retain.

'The Serbs pretend they don't speak Albanian,' explained one officer, 'and the Albanians pretend they can't understand Serbian.'

On the Albanian side of the river, Mitrovica was alive with construction, the new buildings splashed in exuberant colours – a homage, one shopkeeper explained, to the similar exercise in surreal urban renewal being undertaken in Albania's capital Tirana. The covered market thronged with people buying bad clothes and bootleg DVDs. I talked to a bunch of young men who were blowing whistles and flapping posters pertaining to the upcoming UN-sponsored elections.

'We want independence,' said one.

What if the people across the river didn't?

'We want the Serbs to stay,' said another, gravely.

Was that what they really thought, or what they knew they were supposed to say to foreigners with notepads?

They laughed at this.

'As long as they do nothing bad again,' said the first, 'they can stay.'

After the Albanian translator peeled off, I walked across the contentious bridge with Lieutenant Mergerlin and two other French officers. Nobody else was making the crossing.

'Nobody else ever does,' said one of the soldiers, but they seemed surprisingly relaxed, given the bridge's history – none wore helmets or body armour, or carried rifles.

'The people are actually really friendly,' said Lieutenant Mergerlin.

The north side of Mitrovica was overlooked by a communist-era monument to miners, which resembled Stonehenge reimagined by Le Corbusier. The north was quieter than the south – fewer cars, fewer people, no construction. The only signs of anything other than sullen defeat were in a shop called Boutique Sasa, whose shelves heaved with defiant T-shirts and mugs commemorating Slobodan Milosevic, Radovan Karadzic and Ratko Mladic. One T-shirt featured a skull and crossbones above SERBIAN CHETNIK: WE'LL BE BACK. Postcards of Milosevic read COME BACK, WE WERE ONLY KIDDING.

'Don't take it seriously,' said the shop's young proprietor, Sinisa Radovic. 'KFOR buy most of it.'

Sinisa ('Call me Sasa') indicated his pennants and flags embroidered with the emblems of the foreign militaries serving in Mitrovica. He poured excellent homemade cherry brandy for himself, me, and the French detachment. Sasa was twenty-six, and had lived in Kosovo all his life.

'I've no future here now,' he said. 'Before 1999, I was studying economics at the university in Pristina. I used to go to Pristina every day. Now, I can't even go across the bridge.'

I asked about his family.

'Just me and my father now,' he said. 'My mother went in 1999. My sister has gone. There are no jobs here for honest people.'

I asked what was keeping him and his dad here, and had almost started inking into my notebook the usual florid rhetoric about how Kosovo was the bleeding heart of Serbia, etcetera, when Sasa pulled me up with brute economics.

'We can't sell our apartment,' he said.

Because, of course, no Serb wanted to buy property in Mitrovica . . .

'And no Albanian wants to live north of the river.'

I felt sorry for Sasa. I was sure that none of the astonishing nonsense that had convulsed his homeland in the late twentieth century was personally his fault. He was another victim of the men on the mugs and T-shirts in his shop. He was a young Serb in early twenty-first century Kosovo, and that was about as dud a hand as you could be dealt. Not only were you a loser, you were supremely unlikely to attract the consolations of sympathy.

'It was two parallel worlds.'

This was pre-war Pristina, as described by Jehona Gjurgjeala. She was twenty-five, a chronic overachiever who'd worked as a translator during the war, for various thinktanks since, and was now standing as a candidate in Kosovo's imminent elections. We were talking in one of Pristina's many agreeable bars. The local wine was surprisingly good.

'At night,' she continued, 'Albanians would go out between eight pm and eleven pm, Serbs after eleven. It certainly wasn't safe to be out after midnight.'

Many Kosovars I met likened Kosovo in the 1990s to apartheid-era South Africa.

'It was just like that,' she continued. 'My father was a manager at a power plant. He was demoted because he wouldn't take an oath of allegiance to Serbia. My mother's a doctor. She was fired for being Albanian.'

One of the many pernicious aspects of any institutionalised discrimination is that it begins to infect the outlook of the victim as well as the oppressor.

Gjurgjeala nodded. 'I remember once, when I was eighteen, two Serbs overheard me in a bar. One of them told me not to talk so loud. The other said it was okay, I was allowed to talk as much as I liked. Now, the second one was a nicer guy than the first, but the mentality is the same. But what kills me is that I said sorry.'

Gjurgjeala could, I was certain, have got a job, and made a useful and profitable life, anywhere she liked.

'I thought about that after the war,' she said. 'About what the point of it all was, whether to have fun, or try to make a difference. If I can't make a difference, then fuck it, I'll go backpacking, but I want to try here. I want to make this place somewhere I can be proud of.'

Kosovans were intensely patriotic, but they were intensely patriotic about other countries. They were intensely patriotic about Albania: the two-headed eagle flags, the statues of Skanderbeg. They were intensely patriotic about Europe, flying the EU flag more prolifically than any citizens of the EU – even the Luxembourgers. They were really intensely patriotic about America. A new Pristina hotel, the Victory, perched a replica of the Statue of Liberty on its roof. There was an Uncle Sam restaurant and a Route 66 cafe. Bookshop windows were piled with the memoirs of Hillary Clinton and Madeleine Albright, translated into Albanian. The election posters of several parties featured the American flag. A plate I bought from a souvenir shop was slipped into a red, white and blue bag emblazoned with the stars and stripes and the phrase, which may have lost something in translation,

ORIGINAL MARINES FAMILY STORE. I was told that on 12 September 2001, the American consular office in Pristina had been besieged by locals volunteering to fight whoever America decided needed fighting. I wondered if America had proceeded since then on the assumption that everyone in Afghanistan and Iraq would be as grateful for their intervention as Kosovo's (nominally Muslim) Albanians.

The most spectacular homage to Kosovo's liberators hung from an apartment building on a main road. Like many of Pristina's streets, this thoroughfare had gone by several names – most roads in the city were named after prominent historical figures, and a desire to keep Pristina's topography congruent with prevailing politics meant that many Pristinans had lived at different addresses without moving. The airport road, known once as Peter the First Street, and then as Vladimir Lenin Street, was overlooked by a banner, four storeys tall, displaying a beaming, waving ex-president, and the words WELCOME TO BILL CLINTON BOULEVARD!. Other streets were named after Senator Robert Dole, Tony Blair, Mother Teresa, Tirana and the Kosovo Liberation Army (KLA).

I'd been trying to organise meetings with former KLA members. I spoke on the phone to Adem Demaci, who'd racked up decades of prison time under Tito for criticising communism, and was later the political representative of the KLA, but he declined, explaining that he was convalescing from illness. I left messages for Hasim Thaci, the KLA commander who'd become a poster boy for the guerilla group during the 1999 war, but nothing came of it. I didn't blame Thaci: there was an election on, and as one of the leaders of the Democratic Party of Kosovo (PDK), he was a busy man. I did, however, meet the man widely regarded as the puppeteer who'd been yanking Thaci's strings all along.

When Xhavit Haliti walked into the cafe, Nino Rota's theme from *The Godfather* appeared on a loop on my internal stereo. This was partly due to Haliti's saturnine, heavy-lidded demeanour, but mostly due to what I'd been told about him. Haliti was a figure around whom much rumour swirled. It was whispered that he was the Zurich-based bagman who'd funnelled funds from the Albanian diaspora to buy guns for the KLA, that before the war he'd been an officer in Albania's notorious intelligence service, the Sigurimi, that since the war he'd mysteriously acquired much property in Pristina, including the Grand Hotel, that several people who'd inconvenienced him now had the opportunity of eternity to compose rueful ballads on their St Peter-issued harps, or the Islamic equivalent. About the only things that could be said about him with any certainty were that he had been involved at a high level with the KLA – he had been part of their dele-gation to the Rambouillet peace talks in 1999 – and was now a senior figure in the PDK, and a member of the Kosovo Assembly.

Haliti had silver hair, olive eyes, and a crocodile smile. If he wasn't a kingpin of the demimonde, he should certainly have been cast as one. I started by asking when he'd decided Kosovo needed to be fought for.

'The idea was always there,' he said, in a bass that made me reach to hold the table still. 'As early as 1985, myself and some colleagues wanted to start a guerilla movement. But there was little funding available. We decided to get properly involved militarily in '91 to '92. We began designing the political structure of the KLA in 1993. We read a lot, about Che Guevara, about the early history of Israel, and tried to see ourselves as these people.'

Haliti had no doubt about Kosovo's eventual independence. Successful revolutionaries, like successful sportsmen and successful artists, need to be able to tune out that nagging inner voice that plagues mere mortals, the one that curbs our wilder impulses by saying, 'This won't work, you idiot, you're making a bloody fool of yourself.'

'There was a period in 1999,' Haliti conceded, asked to search his memory for a low point, 'when there was a crisis. When the bombing started, and people were forced out of their homes by the Serbs, many Kosovars came to the KLA and said, "What the hell have you done?" We said we'd build them new homes. It was difficult, but I never lost faith.'

I asked if he'd been surprised when the guerilla army he'd helped conjure into being found itself in the position of having NATO, the most powerful military alliance ever forged, acting as its air force. As the realisation of crazy dreams went, that took some beating.

'I can't say I was surprised,' he mused, cracking one knuckle with a noise like a pistol shot, 'because I was involved in the process. But if we hadn't had support from NATO, we planned to continue guerilla warfare for at least twenty years.'

The more espressos we slurped, the more Haliti's attitude softened, from bored contempt to what I like to think was amused contempt. He invited me to join him and other PDK types in a restaurant later that evening. One PDK candidate at the dinner, Enver Hoxhaj, agreed to take me out for a day's campaigning. When I met Hoxhaj at the Grand Hotel on the appointed morning, it was clear he'd asked me along as much for the company as anything else. Enver's electoral apparatus was not extensive: just him and his red Mercedes. Thirty-five-year-old Enver had until recently been a lecturer at the University of Vienna – not a lifestyle that anyone would forsake lightly.

'Balkan people feel a deep connection to their land,' said Hoxhaj, his English tinged with a slight German accent. 'That's why I came back.'

As we left Pristina's brutish browns and greys for Kosovo's Irishly green countryside, I asked about his connection to this land. When Enver was born, Albania whimpered beneath the boot heel of the more-Stalinist-than-Stalin dictator Enver Hoxha. Enver Hoxhaj was surely a burdensome name to be campaigning under. Wasn't it like running for office in Romania with the name Nicolae Ceausescuj, or in Uganda as Idi Aminj?

'Well, it's a name everyone remembers,' he laughed. 'Though I get a lot of jokes. Mostly the one where people tell me they're worried that if they elect me, I'll keep the job for forty years.'

We headed south, to villages around the area where Enver was born. We passed several roadside memorials to KLA fighters. I saw dozens of these in Kosovo, ranging from black tombstones with a portrait of one fallen guerilla etched in grey, all the way to a group tombstone in the shape of an enormous black eagle, complete with wings and tailfeathers. Enver was in Vienna during the war. Like much of the Kosovar diaspora, he endured the twin horrors of watching his homeland ransacked, and being unable to contact a family he knew were caught in the chaos somewhere.

'I didn't hear from my parents for three months,' he recalled. 'They left their home and walked out of Kosovo, up through the mountains, into Albania. This is the main reason that people here want an independent Kosovo, so this kind of thing doesn't happen again. Fear plays a role in every ethnic conflict. People want to feel safe. But it's not just a reaction to discrimination, or even to genocide. It's about the desire for a better life.'

In Suhareka, we met some local PDK staff, before proceeding in what was now a slightly more impressive two-car convoy to Enver's first campaign stop. Leshan was a dumpy, muddy village – or a villagey, muddy dump – whose unsealed roads were untrafficked enough that people stopped to watch our procession. As the cars lurched from puddle to puddle, scattering chickens and dogs, I remarked to Enver that he obviously really wanted the votes of these people.

'You have to understand,' he said, 'that this is something quite new. The usual Balkan thing has always been mass rallies, expecting the people to go to the politicians. We're making an effort to go out and talk to people. Plus, the PDK has a bit of bridge-building to do around here.'

There was an embarrassed grimace.

'Two years ago,' continued Hoxhaj, 'the Mayor of Suhareka, a popular politician, from the Democratic League of Kosovo, our opponents, won an election and was celebrating his victory. One of our supporters shot him.'

Enver's meeting was held in Leshan's school. Outside, fifty or so men waited to greet us, and we visitors were obliged, according to local custom, to shake hands with all of them. This was sweet, but would have been time-consuming in larger settlements. The classroom set aside for the rally had a picture of Skanderbeg on the wall, joined by a poster of Hasim Thaci. There were no women present, and the men were delineated along generational lines by their clothes. The old chaps sported traditional baggy trousers and conical white hats, which gave them the appearance of retired circus clowns. The middle-aged wore bad suits, which looked like they'd been purchased in about 1977 and had since had the mildew thrashed off them twice a year for weddings, christenings, and funerals of unfortunate local politicians.

The young dressed in shapeless bootleg tracksuits, which looked as slovenly and slobbish as the shapeless name-brand tracksuits favoured by young people in London, but would at least have been cheaper.

All were profoundly courteous. At one point during the opening speech by some local panjandrum, there was a round of applause, and everyone turned to look at me. 'Greetings to you,' translated a young bloke at a nearby desk. The language barrier prevented me from following Hoxhaj's speech, but he got a decent hand at the end, and many questions – all of which, he later told me, were about statehood, and when Kosovo might expect it. When we left the school, the men of the village arranged themselves into another queue, and we had to shake all their hands again.

We headed further south to Prizren. Hoxhaj wanted me to see Prizren because, he said, it was where Albanian national identity was invented, and because the local *cevapcici* – the ubiquitous Balkan meatball – was the best in the world. Prizren had been, until recently, a pretty town, pretty enough that it might have served as the foundation of a Kosovar tourist industry. In March 2004, it had been substantially destroyed in anti-Serb riots. Much of Prizren's Old City was torched, including several centuries-old Serbian Orthodox churches and monasteries. Before the 1999 war, Prizren's ethnically Serbian population was estimated at 9000. By 2003, that was down to thirty-six, and since March 2004 that last few dozen had been camped at a nearby German KFOR base. It would be surprising if they ever returned. Enver did not regard this as a success.

'Idiots,' he said, as we contemplated the wreckage of the nineteenth-century St George Cathedral. 'Huge idiots. All through the war, none of these Serbian churches were touched, and now look at it. This is the work of crazy people. Idiots.'

There was, I felt obliged to point out, PDK graffiti on several of the gutted churches. Hoxhaj winced. 'I tell you,' he said, 'if I could get my hands on the party, we'd be rid of these extremists and morons very quickly.'

I felt Enver's embarassment. He'd brought me here because he wanted me to see the town in which his national identity had taken root. A willingness to burn down your own city to frighten off a few dozen elderly Serbs wasn't much of an advertisement for a people. As we walked among the ruins, Enver's gloom intensified, and I wondered if he was thinking that the life of a Viennese academic seemed rather appealing.

On the other side of the Bistrica River, across Prizren's famous Ottoman stone bridge, we found what Enver wanted me to see, and his mood lifted. Inside a neat courtyard were some terrace-style houses, and a small mosque.

'This,' he explained, 'was where the League of Prizren first met, in June 1878. This is where modern Albania started.'

The houses around the mosque, I observed, looked quite new.

'Reconstructions,' sighed Enver. 'The Serbs burned it all down in 1999.'

The League of Prizren, Enver continued, was founded by Albanian intellectuals to create the first Albanian homeland since the Ottoman Empire subsumed the region in the fifteenth century. The impetus for the League's formation was the Treaty of San Stefano, signed in March 1878 to formalise the Ottoman defeat by Russia in the 1877–78 Russo–Turkish war. The treaty diced the territory occupied by Albanians and distributed it among neighbouring Christian states – Bulgaria, Serbia and Montenegro. A pow-wow of Albanian honchos constituted itself as the League of Prizren. They claimed to be after autonomy, not independence – better to be subjects of their Ottoman co-religionists than minorities in Christian lands – but took the precaution of raising a small army.

In July 1878, the League wrote to the Congress of Berlin, where the Treaty of San Stefano was being revised in accordance with Austro-Hungarian and British concerns about Russian influence over the Balkans. The League wanted an Albanian province within the Ottoman empire. They received not so much as a standard reply ('Dear funny-hatted malcontent from faraway land about which the Iron Chancellor could not give two puffs of cigar smoke, Thank you for your interest in the deliberations of the Great Powers. Unfortunately . . .'). Their lands were handed to Montenegro and Serbia.

The League did what Skanderbeg had done four centuries previously, and what the KLA would do a hundred or so years hence: fought. They seized several towns in Kosovo and demanded independence. Unlike their spiritual descendents of the 1990s, however, the League of Prizren were not able to call upon a foreign alliance equipped with stealth aircraft and cruise missiles, and by 1881 Ottoman forces had recaptured Prizren and killed, deported or imprisoned the League's leaders. A noble story, though I noticed that the complex contained little in the way of commemoration of the Second League of Prizren, which formed during World War II and, seeking sponsorship of Greater Albania from Nazi Germany, raised an Albanian division of the SS.

Hoxhaj took me for *cevapcici*. It was, as he'd promised, the best I'd had, washed down with *kos*, a yoghurt made from sheep's milk. I asked him if he thought it was weird, to be campaigning for office in a country which didn't exist, and whose national identity was on loan from somewhere else – someone else's flag, someone else's anthem.

'The paradox of Albanians,' said Hoxhaj, 'is that for most of the twentieth century, Albania was an independent country full of dependent people, and Kosovo was a dependent country with independent people.'

Growing up in Kosovo, it had been impossible for Hoxhaj to visit the Albania ruled by his near-namesake, but possible for him to watch Albanian state television.

'We believed it,' he said. 'We thought Albania was this golden paradise. The first time I went there, in 1993, I was shocked. It was terrible.'

On the way back to Pristina, I asked Hoxhaj if there was a modern equivalent of Prizren, a site which a future independent Kosovo might regard as its birthplace.

'Prekaz,' he replied. 'You have to see Prekaz.'

My friend Nick, the paratrooper turned security contractor with whom I was staying, volunteered to drive me.

'It's up in Drenica,' he said. 'Hillbilly country.'

Our journey to Prekaz was soundtracked by Bruce Springsteen CDs, Nick's thoughtful deconstructions of Springsteen's lyrics, and Nick's expletive-strewn critiques of local driving mores. (One terrible day two years later, Nick's incessant, furious running commentary on a vexatious world would be prematurely silenced when his immense heart proved imperfectly constructed. The world is poorer for the absence of the man who coined the word 'baboonery' – a noun describing the baffling, self-destructive and usually irksomely noisy behaviour of foreign persons.)

Prekaz was a shrine to modern Kosovo's pre-eminent national hero: Adem Jashari. Jashari was a KLA commander who'd died, aged forty-two, along with dozens of his family members, in a battle against Serbian soldiers in March 1998. Jashari was Che Guevara and Ned Kelly crammed into one camouflage suit. We knew we were nearing our goal when the Land Rover stopped rattling from incessant potholes and began to purr contentedly along a new, smooth road.

The Jashari shrine was a sprawling complex. On one side of the road was the remains of the Jashari family compound, encased behind scaffolding which enabled visitors to peer into the bullet-pocked rooms in which the clan had perished. Across the street was the family graveyard. As we approached, two soldiers in uniforms bearing KLA shoulder flashes emerged from a guardhouse and stood to attention beneath the Albanian flags fluttering above the gate. The simple wooden graves poked from between bouquets left by previous visitors.

At the souvenir shop, I bought a Jashari keyring, and pamphlets glorifying the family. 'He is entirely airy,' said one of Jashari, 'in and out of us. Take a deep breath and you will feel him in every cell of your body.'

'I dunno,' said Nick. 'It's a bit maudlin, isn't it?'

It was, but we were thinking of the war memorials we were used to: sombre, sorrowful, dignified. The Jashari complex wasn't really a memorial at all, but an expression of still-throbbing rage. A few decades hence, it might be a Kosovan Gallipoli, or perhaps a Kosovan Glenrowan, but in the early twenty-first century Prekaz was, like

Kosovo's recent history, an open wound. We climbed back into the Land Rover and drove on, and around the corner stopped, because Nick was suddenly laughing so hard he couldn't see straight. As soon as the road was out of sight of the memorial, the pristine bitumen abruptly ceased, giving way to a rocky, bumpy, unsealed gravel track.

Whatever Kosovar nationality was, and whatever Kosovan statehood might yet look like, people had made colossal sacrifices to achieve them. I'd been given Albin Kurti's email address by Erion Veliaj of Mjaft! in Albania, who described Kurti as an 'icon' of Kosovan resistance to Serbia's rule, and 'very savvy, very articulate, very un-normal'. I met Kurti in the lobby of the Grand Hotel. He seemed an unlikely firebrand. His thick black glasses, ungovernable black curls and perpetually quizzical expression lent him the air of a distracted boffin, more naturally suited to bubbling test tubes. I was unsurprised to learn that his academic background was in electrical engineering. Albin was now the engine of a civil activist organisation called the Kosova Action Network, his moral authority derived from the imprisonment he'd endured under Milosevic.

'Two years, seven months, two weeks,' recalled Albin. On 13 March 2000, Albin was sentenced to fifteen years' imprisonment, after being convicted of – he recited, not without pride – 'endangering the territorial integrity and sovereignty of Yugoslavia'. He was twenty-four at the time, already a much-arrested student activist. Kurti refused to recognise the court, convened in the southern Serbian city of Nis, declined a lawyer, made a statement in which he referred to Slobodan Milosevic, accurately if tactlessly, as a 'fascist', and told the judge, 'I don't care how long you sentence me.'

'On 10 June 1999,' he says, 'a few weeks after I was sentenced, they transferred me to a jail in Požarevac.'

• Milosevic's hometown.

'Exactly,' nodded Albin. 'I thought that was pretty funny of them. Then I went on a tour of Serbian prisons. I was beaten pretty constantly for the first year, there were a few mock executions, then they left me alone. I'd become quite famous by then. A lot of people died in prison, though. In Lipyan, four people died that I know of – that I saw.'

What I was hoping Albin could explain was what his struggle was ultimately about, why Kosovo mattered, and mattered to the extent that he was prepared to give his young life for it – Albin's jail sentence could easily have become a death sentence.

'There's a need for freedom more than a need for independence,' he acknowledged. 'Independence is still important, because if independence isn't achieved, then ethnic radicalisation will take place. When things are uncertain, people seek shelter, and nationalism is a shelter.'

I wondered if Albin considered himself a nationalist, or even a patriot.

'I'm a human being first,' he answered. 'Then I listen to these records, and read those books. Then I'm an Albanian, and then I live in Kosovo. Mostly, I'd identify myself as a student. I'm trying to learn.'

He'd have been educated as Yugoslav, though, right?

'Yeah,' he said. 'But after about 1987, Yugoslavia was like Wile E. Coyote in the *Roadrunner* cartoons, in those scenes where he's run off the cliff but hasn't realised there's nothing underneath him.'

Albin told me to meet him at the Grand later in the week, when he and his organisation would be demonstrating against the elections, which he believed were a charade – in his view, a government more answerable to the UN than to its electors was no government at all. I arrived at the appointed hour to find Albin and his associates gathered on the hotel's forecourt, along with a donkey on the end of a rope. The creature was draped with a bedsheet, on which were written the words Votoni per mua! (Vote for me!). Albin was arguing with a passing UN election monitor. She was American, to judge by the accent.

'You're making the election look like a big joke,' the woman complained.

'The election is a big joke,' said Albin.

'You can't tell people to vote for a jackass,' continued the woman, who had an extraordinary knack for setting up punchlines.

'Why not?' replied Albin, inevitably. 'They usually do.'

With that, Albin and his followers set off through Pristina, mascot in tow. I watched them go, thinking what a finer, happier place our world would be if more of its malcontents were like Albin: funny, smart, decent, in no hurry to hurt anyone, yet willing to absorb extraordinary amounts of pain. He led the donkey with the insouciant poise of someone who knows he has met one of the sternest tests a man can face, and passed. He'd been challenged to back his principles with his health and freedom, and he'd done it.

I'd like to think I have sufficient steel inside my spine that I'd go to prison for my beliefs, but due to my good fortune in living where I can think and write and say and do more or less what I like, that particular push has never come to shove. When I went to prison a year later, it wasn't for my beliefs, but for someone else's.

18

And I'd thought the previous day had broken all previous personal records for weirdness. I'd spent it driving jarring red dirt roads in the company of Nfor Ngala Nfor, vice-chairman of the Southern Cameroon National Conference – an illegal organisation whose quaint goal was the establishment of a separate state comprising the two of Cameroon's ten provinces which spoke English rather than French. We'd driven from Bamenda, the biggest town in the region, into the hills to Kumbo. After a breakdown-induced delay, we'd proceeded as far north as Nkamba. Here, Nfor had introduced me to a meeting of the local chapter of the SCNC, who'd been waiting in their meeting hall for hours. They'd fed me a delicious lunch, then queued to outline their grievances against the government of Cameroon, who they believed favoured the country's Francophone majority.

On the way back from Nkamba, we'd dropped by a village called Binka. A crowd of forty or fifty, clad in colourful traditional dress, or smart suits, or combinations of both, sat on two benches in a clearing. On the other side of the clearing was the village chieftain, or Fon. The Fon of Binka was a grinning apparition with a voice like thunderclaps, clad in black embroidered robe and hat, and a necklace of lions' teeth. The Fon delivered a passionate speech affirming the rightness of the SCNC's cause, and its peaceful methods: 'We did not join Cameroon by the spear,' he bellowed, in reference to the 1961 referendum which created the modern Cameroon, 'so we shall not leave by the spear.'

At the conclusion of his oration, a bearer appeared with a wicker basket containing a chicken. 'We had planned,' roared the Fon, 'to kill this for you. As you were late, we are giving it to you so you may do it yourself, later.'

A couple of villages down the track, I awarded the bird its freedom – an act which, not long afterwards, would confirm my long-held suspicion that the concept of karma is a crock. Three days later, a picture of the Fon presenting me with the chook would be on page two of Cameroon's biggest English-language newspaper, the *Post*. On page one would be a picture of me, in a Hawaiian shirt I wouldn't have worn if I'd known there was going to be a photographer present, under the headline AUSTRALIAN JOURNALIST DETAINED IN BAMENDA.

I daresay that at the moment I was arrested, things would have looked pretty bad to an observer unaware of the subtleties of the situation. I was at an illegal meeting of an illegal organisation. At the moment the police arrived, a senior official of said illegal organisation had finished a speech in which he'd pronounced me a roving ambassador for said illegal organisation, and placed atop my head a cloth hat emblazoned with the insignia of said illegal organisation. While I didn't feel like I'd done much wrong in the grand scheme of things, I also recognised, as the khaki-clad gendarmes scuffled through the crowd, that I didn't, on balance, have much of a case.

There were many and complex reasons why an African country was rendering itself asunder over the competing claims of two imported European languages – two imported European languages, at that, which nobody much in Cameroon spoke as recently 1916, when British and French troops seized what had, until then, been a German colony. I'd come to Cameroon to understand these reasons, and to understand a bit more about nationalism, what creates and drives it. A sense of nationality is, like love and faith, one of the few human universals. Go anywhere, meet someone, ask them about themselves. They'll tell you their name. Then, probably, what they do for a living. Then they'll tell you where they're from. A sense of nationality is also, like love and faith, something that doesn't bear much logical scrutiny. It's reasonable that we define ourselves by our names: they're what everyone calls us. It makes sense that we define ourselves by our work: whether it's work we enjoy or endure, it's what we spend much of our waking hours doing, and often something we project as a signifier of status. But there's little rhyme or reason in the importance we place upon our nationality, still less the pride we take in it. My Australian nationality is nothing but fluke. I'm grateful for it, but I didn't do anything to deserve it.

Nationality matters, though. Perhaps not as much as love or faith, but it matters. When I travel, people generally assume that I'm American or British. I'm always quick to correct them. I don't really understand why I do that, but because I do that, I understand something of how it must hurt when your answer to the question of where you're from elicits responses of 'Huh?' or 'Does that exist?'. Maybe our nationality is just something we're happy to advance as a cartoon of our identity. I can go anywhere in the world and tell people I'm Australian, and it means something. In 1998, I was the first foreigner ever to walk into the village of Panggi, in the north-eastern Indian province of Arunuchal Pradesh. When I explained where I was from, the locals – who had established a cricket pitch between their totem poles – asked me about Dennis Lillee.

However, if you have to tell people that you're from, say, the Republic of Southern Cameroon, you're doomed to a lifetime of complicated exposition. This, indeed, was another reason I went to Southern Cameroon: I'd never heard of it. In June 2005, at the general assembly of the Unrecognised Nations and Peoples Organisation (UNPO) in The Hague – the same event at which I'd met Abkhazia's deputy foreign minister, Maxim Gunjia – I'd spent a lot of time talking to the SCNC delegation. They'd intrigued me initially because they were the best-dressed emissaries in attendance, illuminating the mostly heart-stoppingly dull conference sessions with shimmering silk robes and bead-festooned wicker hats. The SCNC's national chairman, Chief Ayamba Otun, and their national vice-chairman, Nfor Ngala Nfor, invited me to visit their non-country. I'd never been to sub-Saharan Africa, and this seemed an ideal chance to rectify this scandalous omission. Getting a Cameroonian visa, thanks to the Cameroonian High Commission's mania for arcane bureaucratic procedure and my desire to evade questions about the company I'd be keeping, was difficult – though not as difficult as getting another Cameroonian visa is going to be.

I arrived in Cameroon at its major air hub, Douala airport. My rucksack arrived, as is traditional when Air France are involved, twenty-four hours later, after enjoying a stopover in Paris. (It is a little known fact that Air France is an acronym, standing for Aircraft Is Running Fucking *Retard* Again, No Cases Expected.) The bad news was that my mosquito repellent was in the rucksack. The good news was that after two days' wear in Douala's damp heat, my shirt had an equivalent effect. While I waited for Air France to effect a reunion between me and my luggage, one of my SCNC contacts, Dr Arnold Yongbang, showed me around Douala and explained the factional rivalries of his organisation. It was hard to tell which was more chaotic. After a couple of days, I still didn't understand – or, to be honest, care – which arm of the SCNC was upset with which other, or why, but I did have my rucksack, and I pushed on to Buea.

Buea was an unprepossessing town of 150,000 or so, huddled at the foot of Mount Cameroon, an active volcano which had belched lava across surrounding countryside as recently as 2000. I met more SCNC members, many of whom seemed to be factions unto themselves, and had lunch with some hotheads from the organisation's militant wing. They favoured open armed revolt to deliver their people from oppression.

'If there is war here,' they intoned gravely, 'we will have the attention of the world. Then, something will be done. The UN will help.'

I asked them if they were, not to put too fine a point on it, entirely fucking mad.

'What do you mean?' they replied.

I meant, I responded, that the Democratic Republic of Congo had been throwing a war for the last decade, which had involved the armies of almost every country around it, left millions dead, and I hadn't seen it on the six o'clock news once. The pits of corpses in

Sudan were long and deep, and nobody north of the Mediterranean was much bothered about that, either. The UN in which they placed such faith had reacted to genocide in Rwanda by withdrawing what troops they'd sent. Another war in Africa wouldn't interest anybody. Non-violent resistance, I thought, in the context of this continent, might have an attractive novelty value. I left hoping they were more convinced than they seemed.

I spent most of my time in Buea with Blaise Berinyuy, a lawyer deferred to by many SCNC activists as 'the prime minister of Ambazonia' – Ambazonia being his preferred name for the Anglophone republic he hoped to wrest free of Cameroon. Berinyuy was punctilious about his appearance, wearing a black suit in defiance of the clammy warmth. In one lapel he sported a badge honouring a friend who had recently died, on his head a black skullcap signifying his position as a Shey, head of his family.

Berinyuy acknowledged that the SCNC's infighting verged on the farcical, but quietly emphasised that the cause was no laughing matter. The anglophones of Cameroon were discriminated against, he insisted, politically, culturally and economically. There was only one Anglophone in a senior government position – the prime minister, Ephraim Inoni, regarded as a puppet of Cameroon's undisputed power, long-serving president Paul Biya. Francophone soldiers and police marauded in anglophone areas. Berinyuy had been arrested several times and beaten, including one thrashing of 120 strokes with a truncheon on the soles of his feet. His house had been smashed up by police.

Berinyuy accompanied me on the seven-hour drive to Bamenda, along roads lined with fields of pawpaw, banana, pineapple and grapefruit. Bamenda was where I was due to meet Nfor Nfor for the ride to Kumbo, where things would go very, if almost charmingly, wrong.

There were a couple of hundred people in Stephen Kongnso's garden. Kongnso, the chairman of the SCNC in Kumbo, was a fizzingly energetic, perpetually smiling man, utterly dedicated to the SCNC and its non-violent methods. I'd visited his rough, dirt-floored house and its beautiful garden with Nfor Nfor a few days previously. Today's plan, as I understood it, was that we were dropping in to say our farewells before heading back to Bamenda. I was surprised to find that a gathering had been convened.

Nfor made a speech, partly in English, partly in pidgin; Southern Cameroon should have independence, he said, 'gear forward, quick quick'. He summoned a call-and-response rendition of the SCNC's motto, prompting the crowd with 'The force of argument . . .' and receiving the reply, 'Not the argument of force,' accompanied by a thumbs-up gesture which appeared to be the SCNC's salute. He paid tribute to other peaceful revolutions, in Georgia, Ukraine and the Philippines, awarded me my honorary citizenship and hat, complimented me on my intelligence and height, and expressed the wish that one day I might return as Australia's High Commissioner to the Republic of Southern Cameroon. Then the gendarmes arrived.

There was some pushing and shoving as the five officers made their way through the crowd, but nothing worse than one of those half-hearted melees which occasionally enliven soccer matches. The officer in charge asked for my passport, and my press card. Seeing as how he said 'please', and figuring there was nothing to be gained by being difficult, I handed them over. The officers allowed the meeting to continue with its ostensible purpose, which was raising funds for the SCNC. People queued to stuff banknotes into a bucket, while chanting defiant slogans at the impassive gendarmes. I asked the top cop what was going to happen.

'You'll have to come with us,' he said, 'and so will Mr Kongnso and Mr Nfor.'

My feelings at this were approximately equally divided between 'Fuck, I'm being arrested in West Africa' and 'Cool, I'm being arrested in West Africa'. (There exists among journalists an undeclared regime of invisible Boy Scout badges, and the Night-in-the-Cells shoulder patch had been absent from my sleeve, let alone the Night-in-the-Cells patch with the coveted Africa clasp, which I seemed about to acquire.) It occurred to me, though, as I noted the hostile glares being directed at the gendarmes, that the situation could turn extremely stupid if not handled correctly. The people at the meeting were not just angry at what they perceived as oppression. They were embarrassed and ashamed that their guest was in trouble.

'Don't worry,' said one. 'We will all come to the station, all of us.'

That was the last thing I wanted to hear, as I was pretty sure that the last place I wanted to be was between a large angry mob and a small group of armed police. Kumbo's dirt roads had soaked up SCNC blood before – in 2001, on 1 October, Southern Cameroon's self-declared Independence Day, three people died when gendarmes opened fire on a peaceful demonstration. Whatever was about to happen, I decided, nobody was getting shot on my account. I grabbed Nfor, who was in huddled conference with several livid-looking fellow activists, by the sleeve of his robe.

For Christ's sake, I told him, get up on a chair now and tell everyone to either stay here or bugger off home, but under no circumstances to go anywhere near the police station. Tell them it's a special request from their honoured guest. Tell them anything you bloody like. Just tell them no protests, no demonstrations, no trouble. Nfor seemed rattled, but mounted a tree stump and ordered restraint. There was, to my inexpressible relief, general assent. Right, I said to the somewhat startled commanding officer, let's get out of here – now. Kongnso, Nfor and I were escorted to the police truck with handshakes and smiles from SCNC members who seemed suddenly, mercifully, cheerful again.

The drive to the police station gave me time to take stock. Though I'd been interrogated, searched at gunpoint, shoved around and mildly assaulted by various law enforcement officials before, this was my first experience of being actually arrested. There were two things I needed to do. One, get the word out. The other, figure out how much trouble I was in. Both, I thought, could be accomplished with one manouevre. I produced my phone from my shoulder bag and asked the gendarme next to me if I could send a message. If he said yes, I thought, this is probably going to be all right. If he said no, and/or confiscated the phone, I was having a bad day.

'Go ahead,' he shrugged.

I exhaled with a force that may have gone close to shattering the windscreen. I texted my friend James Brabazon, a film-maker with much experience of Africa, and of some of the continent's correctional facilities. 'Arrested Kumbo,' I wrote. 'Seems OK. Will keep you posted. Call High Comm if you don't hear soon.' 'OK,' replied James, 'I'm in a mosque in Paris.' I remembered – he was making a documentary about the riots which were gripping the French capital. 'Am getting contact numbers. Standing by.' Before I left for Cameroon, James had taught me some foreign correspondent slang specific to Africa. If things went slightly wrong, the situation would be described as 'bongo'. If things went badly wrong, they could be said to have gone 'deep bongo'. This looked like the shallow end of bongo, but I resolved that, whatever happened, I wasn't leaving Cameroon without an actual bongo for James.

The police station at Kumbo was a yellow-walled bungalow on a hill overlooking the town. Inside, it was bare, functional, rather lacking in a woman's touch: ancient typewriters perched on rickety wooden furniture, battered filing cabinets were swaddled in cobwebs. It was clear that both Nfor and Kongnso were well known to the gendarmes. I introduced myself formally, thinking again that the response would be instructive. Again to my relief, the two senior gendarmes accepted my handshake, and introduced themselves as Captain Dieudone Eteme and Senior Warrant Officer James Akama. Kongnso commenced an impassioned speech about Francophone oppression.

'Shut up, Stephen,' said Captain Eteme, rolling his eyes.

Nobody seemed to know what to do with us. We sat around the main room of the police station for a bit. Feeling adventurous, I went outside to sit around on the verandah. My phone buzzed.

'By the way,' read the message from James, 'you are a cunt for not doing a security protocol for this trip.'

This may have been true, but James was accustomed to working for television, which provided budgets for advance research, fixers and the like. For print journalists, especially freelance ones, 'security protocol' usually means 'hoping very hard that nothing goes wrong'. I was summoned back inside, and asked to turn out my shoulder bag.

The mood among the gendarmes soured as they examined the contents. In Nkamba, I'd been handed a folder, which I'd stuffed in my bag and forgotten about. I was as alarmed as the gendarmes to discover that it was full of heavy-going SCNC fulminations against Cameroon's government. The gendarmes asked me to make a written statement. I offered a bland account of the facts of my trip, and was asked to read it back before signing it.

'We will take you,' said Captain Eteme, 'to the magistrate.'

A short drive deposited me in the office of Ngu Ngwa Augustine. Captain Eteme explained matters, and Augustine lofted an eyebrow at me. I decided to essay a minor offensive. I told Augustine I'd already raised the alarm. I told him that arresting journalists looked bad. I said that if they let me go now, this wouldn't be a story, but that if this went on much longer, it would.

'Yes,' agreed Augustine. 'But we will be keeping you tonight at least.'

I asked if I was being charged with anything.

'I don't know yet,' he replied.

I asked if I could call the British High Commission in Yaounde – Australia had no diplomatic mission in Cameroon. Augustine opened a desk drawer, produced a phone directory and tossed it across the office. The British High Commission explained that, although I was a resident of the UK, Canada had consular responsibility for Australian citizens in Cameroon, so I'd have to take it up with their High Commission. I did. The Canadians promised to dispatch a nun from a mission in Kumbo. I was driven back to the police station.

I then had to decide who else to tell. I had spent much of 2005 breaking up, incrementally but amicably, with my long-time girlfriend Roni. In the weeks before departing London for Cameroon, I had fallen unexpectedly, uncharacteristically suddenly, and quite overwhelmingly in love with a woman I shall refer to as Lucrezia. This didn't appear to be a problem, as she claimed, often and at length, to feel the same about me. Long road trips had been taken, ardent emails exchanged, and a future sketched, without provoking my usual wretched urges, in such circumstances, to bolt for the nearest boat/plane/bus/taxi/donkey cart/third boxcar, midnight train. Shortly after I returned to London, this would go sensationally wrong, to a degree which would make me wish I'd stayed in Kumbo, confessed to espionage, set fire to the police station and lamped magistrate Augustine with his hatstand, but as I texted James and told him to corral the electronic mob and pass round the virtual pitchforks, I had no inkling that I would be spending the ensuing months contemplating incarceration with wistful fondness. Aiming to cut a nonchalant, Indiana Jonesish dash, I texted Lucrezia. She replied; she still loved me. I returned to the police station feeling supremely, perversely content with the world and all its workings.

The Canadian nun arrived. Sister Noreen asked if there was anything we needed. I explained that while the gendarmes had been exemplary hosts in every other respect, we were hungry. She drove off, promising to return with food. One of the sergeants overheard, stalked to an adjacent accommodation building, and returned with his teenage son. 'Tell him what you need,' said the sergeant, 'and I'll send him to the market.' My cake-with-a-file-in-it joke fell upon stony ground. I settled for bottled water, bread and cooked vege-tables. Captain Eteme, apparently horrified that his hospitality had been slighted, produced a bottle of claret. Sister Noreen returned with peanut butter sandwiches. Nfor, also permitted to keep his phone, called someone and told them to retrieve my rucksack from Stephen's house.

Delighted to have something new to do, Captain Eteme and WO Akama asked me to unpack it. They were justly uninterested in my clothes, briefly diverted by my books (Bob Dylan's *Chronicles*, Michael Bywater's *Lost Worlds*), faintly intrigued by the knot of cables relating to my camera, iPod, phone and computer (the latter was stowed, I hoped safely, in Bamenda), and downright puzzled by a small, white, furry clockwork rabbit.

'What's this?' asked Captain Eteme, not unreasonably, twirling it between thumb and forefinger.

I explained that my girlfriend was a singer, and that this was the lucky mascot that she took on tour with her, and that she had lent it to me for this trip, which was very sweet of her, for all the fucking good it was presently doing me.

'Does it have a name?' grinned Captain Eteme.

Yes, I said. She calls it The Chicken.

'But it's a rabbit,' he replied.

I conceded this point. We shrugged at each other, adversaries briefly bonded by bafflement at the mysteries of womankind.

'A lucky charm,' he smiled. 'I think I'd leave it with her next time you go anywhere.'

To my relief, he didn't undo the zip which sealed the waterproof lining at the bottom of my rucksack, in which I'd stashed the fairly ripe SCNC propaganda I'd been given back in Douala and Buea, which I'd intended to post to London when I got a chance. If Captain Eteme is reading this, he'll find all of it behind the wardrobe in the room I was later given for the night.

I spent the afternoon on the police station porch, getting the gendarmes to identify passing birds and lizards, asking to see their photos of family and home – all of the gendarmes, just as the SCNC had told me, were from Francophone provinces of Cameroon – and fielding calls and texts. I'd been about the last person in London to submit to mobile telephony, but I don't think I've ever loved anything non-organic as much as I loved my palmOne Treo that afternoon and evening. I couldn't imagine what a lonely experience this would have been without it. The BBC World Service called. The National Union of Journalists in London. The Committee to Protect Journalists in New York. The Canadian High Commission in Yaounde. The Australian High Commission in Abuja, Nigeria. The Department of Foreign Affairs in Canberra. I made sure the gendarmes could overhear me saying where I was, and spelling out the names of the officers.

I called my parents in Melbourne when I figured they'd be awake. 'Ah well,' said Mum. 'I suppose it was bound to happen sooner or later.' Supportive messages and terrible jokes arrived by text message from friends. The world felt extremely and comfortingly small. And then, when I tried to explain to two West African revolutionaries and a station full of policemen why I was laughing at 'What's got nine arms and sucks? Def Leppard', incomprehensibly large.

Later that afternoon, the magistrate, Ngu Augustine, turned up at the police station. He asked me to unpack my bag, again, which meant that, again, I had to explain why I was travelling with a clockwork rabbit called The Chicken.

'A lucky charm?' he smirked. 'It's not doing much good, is it?'

No, it wasn't. Augustine asked me to follow him into an office, and shut the door behind him. A curious conversation followed. He asked what I thought of Southern Cameroon. I returned rhetorical blanc-mange, saying that I didn't have any fixed opinion, but hoped the differences could be resolved peacefully. Which, for what it was worth, was true. He asked if my arrest would change what I might write about Cameroon. I said that I suspected I'd mention it. He explained that he was from around here, and therefore part of both the Anglophone minority and the allegedly repressive Francophone establishment – and quietly fond of Nfor, whom he regarded as sensible and intelligent.

The suspicion began to develop that I was being played. Other than the fact of arresting me, everyone was being courteous and pleasant. When I emerged from my interrogation by the magistrate, I found that SCNC sympathisers from Kumbo had been allowed to deliver food, a glorious banquet of rice, chicken and vegetables, garnished with stewed huckleberry leaves. Stephen and Nfor shared it with the gendarmes as if this was utterly unremarkable, and the gendarmes chatted convivially with Stephen and Nfor as they ate. My phone, which I'd not only been allowed to keep, but charge – in an illustration of Cameroon's historic Anglo–French schism, the station offered a choice of two-pin or three-pin sockets – kept buzzing. I stepped outside to return a few calls.

'Who were you talking to?' asked Nfor, joining me on the porch after I'd finished.

The NUJ, I told him, the CPJ, a couple of newspapers, the Australian High Commission in Abuja, the Department of Foreign Affairs in Canberra, the BBC World Service, again.

'Excellent,' said Nfor.

More amused than angry, I accused him outright. You set this up, I said. You called an illegal meeting, knowing the gendarmes would bust it, and you brought a foreign journalist, who you knew they'd arrest, and you knew that would get your obscure struggle on the news all over the world.

'Andrew,' he beamed, 'I believe you were sent to us by God.'

What concerned me more at this point was the identity of the power that might send me back home again. I wasn't frightened for my own safety – everyone was being cool, they had nothing to gain by mistreating me – but a couple of the calls and texts I'd had weren't encouraging. 'It's hard enough to get anything done quickly in West Africa at the best of times,' said the friendly woman at the Australian High Commission in Abuja, 'let alone over the weekend. I'd resign myself to a few more days, if I were you.' A few more days, I thought, and the novelty could wear off. 'Usually a bad idea to get lifted on a Friday,' texted James. I loved the 'usually'.

The gendarmes manning the night shift arrived. It was a good sign, I thought, when the incoming sergeant picked up a centipede which had wandered into the building and carried it gently back outside. I stayed that night on a mattress in a dusty office at the back of the police station. I wrote down every phone number I thought I might need on a piece of paper, which I stuffed under the sole of one boot. I sent more texts to friends, few of whom pretended to take matters seriously. Lucrezia pined gratifyingly, and little else mattered to me.

Finding sleep hard to come by, I tried to make sense of the disparity between the day's events, and prison as I'd always understood it from Johnny Cash records, by imagining how a song called 'Kumbo Prison Blues' might go. 'I got plenty of journalist friends,' ran one verse, 'My case is widely reported/I got sweet dreams of you to dream, until I get deported.'

Magistrate Augustine returned on Saturday morning. 'Pack up,' he instructed. 'You're being moved to Bamenda.'

I asked if this was good news.

'Would you rather stay here?' he asked.

I climbed into one four-wheel drive, which contained Augustine and a uniformed gendarme, while Stephen and Nfor were shown into another car, also under armed guard.

'Don't worry,' said Nfor. 'This is usual. We will see you in Bamenda.'

Again, I figured that what I was allowed to do would be a useful indication of the depth of the soup I was in. Augustine didn't object to me sending texts, or to my taking pictures of the green hills through which the road wove – or, even, to my taking a picture of him at the wheel. These, I thought, were encouraging signs. We pulled up beside a house.

'My home,' said Augustine. 'Do you want some lunch?'

I said yes, because I was hungry, and because I wanted to know how much more surreal a prisoner transfer could get. I only had to wait three courses for the answer.

'Do you mind,' asked Augustine, 'if my wife and daughter ride along to Bamenda with us? They want to go shopping.'

This was fine with me, but there were baleful sighs from the uniformed gendarme in the car, who had been enjoying his role as escort to a foreign prisoner. Theatrically grumpy and officious, he wasn't the sort who'd joined up to ride shotgun on shoe-buying expeditions. He sulked out the window as Augustine's wife and astonishingly beautiful daughter adjusted each other's makeup. I texted home updates of my progress.

'Okay,' replied James. 'Fingers crossed.'

'Do you think,' asked Lucrezia, 'this might be an incredibly elaborate practical joke?'

That possibility had occurred to me. The thought that I would shortly be entertaining similar suspicions about our relationship had not.

Our two-car convoy eventually reunited at another large house, Augustine's abode in Bamenda. Nfor and Stephen, Captain Eteme and a couple of the gendarmes from Kumbo were already waiting at the gate, as was a delegation from the local SCNC office. To nobody's surprise but my own, Augustine invited everyone – gendarmes, prisoners, SCNC – in for a drink. As his daughter emerged from the kitchen with a bottle of Johnnie Walker and tumblers on a silver tray, I apologised for any appearance of pushiness, and asked Augustine if he could possibly tell me what was going on.

'We're taking you to Bamenda gendarme headquarters,' he said, sipping his scotch. 'You'll meet the attorney-general there. He'll decide what to do with you.'

Bamenda's gendarme headquarters was a yellowing fort which glowered at the city from a hilltop. Nfor, Stephen and I were parked on chairs in the lobby. The gendarmes here were much less amiable than the ones in Kumbo. They took my camera and my phone. I tried as far as I dared to talk them out of this, pointing out that people were expecting me to check in, but behind the sergeant I was talking to I could see Augustine shaking his head. He was leaving, and so was Captain Eteme.

Where's the attorney-general? I asked Augustine.

'Maybe tomorrow,' he said. 'It's not up to me now. I have to go.'

'Good luck,' said Captain Eteme, and I tried to tell myself that he hadn't looked like he thought I'd need it.

I waited, and read, and paced the balcony, while Stephen and Nfor were questioned in an office. Again, local SCNC activists brought food and water. The gendarmes talking, smoking, polishing their rifles, weren't friendly, but they weren't hostile. After three hours of questioning, Stephen and Nfor emerged from the office. They looked worried.

'They're taking us away,' said Nfor. 'I think you'll be okay, though.'

They followed three armed soldiers into a pickup truck. I watched the tail-lights disappear into the darkness, and felt suddenly very alone.

'Mr Mueller,' boomed a voice from inside the office. 'Please come in, and bring your bags.'

The voice belonged to the commanding officer, Lieutenant Colonel Benjamin Bogmis. Also in his office were the sergeant who'd taken my phone, and another man, in civilian clothes. I hauled my bags in and offered handshakes, which were returned by Colonel Bogmis and the sergeant, who introduced himself as Henry, but not by the plainclothes man. Trouble, I thought, or just a bit of a wanker.

Again, I was asked to unpack my bags. Again, the wind-up rabbit provoked amusement. A lucky charm, I explained again, lent by my girlfriend, though despite appearances it was called The Chicken, and it was evidently selective in bestowing its blessings. Colonel Bogmis and the sergeant laughed. The plainclothes man didn't.

'It is being lucky for you,' he hissed. 'You are still alive.'

Fortunately, the ineptitude of the threat prevented it from being in any way frightening.

Colonel Bogmis explained that they wanted me to write a statement covering every aspect of my trip. I was issued with a biro and a ream of paper.

'Read it out as you write it down,' instructed Colonel Bogmis.

Always start with a joke. '*I hope you realise*,' I dictated to myself, '*what a bargain you're getting here. I can make up to forty pence a word for this kind of thing.*' Even the plainclothes man laughed at this. Feeling that I had the audience on board, I ploughed on. It was the truth, pretty much – that I'd met Nfor in The Hague, that he'd invited me to Cameroon, that I'd come to Bamenda to meet him, that I'd gone to a meeting, and they knew the rest. When they asked who I'd met in Buea and elsewhere, I evaded or invented, hoping that my testimony wouldn't lead to some hapless soul getting his door kicked in just because his name corresponded with one I'd made up. When they asked about my journalistic background, I skipped over the political and foreign reporting I'd done, and rocked on about the bands I'd toured with as a young writer on *Melody Maker*, grassing up Pearl Jam, The Cure and Radiohead, among others.

'My brother,' volunteered Henry, the sergeant, 'is in a country and western band in Los Angeles. I cannot remember their name, however.'

It was, as I'd intended, getting ridiculous. Colonel Bogmis sent out for water and biscuits. Even the plainclothes man, when he asked me to flick through the photos in my camera, was mostly interested in the ones of my friends, family and girlfriend that I'd loaded onto the memory card. Eventually, Colonel Bogmis asked if there was anything I wanted to add to my statement. Yes, I decided, there was. I bashed out a couple of paragraphs of tribute to the beauty of Cameroon, to its talented and determined people and, while we were up that way, the gallantry of the country's law enforcement officials. '*Annoyed though I am*,' I wrote, '*I am sure that Cameroon is absolutely the best place in West Africa to get locked up.*'

'You're a strange man,' said Colonel Bogmis.

I hadn't finished. I wrote extended thanks to Captain Eteme, whose permission to keep my telephone in Kumbo had made matters much less unpleasant than they might have been. It wasn't a subtle ploy.

'You can make one call,' sighed Colonel Bogmis.

Two, I ventured. One to my folks, and one to my girlfriend. She'll be worried about the rabbit.

'Ah yes,' smiled Colonel Bogmis. 'The Chicken. You must love her very much. Two calls, then. But be quick. It's getting late.'

I rang my parents in Melbourne and Lucrezia in London. While harvesting texts which had arrived during the evening, I fired one back to James. I looked at my watch. It was nearly one am. I handed the phone back. Colonel Bogmis placed it carefully on his desk next to my camera, which he also appeared disinclined to return. I assume, I said, that I'm staying with you gentlemen this evening.

'At another place,' said Colonel Bogmis. 'You'll be driven there.'

Sergeant Henry carried my bags outside and loaded them aboard a pickup, in which a driver was already waiting. He gestured towards the back seat. I got in, and two young soldiers, each toting rifles, sprang from the shadows and sat either side of me. The driver started the truck. I tapped his shoulder. Stop, I said. Stop. I turned to the soldier on my left, slowly reached over him to the door handle, and motioned that I wanted to get out. I walked back into the building and knocked on Colonel Bogmis's door.

'Mr Mueller,' he sighed. 'We can't keep you away.'

I was wondering, I said, if we could ask the escort to dispense with the artillery. I don't much care for guns, I explained, and they seemed unnecessary. It wasn't like I was going to run away to Bamenda and blend into the background. Again, I was gauging the situation. If he waved me off with an unarmed escort, it meant I wasn't being taken seriously, and I very much wanted Colonel Bogmis to regard this as the least serious case that had ever crossed his desk. He sighed again, and followed me out of the building to the truck. He said something to the soldiers in French. They handed him their rifles, and we drove into the night.

The commanding officer at the military prison sauntered into a tiled reception area dressed in extravagant floral pyjamas and thongs. He looked extraordinarily like Eddie Murphy. 'Major Ango,' he said, offering his hand. 'At your service.' I've been received with less civility in hotels with five stars next to the door.

I was almost disappointed not to be asked to unpack my rucksack again. My riff about the wind-up rabbit was getting bigger laughs with every telling. Major Ango told me that I'd have to leave my rucksack in the reception area. 'You can keep your shoulder bag, and anything else you need,' he said. 'I'll show you to your cell.'

Cell. Until now, I'd done pretty well at regarding my arrest as the farce that it clearly was, but the word 'cell' struck like a cannonball in the stomach. Major Ango must have sensed that my imagination had become suddenly crowded with visions of crapping into a bucket next to a 200-kilogram maniac with furry knuckles who insisted on being addressed as 'Susan'.

'Don't worry,' he said. 'It's all yours, and it's very clean. I've just finished a postgraduate degree in human rights.'

I couldn't think of anything I might have wanted to hear from him more, short of 'There's satellite television, a swimming pool on the top floor, and the minibar is complimentary. Actually, you know what? Bugger it. I'll call you a taxi.' Down a corridor from the reception area were two cells. The doors were made of solid blue metal. On the one opened to me, some wag had attached a yellow Post-it note bearing the scrawled word 'Hilton'. Inside, a flourescent light illuminated two square metres of concrete floor, a stretcher bed covered in a khaki blanket, half a dozen bottles of water, a couple of open vents high in the yellow walls, and the moths and spiders which had entered through them. None were troublingly large. There was graffiti on the walls, most of it religious, one offering observing that NO WOMAN IS GOOD. The door shut behind me with a western-movie clang, and I heard the bolt slotted home. Again, I thought to test the limits of my limitations. I banged on the inside of the door. Major Ango opened it.

'Can I help you?' he purred.

I pointed out that the toilet was outside the cell. If I wanted to use it during the night, I'd have to wake him – and everyone else in the building who could hear me hitting the door. If he left the door open, I could help myself.

'Fair enough,' he shrugged, and walked away, leaving the door ajar.

In the morning, I sat on the balcony outside the reception area with Major Ango, who hadn't changed out of his billowing pyjamas.

'Things in Cameroon are getting better,' he said, 'but it takes time.' He indicated a building across the road. 'Used to be a prison,' he said. 'Just for political prisoners, up until the early nineties. Now there aren't any political prisoners, so it's an army barracks.'

Major Ango served nine years in President Paul Biya's Close Protection Unit, travelling the world with Cameroon's long-ruling quasi-tyrant. 'He's a realist,' insisted Ango. 'He knows that things have to change, but also that they have to change slowly.'

Our deliberations, about politics and passing lizards, were interrupted by visitors. Another SCNC delegation, led by Nfor's wife, Marie, dropped off some food. It was a wonderful feast of steamed vegetables and rice, and a heartbreakingly generous gesture on her part. I asked if she knew where her husband was, or when she'd see him again.

'No, and no,' she smiled, sadly. 'But don't worry. This happens often.'

Colonel Bogmis turned up, wanting to go through my written statement again. Seeking to put him on the defensive, I loftily informed him that I knew that this was a standard interrogation technique, to catch me out by seeing if I could remember to tell the same lies twice

– and that it wouldn't work, because I'd told the truth from the start, so there.

'No,' he replied, amused. 'That's not it at all. I just can't read your handwriting.'

I suggested that the easiest thing all round might be throwing me out of the country on the flight I had tickets for anyway. Tomorrow night, I said. Just think of it. We wouldn't have to be each other's problem ever again.

'Mr Mueller,' grinned Colonel Bogmis, 'I think you will be making your flight.'

He produced my phone, my camera, and an exercise book.

'Check that they haven't been tampered with,' he instructed, 'then sign here.'

I did both of those things.

'Now wait.'

He left. I waited. I sent texts to Lucrezia, and my friends, confirming that I was alive and cautiously optimistic. Major Ango and I talked about football. His son was playing for a club in Yaounde, and had hopes of one day wearing the shirt of the national side, the Indomitable Lions. Given Cameroon's failure to qualify for the following year's World Cup, I secured his support for Australia, pending our passage past Uruguay in the play-off. I received another visitor, a chattering force of nature in a black suit.

'I am,' he declared, 'Harmony.'

Okay, I said, perplexed even by the standards of the last forty-eight hours.

'I'm your lawyer,' Harmony informed me.

This was news to me.

'Really,' he insisted. 'Don't worry, there's no fee. Get your things. I'm taking you to the attorney-general.'

'It has been a pleasure having you,' said Major Ango, bowed, and vanished upstairs with a swish of pyjamas. I gathered my bags, and followed Harmony to the gate, where a car was waiting. En route to the attorney-general's office, Harmony explained that he worked regularly for the SCNC. 'I've made a lot of calls,' he said. 'And I haven't been the only one. Your friends in London and New York have been making a lot of noise. It's not easy to get the attorney-general to come to his office on a Sunday.'

The attorney-general, Eneke Bechem, was a jovial puffin who worked in an office lined with dusty, leather-bound volumes of legal texts. He subjected me to an exceedingly gentle reading of the riot act, chiding me for my irresponsibility and my naivete. The official consensus seemed to be that, far from being a dangerous foreign provocateur, I was essentially a harmless imbecile who'd had no idea what he was getting himself into. I was content to go along with this on the grounds that it seemed likely to get me off the hook faster, and was more or less correct.

'So,' said Attorney-General Bechem, 'we will not be pressing charges.'

So . . . ?

'You may leave.'

I asked about Nfor and Stephen. I didn't like the idea of anyone being locked up for showing me around their country, and I was uncomfortable about going home if they were still in prison.

'There's nothing you can do about that,' said Bechem. 'Now I understand your flight is tomorrow night. There are buses all night from Bamenda to Douala. You will leave this evening, with two armed gendarmes.'

Er, no, I said. The attorney-general raised his eyebrows; Harmony rolled his eyes. A few things, I began. Eyebrows lifted higher, eyes rolled further. A private car, not a bus, with a friendly driver, and at least as many SCNC representatives as gendarmes. No guns, no uniforms. And I didn't want to travel overnight. I'd stay at a hotel in Bamenda and leave the following day. There'd be time to make Douala for the midnight flight, and besides which I wanted to go to Bamenda's craft market in the morning to pick up a present for Lucrezia, a bongo for James, and maybe an Indomitable Lions shirt for my young nephew in Sydney. I pitched this condition last, hoping it was quirky and flattering enough to win the attorney-general over.

'Dear Lord,' he said. 'You're hard to get rid of. But the craft market is worth seeing. Report to the gendarme headquarters at around midday, if that's okay.'

Not even the monkeys scampering and screeching inside the hotel's roof could keep me awake.

As I left the hotel, the agreed car, driven by a local SCNC activist, was flagged down by a trio of men in traditional dress, apparently on their way to see me. I got out of the car. They made heartfelt speeches expressing their thanks for my visit and sorrow for my inconvenience, and presented me with a straw bag, into which the words GREETINGS FROM SOUTHERN CAMEROONS were woven. When I emerged from the craft market, toting a wooden lion for myself, a tribal necklace for Lucrezia, a carved elephant for Roni and a bongo for James, four more men in traditional dress awaited, along with a waist-high wooden statue of a crouching figure in a winged helmet, clutching a pot with a removable lid. This handsome gift still sits in one corner of my lounge room in London, the injuries he suffered at the hands of Air France's baggage-hurlers having proved mercifully repairable. I call him Keith, because he looks like a Keith.

We met Harmony at a local courthouse. He hustled out to the car, his traditional lawyer's rig as splendidly incongruous against a background of palm trees as someone in a Panama hat emerging from the Old Bailey. He introduced his young assistant Valerie, who'd been drafted as my chaperone for the drive to Douala. At the gendarme headquarters, we collected my official escort – plainclothed, as requested, armed only with a walkie-talkie. He was a sergeant, built like a bouncer, who introduced himself as Petou. As would become deafeningly apparent over the next seven hours, Petou had the loudest laugh in the world, and found absolutely everything hilarious.

An hour out of Bamenda, Petou's walkie-talkie and Valerie's phone summoned their owners simultaneously. Both were absorbed in conversation which, to judge by their frequently exchanged glances, had something to do with the relationship between the organisations they represented. I couldn't figure out what was going on, as Petou's bellowing in French, punctuated by window-rattling eruptions of laughter, obscured Valerie's worried whispering in English. Their conversations ended at almost the same time, as if they'd been speaking to each other.

'There has been a raid,' said Valerie. 'The SCNC headquarters in Bamenda. The gendarmes have taken files, documents, furniture, pictures, everything.'

'HA HA HA HA HA,' roared Petou, whose laughter really was of pure, whimsical joy, without the merest undertone of malice. It was also quite infectious. I started giggling.

'They think you must be a spy!' whooped Petou. 'A HA HA HA HA HA! They think you must have brought important documents for SCNC! A HA HA HA HA HA!'

I muttered that they were going to be disappointed, as I hadn't brought the SCNC so much as a Tower Bridge fridge magnet.

'A HA HA HA HA HA!'

There was a lot of this as we progressed towards Douala. The four of us did as all such multi-party all-male blind dates do, and swapped tales of home, of family, of women. This took Petou longest – partly because he had, as he explained, at least three wives and a number of children he didn't seem too clear on, mostly because his anecdotes were so often derailed by violent gusts of laughter. We stopped in a couple of markets to look for infant-sized Indomitable Lions shirts ('For your nephew! A HA HA HA HA!') and at a roadside stall for plaintains, bananas and coffee (we briefly lost Petou; it didn't take long to find him). We discussed politics, with inevitable reference to Cameroon's linguistic schism, which made Petou laugh until he wept, but then everything did. I suspected that it was only his formidable size that prevented colleagues who had to spend longer stretches in his proximity from burying him up to his neck in an anthill and plugging his mouth with honey. The Australian High Commission in Abuja, Nigeria, checked in by phone every hour to confirm that I was still alive and heading towards Douala. Petou found this hilarious.

'Abuja! One time I was in Abuja! A HA HA HA HA HA!'

At Douala's sweltering airport, our eccentric quartet – three of whom who were possibly suffering some species of post-traumatic stress disorder – checked Keith and my rucksack aboard the flight. An

Air France representative with a clipboard approached.

'The flight is overbooked,' she said. 'We are offering people willing to fly tomorrow night 150 euros in compensation.'

Lady, I said, you couldn't buy me off this flight for 150,000 euros.

'A HA HA HA HA HAAAAAAAAAA!'

Only this time it was all four of us.

The moment the wheels lifted off Douala's bumpy tarmac was about the most perfectly blissful of my life. I was safe, I had a tale to tell and I was hours (in theory ten, in practice, between Air France's inability to effect connections and Lucrezia's no less erratic time-keeping, thirteen) away from a Heathrow reunion with someone who, I thought, might turn into a happy reason to spend less time undertaking the sort of quixotic quests which fill this book. I was beginning to realise that the amount I loved one woman had become more exciting to me than the reasons lots of people I didn't know hated each other.

I never got a chance to explain all that, at least not in ideal circumstances. A couple of weeks after I got home, Lucrezia ditched me to get engaged to the ex-boyfriend she'd spent much of our brief, if intense, time together expressing relief at being free from, on the grounds that he was, by her description, obsessive, possessive, violent, addicted to a dozen drugs and chronically unfaithful with both genders (but, presumably, a heck of a cook). It would be an exaggeration to report that I coped with this, and her ensuing operatic phone calls and bewildering emailed mea culpas, well, or indeed at all. It nearly did what the armed yahoos, unexploded landmines, kamikaze taxi drivers and intestinal parasites of sixty-odd countries had thus far failed to do, and put me into hospital. I avoided that, just, but I became very ill, tedious and, to people who cared, worrying. For several months, I ate little, slept less and felt generally like I'd had the top flipped off my head and a twin-beater mixer rammed into my brain. It was unpleasant to a degree which was almost interesting.

I lead a fortunate life. Usually, when faced with wilful recklessness and/or mendacity, I have the option, at least when not in prison, of deciding that I'm any or all of annoyed, scared and bored, and going home. This time, I had to live with it. This book was, substantially, typed with one hand while I tried to corral my marbles back into one sock with the other.

It might be tempting to ascribe this arguably absurd but nonetheless frightening meltdown to pent-up angst that had been deferred during years of seeking to understand why nations, peoples and faiths seemed so self-destructively keen to create unnecessary misery for themselves and others – to suggest that, maybe, that this broiling reservoir of bewilderment had been tapped by the self-destructive keenness of one person to create unnecessary misery for herself and me. It might even be tempting to draw melodramatic comparison between the effects of political and personal betrayal. It would not be nearly as tempting as it would be wrong, to say nothing of punchably pompous. People who make a show of feeling the pain of others – and some of them are journalists – are invariably full of crap. We all (this also applies to nations, peoples and faiths) feel our own agonies most acutely, however trivial in the broad sweep of events.

I mean, I felt bad that lots of Iraqis had been killed for no good reason, that Palestinians were terrorised, that Bosniaks decayed in mass graves, that my fellow citizens of London had been massacred on the tube. I felt worse about this. It was as simple and as complicated as the fact that nothing bursts like a heart suddenly inflated with hope. Falling in love has in common with travelling to volatile places that it is a leap of faith from an extremely high spot. It involves investing large quantities of trust in people you often don't know that well. Up until this point, as a traveller and a lover, I'd called most of these judgements right, though in practise I'd been better at actually doing the travelling than the loving, doubtless because travelling is easier for the preternaturally lazy and impatient. I was probably due a mis-step on one front or the other, and in the more philosophical moments that were granted me during my unravelling, was occasionally able to recognise that this was at least preferable to winding up posing for pictures in an orange jumpsuit next to an angry miscreant reciting scriptures and brandishing a scimitar.

I survived, shellshocked but still standing, thanks to a doctor supportive of my horror of medication, patient friends, and a professionally concerned woman with a clipboard who allowed me to talk, and talk, and talk, at a rate vexingly equivalent to a decent half-case of wine an hour, until I started boring myself. I derived additional succour from the admittedly extreme therapy of forming a country band with two members of Jesus Jones, the bassplayer from Sum Demeana and the scandalously under-rated Shetlandic chanteuse Astrid Williamson, and going on tour in Albania – 'Kumbo Prison Blues' got to be heard after all.

As for Southern Cameroon, while I bear no grudge against anyone concerned, I cannot quite overcome the suspicion that I was staked out as bait in a PR trap by the SCNC. Some of the subsequent press coverage in Cameroon, much of it amplified by quotes from the SCNC's competing factions, was ridiculous. One quote attributed to me – 'This is the worst thing that has ever happened to me, but the best thing for Southern Cameroon' – was something I'd not only never said, but never thought. Nfor and Stephen were freed three weeks after I got home, by (according to Valerie's email) a judge who referred to the release of 'the Australian' and declared that 'What's good for the goose is good for the gander'; I didn't dare ask Valerie who His Honour perceived as the goose. Over following months, though, I'd receive depressingly regular bulletins informing me of Nfor and Stephen's continuing arrests and harassments. In February 2007, Nfor smuggled a message to me out of Bamenda's Central Prison, where he was, once again, being held without charge following yet another raid on the SCNC's headquarters. 'Why,' he asked, 'is UK vocal on Kosovo but mute on British Southern Cameroons?' I thought I'd wait until Nfor was back out of jail before starting an involved discussion about Britain's chronic, and often counter-productive, bashfulness at any echoes of its imperial past.

It had been while I was typing some notes at the departure gate in Douala for a story for the *Independent on Sunday*'s foreign pages, and trying to find a frame of reference for my weirdly amiable deportation, that it occurred to me what Southern Cameroon reminded me of.

My egress from Cameroon, I wrote, had been like getting thrown out of Northern Ireland during the Troubles, and being driven to the airport by a member of Sinn Fein, one of their lawyers, and a British soldier from the Parachute Regiment. Like Northern Ireland, Southern Cameroon bumbled on the brink of conflict because a substantial part of its population, even in a post-imperial world, wanted to retain trappings of Britishness. No other empire commanded such loyalty among former constituents, but Britain always seemed more embarrassed than proud – although, granted, not always without reason.

19

Northern Ireland's interminable internecine conflict had, like most interminable internecine conflicts, been largely conducted with the standard weaponry of urban strife: guns, bombs, Molotov cocktails, handy chunks of rubble. It had also been fought, to a greater degree than usual, with paint. Throughout the Troubles, Republican and Loyalist neighbourhoods staked their claims with extravagant murals depicting the mythologies of their rival creeds. In Belfast, despite the peace ushered halfway in by the 1998 Good Friday Agreement, IRA hunger striker Bobby Sands was still garlanded in gold and green on the Catholic Falls Road, William of Orange remained triumphal above red, white and blue kerbstones on the Protestant Shankhill, and balaclavaed figures clutching Kalashnikovs haunted the brickwork of both districts.

On the side of a terrace house on a street off Newtonards Road – a staunchly Loyalist Belfast high street, where shops posted portraits of Queen Elizabeth II in the windows, and sold Ulster Volunteer Force coffee mugs – there was a huge painting of a moustached, mulletted figure looking like he might have played football for England in the early 1980s, or in a German heavy metal band anytime, surrounded by the insignia of two Loyalist paramilitary groups: the Ulster Defence Association and the Ulster Freedom Fighters. The picture was of Michael Stone, the man I'd come to Belfast to meet. Arcing in a semicircle above the picture were the words HIS ONLY CRIME WAS LOYALTY.

This somewhat generous assessment of Stone's paramilitary career was not shared by the judge who, in 1989, sentenced Stone to the sort of multi-century jail term one can only reasonably expect to finish in a brass-handled box, including six life terms for six murders. Three of these killings were assassinations carried out on behalf of the UDA and/or UFF between 1984 and 1987, and three were committed on 16 March 1988, at Belfast's Milltown cemetery, when Stone, armed with grenades and a pistol, launched a solo attack on the massive funeral of three IRA volunteers killed earlier that month on Gibraltar by Britain's SAS.

The news footage of the incident is enduringly bizarre: a flat-capped Stone charging at the thousands of mourners to a soundtrack of shots, explosions and screams before fleeing for his life, firing behind him as he runs. Stone was saved, just, from the understandably murderous wrath of the mob by the police. His rampage killed a thirty-year-old IRA volunteer, Caoimhin MacBradaigh, and two twenty-something civilians, Thomas McErlean and John Murray. More than fifty others were injured. There are few places where the perpetrator of such a crime could expect to see another view not obscured by bars and wire, but when I arrived in Belfast, Stone had been free a little over a year – a beneficiary, like many imprisoned paramilitaries, of the Good Friday Agreement. Stone was either a genuinely reformed character, or the most monstrous charlatan – or in the grip of a deeply peculiar midlife crisis. The former hitman was now an enthusiastic cheerleader for peace, and was about to hold the first exhibition of his art.

Stone's art wasn't explicitly political – his paintings and sculptures favoured a lurid surrealism inspired more by Salvador Dali, Pablo Picasso and Max Ernst than by King Billy and Edward Carson. But after I'd submitted to Stone's circulation-staunching handshake, in an office on Newtonards Road, Belfast's murals seemed a good place to start, especially as he featured in one of them. They were a bit creepy, I offered, but I thought they were generally graphically striking, and historically literate.

'Especially Republican wall murals,' Stone enthused, startlingly, 'but Loyalists are catching up. I give advice to the guys who do the murals around here. There's a large one of me on Templemore Avenue.'

I told Stone I'd seen it.

'Well,' he said, 'I'm the only living Loyalist, or Republican, to have a mural done with his face and name on it. I was privileged to have that done, and I'm proud of it . . . granted that the guy in the picture looks like Super Mario.'

The side of another building near where we were sitting was plastered in purple, yellow and orange tribute to the Red Hand Commando paramilitary group, though the effect was marred by the billboard advertisement for Harp lager slapped across the middle of it; in that setting, the Harp slogan HAD ONE LATELY? acquired an air of menace I doubted was intended. There were more murals further up Newtonards Road, where the famous yellow cranes of the Harland and Wolff shipyard rose in the background like immense suitcase handles. An Ulster Defence Association mural sought to depict the UDA as heirs of Cuchulainn, the warrior hero of Irish myth, next to a slogan demanding IRISH OUT – the UDA were clearly of the belief that they weren't making Irishmen like Cuchulainn anymore. A work by the East Belfast brigade of the Ulster Freedom Fighters featured a balaclavaed gunslinger next to a defiant text about freedom; the footpath garbage cans in front of it had been patriotically painted red, white and blue.

I wanted to meet Stone because the story behind his career shift from paramilitary to painter struck me as worth the trip to Belfast in itself, and also because I thought Stone might be able to tell me something about identity, and why people will kill and die for it, even when they live in a First World city. Northern Ireland had been enjoying peace, or at least an absence of all-out conflict, since 1998, but the visual rhetoric of these murals remained uncompromising and unmistakably violent. Where, I wondered, was the mural of a UFF paramilitary, petunias spouting from the barrel of his Armalite, hoisting a pint with the ghost of Bobby Sands? Could a place really be said to be at peace when its public spaces were overlooked by the glares of masked gunmen? Weren't these paintings just war by other means?

'Aw, they're just marking their turf,' said Stone. 'Outside my home, the UVF have stuck a big flag up. So the UDA came round and stuck two on top of that.'

I'd noticed this on Newtonards Road, as well – every streetlamp wore a corsage of the incongruously pretty banners of Loyalist paramilitary groups, all of them bunched up towards the top of the poles to which they were tied. In the grand tradition of violent radicals down the ages, Ulster's Loyalist groups loathed each other at least as much as they hated their common enemy.

'I can see that if you weren't a local it'd be comical,' said Stone.

Stone was still coming to terms with his freedom, such as it was.

'I have three safe houses,' he said. 'They are fortified homes, bulletproof windows, steel shutters. I have twenty-two dogs – dobermans, rottweilers, bull mastiffs, pit bulls. I have hi-tech security systems, I wear body armour when I go out, I have Special Branch watching me. Not that I'm going to do anything – my war is over – but they're frightened that dissident Republicans will take me out and I'll be the spark to start the Troubles again.'

Stone, forty-six at the time of our meeting, was easily the most recognisable of the freed Loyalist prisoners – indeed, as a living icon of the Troubles, he ranked behind only the real kingpins, the likes of Ian Paisley, Gerry Adams and Martin McGuinness. Stone's signature topiary had acquired a few grey strands in the thirteen years since his assault on Milltown, but he was still the man in that video clip. He seemed unsure what to make of his celebrity – or, as he solemnly corrected me, infamy. Most of the stories he told me about his new life were against himself: two young Glaswegians who'd brandished their Celtic scarves at him in an airport lounge and shouted their fervent hope that his plane crashed; shoppers in local grocery stores who asked him to sign boxes of cornflakes. He claimed to feel dismay about this, and anguish at his circumscribed circumstances, saying that he never went into the centre of Belfast for fear of assault, or worse – but, I thought, if he had a shave and a haircut he'd have been able to wander unnoticed anywhere he liked. He wasn't, I suggested, entirely displeased with being identified as Michael Stone – and it was difficult to believe that the people buying his works weren't paying at least in part for the frisson of owning something created by a killer.

'I'm asked if I'm trading on my name,' he said. 'But my name is all I have, and I'm proud of my name – one of my sons is Michael Stone, one of my grandsons is Michael Stone. Look at Adams and McGuinness. Would they have made it in politics without being former Republican activists? They're bad boys. But you have to have your hands bloodied. How can you speak for men of violence if you haven't been there yourself? I agree that it's sad, but there it is.'

Stone began sketching shortly after his arrest in 1988.

'I was remanded in custody,' he said, 'and put on a Rule 25 – that's a twenty-three- or twenty-four-hour lock-up in solitary confinement. And I was in the PSU – that's the Prison Segregation Unit, at the old Crumlin Road jail. They kept me there for a year under Rule 25. Boys did go mad. They mutilated themselves, slit themselves with razor blades and whatnot, but they were ordinary criminals. A guy in for rape sliced his own scrotum open, and I witnessed bits of that going on outside his cell when they took him away to the funny farm.'

Despite such diversions, Stone began to find solitary confinement tedious.

'I kept fit,' he recalled, 'did press-ups, running on the spot. But I got bored, so I asked a senior officer if I could have a sketch pad and watercolours, and he laughed, because this guy's in for multiple murder, you know? But they gave me a writing pad and a pencil. There were fifty or sixty pages in the pad, and they'd numbered every page, in case I was writing notes and sneaking them out to accomplices – every page had to be accounted for. I was given the pad at ten o'clock every morning and it was taken away at two o'clock every afternoon. I'd do sketches from memory, or draw the cell. I got bored drawing the inside of the cell, so I asked the screws if they could leave the peephole in the cell door open. And I sketched the screws sitting in the corridor – signed them, gave them to the screws as wee keepsakes. That's where it took off. It wasn't the butch thing to do, art, but it relaxed me.'

After being sentenced, Stone was transferred to the Maze – the infamous H-Blocks. Here, Stone furthered his interest theoretically, in the prison library, and practically, with the acrylic paints available to prisoners. He painted on linen handkerchiefs before graduating to two-foot by two-foot bits of plywood brought in by visitors, and larger boards fashioned from the backs of prison lockers or canteen tables. 'I also took the linen sheets off the bed and used those as canvases,' he laughed. 'But when the screws caught on, they took the linen sheets away and gave us polyester ones. Which itched like fuckin' hell.'

Since his release, Stone's art had become his full-time occupation, as his paint-spattered shoes and trousers attested. He was encouraging local children and fellow ex-prisoners to forsake bomb and bullet for brush and easel.

'The probation board have given up on a few of them,' he explained. 'They're fourteen, fifteen years old, breaking windows, breaking into homes, and where street justice could have taken over, they're in with me now. I've turned them around. They're still wee devils, and I can't get them into the surreal and the abstract stuff, but they're doing a bit.'

He accepted that he mightn't be everyone's idea of a role model.

'I used to get a bit of the hero worship,' he acknowledged sheepishly. 'Mr Stone, they used to call me. Then it was Rambo. Now it's just Michael. They want to know how to draw the Ulster flag and the Union Jack, but they're moving on – they draw David Beckham and WWF wrestlers. As for the gunmen on the wall murals, that's part of me and it's part of Ulster Loyalism. So the guys come around, and I teach them how to grid their work on murals, and they're doing more cultural stuff now – Cuchulainn, Lord Carson, James Craig, the founders of Unionism. They keep the gunmen because it's part of our history, and because they'd kick my arse if I told them to take the gunmen off. I used to be one, remember.'

Stone emphasised that he was no longer involved with paramilitary activity – he repeated the phrase 'My war is over' in the quantities of mantra. Like Northern Ireland as a whole, though, Stone seemed unable or unwilling to completely abandon the grimly romantic trappings of tribal conflict. A UFF unit provided security at the opening of his exhibition. There were, he said, three or four paramilitary types watching the entrances to the building we were sitting in. Wasn't it time Belfast's young men packed this stuff in?

'We're proud of our traditions,' he argued. 'If you don't have a history, how can you build a future? The Loyalist cause is a just cause, and it's one I still believe in.'

Stone accepted the defining contradiction of Loyalism: that most of the Britain to which his people were so fiercely devoted generally regarded the Loyalist cause, on the infrequent occasions they regarded it all, with bewilderment or revulsion. But he evinced little of the paranoia usually characteristic of Loyalist rhetoric. His belief that Ireland was unlikely to be unified anytime soon was based on appreciation, unarguably well-informed, of a few brutal truths.

'It won't happen,' he said. 'Not with 1.3 million Protestants, with at least half a million of those thinking the way I used to think. It'd be role reversal. You'd have Loyalist paramilitaries blowing the shit out of everything. Can you imagine the Garda Siochana [Irish police] or Irish soldiers patrolling Loyalist areas? Loyalist paramilitaries would have what the Provos always had that we didn't – a uniform to shoot at.'

On that crazy day at Milltown in 1988, Stone nearly jolted Northern Ireland's destiny onto a path unimaginably different from the one it had since followed. Knowing that an IRA funeral would attract the high command, he went to Milltown intending to kill Gerry Adams and Martin McGuinness. Stone believed that McGuinness okayed the IRA bomb that slew ten civilians and a policeman at a Remembrance Day service in Enniskillen the previous November. As well as exacting revenge for that atrocity, he hoped that bumping off the IRA's leadership would provoke full-scale war.

'Aye,' he confirmed, outlining his strategy. 'Never mind another twenty years of bodies dumped on street corners, or no-warning bombs; let's be having you.'

Whatever Stone thought he might achieve by becoming the Gavrilo Princip of Ulster, it is unlikely he imagined that, come the dawn of the twenty-first century, he would be establishing himself as an artist, and Martin McGuinness would be the minister of education responsible for the schooling of Stone's grandchildren.

'McGuinness drives by my home every day to go to work,' giggled Stone, 'and I think of the time I went down to the Bogside in

Londonderry and stood outside his home with a pistol down the back of my trousers, and kicked a ball against his back fence hoping he'd come out.'

I asked how he felt now when he saw the footage of Milltown.

'Sad,' he answered. 'Sad that I was angry enough to go there after those specific targets – McGuinness and Adams. Sad that other Loyalists felt they had to take retaliatory action, and sad that the Republicans felt they had to commit atrocities like Enniskillen. It was a sad time.'

I wondered if he wished he hadn't gone.

'I wish I hadn't had to go,' he replied. 'I wish at sixteen years old I hadn't joined the UDA to defend my country and my community, as I see it. With hindsight, you can pontificate, and analyse, and moralise, but . . .'

There was a pause. Quite a long one.

'I've killed men who've been as close to me as you are now,' he continued, without departing from his gentle, sing-song lilt, 'and I've heard their last words and shot them in the head. There was one, an IRA member with a number of kills under his belt, big lump of a man, and he shouted for his mammy. That never leaves me, but I have to live with it. There's nothing smart, nothing brave about killing another human being. It's cold, it's callous. You have to be that way, you don't see the real person. When I killed people, I wouldn't look at a newspaper or a television afterwards, because then you see the family. Yes, he was a soldier – and I don't see IRA volunteers as terrorists, they're soldiers, same as I'm a Loyalist soldier – but there's his parents and his children and the human side of it.'

Did he regret his failure to kill Adams? Or was he resigned to the curious cult of St Gerry the Peacemaker?

'I don't begrudge Adams that,' Stone shrugged. 'If he'd done it years ago, and if the peace process had happened years ago, I wouldn't have gone to prison, the six guys I killed wouldn't be dead, the people I've injured wouldn't be carrying those scars, the people the IRA and Loyalists killed would still be alive. It's a pity it didn't happen years ago. Once, whenever they came on television, I couldn't look at them. But, peace process, eight years later, I could tolerate it. Now I can watch them. They've moved on. I've moved on. You pass the odd car, maybe a Nationalist driving by a Loyalist area, and he'll give me the finger, and so what? I can handle that. The guys with me might talk about getting his registration, but I just tell them to behave. Forget about it, you know.'

Stone said he wanted to live as normal a life as he could – play with his dogs, paint, try to construct some sort of family life. He was engaged, to a woman he'd known since before he went to prison, and had nine children – he'd become a father for the first time at sixteen, the same age at which he began his first prison sentence, for theft of weapons.

'My kids don't know me,' he said, looking by some distance the saddest he did all afternoon. 'They're between thirty and fourteen, from two marriages and two other relationships – I used to be a devil for the women. I'm trying to get to know them now. Plus there have been a few since I got out saying their daddy is Michael Stone.'

I asked what his oldest son, for example, made of him. Stone's response was either incredibly oblique, or suggested that there were some things they didn't really discuss.

'He laughs at my ponytail,' said Stone.

The Engine Room Gallery, a refurbished flax mill which was hosting Stone's exhibition, was only a short walk up Newtonards Road, but a lift had been arranged. This was partly because of the limp from which Stone had suffered since Milltown ('Aye, I got a bit of a kicking,' he said, as we headed downstairs to the street, 'but all's fair in love and war'), and partly because of Stone's reluctance to walk the streets even in this heartland of Loyalism. We were ushered into a car whose front seats were occupied by two large men with little hair, and many tattoos of lions, Union Jacks and red hands.

As he showed me around the gallery, Stone seemed caught between pride and uncertainty, repeatedly asking what I thought. Colourful, I said.

'Some of them are garish,' he agreed, 'but that's intentional. Where I was, everything was bleak – black asphalt, grey walls, silver razor wire – so the colours were a wee bit of escapism. I know a lot of it's mediocre, but there's a few nice pieces here. I know I'm not a genius. I'm just trying to find my way.'

I said, honestly, that I liked a couple of the paintings, especially one of a multicoloured striped rhinoceros, but that I wasn't sure how comfortable I'd feel having Michael Stone's signature on my wall. The common difficulty of separating the art from the artist seemed especially acute in this case.

'Yeah, I can see that,' he said. 'A lot of people who buy them do it through third parties. Belfast businessmen who have Catholic customers or employees or friends – I think they hang them in their Spanish holiday homes.'

Stone made us tea in the gallery's kitchen, and we chatted further about art, and books we'd been reading. He was a bright and not insensitive man, but he'd done dumb, terrible things. He didn't seem to have figured out whether he saw himself as a victim of his circumstances, or the author of his misfortunes.

Was it, I asked, figuring that I might as well go for the big one while I was here, all worth it?

'It was and it is,' he replied. 'It's life and death. Too many good men, too many good Loyalist volunteers, too many security forces, too many innocent civilians have lost their lives. Too many prisoners have spent thousands of years in prison.'

This was just stupidity feeding on itself, though, like continuing to smack yourself in the face with a tea-tray because you've been smacking yourself with a tea-tray all afternoon, and you don't want to admit to yourself or anyone else that it was an imprudent thing to start doing in the first place.

'We're proud of our Britishness,' insisted Stone. 'My great-grandfather, grandfather and father were all British servicemen. My great-grandfather was gassed at the Somme, my uncle drowned in a submarine. The flags, the symbolism, that's all part of our identity. I could never say I'm Irish. I'm British. We're more British than the British over here.'

This was certainly the case, but even if Loyalism's total nightmare scenario came to pass – a unified Irish republic, with a Sinn Fein majority in its parliament – it was hard to imagine Taoiseach Gerry Adams outlawing the English language, banning images of Queen Elizabeth, forcing Michael Stone to wear a hat shaped like a pint of Guinness on St Patrick's Day, and setting light to Protestant churches.

'It was never anything to do with religion,' said Stone. 'And believe it or not, it was never really anything to do with politics. You were young, you think they're blowing us up so we'll blow them up, they're shooting us so we'll shoot them.'

This crass, wearisomely common, moral arithmetic had turned Michael Stone into a killer six times over.

'There is,' Stone said, contemplating his mug, 'a futility in politically motivated violence, I recognise that. One of my works is a series of shapes in black and white and two shades of grey. It's called *Not Everything In Life Is Black And White*.'

Or green and orange.

'Exactly,' he said. 'My brother's married to a Catholic girl, and what? They're not from the planet fuckin' Zorg. That's what I tell people, guys my age who've never even met a Catholic. It's the old fuckin' dinosaurs like myself who haven't moved on – but I have.'

It was, I thought at the time, a shame that he'd taken such a gloomily scenic route to do it. But I believed Stone then, and I believed him when I bumped into him a year later, on Gibraltar of all places. We shared tea and scones in a hotel cafe, and he reiterated his enthusiasm for peace, and sorrow for Northern Ireland's lengthy and unnecessary travails.

In November 2006, though, it became bafflingly, farcically clear that Stone hadn't moved on at all. In what was either an attempted reprise of his solo charge at Milltown, or a woefully misconceived promotional stunt for his autobiography, Stone, armed with a pistol and homemade explosives, launched a lone attack on Stormont, the seat of Northern Ireland's dormant government, as local politicians tried to figure out if they could tolerate each other sufficiently to engage in politics like grown-ups.

As a display of hostile defiance, Stone's kamikaze onslaught looked, on its own merits, pretty impressive right up until the point at which he was wrestled to a ranting standstill by a middle-aged usher and female security guard. The Loyalist battle cry 'No Surrender' curdles the blood rather less when the warrior declaiming it is incapacitated by a half-nelson administered by a blonde. Tuning in to see Stone's second peculiar contribution to the televisual mythology of Northern Ireland, I noted that what he'd apparently unlearnt about the desirability of peace, he'd at least picked up in tonsorial fashion – the mullet was gone. Perhaps some conniving Delilah had discerned that the ponytail was where he stored his commonsense. 'No sell-out!' Stone bellowed, in the grip of his captors, to a crowd of reporters whose amusement was ill-disguised. The unfinished graffito – 'Sinn Fein IRA Mur . . .' – he'd left on the masonry was an almost endearingly hapless touch.

The following month in Belfast's High Court, Stone's defence lawyer submitted the droll elucidation that his client, far from mounting a murderous assault on the seat of Northern Ireland's sputtering democracy, perish the thought, had actually been staging 'a piece of performance art replicating a terrorist attack'. It was a potentially interesting precedent ('While it may look to the unwitting observer like I stole the plaintiff's phone and broke his nose, Your Honour, the reality is that it was a piece of performance art replicating petty theft and a bloody good hiding, heavily influenced by the early 1970s "Aktions" of Joseph Beuys, Sir.' 'Very good. Case dismissed.'). But, all things considered, I thought my chances of ever again enjoying scones with Stone were remote.

I did wonder, though, what Stone had been thinking when he lit out for Stormont that morning ('I'm one of the most notorious terrorists in the western world, I'm turning up unannounced at one of the most heavily guarded installations in the United Kingdom . . . yes, however you look at it, this is an entirely excellent plan, and nothing can possibly go wrong.') Most people I interview get interviewed by lots of hacks, so I never assume that any of them will remember as much of our conversation as I do, but I did recall asking Stone why non-violence wouldn't have worked in Northern Ireland, and telling him about the kids I knew elsewhere in Europe, who'd mounted revolutions by using graffiti and prankery to mock their oppressors. Maybe Stone had listened after all, but not quite grasped the subtleties of such tactics. Perhaps I just hadn't explained myself very well. More likely than either, of course, was that Michael Stone was just plain violent, and dangerous, a bad man granted a perverse legitimacy, even lustre, by the violent times and the dangerous place in which he had lived.

One ceaselessly interesting aspect of conflict is the manner in which it extracts the worst from the worst and the best from the best, the way war makes people more of what they already are, whether cowardly, brave, stupid, smart, cruel, kind, follower, leader. One of the most depressing aspects of the early twenty-first century was that outright victories for the good guys – and unequivocal trouncings for their opposite numbers – were few and far between. They did happen, though, and the most heartening of them all occurred in a place which, during the dusk of the twentieth century, had been about the last place anyone would have expected such a stirring, Sunday-matinee climax.

20

I was never much of a student revolutionary, but then I was never much of a student. My tertiary education was noteworthy only for a retrospectively inexplicable determination to confirm that my failure to complete the first year of an Arts degree had been no fluke, by returning the following year and repeating the feat. The only demonstrations I attended were against the building of an ugly monorail through the middle of Sydney and the imposition of an administrative charge on Australian university students. The latter protest did at least involve a mildly exciting occupation of some building or other, and a bit of a dust-up with the New South Wales police, who got a trifle carried away by their first opportunity since the Vietnam War to seize spoilt young people by their long hair and heave them down staircases. But, with the exception of those students who were injured – and there were a few – I'm sure everyone involved, in uniform and not, enjoyed the day out enormously.

This is why people sign on for their stint as student revolutionaries: it's fun, or at least it's fun if you're lucky enough to live in a place where it's never going to be a life and death issue. (Those who campaign on international trade and finance may argue that these are life and death issues for other people, and they're right, but they're unlikely to end up making defiant speeches to firing squads themselves.) It's fun being a stridently right-on, witheringly self-righteous creature, wearing terrible hair, worse clothes, shaking a fist at the world, maintaining a headful of half-understood ideology gleaned from Rage Against the Machine choruses, adorning your walls with photos of a dopey Argentinian murderer gazing into the middle distance, and perhaps on very special occasions coming in for some light tear gassing. And there is nothing necessarily bad about any of this. Even silly ideas occasionally gestate into inspiration. Questioning, however reflexive and reactionary, sometimes provokes constructive thought. And if it doesn't, if these rebellious impulses do nothing but fill the air with dim, chanted slogans and annoying whistle blasts, then it at least provides work for smug commentators who derive their livelihoods in part from mocking the convinced.

In Serbia in the 1990s, being a student revolutionary was more than a holiday from responsibility, or a subsidised opportunity to figure out one's politics. A generation of young Serbs grew up without the luxury of being able to imagine a defining struggle, nor to delude themselves about the stakes it was being played for.

'It was my birthday,' said Branko Ilic. Branko wasn't your typical student revolutionary. Your typical student revolutionary, full as they may be of grandiloquent rhetoric, is as likely to realise that nobody has ever looked good with a pierced lip as they are to actually bring down the system. Branko, as nominal figurehead of a remarkable and inspirational movement called Otpor!, had done exactly that – brought down the system, that is, not pierced his lip – not long before I met him.

'On 4 October,' Branko continued, 'at eleven pm, I was sitting here, and I looked at the date over there on the pinball machine, and I realised that I'd almost forgotten that tomorrow would be my birthday. I knew, of course, that tomorrow would also be the big rally, and that it could be the last day of the Milosevic regime. I thought, Tomorrow, I'll be twenty years old, and I'll be free or I'll be dead.'

I'd spent the day before I met Branko following the trail of Belgrade's splendid revolution, which had occurred a fortnight previously. Chaotic though it had looked on the news, there had been little mindless pillage on 5 October. Belgrade's enraged citizenry had hit their targets with a precision that might have seemed an uncanny echo of NATO's surgical missile strikes of the year before, except that the Serbian revolution hadn't demolished any foreign embassies by mistake.

People were still wandering in and out of the smoke-blackened parliament building, exhibiting the incredulous delight and relief of a long-abused woman who finally does the proper thing and clatters her violent husband with a frying pan.

'If we'd known it was going to be that easy,' said Milica, my friend and fixer, 'we'd have done it years ago.'

Milica directed myself and photographer Alan Clarke, on assignment for the *Face*, along the course of Belgrade's rage. After seizing the parliament, this meticulous revolution had set about the headquarters of Slobodan Milosevic's Socialist Party, the office of the Yugoslav United Left (the party of Milosevic's termagant wife Mira Markovic), the perfume shop Scandal, owned by Milosevic's gangster son Marko, a couple of police stations and, most cathartically, the complex that had housed Radio Television Serbia (RTS), the dark heart of Milosevic's propaganda machine. NATO's targeting of the same building during the Kosovo war had provoked uproar, within Serbia and without, but the mob had happily finished what the previous year's air strikes had started. On 5 October, RTS had burned with such fury that the footpath alongside it was an eerie monochrome mosaic: the soot-blackened glass from dozens of shattered windows had melted into the grey asphalt.

The postcard-sellers on Kneza Mihaila Street, the busy pedestrian arcade that wound through the centre of Belgrade, were – as they had been on my previous visit, seven months earlier – a useful barometer of their city's mood. Joining the wry, bitter cards that commemorated NATO's bombing campaign was a cartoon of a glum, familiar-looking man in a grey suit, holding a pistol to his own head. The caption read SPASI SRBIJU, UBIJ SE!: Save Serbia, kill yourself!. On the reverse of the card, a pre-printed letter in Serbian translated broadly as 'Goodbye, and good riddance', and the address of a suggested recipient was thoughtfully filled in: a Mr Slobodan Milosevic, 11000 Beograd, Uzicka 16, Srbija.

Some Belgraders I spoke to thought he might still be there, at home, others that he'd vanished to a mountain hideout, still others that he'd decamped to Minsk or Moscow. The great and encouraging thing was that nobody really cared. Slobodan Milosevic had suffered the most ignominious end imaginable to a dictator's career: a tyrant nobody could be bothered to lynch.

Branko Ilic, a Spanish and philology student at the University of Belgrade, was the most prominent figurehead of Otpor! (Resistance!). As was the case with thousands who rallied to the Otpor! name, Branko's had been a life defined by the man who ran what used to be Yugoslavia into a slough of blood and nonsense. Branko was nine years old when Slobodan Milosevic embarked on his disastrous tenure as Serbia's leader, ten when the Yugoslav national army stormed Croatia, eleven when the Bosnian Serb army began pillaging Bosnia-Herzegovina, twelve when Yugoslavia's economy collapsed to the extent that a 500,000,000,000 dinar note was circulated – and still wasn't worth anything – eighteen when NATO aircraft bombed his country in retribution for Milosevic's pogroms in Kosovo.

'We were always threatened by something, all our lives,' said Branko. 'That's why nobody could make us afraid.'

And so Branko came to spend his twentieth birthday on the back of a flat-bed truck with a megaphone, yelling through the tear gas, trying to prevent panic among the crowds that milled around Belgrade's handsome parliament building on the strange and wonderful afternoon of 5 October, doing his bit to topple a dictator. When I asked Branko if he had anything special planned for his twenty-first, he laughed – but he knew, now, that he could afford to: he and a generation of young Serbs had taken their lives back. The happy ending, and the promise of a new beginning, hadn't always looked assured.

'I've been worried,' shrugged Branko, who'd racked up his tenth arrest in the summer of 2000. 'One week, I lived in seven different apartments. I remember once, we were in a cafe, making plans, and seven cars pulled up in front – the waiter told us, and let us out a back window.'

Branko and I were talking in a cafe in Belgrade University. At nine o'clock on a Tuesday morning, the campus was otherwise deserted – Serbia's students had some things in common with their indolent western counterparts. Branko was shortish, and softly spoken, his occasionally halting English accented only slightly. While he talked, he absent-mindedly stroked the lamp on the table between us, as if it were some luminous green cat. Outside, in a courtyard, the concrete walls were upholstered with Otpor! stickers and slathered with Otpor! graffiti, mostly repetitions of Otpor!'s favourite anti-Milosevic slogan, 'Gotov Je!' ('He's finished!'). The graffiti was in Serbian, except one dominant English exclamation, daubed in bright red: POWER TO THE PEOPLE!. This, Branko explained, had been sprayed by an American television reporter, seeking to give her piece-to-camera a background illustration that she felt might be understood by her viewers.

'I never saw Otpor! as a political party,' said Branko. 'I am sure huge numbers of people will leave Serbia now Milosevic has gone, and we will lose the confidence we have now. Maybe we got some kind of political education these past two years, but this nation, especially the youth, still needs a cultural education. So I hope the role of Otpor! will be some kind of social movement that will spread cultural education in Serbia.'

Branko was difficult to reconcile with the mental image I'd formed from conversations with other, even younger, members of Otpor!. To the adolescent rank and file of the movement, Branko was a peculiarly Balkan pin-up figure: Che Guevara multiplied by Kurt Cobain, though with better-trimmed facial hair than either. ('I remember Branko on the truck,' one Otpor! activist had positively squealed, when asked for her recollections of the uprising. 'He was so cool.')

When I alluded to this devotion, Branko rolled his eyes, and gallantly trotted out the line that Otpor! had no leaders. He would, at least, admit to being one of the founders of the movement, which began as a coalition of disparate student opposition groups towards the end of 1998. Branko had arrived at Belgrade University with form as a troublemaker – in his hometown of Arilje, he had been suspended from school for organising a protest against the rigging of local elections.

Nevertheless, Branko told me, he'd initially felt that the other early Otpor! conspirators – some of them grand old men of twenty-two or twenty-three – needed convincing of his commitment. The opportunity was provided by a visit to the university by Vojislav Seselj, leader of the quasi-fascist Serbian Radical Party, and commander of a Bosnian Serb army militia responsible for some of the most hideous excesses of the Bosnian war. Branko dropped a flag bearing Otpor!'s clenched fist logo on Seselj's head from an overhanging window. 'After I let go,' he remembered, 'I saw Seselj's bodyguards charging into the faculty and I ran. My heart was beating very fast.'

As Otpor! became an increasingly potent force, and Belgrade grew ever more plastered in government-sponsored posters denouncing the students as traitors and terrorists, Branko became a correspondingly well-known identity, and the risks grew proportionately larger. There were few occupations on Earth more dangerous than that of a public figure in the last months of Milosevic's lunacy. In 2000 alone, the high-profile casualties of Belgrade's gang rivalries and political feuds included the war crimes suspect Zeljko Raznatovic (aka Arkan), Yugoslav defence minister Pavle Bulatovic, Yugoslav Airlines general manager Zika Petrovic, provincial politician Bosko Perosevic and, most incredibly, Ivan Stambolic, the former Serbian president and one-time patron of Slobodan Milosevic. Stambolic, a reflective and changed man, had become friendly with Otpor!. On 25 August, he went for a jog near his home. He hadn't been seen since. (His corpse was found in a ditch in northern Serbia in 2003.)

Though Branko was now free to think and speak without the worry of ending up in the Danube River wearing concrete flippers, he professed reluctance to pursue a career in conventional politics. Like many of his western contemporaries, he was weary of the dishonesty, corruption and self-interest of political parties. I couldn't help wondering, though, if Branko felt some sense of anticlimax, some nagging worry that life, though it may get easier, might get a lot less exciting . . . Did he, I asked, apologising in advance for the weirdness of the question, think he'd miss Slobodan Milosevic?

'No,' he laughed. 'Actually, I think it will be more strange for our parents and grandfathers. We were kids when he started his dict-atorship. We have other things to do now. Some of us have already forgotten him.'

Serbs had lived through too much not to be realistic, though, and Otpor! weren't losing sight of Thomas Jefferson's assessment of the price of freedom: eternal vigilance. Already, their anti-Milosevic posters had come down. They'd been replaced by cartoons of a bull-dozer, just like the one driven through the gates of RTS on 5 October It was accompanied by a message for Yugoslavia's new rulers: 'We are watching you.' Branko and the rest of Otpor! may have forgotten Milosevic, but they weren't about to forget what their city had been like, as he turned it into a grotesque combination of 1920s Chicago and 1930s Berlin. When situations change – and especially when they change quickly – the balance between advancement and reversion is a fine one. Serbia's journey towards civilisation over the next few years would rather resemble the progress of a very drunk man motoring home on a very foggy night – slow, hesitant, prone to undig-nified mishap. The important thing, though, was that despite the often debatable competence of the occupant of the driver's seat, they were travelling away from where they'd been.

21

BELGRADE, SERBIA
MARCH 2000

Seven months before the revolution, Belgrade was a city of a thousand jokes about one man. The best gag went like this: a Belgrade resident is driving in his rusty, backfiring Yugo sedan, searching for somewhere to park. Eventually, he finds a spot outside a grand building and reverses into it. An armed sentry rushes up to him and says frantically, 'Hey, what are you doing? This is where President Milosevic lives!' 'Thanks for telling me,' replies the motorist, getting out of his car. 'I'll make sure I lock it.'

At that strange – well, stranger than usual – point in Serbian history, there were a couple of difficulties with flying to Belgrade to report on it: you couldn't fly there, and you couldn't report on it. An international air embargo had turned Belgrade's airport into the aviation equivalent of a pub with no beer. The Yugoslav Interests Office in London sounded, when I called, as likely to toss visas to journalists as they were to throw a surprise birthday party for Tony Blair. Photographer Dave Thomson and I, on assignment for *Loaded* magazine, secured our Yugoslav passport stamps with the ludicrous pretence that we were a travelling partnership of an impressionist photographer and a poet, creating works inspired by European capitals. We flew to Budapest, from whose airport's departure terminal operated one of those improvised enterprises always inspired by war: a minibus shuttle to Belgrade.

It wasn't until we reached the Serbian border, after a long drive across the hypnotically featureless plains of southern Hungary, that Dave and I realised we should have rehearsed our cover better. It had been an easy yarn to write on the application form, albeit to a soundtrack of barely stifled sniggers. Explained out loud to the scrawny, moustachioed Serbian customs officer on duty at the border, it sounded as ridiculous as it was.

'So,' said the customs officer, nodding towards Dave. 'You are a photographer, an artist.'

That's right, we confirmed, helpfully holding open Dave's rucksack to reveal his cameras.

'And you,' he said, squinting at me, 'write poems.'

I nodded in what I hoped was a suitably profound manner.

'You wouldn't be journalists,' he said.

Heavens no, we said, in tones of horror. If either of us had thought to bring a lace handkerchief, we'd have been dabbing our foreheads and affecting vapours. But we were rumbled, and no doubt deservedly. We were as convincing as a pair of anteaters on stilts trying to gain admission to a giraffes-only golf club. The customs officer studied our passports further, pausing long enough at the stamps I'd have preferred him to skip – Bosnia, Croatia, Pakistan, Afghanistan, Lebanon – for me to form discouraging prejudices about Serbian prison gruel.

'Definitely not journalists,' he said, and smiled.

He kept smiling, and when we realised why, we started smiling too. It was a glorious spring day. Before our minibus had shown up, the customs officer had been ensconced in a deckchair with a couple of thick thrillers, and an espresso cooling on a silver platter. If he busted us for being journalists taking the piss, that'd be his afternoon, possibly his evening. He'd have to make phone calls. Involve higher authorities. Fill in, the Balkans being the Balkans, a heap of forms so tall that the skeletons of past explorers would be entombed in its icy upper reaches.

'A poet and an artist,' he grinned. 'Get on the bus. Get the fuck out of here.'

Pleased though Dave and I were to have reached our objective, crossing the Danube on a pontoon replacement for the bridges destroyed in the bombardment, we nevertheless arrived in Belgrade harbouring trepidations. We were coming to town for the first anniversary of the beginning of the bombing campaign that NATO had launched the previous April. We knew that we'd be taken for citizens of NATO nations. In a worst-case scenario, we'd been hoping that emphatic protestations of Dave's Scottishness and my Australianness would confuse any lynch mobs long enough for us to dive into the river and swim for it.

But in a week in Belgrade, we barely attracted a hostile glance. We found people who were as generous with their food and drink, of which they generally had too little, as they were with their time, of which they generally had far too much – unemployment in stony-broke, sanctions-strangled Serbia being the rule rather than the exception. People we'd never met invited us to attend their birthday dinners, and beautiful waitresses with terrible teeth asked us to parties as we sipped our morning coffees. On 24 March, the date on which the air campaign had begun a year before, we wandered unmolested through the events commemorating it, whether half-hearted pro-government rally or wishy-washy opposition demonstration. I tried to enter into the spirit of things by buying, from a street vendor, a rosette in the colours of Serbia's flag with a black and white target in the middle of it. I wasn't sure what it marked me as for or against, but it didn't matter. By lunchtime, everyone had gone home.

Belgrade didn't look like the capitals of dictatorships were supposed to. There were no soldiers on the streets, save for occasional conscripts in uniforms five sizes too big, as if designed for a fondly imagined army of seven-foot Serbian supermen. We only found police in significant numbers when we went to the football to see Yugoslav league leaders Partizan Belgrade at home to already-relegated no-hopers Borac. Though it is traditional among despots to rebuild their fiefdoms in their own image, there were no statues of Milosevic in Belgrade, and no heroic portraits. I saw just one laudatory image of his hedgehoggish face, on a placard wielded by a deranged old woman; she had lovingly written 'My hawk', in Serbian, on his collar. The only other representations of Milosevic available were less reverent, appearing on postcards sold freely from footpath stalls. One showed a still of Milosevic taken from a television appearance during the NATO bombing, his triumphantly lofted hand photoshopped to extend a middle digit to the audience. The caption was characteristically sledge-hammer Balkan sarcasm: PRESEDNIK MILOSEVIC NAJAVIO OBNOVU I RAZVOJ ZEMLJE! (President Milosevic proclaims reconstruction and development of Serbia!).

It said much about Serbia's confused state of mind that the same stalls were also selling souvenirs which took an obdurate pride in those Serbian traits which reappeared through any study of Serbia's past, or any round of drinks with Serbian people: self-mockery, self-regard, self-pity and self-delusion. They coalesced wonderfully on a badge which chronicled centuries of Serbian bloody-mindedness thus: OTTOMAN EMPIRE – NO MORE; AUSTRIA-HUNGARY – NO MORE; THIRD REICH – NO MORE; NATO – WORKING ON IT. (The failure to include a line acknowledging YUGOSLAVIA – NO MORE indicated a fairly selective reading of Serbian history.) Other postcards bore pictures of explosions beneath a jaunty GREETINGS FROM BELGRADE, and pictures of the American stealth fighter which had come down during the air campaign, with a caption gloating SORRY – WE DIDN'T KNOW IT WAS INVISIBLE.

Belgrade had sights as well as souvenirs to offer visitors interested in recent events, and Dave and I got around to most of them, aided by a black market exchange rate that made Belgrade taxis about as expensive as London buses (the official rate was six Yugoslav dinars to the deutschmark, but most waiters, shopkeepers and street-corner fruit-sellers were trading at twenty-two). In the centre of town, the two orange office blocks that had once housed Yugoslavia's Ministry of Defence were both collapsed from the middle outwards, like a pair of mistimed souffles, with scarcely a scratch on the surrounding neighbourhood. The Radio Television Serbia building, petulantly and pointlessly whacked by NATO on 23 April 1999, with the loss of sixteen civilian lives, resembled a cake which some almighty dessert knife had taken a slice out of. However idiotic – even criminal, under

Article 79 of the Geneva Conventions – NATO's decision to hit RTS, the precision was awesome. It's still the only place I've seen bomb damage with right angles.

Two memorials near RTS reflected the divide between the country and its leadership. Closest to the building, a white tombstone bore the names of the dead beneath the reasonable question WHY? – it had been paid for by the families of the victims, not Serbia's government. The official war memorial was a short walk away in the park by St Marko's church: a ghastly faux-bronze statue of a little girl, standing in front of the words WE WERE JUST CHILDREN in Serbian and, lest the point be missed, English. It was dedicated to children killed by the NATO bombardment. While children certainly had been killed by the NATO bombardment, and while this was certainly terrible, it was difficult not to feel nauseated by this sentimental agonising, manufactured as it was by the people who'd orchestrated the horrors of Srebrenica, Vukovar, Gorazde, Sarajevo, Racak and any number more.

'Jesus Christ,' growled Dave, who'd seen much more of Serbia's rampage in Bosnia-Herzegovina than I had. 'I'd kill for a can of spray paint.'

Across the Sava River in New Belgrade, we saw what was left of the Chinese embassy, and the gutted ruin of the Usce business centre. Outside town, next to the international airport, was Belgrade's aviation museum. There was no doubt about the stars of the show. Busloads of Serb schoolkids photographed each other next to the tailfin of the American F-16c which came down near Nakucany on 7 May 1999, and the pilot canopy – emblazoned with the name of Captain Ken 'Wiz' Dwelle – of the F-117a Nighthawk stealth fighter that crashed near Budjanovci on 27 March. The museum's staff were so proud of these trophies that it seemed churlish to point out that NATO had flown 38,008 sorties the previous year: a strike rate of one in 19,004 mightn't be all that much to boast about.

We also swung by the Intercontinental Hotel, where the infamous paramilitary commander and gangster Zeljko 'Arkan' Raznatovic had been assassinated two months earlier. Many in Belgrade, including our taxi driver that day ('Shithead,' he snorted, when pressed for an opinion), expressed relief not just at Arkan's passing, but at the fact that it had driven his widow, Serbian pop idol Ceca, into a year of traditional silent mourning. Another joke doing the rounds noted that the 'businessman' boyfriend of Serbia's second-biggest pop star, inflatable doll lookalike Jelena Karleusa, had also been offed, hopefully condemning her to twelve glorious months of grieving quiet, and speculated that Belgrade's underworld was being terrorised by a gang of vengeful music lovers.

'Underworld' was the wrong word for Belgrade's criminal classes. With their patron and protector Milosevic still in office, they were as unabashed as Capone's men prior to the intervention of Eliot Ness, and dressed similarly. One night, Dave and I asked some people we'd met to take us to what they thought was the coolest place in Belgrade.

'Club Nana,' decided Jasmina, a pretty redhead who we'd have followed if she'd said, 'Commandant Bloodstain's Leather Dungeon, and it's bring-a-foreign-gimp night'. Club Nana's entrance lay beyond several ranks of Porsches and Volvos, and was guarded by a bouncer who looked as if he valet parked by picking the vehicles up like Matchbox toys.

'Welcome,' he said. 'My name is Vladimir.'

Vladimir was an easy six-and-a-half feet. He had a nickel-plated Smith & Wesson .38 revolver stuffed into his waistband at a jaunty angle, and a handshake that suggested he had been forced to waste little of his life searching for a nutcracker.

'Anybody gives you trouble,' said Vladimir, 'tell them you're my friend.'

'I told you it would be cool,' said Jasmina as we entered. Jasmina clearly looked upon Club Nana, and its clientele of sharp-suited gangsters and their barely dressed escorts, with the same wide-eyed hunger with which a different kind of wannabe regarded London's then-inexplicably-fashionable celebrity haunt the Met Bar. This was understandable – with Yugoslavia's legal economy ruined by an inept, corrupt government and silly, counter-productive United Nations sanctions, the criminal classes were the only people in Belgrade who could afford to enjoy themselves.

Dave and I huddled uneasily in a corner. We were the only men not wearing Armani knockoffs – Jasmina had secured our entry with spectacular lies to Vladimir about the scope of our journalistic influence. If this had been a film, the music would have stopped as we walked in, and we both wished dearly that it had. The bereft hush of Ceca and Jelena Karleusa had not, sadly, extended to a moratorium on their recorded output. Both women were practitioners of an indigenous Serbian pop called Turbofolk – a hybrid of sentimental, nationalistic Balkan peasant ballads and Euro-techno. Turbofolk resembled the 'Horst Wessel Lied' remixed by Stock, Aitken and Waterman, though even worse than that sounded, especially at this volume.

'I'm going to take some pictures,' yelled Dave. Something about the way we were being regarded by the other customers made me concerned that this could be the last sentence he ever uttered. I suggested he clear it with the management.

'They said,' he reported, upon returning, 'that I could do it if I didn't mind leaving here in a bag. But Vladimir said we could take one of his gun, if we like.'

Wandering Belgrade's streets, Dave and I couldn't understand why nobody, aside from tone-deaf mafiosi, hated us – or, so far as we could tell, where we'd come from. There was some anti-western graffiti: FUCK NATO, NATO KILLERS, the equation of the NATO compass emblem with the swastika (a favourite trope of Serbia's propagandists had been likening NATO's assault to the rather less discriminating air raids by the Luftwaffe of April 1941). There was, however, a lot more graffiti celebrating Pearl Jam, Metallica and Depeche Mode. The queues at McDonald's were bemusingly long, given that quite aside from ideological considerations, the fare available from any streetside burek-peddler was fantastic. Billboards advertising American products went undefaced, even the ones whose situation next to missile-ruined buildings lent them the aura of exultant captions (LUCKY STRIKE – AN AMERICAN CLASSIC).

Milosevic's government was still pushing the line that Serbia had been the undeserving victim of western aggression and conspiracy: Belgrade was covered in posters depicting US Secretary of State Madeleine Albright as a puppet-master with one hand up Kosovo Liberation Army commander Hasim Thaci, and the other inside a figure representing Otpor!, the student resistance movement whose graffiti was more abundant than that about NATO, Pearl Jam, Metallica and Depeche Mode combined.

However, nobody we met seemed like a cowed, craven subject of a terrorised Orwellian despotry. Belgraders' opinions of their government, and especially their president, kept the air in bars and cafés a luminous shade of blue. The sonorous cadences of the Balkan accent suited English swear words better than any other, and when Belgraders discussed their politicians ('Motherfuckers') or their politics ('Bullshit') or, by extension, the demolition of their nation's civilian infrastructure in retaliation for the insanity of their leaders ('Motherfucking bullshit'), they cursed with a rich, luxuriant vehemence.

I hadn't been to Belgrade since I'd backpacked around Yugoslavia in 1990, but Dave vaguely knew some people who vaguely knew some people who vaguely knew some people. These tentative leads delivered us an entire villa to stay in, and a woman called Milica, who proved to be the ideal fixer – someone who knew everybody, and everything, and spared us a great deal of wasted time and shoe leather. She took us to the studios of radio station B92, which was the generally accepted front for anti-government feeling, and as such had experienced some fairly severe overregulation from the Milosevic regime. They'd been chased out of their studios shortly after NATO had started bombing, and had started broadcasting again five months later. Their new studios were in a high-rise block with views over the wreckage of the ministry of defence buildings. I was introduced to Toma Grujic, B92's music director. He seemed exhausted, fed up, as if the weight of the Milosevic's pettiness was physically pushing him down in his seat.

'They don't bother us much now,' he sighed. 'We're just, you know, in with this whole bunch of traitors, and servants of NATO, and so on.'

Even sarcasm sounded like an effort.

That night, at a dinner party in a loft whose interior could have been cut out of one of those thick, unreadable architecture magazines only ever found in the waiting rooms of television production companies, our hosts elaborated on their conflicting loyalties.

'The night NATO started bombing,' said Stjepan, a hairdresser, 'I was lying in my bath with my boyfriend, watching old American movies, which we love. You can see why we're confused.' Stjepan was the name I gave our host in my original article. He hadn't wanted his name printed anywhere near an admission of his homosexuality, which his family and some friends were unaware of, and which was still taboo in the Balkans. Given that Stjepan could conceivably have been expelled from the Village People on the grounds of excessive campness, I despaired of the average Serb's powers of observation. Stjepan, mind-bogglingly, had at one point served in Milosevic's Yugoslav National Army, during its attack on Dubrovnik in 1991.

'It made me so sad,' said Stjepan. 'Such a beautiful city. I could not stand to watch.'

I asked if he'd done anything about it.

'Yes,' he said. 'Deserted.'

Other talk around the table was of shortages due to the UN sanctions. The truth was, as is invariably the case under such strictures, there were no shortages. Everything was available, as long as you had money, but most people in Belgrade – at least, most honest people in Belgrade – didn't.

'The sanctions are nonsense,' said another diner. 'It can be hard to get milk, soap, sugar, tampons, petrol and cooking oil, but only if you don't have the deutschmarks. All they do is keep us poor and Milosevic in power. What good does the West think will come of locking us in a cage with a lunatic?'

Later on, as the empty bottles began to form a crowd, there was the inevitable Balkan flexing of conspiracy theories, as much a regional specialty as plum brandy and idiot politicians. All the greatest hits got a run: NATO was really the military wing of the Albanian mafia, as if billions of western taxpayers' dollars had been spent to protect the bootleg cigarettes racket of someone called Enver; the whole war had been a romantic gesture directed at the raffish young KLA commander Hasim Thaci by a besotted Madeleine Albright; Milosevic had been working for America all along; varying combinations of Milosevic, the CIA and the Albanian mafia were responsible for flooding Belgrade with weapons-grade Albanian grass, although I detected no overt coercion from government agents whenever another Kalashnikov-sized spliff was passed around the table.

I didn't think anybody really believed any of this hogwash. They just hated the containment of their lives, of their potential, by the stupidity of their circumstances so profoundly that they had to believe it was something they could do nothing about. Nobody in that room had, at that moment, the remotest inkling that, just seven months later, they'd be gathered in front of their parliament building demanding an end to Milosevic's madness while bracing themselves for a Balkan Tiananmen. I certainly didn't.

'We had fifty years of communism,' said Miljana, a student, 'and then ten years of Milosevic. Serbs have no sense of responsibility, and no sense of future. Nobody thinks further ahead than dinnertime.'

Part of me had wanted to find Belgrade, and the Serbian people, dislikable. I thought Serbia's government and its proxies bore the overwhelming responsibility for turning Bosnia-Herzegovina into a slaughterhouse. I had been entirely in favour of NATO's intervention. I thought one of the great missed chances of modern history was the telegram that George H.W. Bush didn't send Slobodan Milosevic in August 1991, a few months after Operation Desert Storm had reversed Iraq's invasion of Kuwait, when the then-Yugoslav army was besieging the Croatian town of Vukovar: 'Dear President Milosevic, it would be no trouble whatsoever – none at all – for our planes to fly over your place on their way home.' I had supported – with a few caveats regarding attacks on civilian infrastructure – the bombing of the city and the people which now received me with extraordinary hospitality.

This is the trouble with all interventions. They're plotted on maps, but the bombs get dropped on homes and workplaces and people. I wanted to meet one of them, and asked Milica if she knew anyone. She did. Dragan Stojkovic, known to his friends as 'Pixie', was a news director at RTS. He'd been in the RTS building at 2.05 am on 23 April 1999, when a missile launched from a NATO aircraft had struck it. We met him in a cafe with a view of the wreckage that had nearly been his tomb.

'I was sitting at a table on the top floor,' he said, 'playing cards with two friends. We never heard a thing until it hit, and then . . . I don't remember anything about the first fifteen seconds, and after that it's still difficult – when I spoke to the friends I'd been playing cards with afterwards, they all remembered something different. I'd like to go back in there one day, and sit at the same table, and see if the memory comes back.'

NATO would have had two reasons for striking RTS at that hour – the cover of darkness, and the likelihood that there would be fewer people in the building. Dragan said that the opposite was the case, and blandly offered an explanation that was shocking however low one's opinion of his country's president.

'NATO were half right,' he smiled. 'The station was never very busy at two in the morning – it could have been run by ten people at that hour. But there were 150 people in there that night. It was still run on the old socialist system, with ridiculous overemployment, but I think the regime knew the building was going to be bombed, and wanted it full.'

The Balkans is the Middle East's only serious rival as the world's principal manufacturer of conspiracy theories, but Dragan didn't seem the credulous sort – journalists usually aren't. I asked if he was sure about this.

'At 1.30 am,' he said, 'half an hour before we got hit, one of the news editors came in and picked up his daughter and his grandson, who both worked there, and took them out for a meal. At 1.30 in the morning.'

He sighed. 'Look,' he said, 'we knew we'd get hit. We even knew which part of the building they'd hit – the control centre. And RTS was a legitimate military target.'

This seemed, in the circumstances, an extraordinary statement. I knew that RTS broadcast the most pernicious rubbish, and I'd have preferred it if they hadn't, but for reasons of obvious self-interest, as well as basic morality, I thought targeting journalists – any journalists – was inexcusable.

'It was a legitimate target,' Pixie insisted. 'It's the machine Milosevic uses to control what gets out and what doesn't. It's maybe not so important in Belgrade, but out in the country where RTS is the only news you can get, it's very important. I knew RTS transmitted lies, but it was a job, and I have a family to feed, and I got to work with friends. I'd just switch off my brain when I came to work.'

Dragan had found new employment as a fixer for foreign news crews in Kosovo; when the locals questioned his accent, he told them he was South African. Like almost everybody else I'd met in Belgrade, he seemed weary and resigned, rather than angry or aggrieved. In a man who'd cheated an attempt on his life so narrowly, I couldn't tell whether this indicated a state of mind which was remarkably solid, or completely unhinged.

'The morning after we were hit,' he said, 'I came down here with a bottle of Jack Daniel's and looked at the building, or what was left of it. I was okay, really – bruises on my arms and legs, not much, though on a psychological level, lots. It's not for me to say who is to blame, and it doesn't matter. I lost sixteen friends, and that is what is important. Everybody is guilty.'

Dave and I spent our last night in Belgrade in a bar that was, in both senses of the word, underground. Many of the people we'd spent our visit with had come here during the air raids, and that night they restored a shred of national honour by dealing Dave and myself a proper hiding, seven frames to two, in a Serbia vs NATO pool tournament.

The conversation turned, inevitably, to the apparent absurdity of a situation whereby NATO had bombed a people who appeared to share their view of who the enemy really was. One of our pool opponents asked the question that has since haunted me every time my taxes have since been garnisheed to help deliver freedom to the oppressed, democracy to the tyrannised, wire-guided munitions to the largely defenceless.

'Everyone knows,' he said, as he chalked his cue, 'that this country has one problem. It is one man. Why didn't NATO launch one missile?'

There were one or two other early twenty-first century societies, I thought, about which the same question could have been asked.

22

For all that we're encouraged to think of the Arab world as a monolith, it's more of an archipelago – Baghdad, like all Arab cities, was an island surrounded by oceans of sand. Unlike most islands, though, Baghdad had no air link – commercial flights had been suspended under UN sanctions. As my plane from London taxied to the terminal at Amman's Queen Alia Airport, it passed three Boeing 727s, in the green and white livery of Iraqi Airways, which had been awaiting permission to take off for just over a decade.

It was coming up for the tenth anniversary of Operation Desert Storm, the vast multinational effort to evict the invading Iraqi army from Kuwait. Despite occurring nine years prior to the dawning of our new era, Desert Storm had been the first twenty-first century war: the first conflict covered by round-the-clock television news, the first to see (or, in the case of Iraq's air defences, not see) the deployment of stealth aircraft and smart missiles. Iraqi losses were massive, allied casualties minimal. The theory, later practised in Bosnia, Serbia and Kosovo, that a cause can be worth fighting for but not risking injury for, had been born in the deserts of Iraq.

I was crossing those deserts because of the war that had been fought since the war, by bomb and by sanction, if rarely by the light of television cameras. The ongoing siege of Iraq, if one dated it to the launch of Desert Storm on 17 January 1991, was now America's longest war since Vietnam, Britain's longest since Napoleon was dispatched to St Helena, and it was lucky if it got the occasional mention on the news just before the skateboarding parrot slot. Before I left London, I called the Ministry of Defence and asked what they'd unloaded on Iraq lately. They told me that since 1 January 2000, the Royal Air Force had flown 1500 missions over the northern and southern no-fly zones, striking targets on thirty-one occasions. British pilots were engaging targets, ducking radar, dodging anti-aircraft fire, dropping bombs and whizzing back to base to paint on their nosecones the silhouette of another missile launcher, weapons dump, command-and-control installation or unlucky camel herd which had resembled, from a distance, something more sinister, and it never made the headlines. It looked like the rhetorical question beloved of generations of peaceniks would have to be updated: what if they gave a war and nobody cared?

I was travelling with photographer Alan Clarke, accompanying me on assignment for the *Face*, and a film-maker called Jamie, who worked with the Mariam Appeal, a charity-cum-lobby chaired by the British MP George Galloway. In 2000, Galloway was still to reach the giddying heights of stardom, or the fathomless depths of hubris, that he would sample by the middle of the decade – with, respectively, his savaging of a US Senate Committee which sought to impugn him as a Ba'athist stooge, and his baffling decision to appear on *Celebrity Big Brother* in the UK, during which, among other exploits which had viewers dashing their heads against floors in an effort to erase the memories, he pretended to be a cat drinking milk from the cupped hands of never-quite-famous actress Rula Lenska. In 2000, Galloway was regarded largely as an amusing eccentric. Journalists made use of Galloway's connections with the Iraqi government, and eagerness to generate coverage of the effects of the UN's sanctions, to secure permission to enter Iraq. Alan and I had done exactly that, collecting our ornate visas from the Iraqi consulate in Amman.

Geography and politics combined to make visiting Saddam Hussein's Iraq feel like stepping off the planet. The desert scenery along the road from Amman to the border was the most malignant landscape

I'd ever seen, flaming red sand perforated by sharp shards of black rock; it could only have been made to look less hospitable by the addition of signs reading DIE, INFIDEL. At Ruwasheid, a town-sized truck stop not far from the border, a restaurant had established a profitable tradition whereby visitors to Iraq deposited their mobile phones – illegal inside Iraq – to be collected upon return, on the assumption that you'd fancy a feed by that point, Iraqi highway catering being an underdeveloped industry. One wall of the restaurant was covered in business cards left by previous satisfied customers. We added ours, consumed an astonishingly good dinner, checked in our phones, and drove on.

The customs officers on the Iraqi side of the border were creepy, officious wankers. It wasn't the fact of their bribe-seeking that grated, but the manner of it. They charged us five dollars to move our bags from the truck into their headquarters, then made us wait twenty minutes. They charged us another ten dollars to search our bags, then made us sit around for another hour or so. They made frequent threats of a compulsory HIV test, which they insisted they could deny us entry without, and which we insisted we weren't taking, even if it meant we had to walk back to Amman. They charged us another ten dollars for, I think, the wear and tear on their seats while we waited. Eventually, after wasting nearly three of our cruelly finite allotment of hours on this mortal coil, they let us go, at a total profit to them of US$150. If they'd just said, 'Fifty bucks each, chaps, and you're on your way,' we'd have coughed up happily, and thrown in another ten for new moustache clippers. It had been a petty, pointless abuse of paltry power – the Iraqi customs guys were, essentially, call centre operators with pistols.

The view upwards through the windows of the Chevrolet truck was enough to stop us sulking, though – a perfectly black sky and a shimmering embroidery of stars. On the smooth dual carriageway rebuilt by Iraq after the Gulf War, there were no hazards other than sleep, and stray camels. The former was kept at bay by continuous coffee, poured one-handed by our driver with the cruise control set at 170 kilometres per hour; as for the latter, we kept our eyes open and our fingers crossed.

* * *

Life in Baghdad in late 2000 may have been hard, but there was plenty of it. On Rashid Street, the shopping district that ran alongside the Tigris River, things were the Middle Eastern idea of business as usual, which is to say that when scenes as chaotic as this occurred in European cities, they were broken up by riot police. Decrepit cars careened in a cacophony of horns, backfires and shouts; donkey carts and nervous pedestrians competed for gaps in the traffic. On the crowded footpaths, tea vendors carrying silver trays of tulip-shaped glasses wove deftly through the meandering shoppers, never spilling a drop.

You could buy anything. There was the sublime: bespoke suits, antique watches, hand-woven carpets, superb copper and silverware, all at the bargain prices common to sanctions-wracked pariah states. There was the ridiculous: 1980 editions of British teen magazines, coverlines including A NIGHT OUT WITH GARY NUMAN and LES McKEOWN: WHAT'S HE BEEN UP TO?. It didn't look like anyone was suffering a shortage of anything, except windscreen spares (the view of Baghdad from any Baghdad taxi was positively kaleidoscopic). But however healthy Baghdad's pulse felt, it was impossible to completely forget that the world – principally America and Britain – was standing on several crucial pressure points. In Mackenzie's Bookshop, I got talking to the proprietor, Lernik Bedrosian. An Iraqi of Armenian descent, she also presented the English bulletins on Iraqi satellite television.

'This shop used to be bigger,' she explained. 'Before.'

'Before' was a popular word in Baghdad. It meant 'before' the epically pointless conflict with Iran in the 1980s that left a million dead, 'before' the Gulf War, 'before' the decade of sanctions and worse that Iraq had suffered since . . . 'before', if you wanted to look for the common element in these unhappy occurences, the rise of Saddam Hussein.

'We can't get books anymore,' said Lernik. 'Everything in here is old.'

Mackenzie's English-language stock was fifth-hand school texts, dog-eared novels and musty reference hardbacks. Nothing predated 1990.

'We miss that connection with literature,' said Lernik. 'And our doctors and engineers make do with books that are ten, twenty years out of date. Why is this?'

I found a coffee-stained 1978 edition of Tom Stoppard's *Rosencrantz & Guildenstern are Dead*, and decided it would make a pleasing keepsake, though I felt uneasy about the idea that my visit to Iraq would result in there being one less book in the country.

Lernik wouldn't take my money.

'You are a guest here,' she smiled.

All foreign journalists in Iraq were dogged by minders from the Ministry of Information. Alan and I were lucky on this front. Mystifyingly considered a low priority by Saddam Hussein's feared Mukhabarat, we were assigned to Sadoun, a plump, camp little chap with a girlish giggle, a droopy moustache and an extraordinary comb-over, which could only have looked more absurd if it had been brushed up out of one armpit.

Sadoun was a model company man, down to his gold-plated Saddam Hussein wristwatch. He was also, as a secret policeman, bloody useless. Every morning, Alan and I would leave the Palestine Hotel, and meet him as instructed in the Melia Mansur Hotel. Every morning, Sadoun would assure us that he was at our disposal. Every morning, we'd punt a few ideas (seeing as how we were here for the *Face*, we fancied visiting youth radio station Shebab FM), which he would ignore (Shebab was run by Saddam Hussein's delightful eldest, Uday Hussein, into whose orbit no Iraqi drifted if they could help it). Sadoun would then offer hints, as subtle as elbows in the throat, about the size of the tip we intended to leave him upon our departure. Alan and I would assemble a tactful answer which did not include the words 'Bugger' or 'all'. Sadoun would then tut about how busy he was, and charge off to a doubtless imaginary 'meeting'. Alan and I would hasten outside and commandeer a taxi, head out for the day and report back in the evenings for a severely miffed debriefing. 'Where did you go?' he'd fume. Nowhere, really, we'd reply. 'Who did you speak to?' he'd sulk. Nobody you know, we'd answer. It was astonishing. Did he spend the intervening hours every day thinking 'Curses! They've outfoxed me again! But how?'

One day, to cheer Sadoun up, and because we thought it'd be instructive to see the Iraq that the regime wanted us to see, we allowed Sadoun to take us on the standard journalistic tour of Baghdad. Guided tours for journalists, a common phenomenon in put-upon hell-holes, operate according to exactly opposite imperatives of guided tours for tourists. Guided tours for tourists show all that is beguiling and glorious about a destination, whereas guided tours for journalists seek to impress with how screwed up everything is. It's like making a visitor to your house look behind the fridge.

Sadoun drove us to the Al-Amiriya air raid shelter, where American missiles had incinerated at least 400 civilians on 13 February 1991. Al-Amiriya was an above-ground shelter, built during the war with Iran to withstand chemical attacks; it had offered the same protection against the American missiles which had punched through its concrete and lead ceiling that an eggshell would against a well-swung hammer. Sadoun pointed to some sooty shadows on a wall, and said they were the outline of a mother and child, silhouetted on the surface as they'd been vaporised.

'Like in Hiroshima,' he said.

From Al-Amiriya we drove to a more jovial memorial to the 1991 Gulf War – the entrance to the Al-Rashid Hotel, which required visitors to walk over a tiled mosaic portrait of President George Bush. 'Bush,' read the English caption, 'is criminal.' There was Arabic writing along-side it, which I guessed read much the same thing, and not, say, 'Although, in fairness, invading Kuwait was a pretty dumb thing to do, and everyone did ask Iraq nicely to leave, and there was a UN Security Council resolution authorising all necessary means to evict Iraqi forces if we didn't, and on top of all that Saddam was given six months' warning of the deadline in which he could have folded his tents and fucked off, leaving America all dressed up with nowhere to go, but the big goose decided to fight, and now look at the state we're in.' Sadoun insisted that I pose for a photo with him, standing on Bush's face.

'Now we are friends,' he gurgled, giving me the least desired hug of my life. 'You will give me very good tip.'

Yes, I replied. Don't do that again.

From the Al-Rashid, we went to a memorial to an earlier war, the stupid, savage exercise in mutual population control in which Iraq had collaborated with Iran during the 80s. The Swords of Qadisiyyah monument, colloquially known as Hands of Victory, was built in duplicate. At each end of a parade ground in central Baghdad, a pair of enormous bronze forearms emerged from the ground, each clutching swords that crossed high in the air. It was supposed to symbolise Saddam Hussein's crushing triumph over the Iranian enemy.

'The swords,' explained Sadoun, 'are made from steel from the guns of our martyrs, just like my watch. The fists are exact models of the president's.'

Around the base of the forearms were piles of green helmets, like a heap of peas stacked against a leg of lamb.

'Iranian helmets,' said Sadoun. 'Look, some have bulletholes.'

Alan wanted to photograph the ghastly thing. Sadoun became agitated, insisting that there were 'sensitive installations' nearby. I advanced my suspicion that the Americans already had a good idea of what and where these were, and were unlikely to be poring over next month's edition of the *Face* in the White House situation room looking for targets. Sadoun was adamant, however, directing Alan's shots with the precision of a surgeon – a surgeon, that is, performing an entirely unnecessary operation on a somewhat bewildered patient.

The highlight of the journalists' tour, which is to say the most wretched afternoon imaginable, was a visit to the Saddam Hospital for Children. As Saddam Hussein's regime saw it, this dreadful place was the epicentre of the tragedy wrought upon Iraq by the UN sanctions under which the country still staggered, pending Iraq's cooperation with weapons inspectors. The doctors dutifully informed us that the patients here were victims of the West twice over – from cancers that had become more prevalent since the Gulf War, which they attributed to the coalition's promiscuous use of depleted uranium munitions, and from the shortage of medicines and equipment to treat them, which they attributed to the sanctions. None of which I doubted, though I couldn't see what was stopping Saddam Hussein from announcing, 'You know what, the welfare of my people matters more to me than my position or prestige, so here's the deal: the weapons inspectors can come back and look at what they like, I'll throw an election, a proper one with other candidates and everything, and if I lose I'll wear it like a good chap, and go fishing.'

There wasn't much gainsaying the end result of the diplomatic impasse. Thirteen-year-old Marwan Khalil Ibrahim lay on a grubby mattress on a rusty iron bed, his face and clothes covered in the blood haemorrhaging from his nose and mouth. His mother, Amonah, her face like stone beneath her scarf, flapped flies away with a square of cardboard. She told me that her son had been diagnosed with leukaemia seven years previously, but that this was the worst he'd been. She'd brought Marwan to the hospital ten days ago. She didn't know when, or if, she'd be taking him home. On an adjacent bed, a younger girl, maybe four or five, played with an empty syringe. The ward smelled like a hospital, but worse.

Marwan didn't look like he posed any meaningful threat to regional security. His faltering grip on life was dependent, explained a doctor who resembled a gaunt, haunted Groucho Marx, on a machine called a cell separator, which removed platelets – the cells which cause clotting – from blood. These were then transfused into Marwan to staunch his bleeding: his drip consumed ten 300 ml bags every day. There was only one cell separator in Baghdad, the doctor said, a contraption of 1970s vintage which broke down frequently. Iraq couldn't import a new one, because under the sanctions regulations such machines were regarded as 'dual use' – presumably meaning that they could be used to treat soldiers, or stripped for parts, or dropped on the heads of Saddam's enemies. I asked the doctor if, that aside, there was any particular treatment he would have liked to have been able to offer Marwan, but could not because of the sanctions.

'Not at this stage, no,' said the doctor.

In the evening, as if we weren't miserable enough, Sadoun had his driver take us to a venue where, he assured us, 'a very important, very interesting' meeting was occurring. Before a conference room full of people at desks taking notes, three men sat below a banner reading BAGHDAD CONFERENCE FOLLOW-UP AND COORDINATION COMMITTEE. The man in the middle, unmistakable in military fatigues, black beret and silver moustache, was Tariq Aziz.

'Mr Deputy Prime Minister,' whispered a theatrically awestruck Sadoun.

Aziz looked as bored as I rapidly became. I hissed at Sadoun that this was a bit dull, it had been a long day, and Alan and I were tired and hungry and thought we might push off. Sadoun's face was an exquisite mask of barely suppressed horror, caught between his duty to keep an eye on us, and a reluctance to conspicuously walk out on Aziz. Suit yourself, I told him, and Alan and I left, strolling into the venue's forecourt and suddenly realising that we had no idea where we were.

'But there,' said Alan, 'is Sadoun's car, and Sadoun's driver.'

So there was. He drove us back to the Palestine, and asked if he should return for his boss. Good grief no, we said, gave him a huge tip, and told him to take the evening off.

Everywhere Alan and I went, we were treated with such kindness that we started to wonder if Saddam had ordered a regimen of overwhelming hospitality, to make visitors feel even guiltier about the sanctions than they already might. The owner of an antiques store invited us to stay for lunch. A silver-haired gent approached me in the street and pressed into my hand two British ten new pence coins dating from 1973; I've kept these on a shelf in my office ever since, and I still hope he didn't think I looked like I needed the money. One night, we persuaded Sadoun to make himself useful and take us to the football to see Iraqi league leaders Al-Zawrah play Al-Sinaah. The game was under way when we arrived. Sadoun led us in through the players' entrance, ushering us onto the athletics track that surrounded the pitch. There was a huge roar from the grandstand behind us. I looked over to the pitch to see what was going on, but nothing much was. Then I realised: the crowd were cheering us.

'They know,' said Sadoun, 'that it is difficult for foreigners to come here. They appreciate your effort.'

Friendly though everybody was, conversation was difficult. In shops and cafes, people were reluctant to complain explicitly, but the devil lurked in the details. The most minor transaction required a thick wad of blue 250-dinar notes, all embellished with Saddam's portrait – the currency, trading at around 1700 dinar to the dollar, was worthless, unless you were buying petrol. (You could fill the 160-litre tank of one of the SUVs which did the Baghdad–Amman run for 3000 dinar, or about US$1.80.) Every taxi driver turned out to be a degree-holding professional (teacher, engineer, radiologist) forced to abandon his vocation because there was no money in it – the ten dollars they could charge us for a couple of hours' driving was two months' wages for a Baghdad doctor. It was hard not to think that, for a people caught between the anvil of Saddam's brutal and stupid dictatorship and the hammer of the outside world's brutal and stupid sanctions, the obvious solution was a change in leadership. The responses, when this was tentatively suggested, could be surprising.

'This isn't a police state,' said twenty-seven-year-old Karim Wasfi. 'This is a state where there is a tradition, which we believe in, of offering a certain level of respect to our leaders. There is discussion, but it is respectful. I don't consider the right to call the president names, or know about his private life, necessarily democratic.'

We got talking to Wasfi one afternoon outside the Melia Mansur Hotel. He was there with his sister Naghin, a reporter for Iraqi satellite television, who was doing a story on some artists who were creating an immense propaganda mosaic on the hotel's forecourt. With coloured sawdust, the artists were depicting an American flag, whose stripes were rendered as bars imprisoning the Dome of the Rock in Jerusalem, held shut by a padlock marked 'Isral' – after all the trouble they'd gone to, it seemed churlish to point out the spelling error. Karim was passionate about Iraq, to the extent that he lived in Baghdad even though he had a choice. He'd been studying in Indianapolis the last four years, and had American residency, but had returned to take up the position of principal cellist in the Iraqi Symphony Orchestra.

'First,' he explained, 'I wanted to prove myself in the country that had attacked me. Then, I wanted to take part in the cultural life here. I want to be a bridge between civilisations. If people can communicate, directly, situations like this won't happen.'

We had coffee in the Melia Mansur's cafe, overlooked by the inevitable portrait of the president. I asked Naghin whether she'd prefer to work for a channel that wasn't state-run. Her reply was, I guess, no more and no less than she could reasonably have been expected to say.

'If the media was free,' she said, 'bad ideas would get out as well as good ones. It's not good to have no control.'

Naghin introduced me to the bespectacled and bearded figure of Khdayr Meri, explaining that he was Baghdad's current literary sensation. *The Days of Madness and Honey*, his memoir of his stint as a psychiatric patient during the Gulf War, was being well reviewed in the (also state-owned) newspapers.

'Freedom must have responsibility,' he said.

I asked if he really thought that a writer's responsibility was to serve the state.

'Sure,' he replied. 'That is the sacrifice we make. But what I am concerned with lies beyond politics.'

But nothing in Iraq lay beyond politics – or beyond, really, one man. It was impossible to escape Saddam Hussein. He appeared frequently on Iraqi television, popping up between the obviously bootlegged movies (the time-codes appeared on screen). The souvenir shops in the hotels sold little but Saddamiana: rugs, watches, clocks, plates, badges, books of his collected ravings. You couldn't open your eyes in Baghdad without seeing his face. One afternoon, Alan and I threw Sadoun another dummy, hired a taxi and set off to photograph as many representations of Saddam as we could. Amir, the driver we'd picked on, got into the spirit of our enterprise quickly.

'But fellows, seriously,' he said, 'you must stop laughing all the time. We will get in trouble.'

We finished with an excellent collection: an enormous painted historical allegory depicting Saddam commanding an army including modern tanks and lance-toting horsemen; a 1970s-style head and shoulders portrait, half a building high, of Saddam in military uniform, with a beach scene reflected in his sunglasses; one of him firing a pistol into the air – above the entrance to a primary school; and my favourite, the tyrant in a fetching beige slacks and waistcoat ensemble, with a bouquet of lilies in one arm and a panama hat tipped raffishly over one eye. Even Amir laughed at that one.

When it became too dark to take pictures, Amir took Alan and I home to meet his family. It was very sweet of him, and one of the most dejecting evenings of my life. While introducing us to his wife, his parents, and his six irrepressible children, Amir told us that he had a brother, who had left Iraq shortly after the Gulf War, and now worked as a doctor near London. They hadn't seen him since, Amir explained, and had very little contact with him – in Iraq email was almost unheard of, phones were erratic, and one might as well have stuffed a letter in a bottle and tossed into the Tigris as entrusted it to the Iraqi postal service. Amir wasn't even sure if his brother knew about some of his nephews and nieces, or that their mother was dying. He asked Alan to take some pictures of the family.

Alan said he could do better than that, and produced a digital video camera from his bag. He showed Amir how it worked – the children were predictably delighted by seeing themselves played back on the camera's small screen – and Amir spent the next couple of hours filming the family his brother had never seen, and the mother his brother would never see again, so that two strangers could act as a link between a family separated by the desire of governments to prove things to each other. The worst of it was how incredibly happy Amir was for the opportunity. I couldn't watch, and waited outside in the garden. It wasn't long before Alan joined me.

After we'd endured the traditional Arab leave-taking – in the Middle East, saying goodbye can consume most of the evening – Amir drove us back to our hotel. He marvelled at the camera, his luck in finding us, his joy at being able to communicate with his brother. As he pulled up, I reached for my wallet.

'No,' he said, wagging a finger.

What?

'You have been to my house,' he said. 'You have helped my family. You are friends. I cannot take money from you.'

I wanted to hit him. Please, mate, I said, don't do this.

'I cannot,' he said, his hands firmly on the wheel, staring straight ahead, ignoring the fifty-dollar note in my hand.

Mercifully, inspiration struck. I told Amir that I respected his values, of not accepting money from his friends. However, he would have to respect my values, which hold that if I'm going to someone's house, I take a gift (usually, granted, a bottle of the second-cheapest red in the shop, but I didn't tell him that). As we hadn't had time to buy anything today, Amir would have to take this money, and buy a gift for his children, from myself and Alan.

Amir thought about this for a long time.

'Okay,' he eventually decided.

Recalling that evening still feels like digesting lightbulbs, particularly the certainty that Amir would have thought none the less of me if I'd trousered my money, shaken his hand and bid him goodbye.

I couldn't find Amir when I went back to Baghdad in 2003. I hope he's okay.

Odai – who I did find when I went back to Baghdad in 2003 – was twenty years old in 2000. He worked in an antique shop which I'd dropped into while searching for a souvenir of Iraq which didn't have a moustache and a pair of sunglasses on it.

Odai had lived in Baghdad all his life, and all he could remember was war. He'd spent the 1980s living in fear of attack by Iran. The windows of his family's house had been blown in by the air raids that fanfared Desert Storm, and he'd been shaken awake by American cruise missile strikes in June 1993 and December 1998. His older brother, a conscript soldier, had taken part in the invasion of Kuwait, and had become unpopular with other soldiers for his refusal to participate in the general pillaging. After the rout of the Iraqi army, his brother had walked back to Baghdad along with other surviving soldiers – many of whom, Odai said, brought their bounty to the shop seeking a quote.

'One man,' said Odai, 'offered me ten gold Rolexes for two hundred dollars, but I didn't take them. It might have made this life easier, but I would have to answer to God in the next.'

Odai seemed a nice kid. I asked him if he liked living in Baghdad.

'There is no freedom here,' he whispered, still smiling. I felt that uneasiness that grips the jittery flyer at the first intimations of turbulence. Iraqis weren't supposed to talk like this, especially not to foreigners.

'Our president,' he hissed, now grinning wildly, 'doesn't care.'

He winked. I got the hint: he was worried that we were being watched. I began nodding, laughing and smiling myself.

'If anyone heard me talking like this,' he beamed, 'or even saw me looking serious, then after you had gone, they would take not just me, but my whole family.'

I asked, all but slapping my thigh, where they would be taken.

'Ha ha ha,' boomed Odai. 'And the sanctions keep us too poor to think about changing anything.'

I then asked why he was telling me all this. I could have been anyone.

'My friend,' he roared, ' I talk to you like this because I am so miserable.'

By now, our hilarity had graduated from fake jollity forced by the absurdity of the situation to genuine mirth caused by the absurdity of the situation. Both of us had tears in our eyes, and I'm sure neither of us really knew whether we were laughing or crying. I left Odai's shop knowing that one whisper from me to Sadoun could ruin, if not end, one brave and trusting man's life, and wondering at the desperation that can drive someone to place the safety of his family in the hands of some scruffy stranger.

I'd think about Odai a great deal after that visit, especially as the dogs of war pawed the sand along Iraq's frontiers in late 2002 and early 2003. I didn't want Odai's city to get bombed – again – but nor did I think he should have to be scared of his government. Ending tyranny, from within or without, is an unarguably noble pursuit.

23

The best new bar in Tirana had opened a few weeks earlier. It was called Living Room, and was created in the image of a mid-eighties Manhattan cocktail lounge, with a full-service restaurant, commodious lounges, gleaming racks of bottles behind a bar manned by crisply dressed staff. Living Room was, however, most noteworthy for what it lacked – walls and a roof. The bar had been built on a roof terrace, overlooking a park, completely exposed. It was entirely insane, and as such wholly in keeping with the spirit of early twenty-first century Tirana.

This summer night, I wasn't sure how long I'd bank on Living Room staying in business. The struggle between the staff's enthusiasm and Living Room's first winter might prove crucial, I thought. However, I was certain that even if Living Room blossomed into a global franchise of the oppressive ubiquity of Starbucks, none of its outlets would host a more remarkable crowd than the one I'd arrived with. They didn't look like much – a few dozen twenty and thirty-somethings, clad in standard-issue urban camouflage of jeans, T-shirts and trainers, yelling at each other over the music, pouring beer from frosted jugs, attempting to consume cocktails without poking themselves in the eye with paper umbrellas. The bartenders probably didn't realise that they were serving the most extraordinary gathering of revolutionaries in twenty-first century history.

The few dozen people – kids, really – drinking in Living Room that June evening had, between them, played significant roles in the overthrow of governments in Serbia, Georgia, Ukraine and Lebanon. The reason they were all in Tirana was to debate, among other things, who might be next.

The occasion was the Tirana Activism Festival. This was the first formal assembly of the youth-led pro-democracy movements which had redrawn Eastern European and Middle Eastern politics in the early twenty-first century. From Serbia came Otpor! (Resistance!), the tenacious termites who'd eaten Slobodan Milosevic's rotten regime from the inside out. From Georgia came Kmara (Enough), who'd helped foment the Rose Revolution which had removed the government of superannuated, corrupt Georgian president Eduard Shevardnadze in late 2003. From Ukraine came Pora (High Time), who had organised the massive street protests in Kiev which brought down the kleptocracy of Leonid Kuchma in December 2004. From Lebanon came Pulse of Freedom, formed from the groups who'd camped in downtown Beirut after the car bomb assassination of former Lebanese prime minister Rafik Hariri in February 2005, and helped force out the pro-Syrian incumbent, Omar Karami. From Belarus, Azerbaijan, and Uzbekistan came delegates from organisations hoping to emulate these successes, and from Kosovo, Croatia, Russia and Macedonia came agitators more interested in reform than regime change, but nonetheless determined for their moderation.

The event was hosted by Mjaft!, the youth-led Albanian civil activist movement. In the two years since I'd first met the founders of Mjaft!, shortly after they'd launched their crusade for democracy and transparency, they'd turned their idea into a major force in Albanian politics – and Mjaft's executive director, Erion Veliaj, now all of twenty-five, into one of the most famous and influential people in the country. Protests, pranks and initiatives by Mjaft! had been responsible for the sacking of Albania's minister of public order for punching a journalist, an increase in Albania's education budget, the dispatch of an Albanian medical team to tsunami-soaked Banda Aceh, and the establishment of an annual three-day music festival. They'd won a

UN Civil Society Award, been invited to speak to politicians in the US and the UK, and had now decided to see what happened when their kindred spirits were collected in one place – which, the first morning, was the Tirana International Hotel, overlooking Skanderbeg Square. Instead of name tags on suits, delegates wore T-shirts and caps emblazoned with the name of their organisations.

A few faces were familiar to me. Albin Kurti, of the Kosova Action Network, who I'd last seen leading a donkey through the streets of Pristina in protest against Kosovo's UN-sponsored elections, regarded proceedings with the benign condescension of the elder statesman. I asked if he had any plans to go legit.

'No,' he smiled. 'KAN is not becoming a political party. We have higher ambitions than that. Our political parties, their ambitions are just to get rich. We don't want to get rich. We want social change.'

Razi Nurullayev, thirty-three, of Azerbaijan's Yox! – it meant 'No!' – had just got out of jail.

'I was held five days,' he said. 'The police grabbed me on the street and pushed me into a car. I thought was being kidnapped.'

The formal opening of the festival was held at Tirana's Academy of Arts. Erion's speech stressed the solidarity that he hoped the weekend would engender. To the organisations which had already dealt tyranny a defeat, he said, 'Your freedom is our freedom,' and to the groups which remained threatened by one despotry or another, he declared, 'We consider your chains our own.' He then asked everyone to turn to the person in the next seat and inform them, 'You are not alone.' He concluded by soaking one hand with red paint, in emulation of the Mjaft! emblem, and making an imprint next to Mjaft!'s name on one of the posters, mounted side-stage, which listed every organisation present. If these kids had retained one lesson from the communist propaganda endured by their parents, it was the power of symbolism.

Delegates from the other organisations followed, giving brief presentations – sort of an activist Eurovision – and leaving their scarlet prints on the boards. Alina Shpak, representing Ukraine's Pora, stressed the terror dictators have of mockery. Razi from Yox! expanded on this idea, announcing plans to bypass the unpleasant regime in Azerbaijan altogether; Yox!, he said, would establish a parallel government. Ako Minashvili, from Georgia's Kmara, made the heartbreaking suggestion that activists still fighting such regimes as those which plagued Azerbaijan, Uzbekistan and Belarus should take consolation in the excitement of their struggles. 'Since we won,' he said glumly, 'life has become quite boring.'

In the lobby of the arts centre I got talking to Ivan Marovic, one of the stars of the weekend. A burly Serb with a laugh that could start avalanches, he'd been a founding member of Otpor! – the clenched fist logo of the Serbian resistance was stitched in white on his black golf shirt. An architect of the revolution which had deposed Milosevic, I knew he'd shared expertise with Otpor!'s spiritual spawn in Ukraine, Georgia and Lebanon.

'I don't exactly feel paternal being here,' said Marovic, 'but coming from Serbia after more than ten years of being the barbarians of Europe, I do feel like we've set a good example, and that feels nice, you know?'

I also knew that he'd met with George W. Bush in Bratislava in February.

'I know this argument goes on,' he said, 'that it's all a CIA thing. The CIA doesn't have a clue about it. The CIA is a hierarchical, secretive organisation. These movements are quite the opposite. They're not hierarchical, and they're everything but secret.'

Otpor! had received American help and encouragement, as had many of the groups gathered in Tirana, leading to widespread whispering that these activists amounted to a sort of Bilderberg Group with eyebrow piercings. The festival brochure produced by Mjaft! acknowledged the sponsorship of Freedom House, and the US Agency for International Development. It was understandable that American involvement in these movements excited conspiracy-mongers. It was less readily explicable why anyone should think that the outside support of Otpor! and their fellow travellers was a bad thing. These groups were defined by their enthusiasm for democracy, and aversion to corruption and violence – it wasn't arming the Contras. But it was worth asking to what degree outside assistance compromised a movement like Otpor!

'We had to [accept their help],' said Marovic. 'We didn't have internal sources of funding. But it was a dilemma. When we protested in 1996, America supported Milosevic against us, because he was guarantor of the Dayton Accords. Three years later, America turns against him, so what are we going to do? Declare Milosevic our friend? No. He's still our enemy. So we got money, but we never got orders from anyone else. That's why we succeeded. When people get orders from abroad, it doesn't work. It's one thing to be supported, and another to be orchestrated.'

Supposing, I asked, someone reading the article I was writing about the festival was seized with inspiration . . .

'Okay,' grinned Marovic, 'a free lesson for readers of the *Independent on Sunday*. You need to reach at least 50 per cent of the voting public. You shouldn't think of people as belonging to one constituency – just their job or their religion or their ethnic group – because people have multiple loyalties. You use the loyalty that suits you, and for Otpor! it was kids – we were kids ourselves. They're rebellious, they hang out in large groups, they're more suggestible. In my family, I was the first to have a mobile phone. Now my father has one and my mother has one. The slang words they use, they got from me. Kids bring new stuff into the family.

'There were three things that made Otpor! One, the unifying of the opposition. Two, the plan: aiming at Milosevic. Three, the non-violence. Army, police, the civil servants, didn't feel threatened by us, so it was easier for them to defect to our side. We made everyone who wanted to defect feel welcome. That's the difference between violent and non-violent resistance.

'It's important that it is a leaderless revolution. That means everyone is safe, because nobody is exposed as leader. The reason I wasn't killed is that we were a leaderless movement. Organisations like secret police, they're not irrational. They calculate: if they kill someone, what's the effect? By killing the owner of a famous magazine, as they did, they stop the magazine. But by killing Ivan Marovic, they achieve nothing, because Otpor! goes on.

'Branding is important, but not all brands are successful. Package is one thing, content another. If they really have a point, they'll succeed. The most important thing when people get together is a vision of tomorrow. That's what kept us together. We wanted Serbia to be a normal country, because we were everything but normal.'

I asked Ivan about Otpor!'s inspirations, assuming that he'd mention Ghandi, King and the Parisian students of May 1968. He did, but also acknowledged one less likely exemplar of insurrection.

'Coca-Cola,' he beamed. 'We realised that there are some really good orange juices which nobody drinks. And then there's this terrible brown sugary water which everybody drinks. Why? Because of a strong brand, and a simple, powerful message. You have Coca-Cola everywhere, on everything, so we put Otpor! on everything – umbrellas, lighters, matchboxes. We branded the revolution.'

This was true. In Belgrade in 2000, Otpor! was a club all the cool people wanted to join, a T-shirt to be seen wearing despite the attendant risks (Ivan was arrested ten times). It was difficult to find a flat surface which wasn't tagged with Otpor! graffiti or stickers – everywhere, you saw Otpor!'s logo and the slogan 'Gotov Je!' (He's finished!). This was a particularly skilful piece of copywriting, proclaiming Milosevic over while he was still in office, making his removal a self-fulfilling prophecy. The key to Otpor!'s lasting influence was their understanding that – to paraphrase Lord Acton – all power is absurd, and absolute power is absolutely absurd. Amazing things can happen when someone points that out, and it's a task well-suited to the impudence of youth.

The festival's schedule had obviously been drawn up by people still the silly side of thirty – the agenda contained such items as 'Celebration of Activism Party, 2300–0300', and then, for an 0930 kick-off the following morning, seminars on 'Activism In Context'. The coffee provided for those who scraped themselves into the Tirana International Hotel on time ran out quickly.

The seminars were characterised by a total absence of fashionable dogmas. Because most of those present were of the first generation of

Eastern Europeans to have grown up free from totalitarian foolishness, they took democracy, peace and transparency as self-evident desirables: these were conversations about how, not why.

The sessions on 'Dressing Up Activism: The Rhetoric and Images Behind Successful Movements' were a dazzling insight into the service that cynicism can provide to idealism. A representative from Pora unleashed an astute, blisteringly sarcastic analysis of the global media beast.

'Foreign media,' he told the meeting, which included foreign media, 'don't care about your problems, and they mostly don't care about you. They care about themselves, and about getting the story they're telling across to the audience. So if you're demonstrating and being interviewed by a French journalist, tell them it's like Paris '68. If it's a Polish journalist, compare it to Solidarity.'

He affirmed the importance of creating news items which conjured a sympathetic impression, of speaking good English, keeping one's message straight, and steering well clear of violence, or the threat of it; I thought it a shame there were no Palestinians present. Yox!'s Razi Nurullayev observed that getting on television or in the papers wasn't always possible – in Azerbaijan, he said, there was little local independent media, and a lack of interest from foreign press. He'd figured out a way around it, though. Azerbaijan's capital, Baku, was a windy city. Yox! planned to print a million anti-government flyers, and leave piles of them in high places.

Other sessions dealt with 'future strategies' – whether movements such as these could ever become something more than a means of directing youthful energy against established power structures. Otpor! and Kmara, having won the battles they took the field to fight, had struggled to find further purpose, and no longer existed as organisations. Ivan Marovic launched this debate in customary robust style.

'When Otpor! started,' he told the group, 'we were seen as kids getting beaten up fighting for freedom, and everybody loved us. Then when we stood in elections in 2003, we got 1.6 per cent of the vote. It was like a cold shower. I mean, we had 80,000 members, and we got 67,000 votes. Not even Otpor! voted for us. That's the problem.

People don't vote for people who are too young, who don't look like a political party. People tend to vote for . . . well, for assholes.'

This, it was agreed, was a difficulty. Everyone had a horror of finding themselves starring in a remake of the final scene of Orwell's *Animal Farm*. ('The creatures outside looked from pig to man, and from man to pig, and from pig to man again; but already it was impossible to say which was which.')

After this session, I had lunch with Erion Veliaj and asked him about the future of Mjaft!.

'We've thought about it,' he said, of an entrance to mainstream politics. 'We get a lot of attention now. Some love us, some hate us, but nobody ignores us. We're a factor. When the party lists here were being decided for next month's elections, most people in Mjaft! had offers, but we're more influential like this, and we're having way more fun. There's no point entering a rotten game. Anyway, we're in no rush. We've got time on our side.'

Erion spoke with the same mixture of rosy-cheeked idealism and ice-eyed realism that characterised all the groups he was hosting. 'We'd read all these articles about the conspiracy theory,' he said, 'so we thought, there are allegations that all our groups know each other and have been organised – we might as well get to know each other and get organised.'

Also at the festival were representatives of Freedom House, an American NGO about which certain rumours had long circulated – mostly due to the fact that Freedom House's chairman, R. James Woolsey, had once been director of the CIA. The Freedom House chaps had been putting up with heavy-handed jokes – quite a few from me – with good humour, and I didn't doubt their personal enthusiasm for truth, justice and the American way. But as long as the Americans were hovering, a lot of people were going to have trouble seeing past them.

'I understand,' said Erion, 'that there's an international context to all this. It wasn't convenient for America for Milosevic to go in 1996, but it was convenient in 1999. It was convenient for America for the Georgian and Ukrainian governments to be removed, but it's not so convenient for the Uzbek and Azeri governments to be removed. There's no denying that there's a foreign influence in this, but there's also a genuine desire for change.'

Erion, I felt bound to observe, had aged more than the two years which had elapsed since we first met.

'I know,' he said. 'There's a lot of people involved now. There's pressure. There are threatening messages on the phone. Of course I worry, but if you don't take a risk at this age, when do you?'

Back at the hotel, Alina from Pora offered another perspective, which explained why these youthful organisations had been so peculiarly effective in this part of the world.

'Older people here,' she said, 'aren't able to make any changes, because of their post-Soviet consciousness. For more than seventy years, people got used to the idea that they were slaves, small instruments in a huge machine, and they couldn't change anything. People our age have an absolutely different way of seeing things.'

The final official activity was a bus trip to Kruja, a glorious redoubt in the mountains north of the capital. Kruja was the citadel from which Albania's national hero, Skanderbeg, defied the Ottoman empire for twenty-five years of the fifteenth century. On this perfect summer's afternoon, Kruja became the site of a less spectacular, but possibly more resonant, act of defiance. On the terrace of the museum devoted to Skanderbeg, Ivan Marovic made a speech outlining what had come to be called the Kruja Pact.

The Kruja Pact had been cooked up in Tirana bars over the weekend, its wording thrashed out by huddles gathered around laptops. The Kruja Pact was emblematic of the groups that had gathered that weekend. It was serious but funny, noble but self-effacing, and unmistakably determined. The Kruja Pact was an echo of Article V of the NATO treaty – known, since its invocation after September 11 2001, as the 'All for one, one for all' clause. The Kruja Pact asserted that an attack by any government on any of the signatories would be regarded as an attack on all of the signatories, and responded to accordingly. The possibilities, given the records of the groups whose representatives took turns to sign the Pact, with arch mock-solemnity, were immense, inspiring and hilarious. Arrests in Baku could lead to demonstrations in Tirana. A crackdown in Minsk may have repercussions in Belgrade. Trouble for activists in Tashkent might mean trouble for Uzbek institutions all over the world.

My photo of the Kruja Pact signatories is still on my office wall. It is probable that people in that picture will become presidents and prime ministers. It's at least as likely that some will end up political prisoners, or worse. But I really hoped that their example might be taken up further afield, encouraging the young of Iran or Zimbabwe or Cuba or Gaza or any of dozens of other misruled basket cases to wonder what miracles might result if sufficient numbers of them uttered the exclamations 'No!' or 'Enough!' or 'Resistance!'

For now, the Kruja Pact's plotters were free to dream and scheme. That melancholy moment, at which the revolutionary realises that it's sometimes easier to get things done when one isn't in power, was still a way off.

24

'When you're in the cabinet,' mused Peter Hain, 'you have to be careful of every word you use. In Northern Ireland, you have to be careful where you put full stops and commas.'

It was late afternoon. We were sitting in the drawing room of Hillsborough Castle, Hain's residence while he was being Her Majesty's Secretary of State for Northern Ireland (when he got a moment, Hain was also Secretary of State for Wales, Member of Parliament for Neath, and a Privy Councillor). It was a space of singular grandness in which, if we'd shifted the grand piano outside, we could have held an indoor javelin tournament.

'I never had a political career in mind,' said Hain, a self-conscious smile suggesting that he realised that this sounded, in these surroundings, ingenuous. 'The thought would have horrified me.'

Hillsborough Castle, an eighteenth century masterpiece surrounded by glorious gardens, was bought by the British government in 1922 to house governors of the then-recently created Northern Ireland. Hain had occupied it for six months when we met, and still surveyed its interior with the gawping wonderment of a tourist. In the lobby, the visitors' book contained signatures of all the British royal family, plus those of the transatlantic alliance who'd met there in April 2003 to put the finishing touches to their meticulously wrought plans for bringing peace and democracy to Iraq – or possibly, given how things had worked out in Iraq, to spend a weekend swigging daiquiris and playing Risk. Hain would also have spent a lot of time in these rooms pondering the most efficacious means of discouraging internecine strife. This was worthwhile work. I wondered why the thought of it would have horrified him. He did what politicians do, and answered a question I hadn't asked.

'I don't mean,' he said, 'that I'd have thought I was selling out, because I've never thought in those terms. I think you find yourself playing different roles, and the way things have worked out, I'm playing this role. It's the same me, with the same beliefs and the same commitments, the same passion about human rights and social justice.'

This was, of course, what anyone in Hain's position would say. It would have been surprising, if refreshing, if Hain had said, 'I couldn't care less about human rights, and you know what else doesn't interest me? Social justice. Social justice can cram it.' However, while it might have been tempting to write Hain's manifesto-speak off as generic rhetorical pabulum, this famously slick politician did have impressive pedigree on the human rights and social justice fronts. In the late 1960s and early 1970s, Hain had campaigned bravely and effectively against the apartheid government of his native South Africa. Hain's family fled South Africa in 1966 after his parents were persecuted for opposing apartheid. In the UK, Hain led protests which caused no end of splendid chaos. Hain fought the law – he led pitch invasions to disrupt cricket and rugby matches between England and South Africa. Hain fought the power – in 1972, he escaped injury when a letter bomb failed to explode, and in 1976 stood trial for bank robbery (he was acquitted of charges widely believed to have been fabricated by South African intelligence). When I alluded to what seemed a laudable record of resistance, Hain became curiously defensive.

'You may regard this,' he said, 'as watching the commas. My job is to understand both where people are coming from, across the community divide, and where we need to get to. To go back over history . . . I don't think it's helpful to anybody.'

There were reasons for Hain's reluctance to discuss his past – and for his careful way of feeling through every answer he gave, parsing as he went for potentially controversial content, and for having the interview taped. The first was that any discussion of the past in

Northern Ireland, as in most places which suffer a history of conflict, was liable to descend into a cacophony of competing grievance. In Northern Ireland, every accusation of Republican/Nationalist malfeasance was answerable with an equivalent charge of Loyalist/Unionist brutality – and both could be marshalled against, or supported by, claims of British treachery. It was such a common mode of discourse that the province had coined a gorgeous neologism for it: 'Whataboutery'. Hain, acutely aware that everything he said would be minutely scrutinised, was at pains not to give anyone anything to yelp 'What about . . .' about.

The second reason for Hain's anguish when I tried to reach the present through his past was that he had, already, contributed to the lexicon of Whataboutery. In the 1980s, Hain made statements in favour of a British withdrawal from, or abandonment of, Northern Ireland. For Unionists and Loyalists, Hain's appointment as Secretary of State must have looked like a referee turning up to officiate a Celtic vs Rangers match wearing green and white hooped socks.

'You can go back to lots of things people have said,' he said, wincing slightly. 'Things Gerry Adams might have said. Things Ian Paisley might have said. At a time when the Berlin Wall was still up, when Nelson Mandela was still in prison. We're in a different world now.'

I explained that I was wondering if Hain's history, in the context of the job he was doing in Northern Ireland, might be more of an advantage than disadvantage. Any Secretary of State for Northern Ireland would have to deal with people who had adopted extreme positions, deployed extreme means. Yet Hillsborough had generally been occupied by figures difficult to picture shaking a fist atop a burning barricade. Maybe this was a way to make use of former militants who might have grown wiser as they got older. If a South African freedom fighter was keeping the peace in Northern Ireland, perhaps some world body of eminent extremists could be established to lend their expertise to mentalities they'd certainly understand. If I were a member of Hamas, I'd be more likely to listen to Saadi Yacef or Martin McGuinness than I would to Jimmy Carter.

'I can understand,' Hain eventually conceded, 'people who've struggled for the cause they believe in. Whether that's Ian Paisley and his followers – because he has come from way out in the cold to being the leading figure in Northern Ireland politics, leading the leading party. It's a huge journey for him. A huge journey for Gerry Adams and Martin McGuinness, as well. And I've been on a journey that I wouldn't have expected back when I was organising demonstrations and protests.'

We'd met the Reverend Paisley earlier that day. Hain had been on a tour of Ballymena, a prosperous Protestant stronghold a short drive from Belfast – Paisley was the local Member of Parliament, member of the Northern Ireland Legislative Assembly, and former member of European Parliament, as well as leader of the Democratic Unionist Party and moderator of the Free Presbyterian Church of Ulster. Paisley had been waiting for us in the cafe of Ballymena's Ecos centre. This was a vast, millennial white elephant, crammed with fatuous consciousness-raising exhibits: daft interactive enviro-horror displays, placards reading – an actual example, this – 'Three billion trees are needed each year to produce enough paper to wipe the bottoms of the world', that kind of thing. Also in attendance were other regional notables, including Ballymena's genial mayor, Tommy Nicholl, and Paisley's son and fellow Legislative Assembly member, Ian Paisley Jr.

While Hain was working the room, I asked Paisley Jr if I might trouble his old man for a couple of quotes. Paisley Jr asked which newspaper I was from, and I explained that I was profiling Hain for the *Independent on Sunday*.

'He won't talk to you,' said Paisley Jr.

This surprised me. While I was aware that the *Independent On Sunday* didn't view Northern Ireland through orange-tinted glasses, I imagined Paisley would have a thicker hide than that.

'Nothing personal,' laughed Paisley Jr. 'He just doesn't speak to Sunday newspapers. Never has. He thinks they're anti-Sabbatarian.'

I half-imagined that Paisley Jr was winding me up. On immediate acquaintance, he seemed the sort. He had a yard-wide grin, and a breezy roguishness contrary to his father's popular image as a brimstone-breathing firebrand – and contrary to some of Paisley Jr's own bizarre public statements, especially about gay people. (Paisley Jr, like many so troubled, had a horror of the mechanics of homosexuality so morbid that it seemed to verge on the interested – something he may have inherited from his father, who once launched a campaign called Save Ulster From Sodomy, provoking the common retort that the initiative was a bit late, as the place was already buggered.)

'I'm not kidding,' he said. 'If you'd said you were from the *Independent*, you'd have got away with it, but you've no chance.'

Feeling like I'd just accepted an especially foolish dare, of the order of tickling a sleeping leopard, I introduced myself to Paisley. I told Paisley that I understood his objection to Sunday newspapers – though I didn't, much – and proposed a deal. I wouldn't quote him directly in a publication whose existence was such an affront to the Fourth Commandment, and I wouldn't write this bit of the feature on a Sunday. Almost disappointingly, Paisley laughed, rather than calling in a lightning strike, and chuntered amiably. Peter Hain was the fifteenth Secretary of State for Northern Ireland since the position was established in 1972. Paisley, who'd dominated Unionist politics for decades, had dealt with them all. He didn't disagree when I suggested that he must have felt trepidation about the present incumbent, but assured me that he wouldn't hold twenty-year-old quotes against anyone, and that he would never, in retribution for some youthful foolishness, instruct a Secretary of State to – and here, I fear, I break my vow to the Reverend and repeat verbatim his deployment of local idiom – 'Get about ye'.

It would be tempting a deluge of angry letters from one half of the province, written in even greener ink than usual for such choleric correspondence, to advance Ian Paisley as a personification of Northern Ireland. Indeed, many Northern Irish Protestants would recoil from such a characterisation, and with reason: it took only a few minutes' idling at www.ianpaisley.org to find views, with Paisley's name attached, which might be charitably described as barking crazy. One 1999 essay, beneath Paisley's byline, asserted that the chamber of the European Parliament had a seat reserved for Satan. When Pope John Paul II had addressed the same institution in 1988, Paisley jeered 'I refuse you as Christ's enemy,' before being escorted from the premises.

Anywhere else in the UK, Paisley would have struggled for an audience larger than a few bemused tourists and heckling tramps in Speaker's Corner in Hyde Park, or some similar haven for ranting cranks. In Northern Ireland, he was probably the most popular politician, and for that reason the epitome of what anyone seeking to understand the place was faced with: a lid of affable charm and ungrudging hospitality atop a cauldron of volcanic nonsense. Anywhere else in the UK, or anywhere else in the First World, Paisley could be written off as a harmless buffoon whose preposterous ravings were without consequence. In early twenty-first century Northern Ireland, however, it was dauntingly easy to find manifestations of superstition which should have gone the way of witch trials.

The next stop on Hain's tour was the St Louis Convent Primary School in Ballymena, which had been attacked by arsonists a couple of months before. Nobody doubted the motivation for this attempt to destroy a Catholic school in a mostly Protestant town. Ballymena's police had taken the pragmatic but profoundly depressing step of issuing Catholic families with fire blankets.

Hain's wasn't the only entourage to pitch up at St Louis's. To audible intakes of breath from the priests and teachers, the unmistakable white-haired figure of Paisley also lumbered into the school. I couldn't swear that the immense ceramic Christ in the lobby didn't arch an eyebrow. After a pause for those present to retrieve their jaws from the floor, visitors were ushered into the school's hall, where what the advance itinerary menacingly described as 'a musical presentation' awaited. Before this began, headmaster Liam Corry explained to the students who Hain was.

'You've heard of Tony Blair?' he asked. 'Well, Mr Hain is the man who tells Tony Blair what's going on in Ballymena.'

Corry went on to express his admiration for Hain's youthful crusade against apartheid and – rather pointedly, I thought – for

Hain's refusal to resort to violence in pursuit of his aims. He didn't offer a similar potted biography of Paisley, though this was probably not so much a deliberate snub as a tacit acknowledgement that no introduction was necessary. Paisley beamed at the children in grandfatherly manner, looking entirely unlike a man who believed, as Paisley did, that they were doomed, hell-bound dupes of a church led by the Antichrist. The threatened 'musical presentation' was a performance by the school's choir, who had been winning local competitions and who were as unobjectionable as warbling schoolkids get. Afterwards, Hain mentioned the arson attack, offered hope that all concerned could put it behind them, and told the kids to keep singing. 'You'll win all the competitions in Northern Ireland,' he assured them, then paused, as if worried about the commas and full stops. 'Of course, I have to be careful here, because I'll go and say the same thing in the next town.' I wasn't sure he meant to say that out loud.

We toured a few classrooms, in which the chorused 'Good morning, Reverend Paisley' of the children was as hesitant as a 'Good morning, Mr Bogeyman'. Outside the school, a scrum of local media gathered. Hain spoke of standing 'shoulder to shoulder' with Paisley against sectarianism. This was a little like standing shoulder to shoulder against apartheid with Eugene Terre'Blanche – but there, I supposed, was the difference between the protests of Hain's youth and the practical politics he had to pursue now. Hain couldn't very well have nodded towards Paisley and said, 'And frankly, if the people of Ballymena had a shot glass of sense between them, they'd stash this old duffer in a facility for the irrecoverably bewildered.' More plausibly, Hain enthused about a new intitiative of Mayor Nicholl, to bring Ballymena's local clergy together for cross-denominational discussions. Incredibly, no such thing had been attempted before.

When questions were invited, someone raised the previous weekend's protests at Newtownabbey's Carnmoney Cemetery. It had not been an edifying spectacle. Catholics holding a blessing ceremony in the graveyard had been abused by a mob of Loyalist protestors.

'Awful,' said Hain. He flailed briefly, as any sensible person would when contemplating such idiocy, and then lit upon the perfect adjective. 'Medieval,' he continued. 'A throwback. And they must understand the image it projects, in Northern Ireland and in the wider world.'

This statement of Hain's isolated one of the key difficulties of conflict resolution – the people who get all the media coverage and, as a consequence, all the political attention, tend to be the ones who don't want the conflict resolved. Northern Ireland was the first war zone I ever visited, arriving as a curious, clueless backpacker in 1990. I assumed that everyone in Northern Ireland would be ablaze with righteous fervour for one side or another. I actually found it difficult to find anyone who cared, or at least who cared more about who governed Northern Ireland than they did about their friends, family and work. I've found the same thing since in the Balkans, Afghanistan, Lebanon, Iraq, Israel, the West Bank and Gaza: what most people want is to be left alone. It would be interesting if, for one day every week, news organisations ignored querulous minorities in favour of the less dogmatic majority: 'Today in Iraq, millions of people didn't murder anyone for holding a contrasting view of the succession to Mohammed'; 'Across Iran this evening, many people wished the United States and Israel no harm at all – and, if they're being honest, inwardly agreed that their president might be a bit of a dickhead'; 'Large numbers of Africans not engaged in inexplicable, poorly organised, internecine slaughter'.

It's never that simple, of course – Ian Paisley had a democratic mandate, as did his equally obdurate opponents in Sinn Fein. But beneath the din created by extremists over nearly four decades of Northern Ireland's Troubles, elements of Northern Ireland had been quietly, efficiently, unnewsworthily getting on with it. Hain's afternoon schedule took in Ballymena's two biggest employers: the vast Michelin tyre factory and the locally owned bus manufacturers Wrightbus. Michelin and Wrightbus were among the principal engines of Ballymena's prosperity – and, as such, guarantors of Northern Ireland's tentative calm. In a town of Ballymena's size anywhere else,

Michelin and Wrightbus might make the difference between boom and bust. In Ballymena, they might have been the difference between peace and war.

Back at Hillsborough, Hain fidgeted when asked to reflect on his transition from scourge of the establishment to pillar of it.

'It's not pragmatism in the grubby sense,' he insisted. 'I don't want to pose or posture or occupy a position because I've got a limousine and a reasonable salary. I want to make change. I've never been an all-or-nothing person. I've always been an all-or-something person. I remember arguing with Tariq Ali, in the sixties and seventies, who told me I shouldn't be leading campaigns to run on cricket pitches or on rugby pitches, I should be digging pitches up and fighting police, because that's fighting capitalism. In my view, that was a lot of old revolutionary balderdash. And whilst he was preaching that rhetoric, we were actually stopping the tour. That defines my whole approach to politics.'

Hain was not entirely above using his radical past to purchase some credit.

'There are people,' he said, 'now leading the world, who as students were marching alongside me in the anti-apartheid movement, and I keep bumping into people who say "I was following you, and now I'm prime minister of this country, or president of that country" . . . It's quite amusing, and then you realise that it's our generation that's in power.' Where, as Hain was discovering, it's astonishing how powerless you can end up feeling, and looking.

Hain, like his predecessors, was dancing the two-steps-forward-one-step-back of what was hopefully the Troubles' last waltz. Four months previously, the IRA had announced an end to its armed campaign. Two months previously, General John de Chastelain, head of the decommissioning body, had verified that the IRA's arsenal had been put beyond use. But recent months had seen Northern Ireland's worst violence for years, rioting convulsing several Loyalist neighbourhoods, and Hain announcing that he no longer recognised the ceasefire of the

Ulster Volunteer Force. A couple of hours after my interview with Hain concluded, former Ulster Defence Association kingpin Jim Gray was shot dead at his Belfast home.

'Unionists and Loyalists,' admitted Hain, 'are in a belligerent mood towards the British government, almost all the institutions of the British state – ironically. That has come at a time when Unionism ought to feel more secure. The IRA have given up bombing and bullets. They have accepted that the people of Northern Ireland will decide its constitutional future. The Irish government has removed its constitutional claim on Northern Ireland. And I don't know whether it struck you today in the same way that it struck me when I started travelling around here six months ago, but there is a lot of prosperity.'

This was true. An uninformed visitor to the parts of Northern Ireland that Hain had toured today would never have guessed that anything was wrong. The houses were large, the lawns neat, the businesses flourishing.

'This is,' said Hain, 'a nice place, full of nice people. I didn't have a negative impression before I came, except the negative impression you get when people are letting off bombs and engaging in this medieval sectarianism. You wonder how people can do that to each other. But I saw what otherwise decent people among Afrikaner-supporting white South Africans did to the black majority there. These were people who worshipped God, looked after their dogs and had tremendously strong family values.'

Any incoming Secretary of State for Northern Ireland must feel like Max, the protagonist of Maurice Sendak's children's book *Where The Wild Things Are* – like a small, perplexed boy in a wolf suit confronting a weird, dangerous place populated by grotesque creatures unknown on our own planet. A Secretary of State faces mythic, demonic figures like Paisley and Adams, and a fluid moral landscape. I wondered if Hain missed the certainties of taking a stand on something so obviously evil and ridiculous as apartheid.

'That was,' he agreed, 'a black and white issue. In every sense. It was very clear cut. But I don't know that I miss . . . I mean, I'm pleased that there aren't those old certainties.'

Hillsborough's first official occupant, Governor James Hamilton, third Duke of Abercorn, had the luxury of twenty-three years in the job, during which all that was asked of him was his stamp on acts of the gerrymandered regional parliament, and his presence at ribbon-cutting ceremonies. Hain had rather more to do, rather less time in which to do it, and – like all peacemakers and keepers – the burden of the knowledge that the people who'd caused the trouble before he arrived would still be there after he left.

25

'George Bernard Shaw wrote, and I paraphrase him very badly, that when a nation is denied its freedom . . . hang on.'

Gerry Adams produced his wallet from his hip pocket.

'Someone gave me this quote on a piece of paper the other day,' he explained, fossicking through receipts and sundry scraps, 'but I can't remember it exactly.'

Neither could I, offhand, but I knew the line he meant. It's from the preface to *John Bull's Other Island*. The complete quote is:

A healthy nation is as unconscious of its nationality as a healthy man of his bones. But if you break a nation's nationality it will think of nothing else but getting it set again. It will listen to no reformer, to no philosopher, to no preacher, until the demand of the Nationalist is granted. It will attend to no business, however vital, except the business of unification and liberation.

'I think that line, if we're thinking of the same one, puts it very well,' said Adams. 'I've been involved in political activism all my life, and I've travelled all over Ireland, and the majority of people want a united Ireland. Have no doubt about that. The symbolism of the tricolour, peace between orange and green. That's what people want.'

I met Adams in Sinn Fein's Belfast headquarters on the eve of the tenth anniversary of the IRA's announcement, on 31 August 1994, of 'a complete cessation of military activities'. Adams' small office was cluttered with Republican memorabilia, which wasn't surprising.

The lack of security was. Adams had many enemies, and had survived several assasination attempts – in 1984, in an attack by Loyalist para-militaries Ulster Freedom Fighters, he'd been shot three times. But, though I had to buzz to gain entry, nobody searched my bag, and Adams was happy to sit by a large window overlooking the busy Falls Road.

'I take precautions,' he said. 'But you get on with your life. The reason that we're here on the front of the road is that we're here on the front of the road. We're a generation of Republicans who've come through the prison camps. [Adams was interned without trial in 1972, served four years between 1973 and 1977 for attempting to escape from a second internment, and was remanded for eight months in 1978 on a charge of IRA membership, subsequently dropped.] We're here now, and we're here to stay.'

Adams was, at the time, in political limbo. Aside from being president of Sinn Fein, a position he'd held for twenty-one years, he was the MP for Belfast West, but didn't sit in the Commons – Sinn Fein MPs wouldn't swear the oath of allegiance to the Crown. He was also the member for the same seat in Northern Ireland's Legislative Assembly, but hadn't had a job there since October 2002, when the Assembly was suspended amid allegations of IRA intell-igence-gathering. As we spoke, talks aimed at resurrecting the Assembly were due. However, given that the largest Unionist party, Ian Paisley's DUP, wouldn't sit in the same room as Adams, it was difficult to to perceive a way forward. I wondered if there was anybody Adams would refuse to deal with.

'No,' he replied. 'If I had to meet people who'd tried to kill me, I'd have no trouble with it. When we negotiated for the release of prisoners, we negotiated for the release of Loyalist prisoners as well, including people who'd been convicted of trying to kill me.'

Last time I'd come to Belfast, it had been to interview one such person, Loyalist hitman turned surrealist painter Michael Stone; Adams absorbed this information with a disinterest verging on the Zen. But given that Stone had told me that he didn't begrudge Adams his role in Northern Ireland's budding government, and that

Adams told me today that, 'If we want to make peace with the Unionists, we have to create conditions in which they can talk to us, listen to us, develop working relationships with us', the visitor to Northern Ireland could only wonder . . . what had Adams been fighting for?

For anyone who had watched British television in the previous thirty years, meeting Gerry Adams was like meeting the monster that cruel babysitters told you lived under your bed. Adams was the public face of a terrorist organisation which had killed hundreds of people, caused millions of pounds' worth of damage to property, and had twice attempted to assassinate Britain's government. Adams was a demon so potent it was feared that his voice could bring the United Kingdom to its knees. In Britain between 1988 and 1994, to the bafflement of all sane persons, it was illegal to broadcast Adams' gentle burr. I always thought that the broadcasting ban, and possibly Sinn Fein into the bargain, could have been subverted out of existence by the first producer who, instead of getting some idle actor to replicate Adams' voice, replaced it with the Swedish Chef from *The Muppet Show*.

Adams, now fifty-five, looked – give or take an encroaching greyness in the famous beard – nothing like the grandfather he'd become five years earlier. He wore jeans and a blue golf shirt, and was brisk and businesslike, but not without charm. When he talked about things he enjoyed outside politics – books, America, walking – he was, whatever baggage one may have arrived encumbered by, thoroughly likable. He'd just returned from a three-week holiday, during which, he said, he didn't read a newspaper. The only interruption to his idyll had been a meeting with Bill Clinton, who'd been in Belfast flogging an autobiography – which, seamlessly enough, was what Adams was doing today with his latest work, *Hope and History: Making Peace in Ireland*.

'I love books,' he said. 'I binge-read, you know. I find it very diff-icult to walk past a second-hand bookshop, and even more difficult to come out of it without a book. I have piles of books everywhere. But if I was to read by choice, I wouldn't read factual or political or polemical books. I'm reading *The Da Vinci Code* at the moment. I just finished one of Roddy Doyle's.'

Adams, author of a dozen books – autobiography, polemic and fiction – appeared as a central character in many more. There was one glaring discrepancy between Adams' account of Northern Ireland's Troubles and pretty much everyone else's. Adams had always insisted that he was never a member of the IRA. Indeed, he wrote about the IRA as if it were an entity with which he had to negotiate, occasionally with difficulty. Other histories of Northern Ireland contended that Adams found contacting the leadership of the IRA less inconvenient than he claimed. Ed Moloney's *A Secret History of The IRA* and Richard English's *Armed Struggle* alleged that Adams was not merely a member of the IRA, but that he'd occupied positions including Belfast chief of staff, northern commander, and membership of the Army Council. Adams' denial of IRA membership sounded as plausible as Paul McCartney insisting that he never joined The Beatles. English's book noted that between April 1971 and July 1973, when Adams was allegedly running the IRA's Belfast brigade, it killed 211 people.

'I have the Richard English book,' said Adams, 'and I met him at an event recently, but I haven't read it. I got the Ed Moloney book and got to about page 25, and then threw it to one side.'

Was there anything in particular that had upset him?

'I just couldn't deal anymore with the turgid . . . lies.'

I didn't know Ed Moloney. I did know that he had reported Northern Ireland with distinction for many years, and that his book got terrific reviews from people who knew the subject. I wondered whether Adams thought Moloney was working to some sinister agenda, or just badly informed.

'I don't know,' said Adams irritably. 'It's obviously legitimate from his point of view. He's involved in writing as a commercial enterprise, so . . .' Adams shrugged. He knew where this was going. I asked him to confirm his line that he was never, ever, a member of the IRA.

'Well, what other line could I take?' he harumphed.

I was tempted to reply, 'How about the howlingly obvious truth?', but thought this could lead to our encounter being abruptly truncated.

Instead, I asked Adams if he was bothered by the widespread assumption that he had been, and still was, a senior member of the IRA.

'It doesn't faze me,' he said. 'What gets annoying is that the issue fades, and it isn't an issue for months, and then somebody writes a book, or I meet someone like yourself – and it's obviously legitimate that you should raise these issues, I'm not objecting to that at all – or some Unionist MP makes some claim, and it becomes news for a day or a week or whatever. But in the normal run of things, no, it doesn't faze me.'

Adams had made his preposterous disavowal of IRA membership many times before, but it was so widely disbelieved that nobody, so far as I'd been able to tell from leafing through the cuttings on the flight to Belfast, had ever decided to see what would happen if one took it at face value. So I asked Gerry Adams why he'd never joined the IRA.

'Well,' he said. 'I think the question is . . . hmm.'

Adams paused, which wasn't something he did often. At this moment, he probably felt as startled and suspicious as Mormon door-knockers greeted by a bathwater-sodden, towel-clad householder with the words, 'I'd love to hear more about the Church of Latter-day Saints – come in and make yourselves at home, and I tell you what, I'll get a few friends round as they, too, are lacking spiritual direction.'

'If you look at the situation,' Adams continued, 'I think it's a legitimate thing for people to have been members of the IRA. I think that the IRA is an organisation which – without glamorising it for a moment, because I don't think anyone should glamorise any physical force structure, whether it's a conventional army or an army of occupation or resistance forces – is an entirely legitimate thing. The IRA doesn't have any monopoly on courage, but I think a lot of extraordinarily brave and good people have been involved in it. But my role has been a different role.'

This wasn't quite an answer to my question, which wasn't surprising, as my question was ridiculous, and Adams knew it was ridiculous, and knew I knew it was ridiculous. I pushed on, observing that Adams' paternal grandfather, another Gerry Adams, was active during the Irish Civil War in the Irish Republican Brotherhood. Adams' father, also called Gerry, joined the IRA as a teenager, was wounded in 1942, aged sixteen, in a confrontation with police officers, and served five years for attempted murder. Two of Adams' uncles were interned for alleged IRA sympathies; one of these, Dominic, was by some accounts IRA chief of staff in the 1930s. A generation later, Adams and four of his brothers had done time for alleged IRA membership or sympathies, and Adams had written of the Long Kesh/Maze internment camp that 'our family association with the camp is such that ever since it opened at least one of us has been imprisoned there'. Given the family background, I thought, he must have been tempted to join the IRA.

'No, no,' he said. 'This could be a misspent youth, but I became involved in Republican activism at a time when there was no IRA, or just a skeletal organisation. The thrust of activism was to build politically. When I became politically conscious, it was against that background.'

There followed a lengthy evocation of the late 1960s, placing the birth of modern militant Irish Republicanism against the upheavals of the period – Vietnam, Czechoslovakia, Paris – and namechecking The Rolling Stones, Bob Dylan, Joan Baez and The Chieftains. Which was fair enough, but didn't quite add up. The world was turning upside down. There was music in the cafés at night and revolution in the air. Adams' hometown was convulsed by sectarian conflict and, as he saw it, occupied by a foreign army. His friends were taking up arms, yet this committed Republican activist had never wanted to fight back. Did he just worry that he'd make a lousy soldier, or what?

'This is phenomenal,' he sighed. 'Here we are on the tenth anniversary of the IRA cessation. Here we are with arguably ten years of a peace process. Yet the IRA is still the sexy story. It doesn't matter what Unionist paramilitaries do, it doesn't matter what British securocrats have done . . .'

I conceded that all parties to the conflict had behaved, at one time or another, abominably. But given that so many of Adams' contemporaries had joined the IRA, did Adams ever feel guilty that he hadn't taken the oath?

'Not at all,' he said. 'In terms of your contribution to struggle, you have to be happy in your own skin that you've done your best, whatever role you have to play. I've never really had time to re-evaluate the whole thing, and I would like to think that if I was in that position, I wouldn't have any guilt about what I did or didn't do.'

The day I met Adams was close to another significant anniversary. It was twenty-five years and three days since the IRA blew up Lord Mountbatten's boat, killing the seventy-nine-year-old cousin of the Queen and former viceroy of India, along with his grandson, his daughter's mother-in-law, and the teenage boatboy. That same day, an IRA ambush killed eighteen British soldiers at Warrenpoint in County Down. What I couldn't get a sense of was how Adams felt about those things at the time. Pleased? Depressed?

'I was sorry for the civilians that were killed that day,' he said, 'especially the children. But you can only judge these events in the time they occurred.'

This was what I was asking him to do, but he didn't. Instead, he offered the briefest glimpse of the ruthlessness often imputed to him.

'I think for combatants,' he said, 'that's your hard luck. That's said in the context of knowing lots of Republican families who've lost sons and daughters. But those people joined that organisation, were on active service, and took the risks. Same as British soldiers, same as all the rest. That's what happens in wars.'

I asked if he could see a difference, other than scale, between September 11, of which Sinn Fein disapproved, and IRA attacks on civilian targets. Because I wasn't sure I could.

'Tell us,' he said bleakly, 'the civilian target you have in mind.'

The first of many that leaped to mind were the 1974 pub bombings in Birmingham and Guildford. Because of the – quite proper – outrage over the imprisonment of ten men who had nothing to do with the attacks, it was often forgotten that the bombs killed twenty-six people and injured dozens more. Those bombings weren't spontaneous reactions to oppression; they were planned, by adults who sat down and had meetings to discuss them.

'The reality,' said Adams, 'is that terrorism is attacks on civilians. That's it. You don't give warnings, you don't try to minimise casualties. Now, when the IRA killed civilians, and this is not to justify it, they did so by mistake. If the IRA had wanted to do those kind of things, presumably they could have done. Otherwise, why go to the trouble of phoning warnings?'

I wasn't convinced that if you planted explosives in a bar, you were absolved of blame for casualties if you phoned the local newspaper to tell them you'd done it just before they went off.

'That's not to justify it,' he insisted, 'but that's the difference. And hopefully, all that is behind us.'

Maybe. When I first visited Belfast in 1990, there were checkpoints on the roads, security barriers outside prominent buildings, bag searches in the shopping malls and, in the Nationalist and Unionist heartlands, an atmosphere of mistrust. If I stopped to take a picture of any of Belfast's political murals back then, it wouldn't take long for someone to appear and ask who I was and what I was doing (my explanation that I was a tourist from Australia invariably resulted in an invitation for a drink). The police got around in armoured Land Rovers, and armed British soldiers stalked the streets.

On this visit, I only saw one police vehicle – a normal squad car – and no British soldiers. Downtown Belfast looked like any medium-sized British or Irish city, though the locals had adopted the dreary contemporary fashion for shapeless tracksuits and nasty gold jewellery with unusual zeal; the place looked like it was hosting a convention of daytime chat show guests. In Nationalist and Unionist neighbourhoods, unharassed tourists photographed the murals; these were also available on fridge magnets in Belfast's souvenir shops. The taxi driver who dropped me at Sinn Fein, who was old enough to remember when driving a taxi in Belfast was one of the world's most dangerous jobs, said he now made much of his living carting visitors on tours of Trouble-spots. 'I've just come from Sinn Fein,' he said. 'Had some tourists from Germany. They got their picture taken with Martin McGuinness.' Sinn Fein also had a shop, where the tourists could have bought coffee mugs, T-shirts, and chintzy tributes to the ten Republican hunger strikers who starved themselves to death in 1981.

Unfortunately, a leaf through an armful of local papers confirmed that Northern Ireland's Troubles were, still, more than a historical tourist attraction. The *South Belfast News* reported that teenagers from rival neighbourhoods were trading sectarian abuse and missiles across the the River Lagan – the golf balls they launched at each other from homemade catapults had broken ten windows in 2004 – and that a recent Loyalist march had ended in a brawl between UDA and UVF supporters. The *North Belfast News* splashed on Protestant families leaving the Torrens estate, claiming intimidation by Republicans; inside was a story about Catholics on the same estate getting their windows broken by Loyalists armed with hockey sticks. The *News Letter* led with a yarn about a local Orange Hall being besieged by Nationalists; at the end, there was a report of a court appearance by four men of Republican bent charged with stabbing two Loyalist bandsmen. The *Andersonstown News* had a story about a sectarian assault on a fourteen-year-old Catholic boy, and a piece on a series of grotesque attacks on cats in the Lower Falls area, though no political or religious motivation for these was discernible. The *Belfast Telegraph*, commemorating the tenth anniversary of the IRA ceasefire, noted that in that tranquil decade, 179 people had been murdered by terrorists, 11,000 had suffered terror-related injuries, and 2300 had been on the receiving end of paramilitary 'punishment beatings', i.e. vigilante justice delivered with baseball bats if the victim was lucky. Also during this time, 5500 illegal firearms had been seized and 1100 explosive devices uncovered.

'One slip,' warned Adams, 'could cause calamity. There are sectarian attacks as we sit here. I think the most telling example of what's happening – and I don't think this was shown on television in Britain apart from one snippet – was on 12 July in Ardoyne, when an Orange parade was forced through a Nationalist area, and of all regiments the Parachute Regiment was brought into Ardoyne, and there was fierce hand-to-hand fighting between local Nationalists and British troops. The generally accepted wisdom, even from our detractors, was that Gerry Kelly [North Belfast MLA and Sinn Fein justice spokesman] and others saved the day. Some young soldiers had been cornered, were obviously armed, and the situation was quite fraught. What would have happened if Gerry Kelly and the Republican stewards had not been there? Those soldiers would have been killed.'

This sounded fantastic. Gerry Kelly was part of the IRA team which bombed Scotland Yard and the Old Bailey in 1973. He shot a warder when escaping the Maze prison in 1983. According to Moloney's book, he was adjutant general of the IRA. The most incredible aspect of Adams' version of events, however, was that the British army did not meaningfully dispute it. Their official response, when I rang and asked, was, 'During the disturbances in the Ardoyne on 12 July this year, ten soldiers and twenty-five police officers sustained minor but not inconsiderable injuries whilst dealing with a deteriorating public order situation. Additionally, items of army equipment were stolen from the back of a Land Rover. Whilst the actions of Gerry Kelly and others at the scene undoubtedly helped in averting what was becoming a very serious situation, it is worth noting that the soldiers and police present showed considerable restraint given the extreme provocation to which they were being subjected.'

It was difficult to know whether to laugh or cry. The spectacle of an IRA veteran coming to rescue of the Paras, whose red berets had been a red rag to Republicans since Bloody Sunday, was an encouraging one, whatever political calculations lay behind it (Sinn Fein's cause would not have been advanced by a lynching). But the willingness of people to smash up their own neighbourhood over whether or not blokes in daft hats can walk down a street whacking a drum was sufficient to make one wonder if Belfast would ever, to echo Adams' borrowing from Seamus Heaney, get hope and history to rhyme.

In 1998, as part of the Good Friday Agreement, the citizens of the Republic of Ireland were asked to vote on dropping Articles II and III of their constitution, which asserted the Republic's historical claim to the six counties that comprise Northern Ireland. An astonishing 94.4 per cent – the sort of mandate once more commonly associated with Iraqi elections – voted to ditch the articles. It sounded like Adams' compatriots in the south weren't all that bothered, didn't it?

'Not at all,' declared Adams. 'Articles II and III were always rhetorical.'

After I said my goodbyes to Adams, it occurred that the Shaw quote he'd mentioned reminded me of something. It was a song called 'Sunrise', by Northern Irish group The Divine Comedy, which had been written as a response to the Good Friday Agreement. The first two verses told the story of the childhood of Divine Comedy song-writer Neil Hannon. 'I was born in Londonderry,' it started, then, 'I was born in Derry City too.' The second verse furthered the defiant wish to stake a claim to both British and Irish heritage: 'I grew up in Enniskillen/I grew up in Inis Ceithleann too'. Then there was the middle eight, an eruption of magnificently reasonable anger. Roared over a thunderous orchestral backing, it could have been written as a rebuke to Shaw: 'Who cares where national borders lie?/Who cares whose laws you're governed by?/Who cares what name you call a town?/Who'll care when you're six feet beneath the ground?'

The accuracy of Shaw's broken bone allegory depended on which bone he meant. Adams doubtless thought it the spine, but what if it was a hairline fracture of the wrist – something which, while annoying, hardly prevented a normal life? Back in London, I emailed the lyrics of 'Sunrise' to Adams' press officer, curious to know what Adams might make of them. I didn't get a response. Adams was a busy man, meetings to attend, a sceptical Unionist community to convince, a nation to forge – and, as he'd said earlier, no time for reflection, no time to wonder whether the prize, if ever it was won, was going to be worth the pile of corpses and rubble that would have been climbed to reach it. It's often the case that by the time you get what you're fighting for, what you were fighting for isn't worth having.

26

I'd been looking forward to the drive from Jerusalem to Erez, the crossing which linked Israel to the Gaza Strip. My map suggested desert views, and I like desert views. My map may have been accurate once, but it wasn't anymore. The road to Erez traversed a part of Israel where the Israelis had put their backs into transcending the physical limitations of the land they had been given by – depending on one's perspective – God, or the UN, or America in league with the International Zionist Conspiracy (the Palestinian driver I'd hired was garrulously of the latter belief). Everywhere was neat, prosperous and green. It looked like Belgium.

The Israeli soldiers staffing the Erez complex that rainy afternoon were struggling for custom. In the VIP office, which dealt with foreigners entering Gaza, the only punters were myself and a balding American tourist in a shimmering pink tracksuit – a man in need of a stylist as well as a new travel agent. He was going nowhere: he had neither an Israeli government press card, nor NGO accreditation, and his protests that he had friends waiting for him in Gaza weren't impressing the soldiers. A couple of bored Israeli squaddies – goofy, grinning kids – wrestled on the reception area carpet.

I had an Israeli government press card, which entitled me to fill in a form seeking permission to enter Gaza. The form asked me to confirm that I had 'no association' with the International Solidarity Movement (ISM) or similar organisations. As an unaffiliated individual merely broadly in favour of all the region's peoples acting the goat a little less, I felt I could answer honestly in the negative. The form also asked for a local contact in Gaza; I invented a plausibly Arabic name and wrote it down along with the direct line of the last editor who'd annoyed me. There was also a declaration I was expected to sign which stated, in effect, that I knew Gaza was dangerous, that there was a war on and everything, and that I'd keep out of the way of Israeli forces and not complain too much if I got winged. I sensed an allusion to the foreigners killed in Gaza in recent years: Rachel Corrie, the twenty-three-year-old American ISM activist crushed by an Israeli bulldozer in Rafah, March 2003; Tom Hurndall, the twenty-two-year-old British activist and photographer shot by an Israeli sniper in Rafah, April 2003; James Miller, the Emmy-winning thirty-four-year-old British film-maker shot by an Israeli soldier in Rafah, May 2003.

Intentionally or not, the Israeli soldier to whom I handed my completed form ratcheted up the pressure slightly.

'Are you sure about this?' she asked.

I said a bit of lousy weather wouldn't put me off.

'I'm serious,' she said. 'Gaza is really dangerous. I wouldn't go in there.'

I gathered my bags and set off through Erez's labyrinthine fortifications. I walked through the truckport, past some metal detectors and the cattle gates through which Palestinians travelled to work in Israel when the border wasn't closed, as it was today and had been for some time. I got lost in the metal maze, and sought help from some Israeli soldiers scooping chow from tin trays. They directed me down a concrete tunnel a few hundred metres long, at the end of which was another checkpoint, manned by six Palestinians in khaki. One toasted bread over a hotplate. He offered me a slice, wordlessly, and I munched on it while the senior soldier considered my papers.

'How long will you stay in Gaza?' he asked.

A few days, I offered.

'Okay,' he said. 'Be careful, habibi.'

On the other side of Erez, it also looked like Belgium – Belgium in the winter of 1917. The view from the taxi stand was of chewed-up roads, ruined buildings, scattered rubble, random rubbish and muddy tracks, along which locals plodded with donkey-drawn carts. There was one taxi at the stand, a yellow-and-rust Mercedes-Benz which, like many vehicles in this part of the world, looked like it had already been used in several car-bombings. The driver quoted me a mildly larcenous price for the ride to Gaza City, but this was a seller's market. He owned the only taxi there, and rain was sloshing down in drenching sheets, like some malevolent deity was personally emptying buckets over me.

The driver explained, in English as halting as his car appeared, that the normal route was blocked. 'Israeli tank,' he said. As we set off, it became clear that this was a stock phrase of his, and a routine phenomenon in the district. 'Israeli tank,' he said, gesturing glumly at a half-demolished barn. 'Israeli tank,' he said, pointing wretchedly at a house missing its roof. 'Israeli tank,' he said, sighing balefully at a car, unhappily similar to his, smoke-blackened and resting on its roof. In an irony I didn't fully appreciate at the time, the only sight which didn't elicit the mournful commentary 'Israeli tank' was an Israeli tank – an Israel Defense Forces Merkava, snuffling irritably between abandoned buildings, forty or fifty metres ahead of where we'd lurched around a corner. From the driver's sudden paleness of countenance, I formed the impression that he was not expecting it to be there. The tank's turret swung quizzically in our direction. It was no time to be constructing whimsical similes, but it occurred to me that the tank resembled an exceptionally large anteater, sniffing a breeze bearing news of a bountiful termite mound.

'Fucking hell,' said the driver, in suddenly perfect colloquial English. There is no higher tribute to the innate hospitality of the Palestinian people than that, when confronted with mortal terror, they would choose to swear in the language of their guest.

This might, I suggested as evenly as possible, be a good moment to reverse. Before I finished the sentence, we were travelling backwards at a speed which sent surges of mud past the car's windows. When the driver had acquired the necessary momentum, he threw the Merc into a violent about-turn, and we charged away from the tank as quickly as the wheels could find traction, swerving crazily in the churning slurry. Both of us hunkered down in our seats, as if moth-eaten head-rests were going to provide much protection from the 120 millimetre shell we were anticipating. Around a bend, behind another half-destroyed house, out of the tank's line of sight, we stopped, and the driver relaxed. I didn't, but then I was blocking the driver's view of what was behind the house, a few metres from my passenger window: two men, clad in black, their heads covered by balaclavas, one carrying a rifle, the other a grenade-launcher. I pointed them out.

'Yes,' said the driver, as if I'd asked about some minor local attraction. 'They are Islamic Jihad. Perhaps Hamas. Something like this.'

Unsure of what else to do, I waved. The chap with the grenade-launcher nodded an acknowledgement, but seemed understandably preoccupied. I waited as long as felt polite for the driver to consider the possibility of some sort of cause-and-effect relationship between the presence of this pair and the prowling tank. As long as felt polite was, in the circumstances, about three heartbeats.

For the love of God, man, I barked at him. Drive!

In the drawer of the desk in my hotel room, where I'd normally expect to find a Gideon Bible, there was a copy of Edward Said's *Politics Of Dispossession*. The hotel was a family-run concern, secluded from Gaza City's streets by a high wall. I was the only guest. The view through my window was of thickets of palm leaves, the soundtrack filtering from beyond them the standard Middle Eastern jazz of car horns. I met my fixer, who I'll call Leila, in the cafe. Leila was a contact of a contact. We'd been introduced via email. She arrived bearing an armful of maps and pamphlets, and a neatly handwritten list of things she thought I should see, people I should meet.

Leila was both a refugee and an exile: a refugee in the sense that many Palestinians consider themselves refugees, which is to say that her ancestors had lost their home a couple of generations previously as the state of Israel fought to establish itself, and an exile from the life she'd been trying to build for herself. She held a degree in civil

engineering and an MBA, and had been pursuing still further education in Ramallah. Four months earlier, she'd got permission to cross
Israel from the West Bank to Gaza to spend a weekend with her family,
who lived north of Gaza City. While she'd been in Gaza, Israel had
closed Erez, and here she still was, her life and studies and ambitions
on indefinite hold. When Gazans called their home the world's biggest
open-air prison, it was to this kind of petty, vindictive, pointless
oppression they were referring.

Leila wore modest clothes and a tight headscarf; women in Gaza
generally did, in contrast to more relaxed, religiously diverse Palestinian cities like Ramallah. She spoke perfect English, distinguished by
a couple of quirks – a regular insertion of the Arabic word 'yani' in the
same places that young American, and Americanised, people deploy
'like', and an odd but endearing mishandling of the word 'mobilise',
which she used whenever she meant 'travel'. Mobilising in Gaza, she
explained, was done mostly by taxi – and in Gaza, every car was a
taxi. On the street outside, she flagged down a random sedan, and
ushered me inside.

'Anyone will take you anywhere,' she said. 'Just tell them where you
want to go, and give them, yani, a couple of shekels before you get out.'

Leila asked me what I wanted to see.

The sights, I suggested.

'There aren't any,' she smiled.

We got out of the taxi at the beach. It wasn't really beach weather.
It was cold and windy, and a fog was organising itself into rain. Even
in the most dazzling sunshine, though, the Gaza City beachfront
would have been as evocative of Bondi as a smack in the face is of a
kiss. It was more rubbish than sand.

'There's more people here in the summer,' said Leila. 'But it's not
much fun for girls, because of course we still have to be dressed like
this.' She indicated her shapeless, observant outfit gloomily.

We trudged back into town. Leila took me to the PLO flag shop, an
institution long beloved of journalists, NGO workers and other trouble
tourists. Tragically, the shop was down to the last of its famous stock
of inflatable Yasser Arafats, and was intent on retaining it as a mascot.

'We won't be ordering any more,' sighed the owner. 'Business is not good. Nobody comes to Gaza now.'

Amid the posters of Arafat and Abbas, I noticed a black, triangular woollen shawl, bordered with a design that included the Dome of the Rock, the initials 'PLO', and the flags of Palestine and the United States. Then I noticed another shawl featuring the same design and the Union Jack.

I'm from Australia, I told the chap behind the counter.

'Oh, I'm sure we have,' he said, opening a cupboard and sifting through dozens of shawls identical to the two I'd seen but with different national flags woven into them. Sweden. Ukraine. Norway. France. Spain. New Zealand, even.

'Here you are,' he said. Whoever sewed the Australian flag into the shawl had forgotten one star in the Southern Cross, but this bothered me rather less than the fact that they'd left the Union Jack correctly in place.

Gaza was an overwhelmingly young place – 64 per cent of Gazans were under the age of thirty, 50 per cent under eighteen. Like all generations of Palestinians since 1948, this surging demographic would have to decide whether to negotiate a necessarily imperfect settlement with their Israeli neighbours, or persist with a war which was not, by any rational analysis, going their way. To meet the future leadership, Leila and I hit the campus of Al-Azhar University. Students on top of the main building were hanging an enormous election poster endorsing Fatah, the faction once headed by the late Yasser Arafat. The poster showed Arafat and his anointed successor, Mahmoud Abbas, in front of the Dome of the Rock in Jerusalem. Those on top of the building were taking instructions from a kid in the courtyard, who was yelling at them over the top of the black and white keffiyeh around his neck. I introduced myself. He was Mohammed, twenty-two, of the Fatah faction of Al-Azhar's student union. He barked a few final directions at his colleagues, then took me and Leila for coffee with a couple of his friends.

'Abu Mazen,' said Mohammed, using Mahmoud Abbas's affectionate nom-de-guerre, 'is the only candidate. I wouldn't work for anyone else. We are absolutely devoted to Fatah.'

Mohammed detected a failure on my part to share his enthusiasm for Arafat or Abbas.

'You do not agree,' he observed, fidgeting with his worry beads.

Not really, I said.

'Why?' he asked. 'Please. Go on.'

Because, I said, I couldn't see where the struggle that these two men represented was going, except into a deeper swamp of blood, guilt, grievance and recrimination.

'Abu Mazen is the only candidate,' Mohammed affirmed.

He wasn't, though. I asked Mohammed if he had any time for Mustafa Barghouti, then polling a distant second to Abbas in the race for the presidency. I explained that if I was Palestinian, Barghouti would be getting my vote, and that if I was Ariel Sharon, he'd be the Palestinian who frightened me most. Mustafa Barghouti was a softly spoken doctor, committed to non-violence. Like no other combatants in the early twenty-first century, Israel and Palestine sought to deploy international opinion as a weapon. If Palestinians stood Barghouti up against a thug like Sharon, I suggested to Mohammed, they couldn't help but look like good guys.

'We are working for Abu Mazen,' said Mohammed. 'He'll fight for our interests.'

We discussed such matters further for some time. It was an amicable exchange of gentle thrusts and gentlemanly parries, and then something strange happened. We were joined by two more members of Al-Azhar's Fatah branch, Sahar and Nadia. It was no reflection on Sahar, and every reflection on every man's inner golden-retriever-suddenly-noticing-someone-with-a-sandwich, that it took me a while to register that she was there at all. Her friend Nadia was absurdly, preposterously, ridiculously, ludicrously beautiful, to a degree sufficient to reduce better writers than I to a tautological stream of gibbered adverbs. She was also aware of, and amused by, the fact, wearing – by Gazan standards – a jumper that was too tight and a veil that was too loose. She could have walked into any room anywhere in the world and turned the internal monologue of every heterosexual male in it into a variation on the theme of 'Hnnggggggghhhhh'. In this room, in this repressed, screwed-up place, the effect she had was more dramatic – and, I thought, revealing.

'Everyone here,' announced Mohammed, 'wants to be a martyr.'

Huh?

'Suicide bombing,' purred Nadia, whose voice was like being drowned in a velvet-lined bath full of warm chocolate, 'is a legitimate tactic. It's a reaction to what the Israelis do.'

'Yes,' agreed Mohammed, nodding gravely. 'Yes, I want that.'

A couple of minutes previously, Mohammed had struck me as a nice enough kid, if a little earnest. Now he was volunteering to turn himself into a hurricane of bones and ball-bearings in a Tel Aviv pizza parlour. I've said my share of daft things in misguided attempts to impress women, but . . .

'We believe that martyrs will go to heaven,' said Nadia.

'Heaven,' echoed Mohammed, with a guilty glance at Nadia that made me wonder if he and she were thinking of quite the same idea of Paradise.

Leila, my translator, had little time for this sort of talk.

'I believe in resisting by staying alive,' she said, 'and getting an education.'

'The death of one,' said Mohammed, 'is justifiable for the sake of the collective. And we have faith in our cause.'

While Nadia toyed with her keyring, which depicted a peace symbol trussed in barbed wire, Mohammed bore the expression of a man hoping that Allah might see fit to reward his sacrifice by reincarnating him as a keyring. But what else could he say, what else could he do? He couldn't tell a girl he was going to be a musician or a poet or an actor or wealthy. He lived in Gaza. He couldn't take a girl to a film, buy her a few drinks and try his luck in the taxi on the way home. He lived in Gaza. The surprisingly plentiful people, back where I came from, who argued that Palestinians had 'no choice' but to become suicide bombers were wrong – Palestinians did have a choice, and millions of them chose every day not to kill themselves, or anyone else. There did, however, seem to be no other framework of aspiration, as far as Mohammed was concerned. He wasn't, I didn't think, seriously planning to do it. He was bullshitting, the way young men do, the way someone his age, somewhere less dreadful, might announce their intention to be a rock star.

I asked what they did for fun. They regarded me blankly. Fun, I prompted. Music, movies, that kind of thing.

'We're already in a movie,' smirked Nadia. 'An ongoing movie.'

'There's no cinema here,' said Sahar.

'We listen to the radio,' said Mohammed. 'It plays songs about the national struggle. There is some theatre, but this is always in the service of the struggle.'

This sounded like hard work. Even in Ramallah, it was possible to have a reasonably boisterous evening out.

'It's not right,' frowned Mohammed. 'People listening to music and enjoying themselves while people are dying.'

Television? I was assuming, by this point, that Mohammed wasn't big on *Will and Grace*, but . . .

'The news,' said Mohammed. 'But only on the Palestinian channels. The enemy's media lies. When CNN and BBC report from here, they say our people are being killed, not martyred.'

The same CNN and BBC routinely accused by Israel of bias in favour of the Palestinians.

'Even Al Jazeera,' harumphed Mohammed, 'reported that George W. Bush had called President Arafat a terrorist.'

There were two obvious responses to this absurd complaint. One, that Fox News reporting the ramblings of Osama bin-Laden hardly made them al-Qaeda propagandists. Two, that Yasser Arafat *was* a terrorist. I didn't make either of them. I just wished there was a way I could get Mohammed to imagine a world bigger than Gaza. More to the point, I wished Israel and Palestine would both understand that their best chance of peace, if that was what either really wanted, was allowing kids like Mohammed to realise that there was life beyond the checkpoints. Nadia presented me with an Al-Fatah pencil case, an Al-Fatah exercise book and an Al-Fatah calendar illustrated with a picture of a keffiyeh-swaddled renegade brandishing a picture of Arafat. I asked her if she was trying to get me arrested at Ben Gurion Airport, and she laughed, then suddenly looked very sad.

'This is endless,' she said.

Out on the street, Leila flagged down a car.

'What did you think of Nadia?' she asked, as the driver tried to find his place in the barely mobile traffic.

Uh, I said, she seemed very, um, nice. I had, I was certain, maintained a dignified, appropriate detachment.

'Did you notice that friend of Mohammed who was whispering to him?' asked Leila.

I had. A burly, silent sort, who'd failed to communicate the impression that he was pleased to see me. I asked Leila if she'd picked up what he'd been whispering to Mohammed.

'He was asking him,' laughed Leila, 'why this foreign man keeps looking at Nadia like that.'

Mohammed and his friends may not have been Kalashnikov-wielding, grenade-tossing militants – not yet, anyway – but in Gaza it wasn't difficult to meet people who were. Leila took me to Gaza's Ministry of Detainees' Affairs, which looked after people who'd been imprisoned by Israel at some time or another.

One room of the ministry was dedicated to artworks created by former prisoners. None were subtle, but many were astonishingly well made. There was a hand-stitched rug portrait of Arafat, a replica prison camp constructed from cardboard and chicken wire, dozens of representations of the Dome of the Rock (and, weirdly, a couple of the Eiffel Tower) built from string and matchsticks. There was also a wall covered with pencil sketches depicting Israeli military hospitality: beatings, solitary confinement, mock executions.

Leila introduced me to someone in charge.

'I understand,' he said, 'you want to speak to someone from Hamas.'

I confirmed that this was the case.

'You want moderate or extreme?' he grinned.

Surprise me, I said.

'You bet,' he said. He made a phone call. 'He's praying,' he said. 'But he'll be with us shortly.'

We were presently joined by a short, stocky, untidily bearded citizen in a polo-necked jumper and thick-lensed round spectacles. He was vague about his personal details.

'It's difficult to talk about,' he explained. 'Because the Israelis have a list, and one day they might send me an air strike. I'm not that afraid – it's a very long list – but I worry.'

We agreed that I could call him Amer, a uselessly generic name, identify him as coming from Gaza, and being aged between thirty and forty.

'At the beginning,' he began, 'I saw Hamas as just a bunch of murderers, but that isn't true. They're educated, intellectual people. I became a member of the party. Then I shifted to the Qassam Brigades . . . sorry, you know who they are?'

The Izz al-Din al-Qassam Brigades, Hamas's military wing, named after a sheikh who was killed rebelling against the British occupation of Palestine in the 1930s.

'Exactly,' he said, pleased that I'd done my homework. 'I participated in one operation. It was during the first intifada. I threw a Molotov cocktail at an Israeli jeep. I was arrested at home an hour later. I think I was sold out by a collaborator. I was twenty-two.'

Not a glorious career as a militant, then.

'No,' he agreed. 'I was in prison for six years, until 1998.'

I asked whether he perceived a difference between the first intifada (roughly 1987 to 1993), during which he'd been imprisoned, and its ongoing successsor (Ariel Sharon's 2000 walkabout on Temple Mount to the present day). The first intifada reinforced a Palestinian self-image of honourable underdogs. It was, not entirely but largely, a revolt of picturesque youths hurling rocks at Israeli soldiers, who tended towards gross overreaction – of the 1378 Palestinians killed by Israeli security forces during the first intifada, 281 were under the age of seventeen. The second intifada placed a greater emphasis on suicide bombings, many by the organisation of which he was a member.

'Some, even in Hamas, believe that suicide bombing should not take place,' conceded Amer, 'but it's not a major movement within the party. It is nonsense that we want to target civilians . . .'

Oh, come on, I said. Hamas hadn't blown up all those buses on the off-chance that the general staff of the Israel Defense Forces might have been catching one of them to work.

'But the Israelis target civilians. Seven, just today.'

Earlier that day, seven children had been killed by Israeli tank fire in a strawberry field in Beit Lahiya, in the north of the Strip, with another dozen people seriously injured. Six of the dead were members of the same family. Amer paused, as if waiting for me to try to justify this carnage. I couldn't, so I didn't.

'So it's a reaction,' he said. 'An eye for an eye.'

Assuming, I ventured, that Amer wanted a future of something other than violence, terror and retribution, what was his idea of a result? What did Hamas's idea of victory look like?

'What I stand for,' he said, 'is a single state from the river to the sea, from the Jordan to the Mediterranean.'

An Islamic state, presumably.

'Of course.'

This, I thought, was going to be a tough sell. I mean, why not aspire to something more plausible, like, I dunno, a statue of Yasser Arafat, sculpted from toffee, on the moon?

'I'm a realist,' he insisted. 'I fight for what I can get. A Palestinian state in Gaza and the West Bank, and a capital in Jerusalem, would be okay.'

I thought of the Israeli settler I'd met, only a few dozen kilometres away and a few days previously. It seemed a world apart and a lifetime ago. Gaza was compressing my perceptions into the tiny dimensions of the Strip, and I'd only just got there. But the Jewish settler's manifesto for peace had been broadly the same as that of this Hamas militant. I didn't know whether everyone's stated desire for peace, and everyone's broad agreement on what peace would look like, was cause for hope or despair.

* * *

I wanted to visit the Strip's refugee camps – although, between Gaza City's dilapidation and the fact that many of the refugee camps had been built decades before much of Gaza City, the distinction between city and camp seemed a semantic one. Leila and I boarded a minibus and headed south along Gaza's coast road. On our right, the scenery was an extension of the rubbish-covered beach of Gaza City. On the left was dense housing, some agriculture, and one vast mudscape, overlooked by a watchtower, which had been bulldozed into being by the Israelis to protect the Netzarim settlement. Netzarim only had seven months to live – it would be evacuated, along with Israel's other Gaza settlements, later in 2005. Leila pointed out the wreckage of two apartment blocks, demolished by the Israelis because their upper floors overlooked Netzarim. We passed a young man, his faced wrapped in a keffiyeh, cradling a Kalashnikov under one arm and striding somewhere. I pointed him out to Leila, who was always heartbreakingly determined to see the best in what passed for her country.

'It's probably a toy,' she said.

We disembarked at the entrance to the Al-Bureij camp. It was hard to miss. Al-Bureij welcomed its visitors with a double arch made of cement, topped with a model of the Dome of the Rock, and daubed in paintings of clenched fists, grenades and rifles. The Arabic writing on the out-facing side of the first arch translated as RESISTANCE, STEADFASTNESS AND MARTYRS CAMP. The second read, somewhat quaintly in the context, AL-BUREIJ CAMP WELCOMES YOU!. On the reverse, the writing read GOODBYE and WE WILL COME BACK ONE DAY TO PALESTINE. On the middle pillar, lest anyone entertain doubt as to what was meant by that, there was a map of the Holy Land which neglected to acknowledge a Jewish state secure within its 1967 borders.

My idea was to meet a local family, and my plan was to do this the same way I usually meet people in Arab countries, by standing in the street affecting an air of bewilderment until a random inhabitant approaches and offers hospitality. It usually takes five minutes at the most. In Al-Bureij, it didn't take that long. A passing woman recognised Leila from a wedding they had both attended. Her name was Hayam.

'Please,' she indicated. 'Follow me.'

She led us to her family home. From the outside, the building looked ugly, ungainly, rickety. On the inside, their apartment was surprisingly large and comfortable. Hayam introduced me to her mother-in-law, who offered me her hand wrapped in a shawl and was too modest or shy to part with her name, and her husband Ashraf. While Hayam organised coffee and fruit, I sat at the kitchen table and glanced around a well-kept middle-class home, replete with crowded bookshelves and potted plants. On the wall were posters of two young, bearded men, rendered in soft focus, against a background of Jerusalem's maddeningly unavailable golden heart. A hand-stitched tapestry of a Holy Land-shaped country called Palestine was framed between them.

Martyrs, I said.

'My cousins,' confirmed Ashraf. 'One was killed by an Israeli missile, the other was shot dead attacking a settlement.'

Apologising for any impertinence, I asked whether having two martyrs marked a family as unusually valiant, or unlucky.

'It's actually five martyrs,' said Ashraf. 'But to answer your question, it used to be a big deal to have a martyr in the family. But not anymore. It is not so rare, these days.'

Ashraf had a degree in computer science, but no job and little prospect of finding one. I apologised again for asking such a question of someone who'd attended five family funerals, but did he think that armed struggle was doing the Palestinians much good?

'We want to solve the problem in a peaceful way,' he said. 'But it has been more than fifty years of struggle now, and the misery never changes.'

Emphasising that I didn't wish to appear insensitive, I explained that that was kind of my point. No sensible person could spend fifteen minutes in Gaza without concluding that Israel's treatment of the people who lived in it was vicious, stupid, counterproductive and several fathoms beneath the standards Israel claimed to set for itself.

But it also seemed fair to wonder how many more of Gaza's young men would be turned into sentimental artworks before it occurred to someone around here that armed struggle was getting them nowhere.

'Wait a minute,' Ashraf said, getting up. 'I want to show you something.'

While he was gone, Hayam told her story. Of Palestinian descent, she'd been born, raised and educated in Algeria.

'I had full rights in Algeria,' she said. That was as dreadful an indictment of Gaza as could be imagined, that Algeria appeared by comparison a Shangri-La of possibility. 'I finished my chemistry degree, but there was something missing, something unique about my homeland. My husband has this yearning for his home village, Kokaba, though he has never been there. His ancestors were forced to leave in 1948. His mother, who you just met, was born on the road from Kokaba to Gaza on 15 May 1948.'

So Ashraf's mother had never been to his hometown either.

This prompted Leila to speak of her home village, Hamama. 'It is green,' she said, 'with space, and no pollution.'

Leila had never been to Hamama. Nor had her father. I explained my failure to understand this implacable determination to see themselves, and to be seen by others, as victims of a war which had been lost two generations previously. I said I couldn't understand why every visitor to Palestine was treated like a stenography service for recording historical grievance. Ashraf returned to hear the end of my next question, which may well have included the words 'get', 'over' and 'it'.

'Because it still goes on,' said Ashraf. 'I'm thirty-one years old. I should have finished my education, travelled, been ten years working. Here, look at this.'

He plonked a cardboard box on the table. Its contents were, in essence, the story of Ashraf's adult life, told through the various Israeli-issued IDs that had been forced upon him. There was a permission to visit Jordan during the first intifada. A laminated security card from the mid-nineties, which confirmed that he had committed no act against Israel. Cards and badges which bore the logo of the IDF and other agencies of the occupying forces. A card which, once upon a time, permitted him to leave the Gaza Strip at Erez. A state of Israel travel document – which, he explained, had still necessitated the torturous acquisition of a separate visa before he could even use it to visit Israel.

'And now I can't go anywhere,' he said. 'I haven't been able to visit my aunt in Rafah for two years.'

Rafah was at the south end of the Strip. It couldn't have been more than 15 kilometres away.

'Today,' said Ashraf, 'satellite television brings us images all the time of peaceful, prosperous places. Palestinians want the same as everyone else. Why are we living like this?'

In the taxi back, I felt as gloomy as the overhanging clouds, too miserable even to ask Leila to ask the driver if there was any reason why he was driving like someone in Gaza City was handing out American passports.

'We could go to the Jabaliya refugee camp,' suggested Leila.

I asked if it was any better.

'Worse,' she said.

Jabaliya was, by some estimations, the most crowded place on Earth. More than 100,000 people were crammed into its 1.4 square kilometres – I'd been to rock festivals where there was more room to move, and better sanitation. Jabaliya's streets were decorated with militant posters. On one, two balaclavaed figures, evocative of those which glowered from the sides of Belfast terraces, carried a mine, while another mounted guard with a grenade-launcher.

'Blow them up wherever they are,' translated Leila, reading the caption. 'Kick them out of the hills and mountains of Palestine.'

We trudged through the camp. Every square foot seemed occupied by buildings or people, until we reached a block-sized expanse of empty land. I guessed that this wasn't the foundations of an exciting new retail and leisure complex.

'No,' sighed Leila. 'The Israelis bulldozed this neighbourhood. They do this a lot. They did it to my aunt's house last April.'

I asked Leila whether her aunt had been with Hamas, or Islamic Jihad. Leila was, mercifully, adjusting to my sense of humour.

'They wanted to widen a road so their tanks could move more easily. Her house was in the way.'

This, I began, may sound like a stupid question . . .

'None of your questions,' reassured Leila, 'are stupid.'

. . . but what sort of compensation had her aunt been offered?

'Stupid question,' said Leila. 'They just turned up, yani, and told her get out, to mobilise immediately. She's forty years old, and has four children. She took what she could carry. Then they demolished it.'

We squelched across the muddy wasteland towards the main road. Some pre-teen boys followed us, making nuisances of themselves, yelling the same inane questions repeatedly, making feints for my shoulder bag. Leila shooed them away and told me to mobilise faster towards the road. She walked backwards behind me, keeping an eye on the urchins. At the roadside, she flagged down a car. As I was opening the door I felt a jagged jolt of pain behind my right ear. The fist-sized rock that had caused it bounced off my shoulder and onto the road. Leila shoved me into the car like a bodyguard protecting an assassination target. I turned around as we drove off, and saw the kids in the distance, laughing delightedly.

'I'm so sorry,' said Leila, who was on the verge of tears. 'Please don't think this is what all Palestinians are like.'

I explained, rubbing my head, that I didn't. I just thought that was what all bored young boys were like, but never mind that . . . the little bastard had hit me flush on the scone from 40 metres. Granted that there were tragic reasons why Gaza's youth might have better throwing arms than most, but had anyone ever thought of teaching these people cricket?

'Cricket?' asked Leila.

It's a game, I explained. Goes on for ages, baffles onlookers, nobody wins.

I'd lugged my flak jacket to Gaza, because I was scared and paranoid, and then didn't wear it because I was embarrassed and self-conscious about the fact that none of the people who had to live there owned one. Wearing a flak jacket when hanging with locals who aren't always feels a gross breach of etiquette, like leaping into the pool during the

Paralympics and idly backstroking home ahead of a field of disabled athletes. So I didn't wear it in Jabaliya and Al-Bureij, which wasn't a problem because nobody shot at me, and I didn't wear it in Khan Younis, which was a problem, because somebody did. Or, at least, I think they did, and not being sure if you're being shot at is worse than knowing that you're being shot at; in the latter case, you at least have some idea of which direction to run.

I'd finagled a ride to Khan Younis with a Palestinian UN employee, who I'll call Ahmed. We'd driven south from Gaza City in Ahmed's staff car, a UN flag flying from its roof – I'd figured that riding with the UN would be safer than taking my (and, more importantly, Leila's) chances with public transport and Israeli checkpoints. It had been bad, or worse than usual, in Khan Younis. The previous week, the Israel Defense Forces had barged into Khan Younis refugee camp after Palestinian mortar attacks on nearby Israeli settlements. The IDF had killed nine people, including a teenage boy and a handicapped man, seriously injured a couple of dozen more, and smashed up a bunch of houses and a marketplace. The final score, according to Ahmed, had been thirteen abodes flattened, forty-odd more damaged, a hundred people rendered homeless.

Ahmed, and a local UN employee who I'll call Omar, were showing me the muddy lot, imprinted with tank tracks, which had been the local market, when I heard shooting – one shot, two shots, three. I'd already been unhappy about standing on exposed ground in view of an Israeli watchtower. There was a fourth, fifth and sixth shot, and I gave voice to my reservations.

'Don't worry about it,' said Omar.

I explained that I rather thought I would worry about it.

'They are probably,' decided Ahmed, 'not shooting at us. They can see that we are UN.'

He indicated the flourescent blue UN bibs we were wearing.

A seventh shot. An eighth.

'It's okay,' said Ahmed, squinting at the tower.

Ahmed's confidence was touching, but I didn't share it. I couldn't help but recall the ghastly footage of the last moments of James Miller, murdered by an Israeli sniper while wearing a flak jacket marked PRESS and walking under a white flag.

'It's probably those kids,' he said, pointing towards a football game taking place on another bit of ground the Israeli tanks had flattened. 'If they get too close to the tower, the Israelis fire warning shots.'

'Yes,' agreed Omar, with the air of a man concurring that it might rain later, 'it's the kids.'

At least, I assumed that's what he said. By the time he'd got as far as 'it's', I was 20 metres away, behind a building. Ahmed and Omar caught up with me presently, clucking amusedly at the new kid in town.

'Khan Younis,' said Omar, 'is a crazy place.'

We plodded further into the camp, following the trail of mayhem the Israelis had blazed a few days previously. The IDF claimed, as they always did, that they'd steamed in responding to attacks by Palestinian militants. This was true inasmuch as mortars had been launched from Khan Younis into nearby settlements, but it also implied that the Israelis had targeted the perpetrators of those attacks. They hadn't. They'd rolled out of their base, walloped whatever was convenient, and gone back home. It was like reacting to a noisy party on the other side of your block by walking across the landing and thumping your neighbour. In the middle of one disarrayed heap of concrete and corrugated iron, a man in sandals, blue trousers and a grey jumper was sitting on what remained of the front wall of his house, talking to his more fortunate neighbours.

I asked Omar what would happen to him.

'The UN can provide some cash assistance,' said Omar, 'but not much. He might rebuild, but a house in this area could easily get knocked down again. Or he might give up and move.'

And become a refugee from a refugee camp.

'Exactly.'

Ahmed and Omar took me to a school which had marked one perimeter of the Israeli incursion. The Israelis had levelled the buildings alongside it, pushing glaciers of mud and rubble through the walls and windows of the classrooms. Out the window, I could see a lone child carting a tree trunk across the wasteland the Israelis had created – firewood for home. I heard a couple more shots from the same watchtower, and retreated behind the wall. When I looked back out, the kid was still toting his load, but it was difficult, in the circumstances, to think him lucky.

The school caretaker, who would presumably have to sweep up this mess, made us tea, and presented me with a sculpture made of seashells. We sat glumly and silently. Above the verandah around the school's courtyard, signs bearing ennobling slogans, in English, hung from the iron beams which propped up the tin roof. The one directly outside the caretaker's room read DO AS YOU WOULD BE DONE BY. I very badly wanted to unbolt it, tuck it under one arm, and walk from Khan Younis to Damascus, via Tel Aviv, Hebron, Jerusalem, Ramallah, Tiberias and Beirut, swatting everyone I encountered en route over the head with it.

Before I left Gaza, I was treated to the mildest fraction of the merest dose of the claustrophobia that every one of the Strip's unfortunate residents mainlines all day, every day. Which is to say that I couldn't leave Gaza. On the day I was due to exit through Erez and return to Jerusalem, I took my bags downstairs to the hotel reception.

'Erez is closed,' said the proprietor's teenage daughter, as she tended her pet terrapins, which dwelled in a tank in the foyer.

I know, I said, already feeling bad that I could leave while she, like every other Gazan, couldn't.

'No,' she elaborated. 'Really closed. To everybody, even you. There was an attack there yesterday.'

I'd been worried about this possibility. After the massacre at Beit Lahiya, Hamas had launched several barrages over the fences. Two rockets had landed inside an IDF base and injured a dozen Israeli soldiers. And now, it seemed, someone had taken a tilt at Erez. I took my bags back upstairs, and called the IDF press office.

'Erez is closed,' confirmed the woman who answered the phone. 'It was attacked yesterday, and we've closed it.'

I asked whether we were talking minutes, hours, days, weeks . . .

'It's closed for as long as it's closed,' she said.

I called the Australian embassy in Tel Aviv.

'Yeah,' drawled the representative of my homeland. 'Not a lot we can do, I'm afraid. Tell you what, though, give me your address so we know which roof to park the chopper on if we have to . . .'

This rarefied Australian sarcasm always made me homesick when I encountered it abroad, the more so as my paranoia launched my imagination into a hypothetical confinement of weeks, months or years. I spent the day sulking, fretting and wondering where Nadia and I might send our children to school.

The following morning, the hotel staff brought news of Erez's reopening, along with my coffee. They seemed genuinely pleased and relieved for me, which added guilt to my not inconsiderable pleasure and relief. I rode to Erez in a taxi with an American NGO worker named Susan. At the entrance to the crossing, foreign media and NGO workers milled irritably, the milling becoming more irritable as minutes of standing pointlessly around collected into hours of sitting aimlessly about. When we were eventually summoned into the long concrete corral, we could see the aftermath of the reason for its closure, the spent bullet casings and bloodstains that comprised the detritus of the previous day's attack. It hadn't been a brilliant operation – an assault by a lone militant, for which both Hamas and Islamic Jihad had claimed responsibility. The gunman had been shot dead by Israeli soldiers, and several Palestinian policemen had also been injured in the incident. The damage to the state of Israel amounted to a small hole in the tunnel wall, and whatever that many bullets cost.

At the end of the tunnel, where Israeli security arrangements began, a voice crackling through a loudspeaker ordered us into two groups, foreigners to the right, the dozen or so Palestinians with permission to cross to the left, and then told us to wait, as if we had much option. In line behind me were an American couple with two young children. I introduced myself because I was intrigued as to what sort of simpleton would bring primary school aged kids to a frightening, dangerous ditch like Gaza.

'We're missionaries,' said the male half of the couple. It instantly struck me as one of the least surprising revelations I'd ever heard.

'Honey,' said the mother to one of their offspring, 'please don't play with the shrapnel.'

The loudspeaker called the Palestinians first, and they charged forward en masse. The observation that orderly queues have never caught on in the Arab world is not an original one, but I made it anyway.

'I once mentioned that to an Israeli soldier here,' said Susan. 'He said, "The day Palestinians start standing in orderly queues is the day we start worrying."'

That said, I admired the Palestinians' attitude. They were less sulky about the process than I would be – or, indeed, was about to be. Each person leaving Erez had to walk through an iron gate into an area sealed by an iron gate on the other side, place their belongings in an X-ray machine, and reveal portions of their anatomy according to instructions emanating from the loudspeaker. When the Palestinians were instructed to roll their trouser legs up, or lift their shirts to expose their midriffs, their compatriots teased them about their physical shortcomings. One fat bloke acknowledged the mockery by slapping himself heartily on the stomach, causing ripples.

Despite the lack of suicide bombings perpetrated by foreign journalists, the Israelis didn't ease off on my account. I walked through the gate, stuck my bags in the X-ray machine, and awaited instructions. I couldn't see any people. Just the loudspeaker and CCTV cameras.

'Roll up your trousers,' said the voice.

I did so.

'Lift up your shirt.'

It was like listening to a record Barry White might have made on a day when he had a headache and couldn't be bothered.

'Turn around.'

I wondered how many had passed before me and been unable to resist the temptation to execute a hokey-cokey.

* * *

As I emerged from Erez, out of Gaza and into Israel, the rain that had sodden my stay in the Strip ceased, and the thick grey clouds that had fouled the sky were parted by sunshine. It was a contrast so corny that no writer of fiction would have dared invent it, and anyway it didn't make me feel any better. Gaza depressed me worse and for longer than any other screwed-up place I'd ever been. A lot of that was for the obvious reasons – the fear, the absence of hope, the lack of any better ideas. A lot more of it was to do with Leila. This world may contain 1.4 million people so appalling that they deserve to live in Gaza, but she wasn't close to being one of them. She managed to get permission to leave a year later, to return to Ramallah to get married. The email informing me of her departure put me in a good mood for about a week.

What with one thing and another, the occupation of Arab and/or Muslim land became a recurring theme of the early twenty-first century. The argument in favour of such enterprises, it was fair to say, was a stretch from being convincingly made. But if anybody could do it, surely it was the people who'd been occupying more places for more years than anyone else.

Well, they were doing their best. But they weren't finding it easy.

27

BASRA, IRAQ
FEBRUARY 2005

Arriving in any conflict zone is a serious business. There's always a moment, when you've crossed a border or passed a checkpoint, when it becomes throat-clenchingly, palm-dampeningly clear that you're in it now, all the way up to your neck – and you have to consider the possibility that somewhere not far away is someone who might, in the next few days, try to kill you. It is no time for frivolity, and nobody knew that better than the passengers on the flight from RAF Brize Norton to Basra – arriving in conflict zones was what they did for a living.

Nevertheless, few were able to suppress giggles at the announcement from the flight deck as we commenced our descent. After reminding us to complete the banal rituals of stowing our tray tables and returning our seats to the upright position, the voice on the speakers instructed us to put on our flak jackets and helmets. Once everyone had sat awkwardly back down, to a soundtrack of swearing as kevlar plates dug painfully into hip bones and helmets banged on overhead lockers, all the Lockheed TriStar's internal and external lights were turned off, and we were told to close our window shades. It wasn't stealth technology, but it was all we had. The British soldiers sat, completely in the dark, at the mercy of forces they couldn't control, with no idea when this trip might end. There are moments when metaphors are too easy.

* * *

'Interior design for a call centre,' mused Major Giles Harris. 'I must have slept through that lecture at Sandhurst.'

We were in a bare room in a complex belonging to Basra's police force. In a few weeks, this would become the central point of contact for any Basran who needed the cops. If their cat was up a tree, if they were pinned by crossfire from a tribal feud, if they spotted someone planting a mine by the road, if they thought the guy next door was hiding an al-Qaeda cell in his shed, they'd be able to dial 115 and reach an operator in this room. Before that could happen, Major Harris, the thirty-one-year-old commander of 2 Company, 1st Welsh Guards, had to organise phone lines, chairs and desks, and decide what colour the room should be.

'White,' he decided. 'Keep it simple. We asked them to paint another office in magnolia, but lost something in the translation. Ended up with this gruesome yellow.'

Harris marked spots on the wall which would become power points.

'For an infantry company,' he said, 'this is quite a step. Our training is about kicking down doors and blowing things up. Forty-eight hours before we got here, they told us we'd be reforming a police force, which is rather more delicate. Fascinating, though.'

By February 2005, the British army had been in Basra nearly two years. I'd flown out with photographer Tom Pilston, at the behest of the *Independent on Sunday*, to see what the soldiers were doing all day. I'd been against the invasion of Iraq. If I'd had my way, 2 Company wouldn't be pondering paint schemes in Basra, but sweltering beneath their bearskins outside Buckingham Palace. I arrived in Basra still thinking the invasion had been pretty dumb, but willing to concede that that was a two-year-old argument, about a war – the war between invading forces and the defenders of Saddam Hussein's regime – which was long over. The coalition soldiers in Iraq in early 2005 were engaged in a different conflict, defending an elected – if ineffectual – government from a rebellion of political fascists and religious lunatics.

The Welsh Guards, an infantry regiment, hadn't been involved in the initial invasion of Iraq – and every soldier in 2 Company who'd had to watch it on television admitted, in the manner of injured foot-ballers forced to sit out a Cup Final, to rage and frustration at not getting to do what they were trained to do: kick down doors, blow things up. Two years later, 2 Company found themselves fighting, like their comrades I'd met in Afghanistan, one of those peculiar modern wars in which the invading army tries to build institutions and estab-lish a civil society, while the country's putative defenders slaughter their own people and commit self-destructive sabotage.

'We've been here four months,' said Harris, 'and not one man has fired his rifle. We've been shot at four or five times, but they tend to be gone by the time we pop our heads back up.'

The members of 2 Company were what might be expected of a Guards unit. The soldiers and NCOs were mostly working class, and fiercely, demonstratively Welsh, many sporting dragon tattoos, some speaking in Valleys burrs that verged on the incomprehensible. The officers, Welsh or not, had polished English accents, and played up to a tradition of foppish eccentricity. The softly spoken, Suffolk-born Major Harris, son of a Royal Navy pilot and grandson of a Military Cross winner, kept crackers and a tin of Gentleman's Relish in a desk drawer, and led patrols to an MP3 soundtrack of Blur, Crowded House and Lynyrd Skynyrd.

Home was Shatt-al-Arab camp, a disused regional airport. The camp was named after the airport hotel, perched on the riverfront. Built by the British in the 1940s, the hotel was crested by a fortuitous watchtower which now scanned the barren surrounding landscape for enemy mortar crews. Inside the hotel, rooms had been converted to offices and accommodation, the dining hall into a mess hall, the lobby into an arena dominated by a vast television screen showing news from home. Shops, operated by Iraqis, sold dodgy DVD players, dodgier DVDs, and framed sets of Saddam Hussein banknotes. There was also an Iraqi barber, and a wandering painter called Ziad, who was making a tidy living turning soldiers' photos into art.

Shatt-al-Arab camp was in a lively neighbourhood. Nights were punctuated by the gunshots and grenade thumps of an obscure but passionate dispute between two local tribes, the Geramsha and the

Halaf. One night during our stay, the sniping escalated into a full-scale battle which, we were told the following morning, left seven dead. I asked Major Harris if they'd ever thought of suggesting to the al-Hatfields and al-McCoys that they gave it a rest.

'The Scots Guards,' he replied, 'went up there once and asked them to put a sock in it, which worked for a bit. Now, we just take the view that as long as nothing comes over the fence, it isn't really our problem.'

Insurgents were dissuaded by a surveillance blimp – which, surprisingly, had not proved an irresistible temptation to some bored miscreant with a Kalashnikov – and illumination flares. These were fired periodically during hours of darkness with a colossal *Whump!*, prompting reflexive lurches in the direction of one's flak jacket before someone said, 'No . . . outgoing,' at which point the challenge was to look as if what you'd actually been doing was reaching for a book with unusual urgency.

On the runways outside the hotel, 2 Company lived in large, dust-coloured, semicircular tents. (These igloos were surprisingly sophisticated – heated at this mild time of year, and air-conditioned during Iraq's brutal summers.) They slept three or four to a tent, decorating their personal spaces with family photos, pin-ups, and Welsh flags – these were also a favourite choice as duvet covers, just ahead of camouflage print. Tom and I shared with one of 2 Company's English interlopers – Captain Dan Hebditch, a Territorial Army officer temporarily posted to the unit. Hebditch, a documentary producer and student of military history, had recently been tasked with distributing 6000 Austrian-made Glock pistols to Basra's police. The job had not been straightforward.

'Word got out that there weren't enough Glocks for all the police,' recalled Hebditch. 'Two hundred cops rioted outside one of their bases. Their colonel sat them down and yelled at them that they were a disgrace to Iraq.'

Ever since, the bespectacled, bookish Hebditch had gone by the not unenviable nickname of Captain Glock.

* * *

After two years of war in Iraq, there were two ways for British soldiers in Iraq to get into the newspapers, neither really reflecting the workaday reality of the 8000 British troops working in and around Basra. The first was to be involved in the squalid abuse of prisoners, which had occurred, and about which I found nothing but a proper degree of incredulous disgust among 2 Company. The second was to get killed, and while 2 Company had been lucky on that front, they'd been inches or minutes away from making the worst sort of headlines. On their first night patrol, one of their Land Rovers was hit by a roadside bomb, injuring three guardsmen. One of these, Guardsman Matthews, sustained what 2 Company's sergeant major, Darren Pridmore, tersely recalled as 'a gigantic hole in his arse'. Matthews, lucky to keep his leg, was evacuated home. He was, apparently, up and about again. On 8 January 2005, about a month before I arrived in Basra, a mortar landed in one of 2 Company's tents. The shrapnel caused a leg wound to one Guardsman Luke, but whoever fired the missile came close to what he would have considered a major victory. Minutes before impact, several men had been in the tent doing an ammunition check, sitting amid boxes of grenades; a mortar in the middle of that could have amounted to the British army's worst day of the conflict. (Guardsman Luke, who also survived the attack on the night patrol, was back home in Wales, bearing a scar on one shin and the inevitable nickname 'Lucky'.)

Most days, however, British soldiers in Iraq weren't hanging detainees off forklifts in bags, or dying in action. They were, rather, doing their occasionally bewildered best in circumstances which were undeniably, perhaps uneasily, evocative of centuries of British history: young troops, far from home, trying to nudge volatile natives towards civilised standards of behaviour, whether in interior decor or legal process.

The Iraqi police with whom 2 Company were working operated out of several establishments in Basra. Over the course of a week, Tom and I made the rounds of all of them, huddled in the limited spare space aboard 2 Company's Land Rovers. Some Iraqi policing initiatives did seem obtuse. Major Harris did an especially commendable job of maintaining a straight face when one officer outlined his plan to forcibly convert the estimated 42,000 right-hand drive vehicles at large in Basra to standard Iraqi left-hand drive; there were, I thought, more pressing issues, but maybe his brother was a mechanic. Other meetings focused on the tiny but cumulatively crucial questions of nation-building. Was it worth the risk of offending the heavily armed local tribes by dismissing their incompetent clansmen from the police? Should they send away to Britain for new police insignia, which would take time, or should they get them produced locally, which would create work, but permit the possibility of surplus being sold to insurgents? How did one establish a body to investigate corruption in a society which, for decades, had known nothing else?

The biggest police base in Basra was a training facility in a British-built World War II RAF compound. The day Tom and I arrived with one of 2 Company's patrols, recruits were marching and drilling in a vast courtyard. Major Harris introduced me to the commander, Colonel Waleed Ahmed. He'd been a policeman during the Saddam Hussein era. I asked him what the difference was.

'It was easier before,' he admitted. 'People were scared, so they obeyed us. One man with a notebook could keep an entire neighbourhood quiet.'

Even as we spoke, in the middle of the day, we could hear shooting outside the base; 2 Company's soldiers, leaning on their vehicles in the sun, traded theories on where it might be coming from, and where it might be going. ('Up,' was the general consensus, probably from wedding ceremonies.) I thought Colonel Ahmed must have been a little bit nostalgic.

'No,' he said. 'This is better.' Though this was, of course, what he was supposed to say.

The biggest combined Iraqi police and British army base was situated in what had been Saddam Hussein's sprawling riverfront palace complex, which he was said to have visited precisely once. After one morning of meetings, we drove there to have lunch in one of the hangar-sized ballrooms of the main palace building, the ornately decorated ceiling of which now looked down on a mess hall. Afterwards,

CSM Pridmore and a couple of guardsmen showed me and Tom around the rest of the complex. Despite the size and splendour of Saddam Hussein's riverside retreat, the overwhelming impression was of cheapness: tacky detailing, sloppy workmanship, graceless flaunting of wealth. The highlight was one of the palace bathrooms, where the gold trimmings on the toilet and bidet had been ignored by looters who'd spotted them for the obvious fakes they were.

'It looks,' said CSM Pridmore, 'like someone in Merthyr Tydfil won the lottery, doesn't it?'

The company's days began with a briefing known as 'Prayers', attended by officers and NCOs. This was a wrap-up of recent events outside the camp wall. One morning, there were reports of two explosions, detonated by persons unknown for reasons no more understood. Other days, there were reports of murders, bleakly categorised as 'De-Ba'athification' (the settlement of scores dating from the Saddam era) or 'Islamification' (the dispatch of those whose behaviour affronted Basra's loopy religious tendency). There were also updates on innovations in local terrorism – 2 Company were told to look out for people suddenly dismounting motorcycles and running off. Snippets from local media were also provided by 2 Company's Iraqi translators.

'Guardsman Gillard is in the papers,' said CSM Pridmore one morning. Gillard was a gangly eighteen-year-old from Rhondda. He'd been in the vehicle that had been bombed the previous October, and had narrowly avoided being scalped by shrapnel in January's mortar attack; he still hadn't told his mother. Gillard was in the doghouse, having returned two days late from R&R. 'There's a nice picture of him with his machine gun,' continued Pridmore. 'The caption says "British soldier helps Iraqi police", but the interpreters think it'd be fun to tell him it's about human rights abuses, so we'll let him flap for a couple of days.'

Much of Prayers was rattled out in the initial-ridden jargon beloved of the military. As Major Harris pointed out locations on the map of Basra in the Ops Room, he talked of MNF (Multi-National Forces), VCPs (Vehicle Check-Points), RTAs (Road Traffic Accidents), RPGs (Rocket-Propelled Grenades, a favourite weapon of the insurgents) and IEDs (Improvised Explosive Devices, roadside bombs, one of which had killed four Iraqi soldiers in Basra the previous week). These reductive terms, which made the briefings sound like spelling bees for the severely dyslexic, were themselves known as TLAs: Three-Letter Acronyms.

The company travelled in groups of ten to twelve, known as 'multiples', in patrols of two armoured Land Rovers, known as 'snatches'. Each snatch had a hole in the roof through which two soldiers stood watch as the vehicle moved. Before leaving camp, each multiple sat through another briefing, at which the route was confirmed, as well as procedures in case of attack by RPG, destruction by IED, or involvement in RTA. Despite the armour plating of the snatches, the proximity of armed soldiers, and my flak jacket and helmet, sitting in the vehicles on Basra's crowded roads felt horribly vulnerable. I asked one guardsman how safe we were.

'In here,' he said, 'small arms fire, no problem. AK bullets probably wouldn't penetrate, but they might. An RPG, that'll go through one wall, and if it does, you'd better hope it goes through the other one. Don't want one of those bouncing around in here. IED, nothing you can do, just depends how big. Some would just take a wheel off. And some would blow the whole fucking snatch a hundred feet in the air.'

The deadliest immediate hazard that faced 2 Company while Tom and I were with them was the odd cheeky urchin bouncing a rock off the snatches as we drove past. Inside the Land Rover, the *thunk* of stone on armour would attract ironic mutters of 'Good shot, kid,' but for the soldiers on top cover, the threat was no less real for being faintly comical – one British soldier on top cover had had his jaw broken by a well-aimed brick.

In contrast to the uncompromising approach of American forces elsewhere in Iraq, British soldiers didn't run red lights, or point guns at vehicles trying to overtake theirs, or award themselves any privileges whatsoever. When we got stuck in Basra's traffic, which was alarmingly often, two or three soldiers from each vehicle swapped their helmets for less threatening berets, and dismounted. This made the patrol harder to wipe out in one whack and increased options for retaliation. Mostly, though, it allowed the soldiers to talk to people, with the help of the Iraqi interpreters who rode with them, doing one of the most dangerous jobs on Earth for US$208 a month.

We were approaching the Shi'a festival Ashura. Due to concerns that the excitable Shi'a cleric Moqtada Sadr might be in town for the occasion, 2 Company had been told to look out for indications of agitation by Shi'a militants. The closest thing we saw was a police vehicle, draped in banners bearing Koranic verse and broadcasting religious music. This represented another difficult diplomatic call 2 Company would have to make – was this the equivalent of a British bobby wishing someone a Merry Christmas, or of a Royal Ulster Constabulary truck blaring 'The Sash My Father Wore' through a loudhailer? In 2 Company argot, such dilemmas were described as 'grey', after the moral area they inhabited. In direct contrast, the company term denoting approval, which I think was an imported Welshism, was 'gleaming'.

Every multiple submitted to a debrief by Major Harris upon return, at which the soldiers pooled what they'd learned. They spoke freely.

'Some police aren't happy about the Shi'a parties winning the election,' reported a soldier one morning. Iraq's first flirtation with democracy earlier in 2005 had been somewhat maddening. At no small risk to their safety, millions of Iraqis had queued to vote for the first time in their lives, and in many cases elected people whose enthusiasm for the furtherance of civil society was doubtful. 'They're worried they won't get to drink or jiggy-jiggy, sir.'

Another day, Major Harris expressed his annoyance at the behaviour of a Psychological Operations (Psy-Ops) team who had joined that morning's patrol. Harris had seen them opening the rear door of their Land Rover and signalling to traffic to stop and let them through.

'That pisses me off,' he said. 'We're not here to stop Iraqis driving around Iraq.'

'It's not a good look,' agreed CSM Pridmore. 'I'll have a word.'

There was, also, frustration with the Iraqi police themselves. Another day, Lieutenant James Aldridge returned from a visit to a VCP.

'There was only one man there,' he reported.

'Was he working?' asked Major Harris hopefully.

'Warming his hands on the fire,' replied Lieutenant Aldridge, 'and facing the wrong way.'

'They know what they're supposed to be doing,' contributed a less diplomatic guardsman, 'because they start doing it when they see us coming. They're just fucking lazy, sir.'

'Well,' said Major Harris brightly, 'we knew this wouldn't change overnight. Anyone got anything positive to say?' He raised a weary eyebrow at me and Tom. 'Make it up if you have to.'

Evenings at Shatt-al-Arab were slow, without even the chance of a drink to ease the boredom. It was a frontline of sorts, so if the troops had to shoot, it was thought preferable for them to be capable of doing so in a straight line. Though there hadn't been an incoming mortar for a month, everybody on base was obliged, come sunset, to collect helmet and flak jacket and repair to the main hotel building, whose brick construction offered better protection than the tents.

In the downstairs rooms, 2 Company diverted themselves until someone, somewhere, decided that the threat had abated for the night – this usually happened around eleven pm – and allowed everyone back to their tents. One of the chief means of passing this time was grumbling about the unfathomable logic of this security regime – as more than one soldier pointed out, it wasn't like the insurgents had to dash for the last bus.

Other amusements included books and days-old British news-papers, personal DVD players, simulated combat on Xboxes, ping-pong, pool and singalongs to the guitar of one of the lance-sergeants (favourites: The Verve, Oasis, Manic Street Preachers). On Thursday nights there was a quiz, accompanied by photos projected onto the wall from a laptop. The highlight was the Name That Guardsman round, in which points were awarded for identifying soldiers within the company from surreptitiously snatched digital close-ups of various portions of their anatomy – the top of a head, a foot, an ear. Other photos projected onto the wall were highlights of 2 Company's tour, particular cheers greeting the pictures of Lieutenant Aldridge's mascot, a toy monkey. A few weeks previously, the hapless stuffed simian had been abducted by unknown guardsmen, dressed in an orange jumpsuit, and photographed being threatened with assorted bladed weapons, before being released unharmed.

Like any group forced into close proximity, 2 Company had developed an initially impenetrable vocabulary of in-jokes. A few months earlier, Tony Blair had visited the camp. By coincidence, the same day yielded a tip-off about a chemical weapons dump, which 2 Company had been dispatched to investigate – what would have been fortuitously timed confirmation of Iraq's vexingly absent WMD capacity had been instantly dubbed 'Operation Knighthood' (the lead proved as false as every other). For radio communications while on patrol, 2 Company had assigned code names to the places they visited regularly. The presidential palace complex was known as St James'. One combined Iraqi police/British army base in downtown Basra, infamous for appalling food, meagre facilities and the violent neighbourhood, was known as the Gurnos, after a particularly grim housing estate in Merthyr Tydfil, the (apparently unlovely) Welsh town whose wealthier citizens allegedly shared Saddam Hussein's tastes in bathroom furnishings. One enterprising lance-sergeant, Tony Warchol, had gone a step further, and named an Iraqi police station after himself.

There was also a good deal of griping, though I didn't read too much into that – few creatures whine like a serving soldier perceiving a sympathetic ear. Some grievances, especially from the younger soldiers, essentially amounted to affront that they joined the army and got sent somewhere dangerous. Other complaints were more reasonable. Each soldier got only twenty minutes of phone time each week, which was hard on soldiers with families (there was a twenty-four-hour internet facility, but this wasn't much use for communicating with toddlers). They were also irritated about poor pay, and about being hopped into for income tax while overseas serving their country. There was much wistful chat about the sums being trousered by former soldiers working in Iraq as private security contractors.

'I'm sure most of the lads have thought about that,' said CSM Pridmore. 'But I still believe in this, that's my drama. Fighting the good fight, and all that crap.'

CSM Pridmore, thirty-five, joined the Welsh Guards from school in Swansea, fulfilling an ambition nurtured since childhood, nourished by the Welsh Guards' exploits in the Falklands in 1982. Pridmore embodied every middle-class milquetoast's nightmare vision of the British squaddie – almost as wide as he was tall, shaven-headed, missing one front tooth, extensively tattooed. Had the only vacant seat on a London night bus been next to him, I rather suspect I'd have stood. But conversations during the longueurs of the evening mortar drill revealed him as something of a hippy. He was a member of Amnesty International and Surfers Against Sewage, and a voracious reader, insatiably curious about the roots of human evil, from genocide in Rwanda and Bosnia to the recently exposed bullying of Iraqi prisoners by some British soldiers. He talked about 2 Company's work with a slightly self-conscious idealism.

'I think that most of the guys feel the same,' he said one evening, 'however much they moan. I feel like we're making a difference here, and I can see how much these guys have grown, as well. There was one guardsman who absolutely didn't want to come, pretended to lose his passport, all sorts. I could have killed him. But he's been great. It has been the making of him.'

Guardsman Balderstone, all of eighteen, sheepishly confirmed this. 'I tried everything to get out of it,' he said. 'But when I went home on R&R, I wanted to come back after a week. I missed the boys.'

The more time I spent with 2 Company, the more relaxed they became about admitting to pride in what they were doing. Guardsmen scrolled through the photos on their laptops, showing stacks of cash they'd retrieved from a payroll robber, drugs and weapons confiscated from an al-Qaeda cell, lines of Iraqis waiting to vote. In a distinguishing quirk of early twenty-first century soldiery, there was even satisfaction at having adhered to the rules of engagement which had kept 2 Company's guns silent. Corporal Andy Thackway showed me his copy of the laminated card, carried by every British soldier, which outlined the extremely limited circumstances in which they were permitted to open fire.

'They went through this with us,' he said. 'If someone shoots at us, then drops his gun, we can't shoot. If someone fires an RPG that kills our mates and then runs away, we can't shoot. Of course, the bad guys know this. The Cheshires, who were here before us, told us they'd had guys shoot at them, then stand there holding their guns in the air.'

If true, this represented extraordinary faith in British military discipline on the part of Basra's militant malcontents.

On night patrol, the soldiers sitting opposite in the rear of the Land Rovers were just voices in the dark, lit only by whatever light flickered through the hatch in the roof. 'I don't get nervous,' said Guardsman whoever-it-was. 'I mean, we were all jumpy after that first patrol got hit – thinking, God, six months of this? But the Iraqis have mostly been really friendly.'

Our first stop was an Iraqi police VCP, next to an arched stone gate. The patrol's leader, Sergeant Julian Hughes, called on the officer in charge. Sergeant Hughes was bearing gifts – oil and cloth for cleaning guns. The police lieutenant thanked Sergeant Hughes for these, and – possibly for my benefit, possibly out of characteristic Arab courtesy – for Sergeant Hughes' help building a new Iraq. The TV in the office showed footage of Ashura – young men flogging themselves with chains and whips. The new Iraq of which the policeman spoke was already drifting from the design on America's drawing board.

'I don't like this distinction of Sunni and Shi'a,' grumbled the lieutenant. 'I am a Muslim and an Iraqi. That will do. This is why we need a strong leader now.'

'Well,' said Sergeant Hughes, 'that's what the elections were for.'

'Yes!' exclaimed the lieutenant, with sudden enthusiasm. 'I choose. If he's good for Iraq, I choose him again. If not, I choose someone else.'

There followed some general chat about the marvellousness of democracy.

'I would like to visit England,' decided the lieutenant.

'Wales,' corrected Sergeant Hughes.

'What's wrong with England?' wondered the lieutenant.

'Too many Englishmen,' grinned Sergeant Hughes. 'They're like the Ba'ath Party. Oppressed the Welsh for hundreds of years.'

On a street full of shops, the patrol pulled up, established a position, and flagged down cars for random searches. This was done with an impressive lack of yelling and gun-waving. Again, the contrast between their techniques, and the behaviour of American troops in Baghdad, who seemed to have learned everything they knew about operating on occupied Arab soil from the Israelis, was stark. When any of 2 Company spoke to the driver of a vehicle they'd stopped, they did so crouched next to the door, looking up at the occupant, their rifle pointed away. It was a terrific gamble – effectively conceding the first shot to the guy in the car – but the deferential body language seemed worth it. In several vehicle searches, not a voice was raised by anyone. That said, 2 Company didn't find or learn anything especially useful, either.

Lance-Sergeant Andy Woosnam invited himself into a mobile phone shop, where a group of men were talking. He returned radiating an air of bafflement.

'The guy in the shop gave me this,' he said, and opened his fist to reveal a chunky gold ring with a scarlet stone set in it. 'Took it right off his own finger. I'll have to think of something to bring him.'

We were returning to base when Sergeant Hughes received a report of a suspicious vehicle parked on a remote road on Basra's outskirts. The patrol drove to a rundown neighbourhood that reeked overwhelmingly of sewage, parked, and awaited instruction. I was confused by the concept, in this context, of a suspicious vehicle. At this late hour, in a place this dark, in an area this dodgy, in a town this dangerous, in a country at war, everything looked suspicious. While the patrol wandered tentatively in different directions, Tom and I waited in the dubious shelter of a half-ruined concrete shack, scanned the surroundings with night vision scopes, and fed each other's paranoia. Was that van driving too fast? Why was that car parked with its lights on? Who were those blokes on that roof and, uh, what was that thing they were carrying? What – seriously, for the love of God, what – were those two chaps doing going for a walk around here, at this hour?

'Hello,' beamed one of them, as they strolled past.

'Good evening,' replied Sergeant Hughes. It was an utterly ordinary encounter. It was also a decision Sergeant Hughes had had seconds to make, with no margin for error.

An hour so after takeoff from Basra, half an hour after the cabin lights had come back on and we'd been permitted to stash our helmets and flak jackets in the overhead lockers, our flight back to Britain ran into extraordinary turbulence. After fifteen minutes of bucking and lurching like a rollercoaster car on the verge of derailing, there was an announcement from the flight deck.

'Sorry about the bumpy ride, ladies and gentlemen,' said the captain, in an accent which ought to have been accompanied by the twitching of a pointy moustache, 'but you'll have to put up with it, I'm afraid. We're being held at this altitude by a Turkish air traffic controller, who I rather think is taking something out on us.'

The vindictive tin-pusher in the Diyarbakir tower wasn't alone. Two years after Iraq was invaded, it was probable that most Britons thought that their soldiers in Iraq, when they thought of them at all, were at best unwitting dupes discharging the dirty work of sinister neoconservative ideologues and/or ruthless oil oligarchs, and at worst outright sadists who beat up prisoners for fun. There were, certainly, many Britons who subscribed to the curious logic that if invading Iraq was wrong two years earlier, then disengaging was right two years later – as if situations remain static, as if our response to them should do likewise.

The anniversary of the invasion was marked in London with another demonstration led by the Stop the War Coalition – a peculiar alliance of old-school the-enemy-of-my-country-is-my-friend lefties, and Muslim zealots whose first act upon reaching power would be to stone their secular socialist allies to death. The slogan on the Stop the War Coalition's banners read BRING THE TROOPS HOME; a shame, I thought, that the placards didn't have room for the parenthetical addendum '(And leave the Iraqi people, millions of whom recently bet their necks to vote, to the tender mercies of Ba'athist recidivists, opportunistic gangsters, and Islamist yahoos)'. Not that 2 Company would ever get – or, for that matter, expect – any credit, but if one corner of Iraq ever became recognisable as modern civilisation, their efforts would have mattered.

It was impossible to predict what Basra might be like later in the twenty-first century. The worst and best case scenarios were easily imagined – respectively, the *Mad Max* theme park of Baghdad to the north, and the gleaming boom towns of Abu Dhabi and Dubai to the south. For better or worse, in Iraq's case the western world had given up on the neither up nor down option, in which the dictator was allowed to continue abusing his subjects as long as he promised not to bother anybody else. Despite that – or, perhaps, given the consequences of intervention, because of it – the western world had acquired a sudden enthusiasm for old-fashioned hypocritical despot-hugging where another oil-sodden Arab tyranny was concerned.

28

On the posters and paintings overlooking the streets and hanging in every shop, hotel, restaurant and cafe, the Colonel was always smiling. In uniform, traditional robes, or one of his iridescent caftan and cap outfits which made him resemble an escapee from a Baptist choir, the Colonel beamed the grin of a man who had gotten away with it – with good reason. Back in the 1980s, when Saddam Hussein was a second-division dictator principally of interest to arms dealers, Yasser Arafat simmered in exile in Tunisia, and Osama bin-Laden was an unheard-of jihadi, Colonel Muammar Abu Minyar al-Gaddafi of Libya was the pre-eminent poster child of Arab/Islamist terrorism, a bogeyman reviled throughout the western world. At the time of my visit to Gaddafi's capital, Saddam Hussein was in jail, Arafat was dead, bin-Laden in a cave burbling threats into a dictaphone. Colonel Gaddafi had not only embarked upon his thirty-seventh year as Libya's unchallenged dictator, but was halfway to reconciling his country with the world. No wonder he looked happy.

Given Libya's recent history, going there as a tourist – or as a journalist trying to write about being a tourist – felt weird. Just twenty years previously, the only people flying to Tripoli from Britain had been the United States Air Force. In April 1986, American aircraft, many launched from British bases, bombed targets in Tripoli and Benghazi, killing 101 people – including an adopted daughter of Gaddafi's, who died when a missile struck the family residence. The American assault was in reprisal for a Berlin nightclub bombing which killed five American soldiers, but it was only one of many clashes between Gaddafi and the West during the 1980s. Libya ran weapons to the IRA, blew up a Pan Am 747 over Scotland, and a UTA DC-10 over Niger (there was, I felt, something especially piquant about researching, as I was, a travel feature on Tripoli for an in-flight magazine). In London in 1984, one of Libya's embassy staff shot dead a Metropolitan police officer, Yvonne Fletcher, who was attending a demonstration outside.

By January 2006, it was possible for anyone to fly to Tripoli from Britain – British Airways had resumed flights in 1999, after the suspension of UN sanctions imposed after Lockerbie (sanctions had been lifted altogether in 2003). Britain had established full diplomatic relations with the Great Socialist People's Libyan Arab Jamahiriya. ('Jamahiriya' translates approximately as 'state of the masses', reflecting Gaddafi's quaint belief that Libya was a citizens' democracy, sufficiently sophisticated to disdain such fripperies as political parties or elections.) Libya had renounced terrorism and its weapons programs. Though Gaddafi remained an accessory to the murder of dozens of British citizens killed by the IRA with Libyan munitions, Tony Blair had visited him. Even America, who still, at this point, listed Libya as a sponsor of terrorism, were edging towards restoring diplomatic relations – a rapprochement which, not long before, had seemed as likely as George W. Bush and Kim Jong-Il duetting on 'I Got You Babe' in a Pyongyang karaoke lounge.

By January 2006, while there were no theoretical impediments to holidaying in Gaddafi's semi-pariah state, there were practical obstacles: the staff of Libya's consulate in London, whose enraging uselessness turned what should have been the only moderately tedious process of securing a visa into a protracted agony that lasted longer than my concurrent romantic relationship, and involved even more despondent banging of my head on my desk. After months of phone calls, faxes and emails, I struggled across London one frosty morning to collect the visa I'd finally been assured was ready. It wasn't. Seized by a sudden understanding of why Americans with ready access to automatic weapons occasionally run wild with them in office buildings, I asked the woman at the counter, who professed never to have heard of me, to fetch her boss. She returned with the vice-consul, a perplexed-looking man in a brown polyester suit. I invited him outside, because I was about to do the one thing that anyone who has spent time in the Middle East knows you should never do with the generally well-mannered people of that part of the world. I was about to lose my temper, theatrically and noisily.

On the freezing footpath, I told the vice-consul, at a volume that would have sent frightened squirrels scurrying up trees across Hyde Park, that I had dealt with the embassies to Britain of dozens of nations, that the surly halfwits in his employ made the Pakistanis look efficient, the Russians welcoming, and that if he didn't find me the visa I'd been promised right now, I'd insist to my editor that we abandon our plans to slather ill-deserved praise upon the tinpot tyranny he represented and instead use those pages of the magazine to do a big feature on what a heck of a place Israel was. I was past caring, for reasons not entirely to do with the obduracy and incompetence of the Libyan Peoples' Bureau, and it was unfair of me to take it out on the vice-consul. He, however, was there. The person I was really angry with was the woman who, shortly after welcoming me home from my mercifully brief incarceration in Cameroon, had dumped me from a daunting height for reasons which at that point were merely inexplicable, and still some weeks from revealing themselves as certifiable. She, however, was unavailable.

The vice-consul seemed to appreciate that he was dealing with a man who had, for one reason or another, disappeared beyond the boundaries of reason. Whether he surmised that I had been propelled off the reservation by the behaviour of his own staff, or by having my heart kicked into a lake of fire, or a combination of the two, he retreated into the building and returned with my passport, visa included, in five minutes. This made me angrier, which I don't think he was expecting. All those months, all those faxes, all those emails, all those phone calls, all that struggling not to yell 'Christ almighty, you can get an entire boatload of semtex to Ireland, but you can't put one stamp in my passport?', and it could be done that quickly?

'Please enjoy Libya,' said the vice-consul. 'We have arranged for a driver and a guide to meet you at the airport.'

Maybe they had. I'd have no difficulty believing that a driver and a guide have been waiting at Tripoli airport since the day after I arrived, clutching a wilting cardboard sign bearing my doubtless misspelt name, beards heading towards waist-level. On the day I landed, however, nobody was waiting for me. I dodged the pestilential taxi touts on the airport concourse, walked out of the terminal, and banged on a window of the cab at the front of the queue until its driver woke.

I was staying at the Corinthia Bab Africa Hotel, a new five-star leviathan perched on the beachfront, two semicircular towers closing ranks around a vast lobby crowned with a stone arch. The overall effect was a Saddam Hussein palace with restaurants. My room over-looked Tripoli's walled old city, the Medina, whose mud-brick houses had sprouted uncountable satellite dishes – dishes which were sucking in images of a world to which the dictatorship was being forced to adjust. The Medina was where I would start, for it was in the Medina that, I figured, lay my best chance of finding the real reason for my visit to Tripoli. I had long rued the absence of any Gaddafiana from the collection of dictator kitsch which dominated the decor of my flat, and I had orders from several friends for watches or T-shirts featuring the Colonel.

They weren't hard to find. Inside the main entrance to the Medina – itself surveyed by a huge poster of Gaddafi, clad in brown robes and clasping his hands triumphantly before a blazing sun – were merchants offering teetering piles of Gaddafi T-shirts and shelves of Gaddafi watches. While I made my selections, I asked the shopkeeper who bought these things.

'Only foreigners,' he said.

He had, I noted, like every other shopkeeper in the Medina, a portrait of the Colonel in his shop.

'Yes,' he confirmed, and busied himself with invoices. In Libya, as in Saddam's Iraq, the mere mention of the leader's name made people visibly uncomfortable.

I was pleased with what I had, but I did better further into the Medina, in a narrow street called Souk Al-Ghizdir. This was where the Medina's coppersmiths clangingly crafted decorative plates, and the crescent moons which perch atop minarets. At the back of one shop, I found a stack of copper drinks coasters into which the Colonel's sunglassed likeness had been engraved in black and green. I've never had any sort of poker face, and the shopkeeper knew he'd made a sale as soon as I spotted them. He wouldn't be talked down from his initial quote of ten Libyan dinar, about four quid, a go. Resignedly, I added up the friends who'd just had weddings, or were about to have house-warmings, or to whom I felt indebted for the hours of my heartbroken whining they'd recently endured, and bought his entire stock.

The best thing about the Medina was that it was no sanitised tourist attraction. It looked and felt like an authentic Arab bazaar, its mazes of shops and cafes, its exquisite mosques, patronised almost exclusively by locals. The worst thing about the Medina was that it was no sanitised tourist attraction. It looked and smelled like some still-aggrieved enemy of Libya's bombed the place nightly with litter. Outside the old British consulate, a stone tablet inlaid in the wall sniffily observed, 'The so-called European geographical and explo-rative scientific expeditions to Africa, which were in essence and as a matter of fact intended to be colonial ones to occupy and colonize vital and strategic parts of Africa, embarked from this same building.' Yeah, okay. But I bet they tidied up after themselves first.

A similarly partisan view of Libyan history was offered by the Jamahiriya Museum. The Roman statues and mosaics, taken from the nearby ruins of Leptis Magna and Sabratha, were worth several times the entrance fee on their own, but they weren't what I'd come for. The top floor of the museum was a shrine to Gaddafi, one hall lined with framed encomiums from organisations which shared Gaddafi's view of himself, though some of these correspondents – the Arakhan Rohingya Islamic Front, the Bangalore Muslim Dalit Alliance – appeared to have little going for them but the ability to print a convincing letter-head.

In the downstairs lobby, pride of place was granted to the turquoise VW Beetle driven by Gaddafi as a young revolutionary. 'This vehicle,' noted the poster above it, 'has been part in serious events, astonishing surprises.' The hastily translated exposition of the car's history went on some distance further, before claiming that the Bug 'has embodied the simplicity in confronting the Mercedes-Benz car which has incarnated clamor, haughtiness and false arrogance.' It neglected to note that when Gaddafi travelled nowadays, he tended to leave the VeeDub parked in the museum and ride in an armoured, erm, Mercedes-Benz – presumably custom-built without the clamor-haughtiness-and-false-arrogance package fitted.

Tripoli didn't feel like the capital of a police state. The only armed soldiers I saw were standing sentry outside a military base. Either I wasn't followed, or I was followed by somebody really good – and given my previous experiences with Middle Eastern intelligence services, who rarely paid me the respect of assigning me their brighter operatives, I suspected the former. Or that the geniuses back at the People's Bureau in London had sent the Libyan Mukhabarat a photo of Rolf Harris. Most public buildings, including the Corinthia Bab Africa, had metal detectors at the entrances, but these were lackadais-ically policed. As long as my bag went through the X-ray machine, the guards never looked up from fiddling with their ringtones – nobody searched my person however many alarms were set off by the camera and phone in my jacket. The moral seemed to be that if you were going to blow up a building in Tripoli, carry the bomb with you.

I popped into Tripoli's plentiful, busy internet cafés perhaps more often than I usually would, in the dim, deluded hope of an email reading, 'Dear Andrew, apologies for recent confusion, I had been locked in a shed by my insane identical twin sister, but she has been returned to her secure ward, I'll meet you at the airport when you get back, and I'll even show up on time.' While I was disappointed on that score, and though the connection was like eating sausages through a straw, I was able to call up any foreign news outlet I liked. I thought of what a friend of mine in Belgrade had said just after the revolution there in 2000, that if the internet as we knew it by then had existed ten years earlier, Milosevic's absurd nationalist crusade, and the resulting conflagrations in Croatia, Bosnia and Kosovo, would never have happened. ('So much changed,' my friend said, 'when people could read British, American, European newspapers every day – they know those papers can print what they like, and they realised that everything we'd been told was bullshit.') I remembered being in Baghdad not long after that, and thinking that Saddam Hussein, or someone close to him, well understood the danger posed to dictators by the internet, which is why it was nigh impossible to use it in Iraq during his rule.

And I remembered listening to those bright young activists plotting in Tirana six months previously, talking of how little of what they'd accomplished would have been possible without modern communications technology. In permitting what seemed to be unfettered access to the internet – my experiments stopped decorously short of trying www.terapatrick.com – Gaddafi was either exceptionally confident of his people's love and/or fear, or extremely naive. Confirming that Libya was a society bestriding shifting plates was as easy as contrasting the infinite media available through dishes and modems with the officially sanctioned product. The English-language newspaper, the *Tripoli Post*, was an entrancingly tedious mix of anti-Israel editorials, and will-to-live-sapping headlines. LIBYA'S CO-ORDINATING COMMITTEE FOR ACCESSION TO WTO HOLDS 7TH MEETING ran one of the more pulse-quickening screamers.

For all that Tripoli was surprisingly relaxed in many respects, it was still a society founded on fear. Before I left for Tripoli, I'd emailed the author and photographer Nick Danziger, who I knew from a day we'd spent together in Nice doing a feature on Helena Christensen – not the most arduous shift either of us had ever put in. I knew he'd been to Libya, so I'd asked him for advice, and he'd replied from his Monaco home. Aside from the ruins at Leptis Magna and Sabathra, he recommended Gaddafi's former residence, the one the Americans had bombed in 1986. It had been a while since Nick had seen it, he wrote, but there was, or had been, some species of memorial to the attack near the building. Cool, I thought. I logged out of the Corinthia Bab Africa's business centre's computer, sauntered across the marble lobby to the concierge, and asked him to organise a taxi. He grasped me meaningfully by one elbow and hustled me behind a potted palm.

'No,' he hissed.

I asked him to elaborate.

'There's nothing to see there,' he said.

I explained that the distinguished reporter and adventurer Nick Danziger had told me otherwise.

'You cannot do this,' he continued, looking in actual pain.

Supposing I just hailed a taxi and went myself?

'Soldiers will shoot you,' he said. 'And anyway, no taxi driver would take you there.'

Nobody in Tripoli wanted to talk about the Colonel – which, given the preponderance of his visage amidst the urban topography, felt a little like turning up to cover a Smiths convention and finding nobody willing to discuss Morrissey. One shopkeeper, who told me that the number of Gaddafi posters had actually been reduced by an order of magnitude shortly after the overthrow of Saddam Hussein, absent-mindedly observed, 'Perhaps he thought he'd be next,' then looked pale and made me swear not to mention his name. When the hotel's PR people took me to dinner, and I mentioned that I'd once inter-viewed the Colonel's son, and presumed heir, Saif Al-Islam Gaddafi, their responses were variations on 'Yessssss . . . he is a very smart man,' followed swiftly by inquiries about the weather in London.

When not wandering the Medina, I lounged in the cafés of Green Square, watching pedestrians struggle through the clockwise lanes of ferocious traffic, reflecting that I'd never need to wonder what it would look like if the 1980s video game Frogger was crossed with Russian roulette. Or strolled the flea market of Sharia ar-Rashid, browsing racks of Abibas tracksuits, Beerok trainers and Timmy Hoflinger jeans. Or photographed the pitches of the street corner tradesmen, who advertised with little sculptures made from their tools – tripods of hammers for carpenters, arrangements of chisels for masons, lightbulbs for electricians, rollers in buckets for painters, surreal arrangements of taps and pipes for plumbers. Or, back in my eyrie at the Corinthia Bab Africa, listened to George Jones and Gram Parsons albums on my iPod while gazing disconsolately out to sea. This was because I was bereft, lonely, angry and felt like a pedal steel sounds. It was also because there wasn't much else to do. The fear of dictatorships is often remarked upon, but the boredom is just as oppressive.

The beachfronts were litter-strewn quarries with waves. The promenade along the harbour was accessible only by crossing a busy freeway. While Libyan drivers were not, on the whole, as crazed as their Syrian and Lebanese cousins, Tripoli's roads were nevertheless irresistibly suggestive of chimpanzees on a dodgem rink; reaching the waterfront was a terrifying wager of my agility on foot against the reluctance of local motorists to get blood on their windscreens. Nightlife consisted of hotel bars full of foreigners complaining that Tripoli had no nightlife, or the cinema on Green Square, which was showing *Basic Instinct*. The allegedly prestigious embassy district of Gargaresh, which the hotel staff had recommended, was a slum of unsealed roads, and dusty shops selling crap. I found one fabulous restaurant, in a refurbished Italian-built villa in the Medina, but everything else I was served filled precisely that many places on my list of worst meals I'd ever eaten in the Middle East. And although, given my state of mind, it was probably a good thing that I couldn't get a drink – the pianist in the hotel lobby didn't look the sort who'd respond to slurred requests for 'Heartaches By the Number' – Libya's total ban on alcohol provoked cravings that verged on the hallucinatory.

On my last day in Tripoli, I lunched at the revolving restaurant on top of the Al-Fatah Tower, a building resembling a spacecraft from a 1970s science-fiction film which had reared up on its twin booster rockets. I dined on congealed spaghetti and a meat sauce I didn't want to think about, and did a few slow laps, reflecting that building a revolving restaurant so people could enjoy looking at Tripoli was as sensible as erecting an enormous brick fence around Florence.

It was perhaps because the view was so uninspiring that my head began to swim with another vision, that of the cell in which Saddam Hussein was confined as he enjoyed the fair trial to which he was being treated prior to his hanging. If it contained a television, there must have been moments in recent Libyan history when the rest of the Baghdad holding facility echoed to the sound of prison crockery clattering against concrete walls. What must Saddam have thought, as he'd watched those astonishing pictures of Tony Blair – looking, granted, like he'd rather be photographed in bed with an assortment of barnyard animals – shaking hands with Gaddafi?

'Let me get this straight,' Saddam must have mused. 'Gaddafi blows up an airliner over Scotland. His embassy staff shoot a police officer in St James' Square. He sends weapons to the IRA, who make at least two attempts to assassinate the British government, one of them while Britain was at war with me over that Kuwait business. He sponsors Islamic insurgents as far afield as the Philippines, and bungs money to the families of Palestinian suicide bombers. Though I'm hardly in a position to judge, his human rights record is terrible. At a personal level he is, by all accounts, nearly as bonkers as I am. And he actually had weapons of mass destruction. But he gets the British prime minister making a pilgrimage to his tent, and I get invaded, arrested and slung in the hoosegow. Is it the moustache?'

Immediately following the attacks on New York and Washington on September 11 2001, George W. Bush announced that the US would 'make no distinction between the terrorists who committed these acts and those who harbour them'. On 20 September 2001, Bush told a joint session of Congress that 'Every nation, in every region, now has a decision to make. Either you are with us, or you are with the terrorists'. It seemed inconceivable that either of these declarations could amount to good news for Colonel Gaddafi, of all people.

Perhaps, to borrow an apposite quip, Washington and London had decided that they'd rather have Gaddafi inside the tent pissing out, than outside the tent pissing in. Perhaps it was an educated bet on the future. In Saddam Hussein's Iraq, the likely succession of one or other of Saddam's demented sons had meant that when Iraqis wished for a long life for their dictator, they were depressingly sincere. Gaddafi's Libya was no less a family racket, but preening diffidently in the wings was that kid of his I'd met at the Ritz in London in 2002, who'd talked a reasonable amount of sense, and hadn't chewed on the furniture. Maybe Saif was the reason that the restaurant I was dining in wasn't an observation post manned by the 82nd Airborne.

The really awful thing about Tripoli was that it was really awfully easy to imagine how it could have been even worse. The country which shared most of Libya's western border, Algeria, another oil-rich Islamic tyranny, had spent most of the 1990s delivering a convincing impression of a nation determined on mass suicide. Algeria's first democratic elections had been won by Islamist cranks, whose beguiling campaign pitch included the promise that any vote they won would be Algeria's last. Algeria's military wouldn't have it, and Algeria descended into a ghastly civil war which saw upwards of 120,000 of its people slaughtered, often with shocking ingenuity, including the use of truck-mounted guillotines to dispatch entire villages.

It looked an uncannily, drearily prescient story arc. In Algeria, before the civil war, before the three decades of one-party rule that preceded the civil war, there had been a bloody eight-year-long revolt against foreign occupation. Was it possible that the story still to unfold in Iraq – the Libya we'd decided we couldn't live with – had been told already? Was there any way it could have been avoided, or could still be fixed? I didn't know. But I did get to meet a man who might.

29

Just up the Avenue de Wagram from the hotel I'd been instructed to report to, restoration work was being performed on the Arc de Triomphe, Paris's glowering monument to French military invincibility (it was built some time ago). The consignment of French soldiery to the ranks of comedy stereotypes, along with British chefs and German comedians, took many defeats to accomplish, but one of its more extraordinary reverses was partly orchestrated by the man I'd come to meet. Half a century previously, Saadi Yacef had been a commander in the Front Liberation Nationale (FLN), the Algerian guerilla group which, between 1954 and 1962, had waged a brutal, merciless and ultimately successful campaign against the occupiers of what had been a French colony since 1830.

On this score alone, Yacef would have been worth a day's outing on the Eurostar. But in Iraq, another occupation of an Arab country had been going on for eighteen months, and Iraq, so far as I could tell from newspapers, blogs and the shaking heads of friends who'd recently been there, was still a distance from being a stable democracy with great galleries and a thriving jazz scene. Despite the optimism I'd found in Baghdad in 2003, it increasingly appeared that the western world had liberated Iraq only inasmuch as someone who whacks a wasps' nest with a branch can be said to have liberated the angry cloud of black and gold marauders besetting him. I figured that if anyone could provide useful insights into how, or if, an occupying army could defeat an insurgency – especially one motivated at any level by Islam

– it might be Yacef. It wasn't just that he'd once run such a revolt. He'd made a film about it.

To understand why every single western policy maker should own the DVD of *The Battle of Algiers*, imagine that in 1996, a couple of years after the IRA 'ceasefire', Martin McGuinness decided to make a movie. Imagine, and this will be the least difficult part of the exercise, that the subject of his film was Bloody Sunday and the period of Northern Ireland's Troubles that surrounded it. Imagine that McGuinness knocked together a script during a stretch in prison, then rang round fashionable European directors to see if they were interested. Imagine that he got one of them – as long as we're imagining weird stuff, imagine Lars von Trier – to sign up, and then imagine that von Trier suggested to McGuinness that, seeing as how the part of the charismatic, ruthless Derry IRA commander was clearly based on him, McGuinness might as well play it himself. Imagine McGuinness agreeing to that, and allowing himself to be depicted ordering the murders of policemen and the bombings of cafes. Imagine, also, that the film – let's call it *The Battle of Derry* – refused to depict British paratroopers as straightforwardly evil, and took pains to portray them as conflicted, even essentially decent, human beings, as much victims of their political masters as the Irish people killed by them.

This is more or less how *The Battle of Algiers* was made. It was filmed in Algiers' Casbah in the mid-1960s, the war fresh in the memories of the suddenly unbound, traumatised population, who served as extras. It featured only one professional actor – Jean Martin, as the baleful but honourable French paratroop colonel, Mathieu. Far from being a tract of strident propaganda, *The Battle of Algiers* inhabited a moral climate as grey as the newsreel stock it was shot on. Yacef, unusually for someone who'd lived in that thin slice of the ethical spectrum where freedom fighter overlaps terrorist, portrayed his own war as a struggle which, while of life and death importance, never contained absolute right or wrong.

'That was important,' explained Yacef. 'When other people,

whether it's America or Russia or France, make films about their great wars, the Germans are always nothing but bad. In *The Battle of Algiers* it's more balanced, and that's how it was. I wanted to relate the way things really happened.'

Yacef, a diffident, hesitant seventy-six-year-old, was in Paris on holiday from his day job as a senator in Algeria. His English was better than he thought it was, but after unburdening himself of the above quote he decided, unexpectedly, that he'd only do the interview in French, one of many languages I don't speak. We prevailed upon the multilingual hotel receptionist, a young Algerian-born chap who regarded Yacef as Che Guevara multiplied by Russell Crowe. He waved away my offer of an hourly rate, insisting that it was an honour.

I asked Yacef if there was one lesson in particular that he hoped *The Battle of Algiers* could deliver.

'The time for colonial occupations,' he said, 'is finished. No country can live as they like in other countries. When this happens, the population will always wake up and make the occupier leave. All the armies of the world cannot stop a revolution – these things are the decision of history.'

The Battle of Algiers, directed by Gillo Pontecorvo – himself a veteran of the World War II Italian resistance – was a critical hit upon release in 1965: it earned three Oscar nominations and won the Venice Film Festival's Golden Lion. Since then, it had been used as a training and motivational tool by the Black Panthers, the IRA and the Tamil Tigers. It had also been used as an instruction manual for armies fighting insurgencies. Its DVD re-release in 2003 was well timed, as the West reacquainted itself with the squalid realities of occupation. The Pentagon's Directorate for Special Operations and Low-Intensity Conflict held a screening, searching for lessons to be learnt in Iraq. ('Children shoot soldiers,' enticed the flyer. 'Women plant bombs in cafés. Soon the entire Arab population builds to a mad fervour. Sound familiar?') Former National Security Adviser Zbigniew Brzezinski recommended it to a Washington conference called 'New American Strategies for Security and Peace'. Yacef seemed bemused.

'I am happy that people are still interested,' he said. 'This is the only movie which speaks so accurately about colonisation. But

America isn't in Iraq for the same reasons the French were in Algeria. If the Americans think all revolutionary wars are the same, they're making a mistake.'

Yacef, it turned out, held views likely to disappoint those who regarded *The Battle of Algiers* as a pre-emptive indictment of America and Britain's Iraqi misadventure. He was fond of America – his daughters lived in Los Angeles, and he spent a lot of time there. 'America is a great country, and a great democracy,' he said, 'but it makes mistakes.'

He was pleased by the unloading of Saddam Hussein, though doubtful about the methods – he believed that there would be all-out civil war in Iraq, followed by the accession of an iron-fisted strongman. ('The problem,' he predicted, 'will be exactly the same.') And, unsurprisingly given the recent dreadful history of his own country, Yacef had no time for the modern jihadi, even if they had learned their trade watching his film.

'Islam,' he said, 'was only a small part of our war against the French – what was more important was that people wanted to be free. These Muslims now are not true Muslims. They want to go back to the time when the Arabs were powerful. They like to pretend it's like when the Prophet was alive, and people were living on the land. They're dreaming about history, only dreaming. Anyway, true Muslims don't kill other people.'

Yacef, of course, killed people. *The Battle of Algiers* unflinchingly examined the linked questions of whether oppression excuses terrorism, which the FLN certainly perpetrated, and whether terrorism excuses torture, which was enthusiastically practised by the French. In 2001, a retired French general, Paul Aussaresses, was convicted of being an apologist for war crimes after writing a book in which he admitted to torturing and executing Algerian prisoners. The torture scenes from *The Battle of Algiers* led to the film being banned in France for many years.

'The movie,' said Yacef, 'shows what happened. You know the scene when the cafe is about to be bombed? The shot of the boy eating the ice-cream?'

It's one of the film's most haunting sequences. We've already seen the FLN bomber given her target. We've seen her waved through the checkpoint at the edge of the Casbah after flirting with the French soldiers. We know what's in the bag she's left under the counter. Before the blast, though, the camera tracks interminably over the people about to die – people chatting, drinking, laughing – and the modern viewer can't help thinking of New York, or Bali, or Jerusalem, or Baghdad, or London, and feel the hideous sensation that they, too, might be living those last oblivious seconds. The child slurping on the ice-cream cone is the agonising peak of the camera's cruel reverie. Then they're all blown to pieces.

'I didn't have to put that shot in,' said Yacef. 'But it is important that it's there. There was a war. That's how it was.'

Yacef insisted that his film shouldn't be read as a field guide for people staging or fighting rebellions, but this may have been the same characteristic modesty that made him think his English wasn't that good. Nobody who has spent time in conflict zones could mistake the authenticity of the film, and it contains many moments which have eerie resonance today. Any politician who wishes to press an ID card upon their population should be strapped down and made to listen to Colonel Mathieu's scorn – 'If anyone has his papers in order,' he tells his soldiers, 'it's the terrorist.' Yacef, I thought, had hard-won knowledge worth listening to.

'When you torture or kill part of a family,' he said, 'when you torture or kill someone's son, someone's mother, all that family will be in the corner of the terrorist. You kill one. You create ten.'

I asked if he thought there was any hope of anything that might resemble victory for America in its current war, and for what it claimed to be trying to bring to Iraq – peace, justice, democracy, and so forth.

'Well,' he said, 'for one thing, they're not France. The French army never wins battles. The Americans have good soldiers. The problem is that in Iraq they're not soldiers, they're trying to be police, like the French paratroopers in Algeria. And they've ended up torturing people just the same.'

Given that we agreed on the desirability of removing Saddam Hussein, I asked Yacef what they should have done differently.

'America should have set up a government in exile,' said Yacef, 'people who would have looked credible to Iraqis in Iraq and overseas. And then America should have told those people to insult and abuse America at every opportunity, so the Iraqi people wouldn't think they were puppets.' He smiled. The old eyes twinkled.

I asked if he was saying it was impossible to export values.

'Very, very difficult,' he said.

Ironically, in Paris as in much of the rest of western Europe, when people weren't worrying about the values America was failing to export, they were fretting about the values Europe was inadvertently importing.

30

The footpaths of Amsterdam were famous for being messy – messy with the doings of dogs usually confined to townhouses, messy with slicks of vomit deposited by scarcely more evolved British stag party revellers, messy with carelessly parked bicycles, messy with litter flung with such abandon that even this visiting Londoner noticed. I'd flown to the Netherlands because Amsterdam's footpaths had recently become messier still, with a simple graffito: two parallel lines, topped by another line, bent at a right angle. This basic illustration of a house had been appearing outside the offices of anti-immigration Dutch politicians, and also outside the homes of Amsterdammers more sympathetic to the Netherlands' recent arrivistes. The symbol could have been an accusatory arrow, or an offer of haven.

The logo was claimed by ASKV, an Amsterdam group that agitated on behalf of refugees. 'It has just been . . . appearing,' grinned ASKV's Bas Baltus. 'Maybe a thousand times in the last month.' Wandering around Amsterdam, I only saw a few. This didn't mean Bas was fibbing – I might have been wandering around the wrong neighbourhoods. What I didn't doubt was that if ASKV's graffiti was to dominate the streetscape like the issue it highlighted was dominating Dutch politics, it would need to be repainted twice outside every house in the country. The Netherlands, a country famous for its militant liberalism, its infinite tolerance of just about everything, was having a radical rethink.

* * *

The Netherlands was haunted by a bald ghost. The assassination of maverick politician Pim Fortuyn, gunned down by a deranged animal rights activist in May 2002, had created a legend. Fortuyn had attempted something new in European politics: an assault upon multi-culturalism and immigration from the left. He believed that a rapidly growing Dutch Muslim population would threaten the Dutch way of life. He was against immigration on grounds of brute practicality: 'The Netherlands,' he declared, 'is full.'

The left, who would usually come down on such views like a tonne of ethnic knitware, didn't know what to do with Fortuyn. He wasn't any of the things people with views like his were supposed to be. He wasn't a bellicose oaf like French National Front leader Jean-Marie Le Pen: Fortuyn collected art, dressed well, read widely and was, by most accounts, personally charming. He wasn't a sinister nationalist like far-right Austrian wingnut Joerg Haider: Fortuyn chose to spend eternity buried near his villa in Italy. He wasn't a fussy wowser motivated by an ignorant horror of all things not heterosexual and white: Fortuyn was gay, and his deputy, Joao Varela, was black. Fortuyn's crusade against immigration, and against Islam – a religion he described as 'backward' – was motivated by a desire to preserve everything that usually got the far right polishing its kicking boots.

Due to circumstances peculiar to the Netherlands, quandaries pertaining to immigration, asylum and Islam were intensified. The Netherlands was small: unless it wanted to be a North Sea Hong Kong, there would have to be some limit on its population. The Netherlands had growing immigrant and Muslim populations. The non-Dutch population of Rotterdam were shortly to become a majority. The Netherlands' Muslim community had doubled in a decade, to 5.7 per cent of the population of 16 million. And I wondered if the precariousness of the Netherlands' geography might have been a factor, whether Fortuynite paranoia about deluges from outside sprang from the fact that the country lay below sea level, at the mercy of shifts in global equilibrium.

Nine days after Fortuyn's death, his party, Lijst Pim Fortuyn, formed barely three months earlier, ran in their first national election. While the sympathy vote should not be underestimated, the result was sensational: Lijst Pim Fortuyn won twenty-six seats, making them the second-largest party in the lower house, and earning them seats in cabinet as part of a coalition government. Following the rapid collapse of this unwieldly alliance, LPF's wings had been trimmed: at the time of my visit to the Netherlands, just eight LPF members sat in the Dutch parliament. However, Fortuyn's influence had, if anything, grown.

Fortuyn himself might have cocked one of his agile eyebrows at recent developments. In February 2004 the Dutch parliament approved a plan to deport 26,000 failed asylum-seekers – including many who had lived in the Netherlands long enough to raise children. Other proposals included automatic refusal of immigrants who didn't speak Dutch, and a ban on Dutch residents under the age of twenty-four importing foreign spouses. Another party founded by Fortuyn – Leefbaar Rotterdam, or Liveable Rotterdam – persuaded Rotterdam's council to deny residence permits to poor or unemployed foreigners. Under policies outlined by Leefbaar Rotterdam, new arrivals would be expected to earn at least 20 per cent more than the Dutch minimum wage, and be able to speak the language. By way of further discouraging riff-raff, Rotterdam council would stop building affordable housing.

All of this sounded pretty extreme, but perspective was needed. So far as I noticed during my stay in Holland, no brown-shirted mobs were holding torchlight rallies. No pyres of books were blazing on the pleins. If the Dutch were becoming crazed by race, asylum, and culture, they were doing it in a very stolid, seemly and altogether Dutch way.

The day I arrived in Amsterdam, ASKV were beginning a marathon protest against the new laws – a bus tour of fifteen Dutch cities. This wasn't as daunting as it might sound. The Netherlands, as Fortuyn's adherents were intensely aware, was so tiny that you could demonstrate in fifteen cities in an afternoon if the lights were with you. I tagged along for the first morning, riding their red bus from Amsterdam to Alkmaar and Haarlem.

It was a bit of a non-event. There was a small crowd outside the mayor's office in Amsterdam; the lone policeman who wandered past couldn't have looked less interested. In Alkmaar and Haarlem, sympathisers armed with balloons met us. Not one passer-by reacted to the signs in the bus window demanding a pardon for the estimated 200,000 refugees in the Netherlands. It would be easy to write the effort off as a quixotic shambles, but the stories of the refugees on the ASKV bus – the unDutchables – were heartbreaking. There was Karim, an electronics and mathematics lecturer who left Algeria in 1994 and, after arriving in Holland, married a Somali asylum-seeker called Mariam and fathered two beautiful, well-behaved children: Ahmed, six, and Nesrin, four. The family lived on 92 euros a week in state handouts, and in two rooms in an asylum-seeker centre. They'd been told they couldn't stay in the Netherlands, but Karim had also been told that Algeria no longer recognised his existence, and neither he nor Mariam saw Mogadishu as an ideal place to bring up children, let alone Dutch children. I asked Karim a dumb question. 'Of course I want to stay,' he said softly. 'Of course I want to work.'

There was Kaba, from Guinea. Kaba had arrived in the Netherlands in 2000. Back home, Kaba, thirty-two, had attracted the attention of the authorities with his role in the youth wing of an opposition party called Rassemblement du Peuple du Guinee. A worried uncle organised him stowaway passage on a container ship. Five million Guinean francs ('About 2000 euros,' reckoned Kaba) bought Kaba fifteen days living in the cupboards of the galley. He didn't know where the ship was going – all that mattered was that it was going away. On arrival in Rotterdam, Kaba was driven into the night, wished luck, and left by the roadside. He had the clothes he'd left home in, no Dutch, no English, no money, and no idea where he was ('Though I thought it might be Europe,' he said, 'because I could see white people.'). The first thing Kaba noticed was the temperature. When he arrived in the Netherlands it was winter. In Guinea, Kaba explained, it was either hot and humid or warm and dry. He'd never been cold before.

Kaba was a citizen of limbo. His application for asylum was denied on the grounds that more senior members of his opposition party were not imprisoned – though they had been, often. 'I tried to explain,' said Kaba, who had taught himself excellent English and Dutch, 'that if you chop down a tree, you cut from the bottom.' He lived on the charity and couches of friends. He couldn't work legally, and worried that if he worked illegally, it might prejudice the appeal he was mounting. Four friends of his marooned in similar nightmares had killed themselves. I had no idea what to say to the guy: my will to live ebbed dangerously if I was put on hold for five minutes.

'I try to remind myself of what is good,' Kaba said. 'It is hard, but I try.'

That night, I strolled along Prinsengracht, one of the canals that meandered through central Amsterdam. There was no more civilised urban environment in the world: rows of handsome terraces, their vast windows yielding views of high walls lined with books, overlooking a still, silent waterway whose pleasantly soporific green-grey gloom was dappled by the butterscotch reflections of becomingly dim streetlamps. It made me heartsick with envy, and I made more money than I needed and owned a flat in London. I tried to imagine how Kaba – who was probably worth less on paper than my shoes – felt when he walked these streets, and failed.

In Rotterdam, I noticed that the citizenry boasted a more varied spectrum of skin colour than Amsterdam. I was annoyed with myself for noticing, because the only reason I noticed was that in Rotterdam, there were people determined to point it out. Around half of Rotterdam's 600,000 people were of non-Dutch descent. The tipping of the balance in favour of the newer arrivals was making political careers for some of the natives. Prominent among these soldiers of Fortuyn was Ronald Sorensen, leader Leefbaar Rotterdam.

I met Sorensen in his office in Rotterdam's stately municipal building. His very appearance was testament to the distance that Dutch politics had veered from European liberalism. Sorensen was grey-bearded, pot-bellied, clad in khaki T-shirt and trousers, and looked like he might have arrived from lunch with Eugene Terre'Blanche. The copy of the Proclamation of the Orange Free State hung on one wall was ill-advised, or wilfully provocative. (The Orange Free State, a Dutch colony in what is now South Africa, ran as an independent country between 1854 and 1900, and was as flagrant an example of immigrants despoiling a native culture as could be imagined.)

'We are not racist,' Sorensen actually said, 'but . . .'

I rolled my eyes. He laughed.

'We don't discriminate,' he continued, 'but . . .'

Go on, then.

'We are not racist,' he insisted. 'We are fed up with being accused of that. The problem has no colour.'

Because we both knew where this was going, I asked if his problem was one of creed rather than colour.

'Yes,' he nodded. 'There is part of the Islamic community which doesn't want dialogue. There is an intolerance towards women, towards homosexuality – the things my generation fought to change in the sixties and seventies. These people volunteered to come to the Netherlands. If they don't like it, there's no reason for them to be here.'

This was a less elegant re-enactment of Fortuyn's effort to outflank multiculturalism from the left. Sorensen became tearful when discussing Fortuyn; a reasonable reaction to the memory of a murdered friend, but there was an unmistakable personality cult developing. The walls of Leefbaar Rotterdam's office were covered with portraits of Fortuyn, including one of him with his beloved King Charles spaniels, Kenneth and Carla.

'I'll tell you why Pim was successful,' said Sorensen. 'In the Netherlands, we have a class system, like in Britain, but ours is defined more by intellectualism than class or money. Pim led a revolt against that elite. He was a stereotypical member of that elite – intellectual, homosexual, flamboyant, a complete affront to Dutch Calvinist modesty – but he said to the people in the streets: "You know what? You're right. And I'm going to say it for you." '

Fortuyn wanted to ensure that Holland remained a society which allowed people like Fortuyn – i.e. gay sociology professors – to go about their business. This was a reasonable aspiration – Rotterdam struck me as a damp, cheerless swamp, but I didn't have to be a gay sociology professor to be certain I'd rather live there than Riyadh.

'Most Islamic countries,' said Sorensen, 'are backward. Pim Fortuyn said Islam has to have an enlightenment, like Christianity did. Or there will be problems.'

That much was unarguable. Islamic countries were, by and large, corrupt, repressive and misogynist, and the degree to which they were those things was generally proportionate to how fervently Islamic they were. But I thought we were a way from keffiyeh-clad guerillas manning checkpoints in Rotterdam's backblocks.

'There is a mosque being built,' thundered Sorensen, 'next to Feyenoord football stadium. The minarets, when they are finished, will be 50 metres high – higher than the stadium. And that stadium is our temple. We asked them to make the minarets more modest, because only 80,000 people here out of 600,000 are Muslims. But they won't.'

Did Sorensen honestly believe that they were doing this on purpose to cause offence?

'Yes. Yes, I do.'

He didn't countenance the possibility that Muslims were just having difficulty believing that anyone cared this much?

'No, I don't. Of course they know. And it's against everything in our history. Even Catholics here never have parades. Making such a show of it is just so . . . un-Dutch.'

So, I thought, was berating people for being a bit different.

'Maybe,' he beamed.

There was a silence, and then, for reasons I couldn't begin to guess at, he announced: 'I'm a Freemason as well, by the way.'

It would have been easy, at around this time, for a Dutch reporter to visit northern England, endure a councillor representing the British National Party, and knock out a piece about how liberal, tolerant

Britain was being hijacked by extremists. The difference was that in Britain, the BNP were generally regarded as a sorry sack of white supremacist buffoons, and had the pitiful electoral support to prove it. In the Netherlands views such as Sorensen's were now a heavy current of the mainstream.

In The Hague, I met with Hilbrand Nawijn, one of Lijst Pim Fortuyn's eight remaining MPs. The LPF's offices were in a building being refurbished to accommodate Dutch MPs. A meeting room had been named after Fortuyn, the only time such an honour had been conferred upon someone never elected (granted that Fortuyn was only deprived of this by his murder). Two enormous – and, though I'm no expert, bloody awful – paintings of Fortuyn hung in the antechamber.

Between July 2002 and May 2003, Nawijn had been the Netherland's minister for immigration and integration, an appointment as risible as handing the health portfolio to Harold Shipman. If a British or Australian MP gave an interview in which they expressed opinions comparable to those which Nawijn breezily shared over coffee, they'd be lucky if their career lasted five minutes beyond publication. Nawijn believed, for example, that it should be mandatory to speak Dutch in the Netherlands' mosques.

'Yes,' he confirmed. 'It's a sign of integration.'

So would be singing opera in Dutch rather than Italian, or conducting Jewish religious services in Dutch rather than Hebrew.

'Also,' he chirped, failing to discern what I'd thought was pretty obvious sarcasm, 'you can control and monitor things. If they are speaking in Arabic, you don't know what they are saying.'

Not unless your security services have thought to hire a few people who also speak Arabic. Those debriefings back at the headquarters of the Algemene Inlichtingen-en Veiligheidsdienst, to give the Netherlands' spooks their official title, must have been dreadfully frustrating: 'We infiltrated the fundamentalist cell, but couldn't understand a damn word they were saying.'

Nawijn may have set a record for the most generalisations about an ethnic group in one hour: Moroccan men prefer to import brides from home rather than marry Dutch women, Moroccans cluster in ghettos, Moroccans are disproportionately given to criminality. All of which might have been statistically verifiable – but was this anything more than the teething pains of any new wave of immigration? What was the worst that could happen?

'I think,' he decided, 'a lot of Dutch people are afraid of Islam. And there are more and more Muslims. How far will it go? I doubt that Dutch people are quite as liberal and tolerant as the outside world thinks.'

The fridge magnets on sale in Dutch cities leaned heavily on the motifs of windmills and clogs. (What a moment it must have been when the Dutch beheld the first foreigner who crossed their border in leather shoes: 'Blimey, what a good idea. These bloody things have been killing me.') However, the Netherlands was also widely identified with less family-oriented merchandise. For many foreigners, the Netherlands was Amsterdam's red light district – which was, I guessed, fine if you liked that kind of thing: money boxes shaped like vaginas, T-shirts depicting Pope John Paul II smoking marijuana and, outside one strip club, a fountain shaped like a permanently gushing penis, complete with revolving testicles. I paused at this, wondering what sort of person could consider the civilisation that created it, and not want to join the Taliban. I didn't have to wonder long: a party of deafeningly drunk Chinese men, and two English peasants in Arsenal shirts, took pictures of each other in front of it.

I dropped in on Mariska Majoor, who ran an organisation whose name epitomised the Dutch knack for reconciling sensuality with sense: the Prostitution Information Service. Majoor spent five years in the eighties working in windows of the red light district, and now dispensed advice and necessities to new arrivals, and souvenirs to tourists. While we talked, two young American girls who'd wandered into the shop stood, and stared, their minds boggling almost audibly.

'I'm sure,' said Majoor, 'that for people who come here from Islamic countries, this must all be a bit of a shock.'

Yes and no. On my visit to Kabul back in 1998, I'd asked two

Taliban officials to describe the West as they imagined it; the Sodom they'd conjured sounded remarkably like Amsterdam.

'I understand,' she continued, 'that it takes time to appreciate that everything is different here.'

The red light district didn't exist in total isolation from the politics of its host nation. There were concerns about immigration here, as well, although little fear of work being taken by incoming Muslims. Majoor believed that the EU expansion scheduled for 1 May 2004 would lead to an influx from the East which could drive up rents on the window booths, and drive down prices charged for services rendered.

'I don't think Amsterdam is becoming conservative,' she said. 'That would be impossible. I think what Pim Fortuyn said – and screamed – spoke for a lot of people. But you can make a mistake thinking everyone thinks like that.'

I couldn't help thinking that if the laissez-faire Netherlands of the popular imagination was in mortal danger, it wasn't from conflict between Muslim marauders and cranky politicians substituting populist table-banging for thought. The great liberal experiment could be ended by the fact that the Netherlands' Muslims and the Netherlands' conservatives had more in common than either party realised: an inflated fear of each other, which was driving people into the dead-end of identity politics.

Back in Rotterdam, I asked Dr Ahmed Akgunduz, rector of Rotterdam's Islamic University, if he'd accept that, as the Fortuynites insisted, there were some things long tolerated in the Netherlands – homosexuality, prostitution, soft drugs – which would always be a mile offside from the Muslim perspective.

'Well,' he smiled, 'there are Christians and Jews who are against those things.'

True enough.

'Now,' he continued. 'Homosexuality, for example. Islam forbids it. But if you ask me how I react to homosexuality in the Netherlands, I have two reactions. First, I am a Muslim, so I cannot allow it in my family. But the second reaction is that Dutch law allows it, and according to my religion, I must observe the law. So I don't agree with the law, but I don't violate it. There doesn't have to be conflict.'

Especially since the Iranian revolution in 1979, Islam had become, for some, an ideology overriding all other allegiances. On that score, didn't Fortuyn, Sorensen and Nawijn have a point?

'There are misunderstandings on both sides,' said Dr Akgunduz. 'Muslims in non-Muslim countries should choose a moderate way. I was visited by a Muslim who expressed extremist views. I asked where he lived, and he said Amsterdam. I asked him, if he didn't like it, why he didn't move to Saudi Arabia.'

Awkward though it was to admit it, I shared some of the concerns of Pim Fortuyn's heirs: I believed that any society that made any concessions to anyone who claimed to speak for God was nodding towards a sleep of reason likely to descend into a coma. I could also see where Dr Akgunduz was coming from. Like him, I was a foreigner in the country where I chose to live – an economic migrant, indeed, there being no threat to my safety at home in Australia, unless some of the bands I reviewed as an overzealous teenage rock critic had memories which defied most research into the long-term effects of solvent abuse. I believed that the onus to adjust was on the newcomer to any country. I believed that if you were going to live in the Netherlands, you should learn Dutch, and something about the Dutch. I believed that newcomers to Britain should learn the language and the history, if only because they could then teach them to the British.

'This country once tolerated everything,' said Omar Altay. Altay was chairman of the Mevlana mosque in Rotterdam. On his desk were the flags of the Netherlands and Turkey, on his wall portraits of the Dutch royal family and Mustafa Kemal Ataturk. He couldn't see why these loyalties should be mutually exclusive. 'Now, they want to blame someone. And I am worried. I don't know how far this is going to go.'

It went further. Later in 2004, the Dutch director Theo van Gogh, who'd made a film, *Submission*, critical of Islam, was shot dead in Amsterdam by a Dutch-Moroccan dual citizen. Stuck to his corpse with a knife was a letter threatening death to his collaborator on *Submission*, Somali-born Dutch MP Ayaan Hirsi Ali, another critic of

Islamic influence on the Netherlands. In 2006, Ali announced that she was leaving the Netherlands. This was the culmination of a sequence of events which could only lead one to believe that a large body of Dutch opinion just wanted Ali gone – she had already been evicted from her government safe house after neighbours complained about the security risk.

Ali's timorous neighbours were an irresistible metaphor for the liberal response to the encroachment of Islam – don't confront, don't provoke, make more and more allowances, and in case of conflict, blame the victim of religiously motivated violence. A lot of what Fortuyn and the Fortuynites said had been paranoid and graceless, but that didn't mean it was entirely wrong. Taking a charitable view, it was possible that the reason Ali's neighbours had concluded that Ali, rather than her persecutors, was the problem that required expunging was that Ali's neighbours were essentially rational people – and, as such, unable to comprehend the immensity and intensity of the irrationality arrayed against them.

By late 2005, they should have figured it out. In September that year, a witless cartoonist on an obscure Danish newspaper drew an unfunny picture of a man with a bomb in his turban. Over ensuing months, a global inferno of imbecility raged. In Damascus, the Danish and – oddly – Norwegian embassies were burned. Danish missions to Lebanon and Iran suffered similarly. Muslim countries announced a boycott of Danish goods, which must have terrified manufacturers of Denmark's most famous exports – beer, pork and pornography. In Afghanistan, Somalia, Pakistan, Nigeria and Libya, the reaction was furious enough to kill. In London, a demonstration outside the Danish embassy was attended by one moron dressed as a suicide bomber. Though the Metropolitan Police inexplicably failed to shoot him, there was some satisfaction to be had from the fact that the publicity attracted the attention of his local cops, who revoked the licence under which he'd been released from his prison sentence for the devoutly Muslim act of dealing cocaine and heroin.

My personal confirmation that some Rubicon had been crossed came the night of the 2006 Super Bowl, for which I had the usual crowd of friends round for beer, donuts and bets on who'd be singing 'The Star-Spangled Banner' ('Saddam Hussein, at gunpoint'). Prior to kick-off, the news led with footage of Muslim protests in Brussels, thousands of residents of early twenty-first century Europe suffused by violent rage at sketches in a newspaper.

One friend of mine, a painfully decent Englishman who I'd never heard utter an opinion not a model of painfully correct liberalism, sighed. 'If they don't like it here,' he asked, 'why don't they just fuck off?'

In the context, it seemed a fair question. So I thought I'd ask someone.

31

At the Dorchester Hotel, the Kingdom of Brunei was celebrating its independence by throwing the most restrained twenty-second birthday party in history. The glasses on the silver trays toted by liveried waiters contained nothing stronger than orange juice. The volume never rose above the gentle rhubarbing of dull small talk. The temptation to set the drapes alight in order to get the place evacuated was overwhelming, but the man who'd brought me here, Sir Iqbal Sacranie, secretary-general of the Muslim Council of Britain (MCB), saw this social ditchwater as fertile opportunity.

'Very useful,' he enthused, at the twelve-beats-to-the-bar pace at which he conducted all conversations. 'I've met the ambassadors from Iran, Sri Lanka, Bangladesh.'

Malawi-born Sacranie was nearing the end of his second, and final, term as the head of the MCB. I was hoping he could help me figure something out: why, in the early twenty-first century, were we lending any – it seemed to me, increasing – credibility to anybody whose sole claims on public attention were the absurd, unproveable beliefs they chose to hold about God? Why, when someone announced that their sensibilities in this area had been affronted, were we – allegedly inhabitants of an age of reason – falling over ourselves to atone and assuage, rather than seeing them off with hoots of derision and last week's tomatoes? I asked Sir Iqbal what he'd been discussing with their excellencies, and his reply – while predictable – was, on this level, profoundly depressing.

'There is,' he said, 'much concern about these Danish cartoons.'

I, too, was concerned about the Danish cartoons. I was concerned that the ridiculous, disproportionate reaction to some feeble sketches in an uninfluential Scandinavian newspaper might be confirmation that in – to deploy an appropriate adjective – fundamental respects, Islam and the West were ultimately irreconcilable.

'Not at all,' grinned Sir Iqbal, and I sensed that he enjoyed an argument, which was going to be just as well. 'In this regard, Britain is an example to the world. Alone in Europe, British newspapers did not reprint these cartoons. It shows what can be achieved when people act responsibly.'

My suspicion was that the restraint of British newspapers derived less from sensitivity to Muslim disgruntlement than it did from a desire not to have their windows broken, or their staff threatened, by maniacs.

'I don't think that's true,' said Sir Iqbal, sounding weirdly surprised that someone could offer such an opinion. 'It is just a question of where you draw a line.'

On this little, we could concur. One way or another, as any Scandinavian cartoonist contemplating plastic surgery and/or relocation to Paraguay might have agreed, where you drew lines was precisely what it was a question of.

Sir Iqbal was a busy man, then more than ever, prevailed upon to explain British Muslims to Britain's government and media, and to explain Britain's government and media to British Muslims. I spent two days with Sir Iqbal on a taxi and tube tour of London as he barrelled through a giddying schedule of press conferences and meetings.

Sir Iqbal had been summoned to meet the Home Secretary the day after the bombings of 7 July 2005. He'd been consulted by British news outlets over the cartoon uproar – and given that no resident of Britain had been able to see the cartoons without searching foreign news agencies online, his opinions were obviously valued. Even the BBC had declined to show them, placing itself in the absurd position of covering every angle of a story except what the story was about. It was like watching a soccer match from which digital technology had excised the ball. Nobody would have been so timid confronting Christian taboos – not long beforehand, the BBC had defied the protests of Christian groups to commission a production of (the apparently blasphemous, according to people who care about that kind of thing) *Jerry Springer – The Opera.*

In some ways, it was unfair to pick on Sir Iqbal. He had not personally burned down any embassies. I understood his frustration that the British Muslims who got all the press were the worst possible advertisements for the faith. No news bulletin ever led with 'Across Britain today, 99 per cent of the 1.6 million or so Muslims who live here got up, put in a day's work, spent time with friends and family, and meant no harm to anybody.' But one dunce dressed up as a suicide bomber could become, if mercifully fleetingly, the most famous Muslim in the country. Holding Sir Iqbal responsible for the picturesque ninnies who'd protested outside the Danish embassy in London, waving banners demanding the beheading of anyone who poked fun at their religion, would be like expecting Tony Blair to answer for the sappy Mosleyites of the British National Party. Sir Iqbal, indeed, dismissed the nuttier Islamist elements with refreshing robustness.

'Loonies,' he said, 'a fringe element, which every community has.'

Some fringes obscure vision more than others, however. In February 2006, an ICM poll found that 20 per cent of British Muslims had some sympathy with the 'feelings and motives' of the perpetrators of the 7 July murders in London. Though I was sure many British Muslims had reacted to the cartoon demonstrations with the same cringing embarrassment with which I, a native of Sydney, had viewed coverage of recent anti-Arab riots on my hometown's beaches, there were those who'd felt genuine, visceral rage at cartoons. Pictures. Jokes. Sir Iqbal, allegedly the moderates' moderate, was one of them.

'We understand,' he began, 'that there are things which we don't like, which hurt us, but it's part of the society we live in – freedom of expression, satire, these are part of western liberal culture. But this editor went out of his way to say "Why shouldn't people be able to draw pictures of the prophet?"'

Well, why shouldn't they?

'The person of the Prophet,' said Sir Iqbal, 'peace be upon him, is revered so profoundly in the Muslim world, with a love that cannot be explained in words. It goes beyond your parents, your loved ones, your children. That is part of the faith. There is also an Islamic teaching that one does not depict the Prophet. This is depicting the Prophet as a terrorist, and also depicting his followers as terrorists.'

This assumed that the values of Islam trump anyone else's – which is what any Muslim does assume, just as any follower of any religion believes that theirs is the sole way, truth and light. If people decided to love a seventh century preacher more than their own families, that was up to them, but surely nobody else was obliged to take it seriously – a non-Muslim was no more obliged to refrain from sketching Mohammed than he was to pray to Mecca five times daily. The bomb-in-the-turban gag was crass, but nothing that couldn't have been dealt with by a brisk letter to the editor, or by ignoring it. The *Jyllands-Posten*, the paper which ran the original cartoon, was a publication with a readership of 158,000 Danes. Islam was a 1400-year-old belief system with 1.5 billion adherents. This was like elephants stampeding over an editorial in the *Daily Flea*, wasn't it?

'Freedom of expression is important,' conceded Sir Iqbal, 'but freedom to insult and abuse to that extent is not part of civil society.'

It was too, I said. So was the manners not to, and the maturity to rise above it if someone did.

'This was a deliberate attempt to provoke,' huffed Sir Iqbal, as if the subsequent rabble-rousing by Arab newspapers and Islamic clerics wasn't.

Our taxi arrived at London's fencing mask-shaped City Hall. Sir Iqbal diverted via the multifaith prayer room – he explained that he always tried to pray five times daily, but was making an extra effort following his mother's recovery from a heart problem. We were attending the launch of a book by Sir Iqbal's deputy, Mohammed Abdul Bari, entitled *Race, Religion and Muslim Identity in Britain*. The speakers, including London mayor Ken Livingstone and contro-versial academic Tariq Ramadan, said what might be expected about tolerance and acceptance. Afterwards, Sir Iqbal prayed again, and we marched to London Bridge for a tube to his next meeting. He enthused en route about Britain's risible new law against incitement to religious hatred, of which he had been a vocal supporter. It had limped onto the books after a splendid mauling in the House of Lords. To Sir Iqbal's chagrin, the new law had been stripped of a proposed proscription of the right to 'criticise and ridicule' religions.

We arrived at a building owned by the Muslim World League, a Saudi-backed NGO. I was intrigued by the concept of offence, as Sir Iqbal had been explaining it. Offence isn't a reflex, like the pain of someone poking you in the eye – it's a choice. If, I began, I drew a picture of a grumpy guy with a beard holding a bomb, should that be outlawed?

'No,' replied Sir Iqbal. 'It hurts, if it depicts a Muslim like that, but no.'

But if I then wrote the word 'Mohammed' beneath it . . .

'Yes,' said Sir Iqbal, 'for reasons I explained earlier. Mohammed is the last prophet of Islam. There is no personality closer to one's heart. It is like . . . my mum is the closest living person to me on this Earth. If she was defamed in such a manner, how would one feel? I'm asking as a human being.'

I wouldn't set fire to anyone's embassy.

'It's not quite that,' he sighed.

But what if the 'Mohammed' caption continued '. . . Smith, of Neasden'? Sir Iqbal ignored this.

'Franco Frattini,' he said, summoning his posse, 'vice-president of the EU, issued a strong statement making it clear that this material is deeply offensive, and doesn't fit in with a culture of freedom of expression. Jack Straw . . .'

Straw, then foreign secretary, had offered a wretchedly pusillanimous statement ('The right of freedom of speech . . . does not extend to an obligation to insult') which had inspired in this viewer an unprecedented urge to put a boot into the television. I'd have preferred to see a British cabinet minister responding to the ruckus with: 'If any of you clowns are right about anything, the cartoonist is going to hell anyway – won't that do? In the meantime, if you want to get excited about actual, meaningful affronts to Muslims, try the Amnesty International reports on Syria and Saudi Arabia.'

'Straw understood the society he was coming from,' parried Sir Iqbal. 'How you have to respect sensitivities.'

I wondered how happy Sir Iqbal was about the fact that the reason that press and polity were being so respectful of Muslim sensitivities was that they were scared, in a way they were not of other faiths. If Muslims came in for, and put up with, the same ragging as everyone else, it'd indicate the acceptance that Sir Iqbal claimed to crave, wouldn't it?

'Interesting point,' conceded Sir Iqbal, though he didn't seem keen to pursue it.

I asked Sir Iqbal if he was familiar with the legal travails then besetting the veteran Italian journalist Oriana Fallaci. He claimed that he was not. Fallaci had written a book, *The Force of Reason*, heavily – even crankily – critical of Islam. Italy had laws against incitement to religious hatred similar to the ones which had been mercifully defanged in Britain. The head of the Muslim Union of Italy, Sir Iqbal's Italian equivalent, had decided to get upset with Fallaci and so, in early twenty-first century Europe, an author was due to stand trial for writing a book.

'Was she vilifying?' asked Sir Iqbal.

Did it matter? She hadn't torched a mosque or handbagged an imam. She'd written a book.

'But the law is there,' insisted Sir Iqbal.

The existence of the law, I suggested, wasn't proof that the law wasn't crazy.

'That's a very personal judgement,' he said. 'What do laws do? They don't end your ability to commit an act. They're a powerful indicator of what is acceptable in a society and what isn't. If you defy that law, you pay the price.'

How, I persisted, could it make sense that writing a book was a crime?

'If,' began Sir Iqbal, 'a book causes social commotion or disruption –'

It was more than likely, I'd started replying, to be the Koran or the

Bible, but there was a knock on the door, and Sir Iqbal had to pray again, and attend another meeting.

A few days later at Waterloo station, I met Sir Iqbal off the train from New Malden, where he and his family – he was married, with five children – had lived for fifteen years. Sir Iqbal had returned to London to visit the East London Mosque for an MCB press conference on another governmental attempt to regulate thought and speech: a planned law against 'glorification' of terrorism. Sir Iqbal, who was in favour of restricting what people could say about religion, was against restricting what people could say about terrorism.

This silly bill would also be scuppered in the Lords, but as the taxi lit out for Whitechapel, all was still to play for. Sir Iqbal, I noted, had recently had a brush with the thought police. In an interview on BBC Radio 4, Sir Iqbal said he believed that homosexuality was 'not acceptable'. Incredibly, this had led to a police investigation. No charges were brought, but I asked Sir Iqbal if the experience had not given him pause to consider where the outlawing of expression might lead. My own view, I explained, was that while I thought his opinions about homosexuality were ridiculous, he had every right to express them, as I had every right to tell him I thought they were ridiculous. From the heat of argument comes the light of truth, and so forth.

'If there is concern,' said Sir Iqbal, 'from certain quarters that I may be breaching a law, then it is proper for them to report me to the police.'

There were burglars they could be catching.

'The question,' he argued, 'is whether by expressing your belief, your religious viewpoint, on a particular form of sexuality which your religion clearly views as unacceptable, is that tantamount to a breach of law?'

If it was, it'd be grim news for publishers of holy texts, most of which flagrantly incite hatred against homosexuals, believers in other religions, and people like me, who think pledging yourself to any faith is no more or less weird than choosing to believe that the world is rhombus-shaped, and borne through the cosmos in the pincers of two enormous green lobsters called Esmerelda and Keith.

'If I may ask you a simple question,' said Sir Iqbal, 'would you oppose incitement to hatred on the grounds of race?'

Of course.

'So,' he continued, 'how would you distinguish between groups of people who are classified racially, like Jews and Sikhs, and those who are not, like Muslims? Are you comfortable saying Jews and Sikhs should be protected, and Muslims and Christians should not?'

I was comfortable saying Muslims and Christians were entitled to the same protections under extant laws, and common courtesy, as trainspotters, goths, bassoonists, fans of particular football clubs, voters for certain political parties, and anybody else who made a choice about who and what they were. Just as it was wrong and stupid to discriminate on grounds of race, it was wrong and stupid not to discriminate on grounds of belief. How else were we supposed to make judgements about people? If Sir Iqbal wasn't permitted to express his quaint views about homosexuality, how would I know he was a homophobic bigot?

'We must be very clear,' he said, bristling, 'what we mean by homo-phobic. It means an incitement to hatred against people. I may not like homosexuals, I may totally disagree with their practices, but I cannot speak on the basis that one should hate the people who practise homosexuality.'

Sir Iqbal, as was usually the case with people who care in the slightest what consenting adults get up to in their bedrooms, discussed the subject with wincing queasiness. As he was uncomfortable anyway, I thought it a good time to ask the question which, I was sure, was the reason he'd looked so relieved at hearing the call to prayer when we'd been talking about Oriana Fallaci. There had been a time when Sir Iqbal had come close to suggesting that writing a book should not only be an indictable offence, but one meriting capital punishment. In 1989, in response to Ayatollah Khomeini's demand for the murder of Salman Rushdie, Sacranie had said of Rushdie that 'Death is perhaps too easy for him'.

Sir Iqbal shot me a weary look. To my mind, I continued, the

Rushdie fatwa was a total no-brainer. A proper response from the British government of the day would have been to call a press conference beneath the nosecone of a Royal Air Force Tornado, and issue a communique forcefully suggesting to Rushdie's persecutors that they had the flight time from Diego Garcia to Tehran to rethink their edict. Surely, this was something every halfway sane person could get together on. Either you were utterly and unequivocally opposed to the fatwa, in spirit and letter, or you were an absolute moral idiot, and possibly a certifiable lunatic.

'I stand by what I said,' he replied. 'I was asked to comment on the fatwa, whether I would encourage or support it. My answer was clear, that we do not accept that the fatwa should be implemented in this country because it is a criminal offence, it's murder.'

And crazy, surely. And just plain wrong.

'If,' continued Sir Iqbal, 'someone carried out an act to bring harm to Rushdie, what would it entail? He would be a martyr. It would be counterproductive. We would lose the debate about vilification.'

And that, apparently, was the reason it would be bad to kill someone for making up a story.

'So, my point was that I as a Muslim had been deeply hurt, as had 1.5 billion people across the Muslim world.'

Almost none of whom read it.

'They were aware of the content.'

Had Sir Iqbal read it?

'I read the relevant chapters,' he said, with the expression of a man recalling a bout of food poisoning. 'I had the painful task of facing journalists to be questioned about it. The reason I said death would be too easy for him was that he would be made a martyr. There was a choice. Should he be killed, or should he be living as he is living now, but facing divine retribution? God almighty takes care of those who vilify God. God can look after Himself.'

If only more of His fans were content to let Him.

'Rushdie,' declared Sir Iqbal, 'should suffer divine retribution, which I believe he is suffering until today. He lives in fear.'

He lived in New York, last I read, with a deserved reputation as a literary titan, a supermodel wife and the royalties of several million book sales. God was, presumably, lulling Rushdie into a false sense of security before He really let him have it.

The press conference at East London Mosque wasn't over-attended – the MCB could have got everyone into one of the minarets. It was at least ironically amusing: the same people who'd campaigned for a law forbidding the criticism of religious belief complaining about a bill which 'would stifle legitimate debate'. The somewhat feline press release expressed concern that the bill 'could put behind bars opponents of the current odious regimes in, say, Burma, Chechnya and North Korea'. The odious regimes of Saudi Arabia, Syria, Iran, Sudan, Libya, Egypt and so on (and on, in the Islamic world, and on) had slipped the memory of whoever drafted the handout.

Afterwards, in a downstairs hall in the mosque complex, there was a memorial service for Zaki Badawi, an Egyptian-born imam whose lifelong pursuit of pluralism – he'd nobly responded to the Rushdie fatwa by offering the author sanctuary in his home – was reflected in a dazzlingly ecumenical roll-up of speakers: the Archbishop of Westminster, the Bishop of Fulham, Rabbi David Goldberg of the Liberal Jewish synagogue (Goldberg, in a rousing oration, identified the Rushdie fatwa as 'the moment at which the clash of civilisations changed from a soundbite to a self-fulfilling prophecy').

On stage awaiting his turn to speak, Sir Iqbal doubtless felt that this added up to an ideal vision of modern Britain, modern Europe, the modern world: diverse, tolerant, at ease. I hoped he was right. Europe's demographic realities didn't suggest an attractive selection of options. Declining birthrates among Europe's established peoples, and blooming growth among its Muslims, were steering the continent on course to become much more Islamic by the early twenty-second century. The response of the secular world I lived in to the sudden arrival of a reinvigorated Islam would preoccupy many future chronicles of these times. Which was kind of where I came in.

32

Peace. Love. Understanding. Fuck off.

'Aw, come on,' said Bono. 'Correct me if I'm wrong, but I hardly said a word on stage last night. It's hard for me to shut up, but I really did.'

U2's second show at Madison Square Garden had been more assured than the frenetic first, U2 now certain of their welcome. Bono wore a Fire Department of New York T-shirt beneath his stars and stripes-lined jacket. Edge sported a glittering Yankees logo on his T-shirt. Bono interrupted U2's ancient hit 'I Will Follow' with an improvised homily to New York ('Twenty years ago we came walking down these streets . . . New York, you lifted me up on your shoulders') and, later, even felt able to attempt a joke. Before 'One', he thanked New York for taking U2 in 'like you've taken everyone in – Irish, Italians, Jews, Hispanics, Muslims . . . no letters from anyone I've left out.' If U2's first night had been the memorial service, the second was the riotous, celebratory wake.

'I want to be able to adore this city,' said Bono now, sounding the worse for his exertions of the previous two nights. 'And I want to grieve alongside it. But at the same time, if artists are not standing up and talking about tolerance . . . I think that's our gig, and I'm ready to take the criticism for it.'

Adoring this city, from where we were sitting, wasn't difficult. The view from the balcony of Bono's flat swept out over Central Park's infinite shades of green to a horizon defined by the silver pinnacles of midtown Manhattan.

'What do you think?' he asked, sounding endearingly anxious.

I thought, I said, that if he ever wanted to look at a view of a car park behind an East London bingo hall, he could call me and I'd get the kettle on.

'It is amazing,' Bono conceded. 'And I thank God for it.'

He wasn't here on September 11.

'I'd just left,' he says. 'Of all the serendipities, we'd been here recording one of the most famous anti-war songs – Marvin Gaye's "What's Going On", on behalf of the Global AIDS Alliance. So I guess I left on September 8 or 9 . . .'

This version of 'What's Going On' also featured Destiny's Child, Michael Stipe, Jennifer Lopez and Britney Spears, among others, and and was selling under the name Artists Against AIDS Worldwide. U2 had taken to incorporating their own version into their encores.

'. . . and a few days later, you never needed to hear a song as much. In the aftermath of September 11, it was the most played song on the radio here, but it stopped as soon as military action in Afghanistan started because some lines had started to jar. Which is a shame, because I think even the militarists realise this is a war you can't win just with ammunition.'

This new war was, I suggested, going to be at least as big a challenge to the imaginations of instinctive peaceniks – a body of people that Bono had rarely strayed far from. People who were capable of spending months, years, planning to fly aeroplanes into office blocks – without ever once asking, 'Is it just me, chaps, or does this seem kind of nuts?' – and anyone who felt represented by such an act, were not people who could, or should, be reasoned with. On that score, I asked Bono if he'd have made the previous two nights' acknowledgements of the IRA's recent and cynically timed disarmament if U2 had been playing in Manchester, Birmingham or London.

'I like,' he croaked, 'the line – I don't know who said it – that just because you have a past, it doesn't mean you can't have a future. I really believe that. That's a fundamental for me. That we can begin again.'

* * *

Pointedly, U2 had not deferred to any tenderising of America's sensibilities by dropping 'Bullet the Blue Sky' from the set.

'That unsettles people,' agreed Bono. 'They know what it's about.'

'Bullet the Blue Sky' was a song about terrorism – terrorism as sponsored and practised by the United States and its proxies in Nicaragua and El Salvador in the 1980s. Like any of America's more thoughtful critics, Bono got angriest with the place when it failed to exemplify the standards it claimed to embody. (At this point, neither Guantanamo Bay nor Abu Ghraib had entered either the language or the wildest nightmares of people, such as myself, fundamentally favourably disposed towards America.)

Other U2 songs had assumed new significances. 'One' was now a lament to that roll-call of the dead. 'Walk On', inevitably, had become a battle cry, which could be taken up however you thought this war should be fought. 'Please', a song urging on Northern Ireland's interminable stagger towards peace, with its words about streets capsizing in September, and glass shards falling like rain, was now freighted with weightier meaning than a phone booth blasted across a Belfast shopping precinct. The song 'New York' itself had been delivered, at Madison Square Garden, against a backdrop of skyscraper silhouettes, originally intended as cartoon homage, but now resembling a feastful of spectres.

Bono was very possibly the early twenty-first century's most high-profile agitator. His campaigning on causes such as AIDS treatment and Third World debt relief had got him into an astonishing assortment of offices. Using his fame as a skeleton key, Bono had taken his case to congressmen and senators, counsellors and advisers, prime ministers and presidents, and one pope.

'Most were smarter,' said Bono, 'and more hard-working, than I thought. It's a very dangerous idea, that all politicians are wankers. If that's a given, you stop voting. Without wishing to be too windy about this, democracy is a blip on history. The moment that lethargy takes hold, your civil liberties will be robbed from you.'

U2 had always worn their beliefs on their record sleeves, providing contact information for organisations including Greenpeace and Amnesty International – and they'd sold more than 100 million of those albums. Looked at like that, the rock star as lobbyist has a democratic logic. Looked at almost any other way, it induced the same pained grimaces as any photo opportunity involving Tony Blair and his Stratocaster (I always thought Blair's choice of axe unfortunately revealing – the Stratocaster is almost exclusively the instrument of wankers, the fussy, prissy cousin of Fender's handsome, no-nonsense Telecaster, the AK-47 of rock'n'roll). The rock singer's job came with a licence, if not a duty, to be unreasonable: nobody, however powerful their voice and skin-tight their spandex, would bring a stadium to its feet with a chorus that went, 'We will engage fully in Europe, help enlarge the European Union and make it more effective' – and that was one of the sprightlier sentences of the manifesto that had returned Labour to power in the UK in June 2001. Conversely, the role of politician demanded engagement, compromise: modern politicians often sought to assume rock'n'roll cool, but no mainstream party leader was ever going to end his conference speech by kicking the amplifiers over. The point being that politics and rock'n'roll had a tendency to make each other look ridiculous.

'True,' said Bono, whose lack of concern with looking ridiculous was generally, I believed, laudable. 'But agitprop had to grow up. In Genoa during the G8 summit in July, I met anarchists, people who love the barricades. I was trying to get to the bottom of their script, and there wasn't one. I asked, what do you want? Can you turn it into a manifesto and can you go after it? They're not interested. My attitude was, if you're just in it for the Molotov cocktails, fuck off. These matters affect peoples' lives.'

That G8 summit was a good example of what I meant. The anti-capitalist demonstrations it had attracted, whether they were clever or pointed or entirely well-meaning or not, had been attacked by Italian police with shocking incompetence and brutality. Many protestors had been injured, and one young man, Carlo Giuliani, shot dead. Bono, on the other side of the security precautions, had been photographed laughing with Vladimir Putin, by any estimation a paragon of everything U2 had ever claimed to be against. How compromised could you allow yourself to get?

'He made a joke,' sighed Bono. 'And I laughed, and the cameras whirred and clicked, and that didn't feel right to me two seconds later, but there it was. The band weren't the only people who broke out in a rash over that photograph. I did as well. But this is how people like me, or Geldof – who will swear his head off in front of anyone – manage to cross the lines, because we don't have to follow the usual rules.'

There was an uncharacteristic pause.

'I'd be very happy,' he decided, 'to be talking to Vladimir Putin, and honoured to be speaking to the leader of Russia. Of course I would. That's not what I'm embarrassed about. I'm embarrassed about appearing smiling in a photograph at a time when people were getting their heads kicked in.'

I'd been wondering how to broach the rumours of the impatience of the rest of U2 with Bono's extracurricular activities, but he'd beaten me to it. So I asked how badly one job interfered with the other.

'Well,' he said, 'the new album might have come out a lot sooner otherwise. But the campaigning helped, because I was coming back to the studio energised by the idea that maybe the world was more malleable than I thought, that if you put your shoulder to the door, sometimes it opens.'

Doors open a sight quicker if that shoulder is a few inches below a famous face, though. Finding examples of the corrupting, corrosive seduction of celebrity in the early twenty-first century was, given the exponentially increasing pervasiveness of media, less difficult than, for example, doing nothing at all.

'Celebrity is pretty useless,' shrugged Bono. 'I figured that if you can find something to do with it, you might as well.'

He was just being ingenuous now. In the early twenty-first century, celebrity was not useless. It was about the most useful thing you could have. It was the only way anyone could get people to listen to them.

'Okay,' he conceded. 'But it upsets God's order of things. It is noxious. As New Yorkers have learned in the last month, nurses and firemen are real heroes. Celebrity is silly, but it is a currency of a kind, and if I can spend it, I will. I don't think this should be my job, but if you find yourself on a football field, the ball lands at your feet, and the goalie is looking elsewhere . . .'

The metaphor died a swift, painless death. But he could understand, I said, why it made some people uncomfortable.

'Of course,' he replied. 'There are three of them in the band.'

Over the three nights of U2's run at Madison Square Garden, the guest list included David Bowie, Denis Leary, Chris Rock, Jann Wenner, Michael Stipe, Moby, Frankie Dettori, Eddie Jordan, Christy Turlington, Ed Burns, Salma Hayek, Sheryl Crow, Huey Morgan, Debbie Harry, Dan Aykroyd, John McEnroe, Kathleen Turner, Trent Reznor, and Michael J. Fox, among others. A couple of months before, the presence of any or all of the above might have been a talking point.

'It has been an extraordinary thing,' said Bono, towards the end of the last show, 'to watch the concept of celebrity turned on its head in the last month.'

As the last chord of 'Walk On' faded that night, the (regrettably temporary, it turned out) truth of this was demonstrated as several dozen New York firefighters filed onto the stage, to a reception so loud as to be physically painful. Bono ushered them around the heart-shaped walkway that jutted from the 'Elevation' stage and then, while the firefighters reciprocated the crowd's applause, led U2 through an aptly rumbustious tear-up of their twenty-two-year-old debut single, 'Out of Control'.

After U2 left the stage, some of the firefighters approached the microphone. One talked about his brother – also a firefighter, killed on September 11. He explained that the dead man always wanted to be a rock singer, but never made it onto the stage, and so he was doing it for him. Others offered brief memories of their fallen friends and colleagues. Not one of them said anything about revenge, although nobody on the television or radio was talking about much else.

For all that Bono had been mocked as a messianic windbag – not least by himself – he still seemed driven as much by doubt as by faith.

'I saw this photograph recently,' he said. 'Anton Corbijn had an exhibition in the Netherlands. He made me go into this room full of Bonos – horrifying thought, I know. And I noticed a shot of me at twenty-one, and the look in the eye was much clearer. Part of me must have thought our critics were right, and that beautiful naivete – that I now see in my own childrens' faces – I went about killing off. I thought it was something that you had to get rid of, and it's not true. Innocence is much more powerful than experience, especially when it has that teenage fearlessness beside it. That's really something.'

Wasn't that just rampaging adolescent ego? The kind that made a grown rock star want to save the world?

'You'd think so,' he said, 'but it's not. Not long after that picture was taken, when we were twenty-three, all of a sudden America was going off for us, and the UK. You'd think that your ego should inflate, but an odd thing happens – it implodes. I can remember times of being paralysed by fear where once I had faith – in myself, in God, people around me. It was gone. At some point along the way I lost my nerve, and replaced it with front. I think I'm getting back to a more courageous place now.'

So, I asked, if you could go and meet the kid in the photo, what would you tell him?

'That he was right. That's what I'd tell him.'

Nerve. Faith. Hope. Maybe saving the world was as simple as that.

33

'He's great, isn't he, Neil Young?' enthused the forty-fifth vice-president of the United States. 'Did you ever see *The Last Waltz*?'

Young's mid-1970s all-star concert film. I had, but years ago. A bit before my time.

'You know he's done quite a similar film for his new album?'

I did. I'd interviewed Neil Young in San Francisco the previous month. I wasn't sure why I'd mentioned this to Al Gore, but I wasn't sure about much. I'd been in Edinburgh for eleven nights of its annual festival, and had accumulated about that many hours' sleep in the period.

'Wait until you see the video for *After the Garden*. It hasn't been released yet. It's fantastic. Of course, I would think so.'

I imagined that quite a few of the sentiments articulated on Young's vituperative anti-Bush philippic *Living With War* were congruent with Gore's outlook.

'They are,' Gore agreed, 'but that video is based on footage from my movie.'

Gore's movie was *An Inconvenient Truth*, a cinematic rendering of the one-man environmental consciousness-raising presentation he had been touring around the world for the last few years. Gore had flown into Scotland that morning for its European premiere, at the Edinburgh Film Festival. We were in a bar, the colour scheme of which seemed to have been chosen by plucking random jelly beans from a bag, in Edinburgh's CineWorld complex. *An Inconvenient Truth* was showing next door.

I'd seen *An Inconvenient Truth* in London a few weeks earlier. It was a calmly shocking explanation of the environmental catastrophe into which our feverish planet was sleepwalking. The message of *An Inconvient Truth* was that however severe the travails of the early twenty-first century, they could be made to look insignificant by the hazards of the latter part of our new era, in which humanity could end up going to war, if it insisted on so doing, in snorkels.

The film, Gore's attempt to save the world, also felt like Gore's attempt to save himself. It secreted the subtext of one unimaginably disappointed man's quest to find purpose after being deprived, in excrutiating circumstances, of the colossal prize for which he had striven his entire life. In 2000, Gore, who had already been a congressman and a senator from Tennessee, and a two-term vice-president, had bid to be elected forty-third president of the United States, and the first of the twenty-first century. He lost to George W. Bush in the closest race in history. Wrangling over the decisive electoral college votes of Florida lasted more than a month, halted only by a 5–4 Supreme Court ruling that declared ongoing recounts unconstitutional, with Bush 537 votes ahead. Though accusations that the Florida vote was fixed had never abated – principally because the Florida vote was fixed – Gore had eventually conceded gracefully. He was, perhaps, mindful that if he'd won his home state – about the least that is expected of any presidential candidate – the shenanigans in Florida wouldn't have mattered.

Few divisions are so narrow yet so deep as that which separates a president of the United States from their vice-president. Anyone who takes the oath of office, even if they catch pneumonia while delivering their inaugural address and die thirty days later, as William Henry Harrison did in 1841, is remembered forever. The vice-presidency is an arena of agonising impotence, haunted by half-recalled spectres and *Simpsons* punchlines, Mondales, Quayles, Humphreys and Barkleys. Thomas Marshall, who did the job from 1913 to 1921, quipped that 'Once there were two brothers. One ran away to sea, and one was elected vice-president. Nothing was ever heard from either of them again.' The job was surely rendered endurable only by the thought of moving up a notch when the guy behind the big desk served his two terms, got impeached, or got shot. Gore had spent eight years as the understudy waiting for his chance to play the biggest part there was, only to suffer – to pursue the analogy to the brink of exhaustion – the show in which he'd hoped to star being abruptly cancelled in favour of a grim farce starring what appeared to be a ventriloquist's dummy that had struck out on its own.

I couldn't understand how Gore, fifty-eight at the time of our meeting, had not gone mad. All of us live just one of the many lives we might have lived if things had worked out differently. By choice or misfortune, there are jobs we don't do, homes we don't live in, lovers we aren't with. However much those lost possibilities may torment us personally, most of us have the consolation that they don't, in the grand scheme of things, matter much. I couldn't imagine how it must have felt to pick up the newspaper every day, and think that if I'd worked harder, been a little luckier, shaken a few more hands in Nashville and Memphis, almost every word outside the sports pages could be different.

Al Gore knew, though. He personified a complete alternative narrative of early twenty-first century history. The scope of his loss in 2000 was reflected in the fact that it was measurable on the most trivial scale I could think of: my own. Had Gore won, this book wouldn't have been written, or would have been different. There are places I wouldn't have gone, people I wouldn't have met, records I wouldn't have heard because they wouldn't have been made. Everyone reading this will be able to identify a way in which the Al Gore presidency that never was would have altered their experience of the early twenty-first century. Especially if they're reading it in Baghdad.

'Rationalise it?' he said. 'How do you mean?'

Since he asked, I guessed I was wondering how, after such an astonishing personal mishap with such globe-altering, history-diverting consequences, a man constructed a framework for living that allowed him to continue, without feeling any desire to retreat to a clocktower with a rifle.

'Well,' replied Gore, 'you move on in life. But let me ask you. You use the word "rationalise" as if, uh . . . I'm to blame for it?'

I didn't have a short answer to that. How much of the early twenty-first century was Al Gore's fault? It would be unfair to blame him for the mistakes and/or mendacity of Bush. It would probably be a bit much to hold him directly accountable for Bill Clinton's errors and omissions, of which there were many. But the thought that he might feel responsible had occurred to me, even if it was just the useless guilt people lash themselves with, over things that aren't really anything to do with them. I flailed, trying to think of a new way of asking what he must have been asked a million times before, not least by himself, and couldn't.

'How do I deal with it?'

Gore echoed the question with mild incredulity, as if it was the first time he'd been asked it, which I was fairly certain wasn't the case.

'I don't know,' he said, contemplating his Diet Coke, 'that I can give you a precise answer. I try to be useful in what I do, and enjoy life, and not dwell on the past. I'm grateful for the opportunities I've had. I think it's important to keep setbacks like that in perspective.'

There was perspective, and there was perspective. Perspective was the refuge of the dumped, the sacked, the ill, the victim of workaday adversity. We were considering, for one thing, a war that wouldn't have happened. Tens, perhaps hundreds, of thousands of Iraqis, several thousand of the troops he might have commanded, now dead and injured, who might still be alive, unhurt.

'Yeah,' he agreed, with a sad smile. 'But you can't change the past. The questions that are important to me are questions about the future.'

This begged one obvious question about his future, the one he knew I was going to ask, and the one I knew he wasn't going to answer, but we'd deal with that later: right now, Gore had a film to spruik. If what Gore was saying in *An Inconvenient Truth* was correct, then every past, present and potential conflict surveyed in this book was, to deploy a weary though appropriately watery metaphor, an argument over bunk space on the *Titanic*.

'I'm always careful discussing those consequences,' he said, 'because one has to be careful not to push the vulnerable towards mistaken feelings of despair. Because there are a lot of people who go straight from denial to despair. But facts are facts, and the reasons for the sense of urgency around the world, especially in the scientific community, is that the most sophisticated computer models tell the scientists that within ten years, without any action to meaningfully change the pattern, we could cross a tipping point which would put us in a climate from which the road back would be far more difficult.'

Gore wanted to talk about his film. I wanted to talk about his reasons for making it. *An Inconvenient Truth* was, despite its warnings of doom, essentially an optimistic work, so I'd discounted the idea that it might be a massive, elaborate huff, Gore telling the planet he'd wanted to lead that it didn't matter because we were all rooted anyway, so there. I did, however, suspect that it must have been, at least partly, a way for Gore to feel important again.

'This film is not therapy,' he insisted. 'It's passion, of long standing.'

This was fair enough. In 1992, the then-senator had published – even more remarkably for a politician, had actually written – a book called *Earth in the Balance*, an ecological jeremiad in which Gore declared, 'We must make the rescue of the environment the central organising principle of civilisation.' So it wasn't like *An Inconvenient Truth* was entirely the equivalent of a redundant middle manager seeking solace in model railways. But surely, just like everybody, Gore had moments of wrenching what-iffery, and surely, for him of all people, those moments must be acutely painful. Hoping to wrong-foot him, I asked if he was a regular reader of the satirical newspaper the *Onion*.

'I'm an episodic reader,' he replied. 'I haven't figured out their online publication date. Have you?'

Wednesdays, I thought.

'Yeah,' he said. 'But they seem to do it piecemeal. I love the *Onion*.'

I asked about one story, a cruel but slightly wistful piece that appeared in November 2001. Headlined GORE DELIVERS EMERGENCY

ADDRESS INTO BATHROOM MIRROR, it depicted the president-who-never-was rattling around his Tennessee home, making unheard speeches and drafting futile policy in response to 9/11, and conferring across a document-covered table with his 'top advisers', two bemused cats called Simba and Stripe. Did this ring true? Had he ever paused, amid doubtless genuine grief and concern at his country's suffering, to rage that it wasn't him at the centre of events?

I didn't get an answer, just a gust of laughter that rocked him back in his chair.

'I had one I preferred,' he eventually replied. 'My favourite was a front page story, with a very nice picture of me and my wife, Tipper, and the headline GORES ENJOYING BEST SEX OF THEIR LIVES. My wife's reaction was: "Who talked? How did they know?"'

The silence that followed this revelation must have ranked high among the most awkward in the history of human discourse. I told the vice-president that I was really – *really* – only interested in the truth behind the first story.

'No, no . . .' he giggled. 'I'm gonna leave that alone. But actually, the best *Onion* story, in all seriousness, was about a month before Bush's inauguration, with a humorous inaugural address which, if you read it now, is prophecy. It is dead on.'

I looked it up afterwards. Dated January 2001, the headline was BUSH: OUR LONG NATIONAL NIGHTMARE OF PEACE AND PROSPERITY IS NOW OVER, above a report of a speech in which the incoming president did indeed pledge tax cuts for the rich, oil drilling in wildlife refuges and 'at least one Gulf War-level armed conflict in the next four years'.

Earlier, I'd attended Gore's speech at the Edinburgh Television Festival. It started the same way *An Inconvenient Truth* did, with well-rehearsed, self-deprecatory schtick. 'I'm Al Gore,' he began. 'I used to be the next president of the United States.' He let the audience laugh, then narrowed his gaze. 'Actually, I don't find that particularly funny.' There was some other cute stuff, about driving Tipper from their home in Nashville to the family farm near Carthage, Tennessee ('I was driving myself . . . I know that doesn't sound a big deal, but I looked in the rear-view mirror and there was no motorcade – ever heard of phantom limb pain?').

The speech was a barnstorming meditation on the history of the relationship between media and power. Without notes, Gore spoke of the uniquely hypnotic power of television. He considered the uses to which that power is put, noting that polls before the invasion of Iraq found that 77 per cent of Americans believed that Saddam Hussein was involved in the terrorist attacks of September 11 2001. He pondered how the internet might alter what he described as 'the information ecology'. He made reasonably seamless reference to Julius Caesar, Thomas Paine, Martin Luther, Napoleon, Jurgen Habermas, Upton Sinclair, Theodor Adorno, Adam Smith and J.K. Galbraith. Summarising his worry that a burgeoning media–political complex could trample democracy, Gore offered the formula that Adorno, of the Frankfurt School of German philosophers, had coined to explain the descent of his hitherto civilised nation into goose-stepping lunacy: 'All questions of fact,' wrote Adorno, 'became questions of power.' I found myself writing things down, not just because I was meeting Gore the other side of lunch, but because I was intrigued and wanted to read up on some stuff – not a reaction often inspired by speeches made by politicians.

When Gore took questions from the floor, it was clear that the audience had similar thoughts. One delegate asked why obvious intellect appeared to be an electoral disadvantage in America; Gore did the electorally advantageous thing and ducked the question. Another audience member asked Gore if George W. Bush was as dumb as he looked. Gore replied that he didn't believe that Bush was stupid, but he did use a word which was much more damning: 'incurious'. Inevitably, someone asked Gore if he was busy in 2008. Gore gently swatted it aside, but – unprompted – emphasised that he would not utter a 'Sherman Statement' (after William Sherman, the US Civil War general who declined the Republican nomination in 1884 with the words 'If nominated, I will not run, if elected, I will not serve'.) Gore exited to a thunderous standing ovation.

At CineWorld, I pursued those questions further. The person who'd asked Gore why American politicians were afraid to display an intellectual hinterland, should they have one to hand, was on to something, I thought. I could imagine the speech Gore had just given being turned back at him in an attack ad – tree-huggin', owl-pettin' Al Gore, spoutin' fancy-pants book-learnin' to cheese-eatin' Yurpeans. It wasn't a uniquely American phenomenon, but it seemed more pronounced there, as everything did. Why did politicians have to pretend to be as thick as the thickest voter?

'I'm not sure that's all that new,' said Gore. 'If you look at the major divide in the economies of advanced nations, it elevates those who have higher education and jobs that give them higher incomes, because the information component of the work is high. The wages for jobs that require less skill and information are the ones which have declined. They're the ones which have been most vulnerable to the new reality of globalisation. If I were in the workforce competing for jobs of that kind, I'm sure I'd feel resentment against some political leader who seemed to be bandying high-falutin' – do you use that word?'

On occasion.

'There's always been a version of that phenomenon. If you go back to the time of Julius Caesar, the division in Rome, among those who were free citizens, was not completely dissimilar. Caesar's base of support was with the plebs, as they called them.'

And now Gore was making a point by recourse to Gibbon's *Decline and Fall*. He couldn't have done that if he was running for office at home, not without being throttled by his advisers.

'Well, yeah,' he agreed. 'Bear in mind, however, that I was not infrequently criticised for doing the same thing when I was in office. There is a toxic quality to politics now, and politicians are penalised for committing too much candour, but I like to think that if the Supreme Court decision had gone differently, and I'd been sworn in as president, I'd have spoken as unreservedly and as passionately in office as I feel the freedom to do now.'

Ah, so he did think about it . . .

'Aw, come on,' he said. 'Why dwell on it?'

Because people dwell on stuff, almost none of which is ever of any concern to anybody but themselves and whichever of their friends have to put up with them moaning about it. Al Gore had nearly become the most powerful man alive. Scintillating though my company surely was, I couldn't imagine it was much substitute for commanding the mightiest economic, cultural and military force ever created.

'Yeah,' he sighed. 'It's too bad. But, you know, in the American system, there's no intermediate step between a definitive Supreme Court decision and violent revolution.'

This seemed an odd thing to say. I asked how far along his plans for violent revolution had got.

'I wasn't toying with violent revolution,' he grinned. 'When I get searched at airports now, I say, "Look, I was mad after the election, but I'm not that mad." But I did have to confront the basic decision of whether and how to accept and embrace the rule of law. What the Supreme Court did was something that, as I've said before, I thoroughly disagree with, but it is what it is, and the rule of law in our system means abiding by decisions by the highest judicial authority. So it wasn't that complicated, in the end.'

While that rumble had been occurring in 2000, I'd been in Baghdad. News hadn't been easy to come by in Saddam Hussein's Iraq, but the dispute over the presidency had filtered through – and the subjects of the dictatorship had been perplexed, but impressed, that a contest for power, and such power, was being resolved without anyone even suggesting violence.

'I've had that kind of reaction very powerfully in a lot of places around the world,' said Gore. 'But there are lots of countries in our modern world which would handle that situation the same way. As for me, if you have a difficult decision, and you make the wrong decision, one sign that you've made the wrong decision is that you just feel . . .'

He arranged his features into a reasonable impression of a man processing the confusion attendant upon waking in an unfamiliar hotel room with a dead hooker.

'Whereas,' he continued, 'if you make the right decision, you feel . . .'

He constructed a facial expression evocative of that blissful relief which descends upon reaching the end of a long half-time queue for the urinals. And shrugged.

Had it really been that easy?

'A lot of your questions,' he said, 'seem designed to discover hidden angst lurking beneath this placid exterior, and really, it's not there.'

I was asking them because in his position, most people would have wound up like Inspector Dreyfus, the long-suffering boss of Inspector Clouseau, at the end of *Return of the Pink Panther*: lashed into a straitjacket and writing our nemesis's name on our cell's padded walls with a crayon held in our toes.

'I don't torture myself with what-ifs,' said Gore. 'There's no point. I focus my energy on leading a productive and fulfilling life, using the skills and experiences I gained to make the world a better place. But let me answer your question in a different way. I like to think that if I had been president at the moment of that attack on 9/11, that I would have done as well as President Bush in rallying the country in the immediate aftermath.'

This was, in the circumstances, generous. But I'd thought much the same at the time. Within his exceedingly narrow abilities as a communicator, Bush rose to the occasion well.

'He did,' continued Gore. 'Speedily invading Afghanistan, that was right. But I would have parted ways with his decision-making after that.'

Historical counter-factuals didn't get much more tantalising than this. Usually, when hypothetical geopolitics are considered, whether in a television studio or a taxi, the discussion is necessarily limited to what could or should happen. This was what would have happened.

'The proper course,' said Gore, 'would have been to persist in Afghanistan – and, if necessary, Pakistan – until Osama bin-Laden was captured and al-Qaeda had been routed. There was an historic mistake at Tora Bora. You could feel it when it happened. He [bin-Laden] was cornered there. The intelligence in retrospect makes that clear. Even at the time, I knew from continuing conversations with people in the national security community that that was where the showdown was going to – should have – occurred. I still don't know why Bush pulled back. I think his next major mistake may have been one of the reasons why he made the first mistake. The next mistake was to withdraw so much military force, and so many of our intelligence assets, and take them to Iraq. In addition to pursuing bin-Laden, instead of invading a country that hadn't attacked us, the president should, in my opinion, have rallied the American people to become independent of such heavy reliance on oil and coal, and use that opportunity to greatly lessen our strategic vulnerability in the Persian Gulf, and simultaneously lead the way in solving the climate crisis.'

Much of this sounded like the sort of speech that might have echoed around Gore's bathroom on 12 September 2001, but I only had forty-five minutes, and I didn't feel like this was the day he was going to confess, 'Screw everything, you're right. I am a broken, bitter shell of a man, my entire existence a hollow mockery, my dreams, when I am blessed by sleep, haunted by the screams of dying Iraqis, and next time I run into that smug, cross-eyed, ballot-stuffing, roll-fiddling son of a bitch Bush, I'll kick his ass through his hat.' So I asked, instead, if Gore had felt weirdly liberated by being able to speak, and think, outside the strictures of party discipline.

'Sometimes,' he allowed, 'but I'm under no illusion whatsoever that there's any position in the world remotely close to the position of president of the United States in terms of the influence one can have. Nothing is comparable. I know that, and I don't delude myself into thinking that what I'm doing now is a subsitute for that, because it's not.'

That didn't sound like something General Sherman might have said circa 1883.

'I don't,' Gore intoned, for what must have been the hundredth time today alone, 'have any plans or intentions to be a candidate for president.'

For such a well-rehearsed statement, it was noteworthy for its flexibility.

'I'm enjoying the business world,' he said. 'I have two very success-ful businesses that I started [interactive television channel Current TV,

London-based ethical investment firm Generation], both focused not only on making money, but doing so in a way that advances good public policy. I'm not being coy. It's just that I've been so many years in the American political process, the internal shifting of gears has not been completed yet. I don't want to hear that grinding sound again.'

It was easy to become misty-eyed about the Gore presidency that never was, and the early twenty-first century that might have been. It was especially easy if you could forget that the Iraq policy of what Gore habitually referred to as 'the Clinton–Gore administration' – I rather doubted that Bill Clinton did the same – was scarcely a success, enforcing UN sanctions which propped up an absurd tyrant while immiserating and impoverishing the people who, if able to think further ahead than their next meal, might well have done the decent thing and hung Saddam Hussein off a lamp-post. Gore was vice-president in a White House which waved through genocide in Rwanda, watched Sarajevo burn for four inexplicable years, and bombed Baghdad and Khartoum for wholly dubious reasons, to no good effect. It was also worth remembering, before viewing Gore through a Vaseline-smeared lens, that the Islamist hooligans who attacked America on September 11 2001 didn't wake up that morning and say, 'Hey, you know what would be fun?'. They'd been planning it a long time, time during which Al Gore was vice-president.

'Sure,' he nodded. 'We asked ourselves those questions. And President Clinton and I asked the commission that was established to dig as deeply as they could, not only into the administration of Bush and Cheney, but also into the Clinton–Gore administration. Upon reflection, I feel that we vigorously followed every lead we had. At that time, though, invading Afghanistan was not considered a realistic possibility. The Republicans in the Congress bitterly attacked Clinton for bombing Milosevic, or doing anything that involved the use of military force overseas, so they would have revolted. Of course, the situation then was not the same. But during the transition period, in December 2000 and January 2001, every member of our national security team conveyed to their incoming counterparts forcefully that they should make Osama bin-Laden and al-Qaeda their top priority.'

Al Gore may not have been a great president, or even a good one, but he would have been a different one, and it was hard not to think, all things considered, that he would have made a better one than the guy who did steer America, and the world in its wake, through the early twenty-first century. It really wasn't working out like it should have, and could have.

When Al Gore told me that he characterised himself as an optimist above all else, I'd asked him if that optimism had ever faltered. He'd paused, for quite a long time.

'No,' he'd finally decided. 'It's partly an act of will. Partly a belief in self-fulfilling prophecies. It's really based mainly in my belief that the political system can and will respond. I've seen it happen. I've watched American politics all my life, and I've seen lots of occasions on which it seemed that nothing was happening, nothing was changing, and then all of a sudden the country quietly crosses the tipping point, and before you know it, dramatic change takes place.'

Politically and personally, this idea appealed to me.

'If you know those possibilities are ever-present,' said the definitive nearly man of our age, 'it's a source of hope.'

This was a commodity which had, at various points in the previous six years, seemed to me a dwindling, and not necessarily renewable, resource. But I was sure I'd seen it somewhere.

AFTERWORD

Even less than forty-eight hours after the event, writing anything pertaining to the election of Barack Obama to the presidency of the United States feels akin to proceeding to the waterline of some Atlantic shore, flinging a thimbleful of tap water into the fathomless brine, and expecting anyone to notice. Few political events in my lifetime have been or will be so scrutinised – possibly because, I think, judging by the fact that Philadelphia's sidewalks, nearly two days later, remain populated by dazed, dishevelled people who give every appearance of having not gone home yet, few political events in my lifetime have made so many people so happy.

At the moment polls on the West Coast closed and the networks called the election for Obama, I was standing amid just one of uncountable spectacular eruptions of human joy taking place all over the globe at that moment – the *moveon.org* party in Philadelphia, to which I'd been invited by some people I'd met in a bar earlier. In between accepting hugs and drinks from delirious strangers, I fielded text messages from no less ecstatic friends around the world, and I thought of the other people I'd spoken to in the time since Barack Obama had announced his candidacy back in May 2007, whose faces had illuminated discernibly at the prospect of him waving from the door of *Air Force One*. The jovial rug merchant in Damascus. The street-corner bookseller in Addis Ababa doing a roaring trade in bootleg copies of *Dreams From My Father* and *The Audacity Of Hope*. The Bruce Springsteen fans I'd met a year earlier while doing a story about following the "Magic" tour through Minnesota, Ohio and Michigan, who seemed – even the Republicans – to think that here might be the man to lead them on what they'd just been singing lustily along to in "Long Walk Home". The journalist in Cape Verde, daring to wonder what it might mean for the beleaguered continent to his east. The barstool philosophers of the Dingle peninsula, expressing solemn approval of the fine Irish name of O'Bama. The Philadelphia taxi driver who'd driven me to my hotel on election day, a native son of Mali still two years from American citizenship and its attendant voting rights, who'd nevertheless attended Obama's last rally in the city, and cheered himself hoarse.

Philadelphia had been a deliberate choice for election night. A few months prior, after nearly twenty years of travelling to and from the United States, I had been – absurdly – to Philadelphia for the first time. I'd been cursing my tardiness ever since. Every so often, I arrive somewhere I've never been before, and as soon as I step out of the airport, or train station, or bus depot, find myself thinking: I'm going to like it here. In all my most beloved cities, including Vilnius, Istanbul, Reykjavik, Beirut, Tirana and Taipei, this instinct has never been mistaken. I'd felt it as soon as the train from New York City had pulled up at 30th Street Station in June 2008, and it had proved, over my subsequent stay in Philadelphia, as unerring as usual. I didn't, and don't, quite get the whole cheesesteak thing – I suspect it, indeed, of being some sort of prank played on tourists, the local equivalent of Scottish tales of haggis-hunting, or Australian warnings of the predatory strain of koala known as the dropbear – but aside from that, I adore the place. It's a great American city on a European scale – walkable, accessible, thus far resistant to the depressing American tendency to outsource a vibrant downtown to satellite suburbs of identikit strip-malls.

Plus, of course, there's the history. It is arguable that Philadelphia has had more influence on the last few hundred years of human endeavour than any other city in the world, because of what happened in a handsome Georgian building a few blocks from where I'm

typing this. On July 4th, 1776, in what was then the State House of
Pennsylvania and is now known as Independence Hall, the Continental Congress approved for publication my single favourite –
for what little the praise may be worth – piece of writing. Every
American reading this will know these words already, but they always
bear further consideration, further admiration, further determination that they never be taken for granted and – though this aspiration
has become recently unfashionable – further hope that they might
catch on abroad: "We hold these truths to be self-evident, that all
men are created equal, that they are endowed by their Creator with
certain unalienable rights, that among these are life, liberty, and
the pursuit of happiness." If the travelling described in these pages
has left me certain of any one thing, it's that the trio of entitlements
that Thomas Jefferson chose to define in that passage are an almost
universally applicable summary of human desire. Though various
political and religious movements in our time have succeeded in
attracting followings to creeds of death, curtailment and the propa-
gation of misery, it's notable that the leaders of said movements
are always careful to put it otherwise in their official rhetoric. The
proverbial poor huddled masses, as the world's tyrants and despots
know better than anyone, really do yearn to breathe free. Any western relativist demanding to know who "we" think "we" are when
"we" seek to promote or encourage "Western" values should pause
to consider what might result were the United States to offer green
cards to everyone from Tangiers to Tehran: the Middle East would
be left, by my estimation, with a population of nine.

The period chronicled in the preceding pages was not always an
easy one in which to be, for want of less imprecise term, pro-America.
I was and am exactly that, however, and I'm not just saying this
because I hope this book will be read by Americans (who, at any rate,
if they're reading this, have pretty much read it by now, and thank
you). Though it's true that little of this book is set in America, pretty
much every chapter is about America in some respect or another. This
is still the one country against which others measure and/or define
themselves. This is still the one country that inspires and infuriates

like no other. And that's because it's a country which has set itself a higher standard than any other.

The early twenty-first century and my meanderings within it have been determined to a large extent by America's reaction to what happened on September 11th, 2001. While America made many stupid and terrible mistakes in its reaction to those dreadful and inexcusable attacks, I submit that those errors were all made for the same reason: that America had the misfortune, at that moment, to be led by people who lacked the courage to be American, as most of the world understands the term. For all the ostentatious flag-waving of the Bush administration, and the bellicose, fist-pumping "USA! USA!" imbecility it encouraged, I am unable to think of any actions which strike me as so definitively un-American as torture, extraordinary rendition, the abandonment of *habeas corpus*, the promiscuous snooping upon one's fellow citizens, the boneheaded adherence to ideology over reality, the encouragement of the notion that our governing emotion should be fear. I have, in my time, spoken with many people who hate America – sometimes with good reason, often without. What they've had in common, whether they've been Hezbollah ideologues, Taliban footsoldiers, Hamas militants, European left-wingers, even aggrieved Native Americans, is that their anger is rooted in a conviction that America is hypocritical, that America does not observe the values outlined in her founding documents – that America, in short, is insufficiently American. It's a compliment paid to nobody else – that your enemies wish you'd be more like you're supposed to be.

The United States is the one country about which everybody cares: I can assure that not a single one of my friends in Britain has ever stayed up till dawn, champagne on ice, anxiously awaiting the results of elections in Germany, France or Spain. There are many reasons why America so dominates the global consciousness: its cultural dynamism, its military might, its economic muscle, its staggering capacity for change and reinvention (in the presidential election held a month before I was born, just forty years before a half-Kenyan black man with a Swahili name won the White House, a third-party ticket of George "Segregation Forever" Wallace and Curtis "Bombs Away" LeMay attracted 13.53 per cent of the vote and carried five states). But all of these qualities grow from an attitude which is less common, around our anxious, querulous planet than many Americans realise – an attitude which your new president made a central motif of his election campaign, and which, I'll warn you now, will form the last three words of this edition of this book.

By the time this afterword is publicly disseminated, President Barack Obama will, inevitably, have revealed himself to be a human being – perhaps, even, a politician (though I doubt, despite some of the more peculiar pre-election insinuations of his opponents, that he will either have press-ganged the population onto collective farms, or replaced the Supreme Court with a scimitar-swishing Shariah invigilator). But his victory, and all that it means and all that it represents, will still have forced America's friends and foes alike to take another look at, and have another think about, America. The likelihood, it seems to me, is that most people will find more to love, and/or less to loathe.

We have heard a lot in the twenty-first century to date, not least from your outgoing president, about a grand, global struggle between good and evil. I'm as certain as I can be that no such dispute is occurring. The universal human conflict is, as it ever was, between the smart and the stupid. In general, I'm still betting on the smart, even if it does often seem that that stupid have the numbers. And so, in a spirit of cheer which I recognise has been erratically present elsewhere in this book, and is only intermittently discernible in this author, I'd like to close by joining in with your new president's signature refrain. I do so not without equivocation: While these three tiny, almighty words have, in the heads and hands of Americans, given man wings, liberated continents, sent people to the Moon and thrilled and connected the world, they've also been responsible for a good many of the sort of harebrained foreign policy initiatives that keep people like me in employment. Nevertheless, I'm as convinced as the optimist you've just elected that the twenty-first century might, despite a largely disheartening start, still be an improvement of most of its predecessors. And, for the first – and I promise, absolutely the last – time, I will presume to speak for the rest of humanity, and suggest that, were we to be asked right now if we find it possible to imagine that America might still have it in herself to lead the way to the light, I reckon we'd have it in ourselves at this moment to answer: Yes, we can.

ACKNOWLEDGMENTS

EVERYWHERE, ANYWHERE
JANUARY 2000–PRESENT

One of the things I like most about travelling is that, by and large, people like travellers. There seems to be something about pitching up in someone else's country and trying to figure out what the locals think they're doing that inspires people to go to extraordinary lengths to be helpful. I would prefer to believe that it's not entirely the same reflex which impels any responsible adult to try to help a wailing, soggy-trousered, ice cream-smeared five-year-old lost in a shopping mall find its parents, but there's no getting around it: were it not for the company, assistance, insight, patience, courage, good humour and kindness of the folks I met along the way, this book wouldn't be here, and nor, in all likelihood, given a few of the locations and situations it describes, would I.

I cannot count – and, in a few cases, whether for their own safety or due to my illegible notes, cannot name – everyone who has gone miles out of their way to assist me, when it would have been easier, safer and more profitable to ignore me, avoid me, or relieve me of my laptop and other fenceable chattels and send me waddling back towards the border wearing a barrel. Properly honouring everyone who has travelled with me, cleared me a path, staged a diversion while I bolted for the exit – or, on one memorable occasion, plagued various tiers of a West African government with requests that they let me out of jail – would have necessitated an appendix of sufficient heft to block the entrances to most bookshops. This, it was pointed out, would have been counter-productive. Plus, I'd end up forgetting someone, and it would obviously turn out that they were the one who was the only suitable donor when I needed a kidney transplant, and this would, I feel, lend unnecessary awkwardness to an already delicate situation. So, all in all, I just hope that every one of my immeasurable legion of St. Christophers knows who they are, and how grateful to them I am.

That said, there are some people who really do deserve to be thanked in person – or, depending on your perspective, blamed by association. I am obliged to every editor that has paid me money for the agreeable task of arranging words next to each other during the period chronicled in *I Wouldn't Start from Here*, but especially to Andrew Tuck and Bill Tuckey at the *Independent on Sunday*, Tim Lusher and Kathy Sweeney at the *Guardian*, Paul Clements at *High Life*, Isabel Hilton and David Hayes at *opendemocracy.net*, Laura Lee Davies at *TimeOut*, Shaun Phillips at *Esquire*, Allan Jones, Michael Bonner and John Mulvey at *Uncut*, and Bob Guccione Jr. at *Gear*. Thanks most of all on this front to all at Pan Macmillan in Sydney – Kylie Mason, Kate Nash, and especially Alexandra Craig, who commissioned this book, and has stayed a lengthier than expected course with commendable forbearance, though it must sometimes have felt like the equivalent of signing a vaguely promising pop group and being presented with a triple concept album of orchestral jazz. Ali Lavau's thoughtful and sympathetic edit of the manuscript was also extremely constructive, and certainly less like being present at my own autopsy than I'd feared. For faith in the idea that this thing may find favour with a non-Australian-speaking audience, thanks to my UK agent, Simon Benham at Mayer Benham, and all at Portobello. For a willingness to inflict it upon the United States, thanks to Richard Nash and all at Soft Skull. Also on that side of the Atlantic, and hardly for the first time, I am unrepayably indebted to P.J. O'Rourke, for generous encouragement way above and beyond the call.

For someone who spends most of their time either out of the country, or alone at home launching querulous diatribes at an indifferent world down an ISDN cable, I have friends of a quantity and quality which endlessly delights and astonishes. All of the following have helped usher this book into existence, whether by offering encouragement, sharing hard-won wisdom, partaking of argument, providing inspiration by example, reading drafts of the manuscript, telling me to shut up and get on with it – or, much more often, just by being themselves. A free run at the posh end of the wine rack is extended – for a limited time only, conditions apply, "wine" in posh end may actually be that frightful-looking slivovitz I bought at Bucharest airport duty-free in 1995 and have been trying to palm off on the unwary ever since – to all the following: Angus Batey, David Bennun, James Brabazon, Robert & Theodora Burrow, Jenny Colgan, Cathal Coughlan, Kirstin Crothers, Shane Danielsen, Heather DeLand, Barry Divola, Steve Dowling, Roni Dutta, Roddy Frame, Adam Free, Ian Gittins, Luke Haines, Adrian Jobling, Cressida Johnson, Jonathan Kaplan, Sean Kemp, Imran Khan, Stuart Kirk, Elisabeth Knowles, John Knowles, Sarah Le Claire, Colleen Maloney, Ben Marshall, Jim Marshall, Jack Marx, Clancy McDowell, Eleanor McKay, Caitlin Moran, Simon Morris, Michael & Patricia Palmer, Peter Paphides, Robert Young Pelton, Simon Price, Martin Quinn, Justin Quirk, Chris Roberts, Mat Smith, Katy Steinmetz, David Stubbs, Neal Townsend, Everett True, Chelsea Walters, Jessica Whittaker. A hearty *yee* and a rousing *haw*, as well, to fellow members of the Blazing Zoos, past, present and honorary: Mike Edwards, Gen Matthews, Alec Pointon, Astrid Williamson, Dan Burke, Robin Colgan, Billy Cerveny, Damon Wilson, Tim Van Der Kuil, Kate Burdette, Matthew Dupuy, Mark Wallis, Jason Moffat, Neil Herd, John Moore.

Finally and least frugally, thanks to my family, who I hope realise that my decision to live about as far away from them as it's possible to get is nothing personal: that's all of the clans Mueller, Stivens, Ahern and Smith, in particular the London-based contingent of Ceinwen, Ceridwen and Hunter. Most love and thanks, of course, to my parents, Des and Gweny, my brother and sister-in-law, Nick and Katriina, my nephew (and, obviously, future Australian opening bat, Geelong centre-half-forward, president-for-life,

UN Secretary-General and Nobel literature laureate) Sebastian, and to my two remarkable grandmothers, Jean Mueller and Sylvia Stivens, to whom this book is dedicated.